STATES OF VIOLENCE

The book brings together scholarship on three differe[...] ining each for what it can tell us about the conditions [...] and the significance of violence to our understanding [...] book demonstrate that states of violence have a histor[y ...] ...ology. Wherever the state does act violently, however, the legitimacy of its acts must be engaged with the real facts of war, capital punishment, and the ugly realities of death. This book calls into question the legitimacy of state uses of violence and mounts a sustained effort at interpretation, sense making, and critique. This book suggests that condemning the state's decisions to use lethal force is not a simple matter of abolishing the death penalty or – to take another exemplary case of the killing state – demanding that the state engage only in just (publicly declared and justified) wars. It points out that even such overt instances of lethal force are more elusive as targets of critique than one might think. Indeed, altering such decisions might do little to change the essential relationship of the state to violence. To change that relationship, we must also attend to the violent state as a state of mind, a state of mind that is not just a social or psychological condition but also a moral commitment or a philosophical position.

Austin Sarat is William Nelson Cromwell Professor of Jurisprudence and Political Science, Five College Fortieth Anniversary Professor, and Senior Advisor to the Dean of the Faculty at Amherst College. Professor Sarat founded both Amherst College's Department of Law, Jurisprudence, and Social Thought and The Association for the Study of Law, Culture, and the Humanities, a national scholarly association. He is former President of that association and has also served as President of the Law and Society Association and of the Consortium of Undergraduate Law and Justice Programs. He is author or editor of more than sixty books, including *The Killing State: Capital Punishment in Law, Politics, and Culture*; *When the State Kills: Capital Punishment and the American Condition*; *The Cultural Lives of Capital Punishment: Comparative Perspectives*; *Law, Violence, and the Possibility of Justice*; *Pain, Death, and the Law*; *Mercy on Trial: What It Means to Stop an Execution*; *When Law Fails: Making Sense of Miscarriages of Justice*; and *Capital Punishment* (two volumes). His most recent book is *The Road to Abolition?* He is currently writing a book entitled *Hollywood's Law: What Movies Do for Democracy*. He is editor of the journal *Law, Culture and the Humanities* and of *Studies in Law, Politics, and Society*. Professor Sarat has received numerous prizes and awards, including the Harry Kalven Award, given by the Law Society Association for "distinguished research on law and society"; the Reginald Heber Smith Award, given biennially to honor the best scholarship on "the subject of equal access to justice"; and the James Boyd White Award from the Association for the Study of Law, Culture, and the Humanities, given for distinguished scholarly achievement and "outstanding and innovative" contributions to the humanistic study of law.

Jennifer L. Culbert is an Associate Professor in the Political Science Department at Johns Hopkins University, where she teaches courses in political theory and jurisprudence. She is the author of *Dead Certainty: The Death Penalty and the Problem of Judgment* (2008).

States of Violence

WAR, CAPITAL PUNISHMENT, AND LETTING DIE

Edited by

Austin Sarat
Amherst College

Jennifer L. Culbert
Johns Hopkins University

CAMBRIDGE UNIVERSITY PRESS

CAMBRIDGE UNIVERSITY PRESS
Cambridge, New York, Melbourne, Madrid, Cape Town, Singapore, São Paulo, Delhi

Cambridge University Press
32 Avenue of the Americas, New York, NY 10013-2473, USA

www.cambridge.org
Information on this title: www.cambridge.org/9780521699761

© Cambridge University Press 2009

This publication is in copyright. Subject to statutory exception
and to the provisions of relevant collective licensing agreements,
no reproduction of any part may take place without the written
permission of Cambridge University Press.

First published 2009

Printed in the United States of America

A catalog record for this publication is available from the British Library.

Library of Congress Cataloging in Publication data

States of violence : war, capital punishment, and letting die / edited by Austin Sarat,
Jennifer L. Culbert.
   p. cm.
Includes bibliographical references and index.
ISBN 978-0-521-87627-8 (hardback) – ISBN 978-0-521-69976-1 (pbk.)
1. Political violence. 2. Capital punishment. I. Sarat, Austin. II. Culbert, Jennifer Louise.
III. Title.
HN90.V5S8324 2009
303.601–dc22   2008046621

ISBN 978-0-521-87627-8 hardback
ISBN 978-0-521-69976-1 paperback

Cambridge University Press has no responsibility for the persistence or
accuracy of URLs for external or third-party Internet Web sites referred to in
this publication and does not guarantee that any content on such Web sites is,
or will remain, accurate or appropriate. Information regarding prices, travel
timetables, and other factual information given in this work are correct at
the time of first printing, but Cambridge University Press does not guarantee
the accuracy of such information thereafter.

For my son, Ben, with the hope that he will grow up in a world where states of violence are less common than they are today (A.S.)

Contents

Contributors		*page* ix
Acknowledgments		xi
1	Introduction: Interpreting the Violent State *Austin Sarat and Jennifer L. Culbert*	1

PART I ON THE FORMS OF STATE KILLING

2	The Innocuousness of State Lethality in an Age of National Security *Robin Wagner-Pacifici*	25
3	Oedipal Sovereignty and the War in Iraq *Jeremy Arnold*	51
4	Sacrifice and Sovereignty *Mateo Taussig-Rubbo*	83
5	Due Process and Lethal Confinement *Colin Dayan*	127
6	From Time to Torture: The Hellish Future of the Criminal Sentence *Thomas L. Dumm*	150
7	The Child in the Broom Closet: States of Killing and Letting Die *Elizabeth A. Povinelli*	169
8	The Lethality of the Canadian State's (Re)cognition of Indigenous Peoples *Mark Antaki and Coel Kirkby*	192

PART II INVESTIGATING THE DISCOURSES OF DEATH

9   Death in the First Person   229
Peter Brooks

10   Open Secrets, or The Postscript of Capital Punishment   245
Ravit Pe'er-Lamo Reichman

11   Ethical Exception: Capital Punishment in the Figure of Sovereignty   270
Adam Thurschwell

12   No Mercy   297
Adam Sitze

Index   309

Contributors

Mark Antaki Assistant Professor, Faculty of Law, McGill University

Jeremy Arnold Graduate Student in Political Science, Johns Hopkins University

Peter Brooks Sterling Professor of Comparative Literature, Yale University

Jennifer L. Culbert Associate Professor of Political Science, Johns Hopkins University

Colin Dayan Robert Penn Warren Professor in the Humanities, Vanderbilt University

Thomas L. Dumm Professor of Political Science, Amherst College

Coel Kirkby Doctor of Philosophy (Ph.D.) candidate. University of Cambridge, Faculty of Law

Elizabeth A. Povinelli Professor of Anthropology, Director, The Institute for Research on Women and Gender, Codirector, Center for the Study of Law and Culture, Columbia University

Ravit Pe'er-Lamo Reichman Assistant Professor of English, Brown University

Austin Sarat William Nelson Cromwell Professor of Jurisprudence and Political Science, Amherst College

Adam Sitze Assistant Professor, Department of Law, Jurisprudence, and Social Thought, Amherst College

Mateo Taussig-Rubbo Associate Professor, University of Buffalo Law School, State University of New York

Adam Thurschwell Civilian Attorney, Military Commissions Defense Office, Department of Defense

Robin Wagner-Pacifici Gil and Frank Mustin Professor of Sociology, Swarthmore College

Acknowledgments

We are grateful to the terrific scholars whose work is collected in this book. We also wish to express our gratitude to the Dean of the Faculty of Amherst College, Greg Call, and the Chair of the Political Science Department at Johns Hopkins University, Jane Bennett, for their generous financial support. Thanks are also due to Michael Donovan for his skilled research assistance.

Chapters 2, 5, 7, 9, 10, 11, and 12 were previously published in a special issue of *South Atlantic Quarterly*, Volume 107, Number 3, Summer 2008. They are reprinted by permission of Duke University Press.

1

Introduction

Interpreting the Violent State

Austin Sarat and Jennifer L. Culbert

If we were conjuring a fantastic nightmare, we would describe the state as a bloodthirsty beast that spends much of its time on the prowl, making war, imposing the death penalty, and spilling blood. We would see this beast busily covering its tracks, clothing its bloodletting in a rhetoric of necessity, the common good, or high moralism. Indeed, it is this combination of bloodthirstiness and rhetorical sleight of hand that would give the state its horrible power in our dreams.

In waking life, the state appears more benign, although it surely comes as no surprise to say that violence of all kinds is done every day with the explicit authorization of state institutions and officials or with their tacit acquiescence. Some of this violence is done directly by those officials, some by citizens acting under a dispensation granted by the state, and some by persons whose violent acts subsequently will be deemed acceptable.[1] Because the bloodlust and bloodletting done, authorized, or condoned by state institutions occurs with all of the normal abnormality of bureaucratic abstraction, responsibility for the blood spilled is often untraceably dispersed. Because state violence seems so ordinary, so much a part of the taken-for-granted world in which we live, it is sometimes difficult to see the human agency involved. Indeed it is this distinctive combination of bloodletting and bureaucracy that makes the violence of the modern state possible in our daily lives.[2]

---

[1] Self-defense provides perhaps the best example of such after-the-fact authorization of violence. See *People v. La Voire*, 155 Colo. 551 (1964); *State v. Gough*, 187 Iowa 363 (1919) and *People v. McGrandy*, 9 Mich. App. 187 (1967).

[2] See Hannah Arendt, *Eichmann in Jerusalem: A Report on the Banality of Evil*. New York: Viking Press, 1963.

Identifying how, where, and when states turn to violence has been a subject of academic interest for a long time. Much of the academic literature devoted to it has been critical of state violence, although recently with the emergence of non–state terrorist activity some might long for the days when states had much more of a monopoly on the most lethal forms of violence.[3] In that literature most scholars have concentrated their attention on one or another kind of violence (*e.g.*, war, punishment, structural violence, etc.). The work collected in *States of Violence: War, Capital Punishment, and Letting Die* draws these phenomena together, laying them side by side to see how one illuminates the others.

From the State of Nature to State Violence

In the liberal political tradition, the state authorizes itself and its violence as a response to our inability to live in a world of ungoverned or ungovernable violence. In this tradition the state is constructed and justified on the basis of narratives of life outside or before the state in a place or time when life is "nasty, brutish, and short." In this context, state violence is thought of as the lesser of two evils: a life without violence might be impossible, but at least in a state a whole life might be lived. To understand such a state-constructing narrative, one must almost inevitably begin with the state of nature and with Thomas Hobbes.[4]

The Hobbesian understanding of life outside the state presents persons as driven by ungoverned will and desire. If persons are to survive the war of all against all to which this condition inevitably gives rise, all power must be transferred to a single entity (or person). This understanding reveals perhaps the cruelest dilemma of the human condition, namely whether human beings should act as they wish but in a perpetual condition of

---

[3] For a discussion of this view see Michael Ignatieff, *The Lesser Evil: Political Ethics in an Age of Terror*. Princeton: Princeton University Press, 2004.

[4] Thomas Hobbes, *Leviathan*, C. B. MacPherson ed., New York: Penguin Books, 1968. Hobbes described the state of nature as a condition of life in which men might live "without a common Power to keep them in awe" (at 185). That condition is one, as every undergraduate knows, of violence or the perpetual fear of violence. Given rough equality of desire and power, men "endeavour to destroy or subdue one another," and are, as a result, "... in a condition which is called Warre; and such a warre, as is of every man against every man." (at 184–185) As Hobbes noted in one of the most famous passages in his work, life in the state of nature is "solitary, poor, nasty, brutish and short" (at 186).

Introduction

insecurity or whether this freedom should be relinquished in the name of a greater security.[5]

For Hobbes, the solution was unequivocal and unconditional. Leviathan, in whom sufficient power is vested to keep "all in awe,"[6] is Hobbes' device for rescuing us from the will, desire, insecurity, and violence of the state of nature. The state or law (in Hobbes the two are hardly distinguishable) is presented as a way of taming violence by producing, through social organization, an economy of violence.[7] It is Leviathan's awesome force, not its moral commitments, that in this account makes it socially valuable. Violence lurks just below the surface, a violence so great and overwhelming as to produce a frozen acquiescence. Should the need arise, however, Leviathan can be counted on to spill blood willingly to prevent an even more gruesome bloodbath. In sum, what brings us to the state and holds us there is fear of what life would be like if the state did not or could not effectively deploy this terrible violence.

Other early modern political theorists understood that if the state were to be powerful enough to keep anarchy at bay, humans would have to relinquish more than their natural powers of self-preservation and punishment to it; they would also have to give up their powers of judgment.

In John Locke's philosophy, for instance, they would have to do so because in the state of nature all persons have equal right to decide their own disputes in accordance with their own interpretations of the natural law. What is more, all people have equal right to enforce their verdicts and to punish those who do not acquiesce.[8] Confusion and disorder naturally ensue. The only solution is a political society in which "every one of the members hath quitted this natural power, resigned it up into the hands of the community."[9] In the hands of the community, this natural power is used to make laws that are interpreted by impartial judges and enforced by the state. People are no longer free to decide their own cases and to punish

---

[5] Duncan Kennedy argued that this dilemma poses a fundamental challenge for liberal political theory. See "The Structure of Blackstone's Commentaries," 28 *Buffalo Law Review* (1979), 205, 211–213. See also Roberto Unger, *Knowledge and Politics*. New York: The Free Press, 1975.
[6] Hobbes, note 4 at 185.
[7] This image is labeled *repressive law* by Philippe Nonet and Philip Selznick, *Law and Society in Transition: Toward Responsive Law*. New York: Harper Colophon Books, 1978, chapter 2. See also J. H. Hexter, "Thomas Hobbes and the Law," 65 *Cornell Law Review* (1980), 471.
[8] John Locke, *Treaties on Civil Government and a Letter Concerning Toleration*, ed. Charles L. Sherman. New York: Irvington, 1979, 56.
[9] Id., 56.

transgressions as they see fit, but they are able to preserve and enjoy their lives, liberties, and estates.[10]

Still, social contract theorists like Locke recognize what earlier theorists like Hobbes also knew: one of the greatest threats to the achievement of political society, is posed by the individual members whom the people have selected to be their trustees or deputies in government. Locke observes that "ill affected and factious men" might spread among the people the idea that the prince or legislative body acts contrary to their trust when in fact "the prince only makes use of his due prerogative."[11] Locke also understands, however, that legislators could "either by ambition, fear, folly or corruption, endeavour to grasp for themselves or put into the hands of any other an absolute power over the lives, liberties, and estates of the people."[12] Hobbes maintains that men never give up the right to preserve their lives, even when the Leviathan is justified in taking them. Similarly, although on a collective scale, Locke sees no alternative but to defer to the judgment of the body of the people, "for who shall be judge whether the trustee or deputy acts well and according to the trust reposed in him, but he who deputes him?"[13] Therefore, despite giving up their natural power to judge their own cases, the people must still be able to judge whether a trustee or deputy acts well.[14]

Sovereignty and State Violence

Social contract theory is not the only liberal political tradition to imagine the state in terms of a relation to violence. In his account of the state, Max Weber also emphasizes its relation to violence. Indeed, according to Weber, what makes a particular association political per se is its relation to physical force. This is clear when Weber defines the state as "a human community that (successfully) claims the monopoly on the *legitimate* use of physical force within a given territory."[15] Weber claims that the state, like all

[10] Id., 82.
[11] Id., 82.
[12] Id., 165.
[13] Id., 165.
[14] Id., 162–163.
[15] Max Weber, "Politics as a Vocation," in *From Max Weber: Essays in Sociology*, eds. and trans. H. H. Gerth and C. Wright Mills. New York: Oxford University Press, 1946, 78.

Introduction

political associations, is a relation of humans dominating humans. Because this relation is supported by means of violence, one might expect people to resist. They do not, Weber argues, because they think this violence is legitimate.[16]

According to this line of thinking, the state gets into trouble only when the violence it exercises cannot be distinguished from criminal violence. In *Discipline and Punish*, Michel Foucault suggests that the sovereign, who once played a central role in public executions, retires from the scene beginning in the eighteenth century when, in the eyes of the public, executions came to resemble the acts of violence for which death sentences were being imposed.[17] Focus shifts away from the execution to the trial and to the sentence as the sovereign distances him- or herself from the violence that is bound up with the practice of justice. In this way, the sovereign comes to appear as a disinterested party whose primary concern is the integrity of the process of judgment rather than its outcome.[18]

State violence is, of course, intimately connected with ideas of sovereignty.[19] As Foucault describes the sovereign of classic political theory, when external or internal violence puts its existence in jeopardy it responds by exercising power, directly or indirectly, over the life and death of its subjects.[20] Specifically, when a subject transgresses the law, the sovereign replies with lethal force, putting the offender to death as

---

[16] Id., 78.
[17] Michel Foucault, *Discipline and Punish: The Birth of the Prison*, trans. Alan Sheridan. New York: Vintage, 1979, 9.
[18] In *Violence and the Sacred*, René Girard offers a slightly different analysis of the rationalization of political power. According to Girard, the judicial system is not concerned with justice but with general security. Its specific concern is to limit and isolate the effects of violence, in particular the effects of violence that are the product of cycles of revenge. The judicial system seeks to stifle the impulse to vengeance rather than spreading or aggravating it. To achieve this goal, the system "rationalizes" revenge. It does so by confronting violence head on so that violence falls on the right victim, the perpetrator of the violence rather than a substitute (as in sacrifice.) When the judicial system is backed by a firmly established political power, it can act with such force that no (vengeful) response is possible. In such a situation, the judicial system possesses "a monopoly on the means of revenge." René Girard, *Violence and the Sacred*, trans. Patrick Gregory. Baltimore, MD: Johns Hopkins University Press, 1977, 22–23.
[19] Austin Sarat, "Capital Punishment as a Legal, Political, and Cultural Fact: An Introduction," in *The Killing State: Capital Punishment in Law, Politics, and Culture*, ed. Austin Sarat. New York: Oxford University Press, 1999, 3.
[20] Michel Foucault, *The History of Sexuality: An Introduction*, trans. Robert Hurley. New York: Vintage, 1990, 135.

punishment for daring to challenge its authority. Even if this course of action is justified in the name of preserving and caring for the conditions that make collective life possible, let alone meaningful, in the exercise of state violence the classic sovereign has been subtly displaced by what Foucault calls "biopower," a power whose main role is to "ensure, sustain, and multiply life."[21] In a regime dedicated to putting and keeping life in order and safe, the state may still exercise the right to death associated with the classic sovereign. To do so, however, it has to describe those who will be put to death as incorrigible monsters or as biological hazards so that their demise and final disposal can be represented as an unpleasant but necessary task that the state reluctantly but decisively undertakes for the well-being of its citizens.[22]

Overview of the Book

The scholarship collected in this book recognizes that violence, as a fact and a nightmare, is integral to the life of the modern state because the state is a creature of both literal violence and threats, real or imagined, of force. Each of the authors acknowledges the complicated character of the state's relationship to violence and so understands the difficulty of accurately naming and defining state violence as well as the difficulty of disciplining that violence and subjecting it to a clarifying academic theory.

What is more, different states hold different capacities for, and dispositions toward, violence. To complicate matters further, an ambivalent "charge" comes with contemplating how the use of lethal force is justified. The authors in this collection recognize that we can easily condemn actors whose exercise of violence is justified in the name of consolidating or preserving state power, but at the same time we want to be able to exercise such violence ourselves. As long as we repress the pleasure associated with such wishes or otherwise defer working through the desire for mastery and the sense of vulnerability that move us to critique the state, the "charge" remains. Wherever the state acts violently, however, the legitimacy of its acts must be engaged with the real facts of war, capital punishment, and the ugly realities of death. The urgency of the contemplation of those facts

[21] Id., 138.
[22] Id., 138.

depends, as we hope to show in the chapters that follow, on mounting a sustained effort at interpretation, sense making, and critique.

This book is divided into two sections, the first, "On the Forms of State Killing," provides an overview of various modes through which state violence appears in the world. The second, "Investigating the Discourses of Death," focuses on one particular form of state violence, capital punishment.

The first section begins with a chapter by Robin Wagner-Pacifici, who argues that despite the necessary role of violence in state formation and governance, the recent transformation of the framing of that violence – from policies of "war" and aggression to strategies for "defense" and protection – has created an odd situation in which the lethality of the state might actually be deemed innocuous. Her chapter examines how the discussion of sovereignty and violence has been transformed by several United States government policy documents, beginning with the Bush administration's *National Security Strategy of the United States of America (NSSUSA)* for 2002. Wagner-Pacifici suggests that the defensive strategies modeled in these documents challenge Weber's conception of the state by breaking down the borders that are understood to limit a state's monopoly on violence "within a given territory."

For Weber, Wagner-Pacifici argues, "the monopoly of force is qualified as legitimate, and its success seems to hinge on this legitimacy," yet Wagner-Pacifici points out that although Weber claims to focus his definition of the state exclusively on means, that is, physical force that can be used for any end, the concept of legitimacy inevitably introduces "ends" criteria. According to Wagner-Pacifici, Weber's assertion that states monopolize violence "within a given territory" implies a necessary demarcation of borders that were once drawn using violence before that violence was monopolized and legitimized. She notes that established states' "deployment of force beyond the borders of the domestic sphere" is presumptively illegitimate. To avoid this charge of illegitimacy, she argues, states qualify their extraterritorial deployment of violence as a measure of defense for their legitimate borders.

This rationale helps to explain the shift toward a more defensive understanding of violence. The 2002 *NSSUSA* announced a new "preventive war" policy, which called for the United States to act against threats "before they are fully formed." The 2006 *NSSUSA*, in turn, reaffirmed the "reasonableness" of the preventive war model. Wagner-Pacifici notes that these documents attempt to reassert the power of the United States in post-9/11 politics but actually work to transform violence into "something nonviolent, nonlethal, innocuous." The actions outlined in the documents are always "defensive, rather than aggressive." The United States is also painted as a conventional state – as opposed to a "failed" or "rogue" state that does not have an effective monopoly over legitimate violence in its given territory – and as such is depicted as "paradigmatic" of "innocuous or nontraumatic" sovereign statehood. In this self-dramatization, the United States is no longer an imperialist nation but rather one that responds to the actions of others. Wagner-Pacifici contends that as a result, in the context of new "wars," "the public may no longer be able to recognize victory when it arrives." The documents in question, by re-situating the United States' means of legitimately using violence, "actually problematize and actively reinterpret many of the key terms of state sovereignty and power."

The next chapter by Jeremy Arnold takes up the issue of reinterpreting sovereignty with an examination of the United States' invasion of Iraq. That invasion, he claims, reveals the buried logic of what he calls "Oedipal sovereignty." According to this logic, *"sovereignty is the cause of the very problems it claims the right to solve."* To better understand the paradox that characterizes this logic and its centrality to the concept of sovereignty, Arnold directs our attention to the story of Oedipus.

According to Arnold, the Oedipus trilogy is intended to teach us that "the figure of death signifies...*security*." The figure of death signifies security insofar as *"death is a limit upon human existence which cannot be transgressed."* Before this limit of human existence is reached, however, there is no death; therefore, there is no security and life could be destroyed. According to Arnold, the Oedipus trilogy teaches us that sovereignty is the political structure that prevents this from happening. The sovereign understands that humans are "destined for ruin," but it is his goal to limit the tendency toward ruination because the context of misery and suffering that surrounds life makes possible experiences of happiness and joy by comparison. To protect life, however, the sovereign must have access to secret knowledge about death. The sovereign must have this access because death is what secures existence, and, to secure the best possible life, the sovereign must "maintain that knowledge as its own."

Introduction

Arnold argues that the Oedipus trilogy is so instructive about the character of sovereignty because it shows us how sovereigns fail and thereby set in motion the logic characteristic of sovereignty. Specifically, the Oedipus trilogy shows us that when the sovereign forgets or fails to protect his knowledge, he is transformed "into a man of passion." For example, trying to escape what he knows to be his fate, Oedipus ends up on the path that leads him to kill his father and marry his mother. This decomposition "is the origin of the political ills that infect the body politic." Once this decomposition occurs, the sovereign begins to create or cause the very problems he must confront.

According to Arnold, the invasion of Iraq by the United States demonstrates this logic. Oedipal sovereignty, according to Arnold, teaches us that the effects of sovereign power could "undermine the very ends of sovereignty." As Arnold points out, in Sophocles' famous tragedy, Oedipus is simultaneously "the cause of, and solution to, the problem of the political." Arnold shows that in Iraq, when the United States claims the right to expel violence from a violent space, the United States is similarly responsible for the violence it seeks to eliminate. When this paradox comes to light, Arnold claims that the war in Iraq cannot be seen as a war of defense; rather it must be recognized as an action that creates the very problem that it is employed to solve. The invasion of Iraq has produced a space of violence where one did not previously exist. In an effort to ensure security, the United States created insecurity for both Americans (by causing terrorist backlash) and Iraqis (by creating a violent space within their borders).

As evidence that "the meaning of death, and the knowledge death provides, is crucial to the success of the sovereign," Arnold turns his attention to how the dead in Iraq are counted. Arnold is specifically concerned with the lack of attention given to the violence against Iraqi bodies and why these bodies do not seem to count. He criticizes the liberal-humanitarian justification for the invasion of Iraq – the notion that the United States is bringing universal rights to the country – for ignoring the human being "in its singularity." According to Arnold, singular dead bodies do not count because (1) they are dead and can no longer bear rights and (2) there is nothing universal in *a* dead body. Arnold's discussion of how different deaths are represented differently by the sovereign – specifically how Iraqi bodies either do not count or are counted "only as part of a *calculus* in which certain bodies can be *sacrificed* for the greater end of liberation" – anticipates

Taussig-Rubbo's argument in the next chapter. It also raises "a criticism of the *instrumental effectiveness* of sovereign power," as Arnold suggests that "the entire logic of means-ends rationality in the context of sovereignty" must be questioned because the ends are always in contradiction with the means. Arnold concludes his reinterpretation of sovereignty by proposing that the best way to "formulate deeper challenges to sovereign power" is to assert that sovereignty kills not as a means, contra Weber, but as an end in itself.

In the next chapter, Taussig-Rubbo is particularly interested in contemporary state efforts to "unbundle itself from sacred meanings." Focusing on state efforts to manage the logic and rhetoric of sacrifice, he explores how the suffering attendant to state violence is presented (by the government) and received (by the public) when that suffering is borne by nontraditional heroic figures, namely (1) private military contractors in Iraq, (2) the families of government-recognized servicemen, and (3) detainees in Guantánamo Bay.

Taussig-Rubbo chooses sacrifice as his focus because the "logic and rhetoric of sacrifice can function as a form of accountability" for citizens to ground claims against the government. When the state recognizes deaths as sacrifices, those deaths come to represent something sacred or significant. Consequently, the state seeks independence from its citizenry when it comes to labeling certain deaths as sacrifices. According to Taussig-Rubbo, the state jealously guards this prerogative so that it alone may designate which deaths are meaning*ful* and which deaths are meaning*less* to reinforce its monopoly on violence. Taussig-Rubbo asserts, however, that the state, despite its best efforts, cannot completely escape the reality "that sacrifice is central to the citizen's relation to the sovereign."

Taussig-Rubbo's first case study involves private military contractors in Iraq. Taussig-Rubbo identifies the use of private contractors as an attempt by the U.S. government to outsource sacrifice to actors whose deaths might not resonate as strongly with the public as the death of a uniformed soldier. When four armed Blackwater contractors were brutally killed in Fallujah in 2004, however, it was difficult for U.S. government officials to continue their designation of private military contractors as "unsacrificeable subjects." Prior to this event, sacrifice in the military sense was usually viewed as something only a soldier could do for his or her nation. In the post-Vietnam era, however, with its gap between the military and society,

Introduction

Taussig-Rubbo observes that "the roles of those giving and receiving sacrifices for the nation are not clearly defined."

This discussion of the murder and desecration of the Blackwater contractors leads Taussig-Rubbo to his second area of inquiry: "instances in which U.S. officials try to 'privatize' sacrifice by... making it a 'family matter.'" Last, he turns to the "counter-sacrificial" policies employed against enemy detainees attempting to martyr themselves while in U.S. government custody. Enemy detainees, like private military contractors, are supposed to be excluded from sacrifice. Taussig-Rubbo suggests that detainees attempting to cause their own death by hunger striking are force fed because their attempts at self-destruction take power away from the state, which is supposed to have a monopoly over violence. Detainees must not be allowed to sacrifice themselves, as it were.

Government action in all three of these examples, Taussig-Rubbo asserts, can be traced to Giorgio Agamben's notion that sovereign power is "that which can take life without the action being considered a sacrifice." Taussig-Rubbo concludes that sacrifice attendant to the state's violent acts seems to be too entrenched in deep national traditions for the public to perceive as insignificant any of the deaths he describes, however. Consequently, "the state's attempt to unbundle itself from sacred meanings is not entirely successful."

Reminding us that there are many acts of state violence and forms of death that the public might not see, Colin Dayan's chapter shifts the focus a bit, connecting the war on terror to the phenomena of supermax (i.e., supermaximum security) prisons. According to Dayan, both in domestic supermax prisons and in secret detention centers overseas (mostly in Iraq), new categories of persons are created who exist in limbo outside of the law. Imprisonment has become lethal, because these persons are devoid of many of the basic civil rights guaranteed in the Constitution. In this age of "new world security," the "legal vacuum" created for these persons leads to a sort of "civil death."

By redefining persons, the state is able to sustain violence that should not exist. The elimination of habeas corpus for "illegal enemy combatants" or "security detainees" prevents courts from hearing cases challenging arbitrary detention or other constitutional violations, effectively giving the state carte blanche to treat prisoners however the state sees fit. Referencing the arguments of Hannah Arendt, Dayan explains: "Not only do these entities lie outside the legal definition of persons, but they seem to occupy a space of incapacitation outside the claims of legality." As "the new acceptance of torture... institutes judicial novelties that the law itself was designed to prohibit," Dayan's argument resounds with Arnold's suggestion that sovereignty tends to create the very problems that it purports to solve. On the other side of the debate, however, White House lawyers justifying the government's actions argue that the labels that they place on dangerous persons are precisely *intended* to "suspend the requirement of due process without in any way touching or harming the core of constitutional and judicially ascertained principles of liberty and justice." The lawyers argue that these enemy combatants *should* be excluded from eligibility for writs of habeas corpus and furthermore that their exclusion protects the liberty of the rest of us.

Dayan sees the current attacks on due process as another instance of a time when ideals of due process have come into conflict with "a philosophy of personhood." In the *Dred Scott* case, for instance, Chief Justice Roger Taney designated Scott as a person lacking the right to bring suits to court, thereby denying jurisdiction to federal courts and condemning Scott and the new category of persons to which he belonged "never to be free of the status that [consigned them] to degradation in the eyes of the law." Like slaves, the "civil rights and legal capacities" of the new categories of criminal created in this new age of security are often "rationalized as dispensable." Concluding with a warning borrowed from William Blackstone, Dayan argues that confinement of the type in Guantánamo Bay, or anyplace in which persons are categorized in a way that keeps them outside of the law, signals despotism and tyranny, because such "secret forms of imprisonment" represent "'a more dangerous engine of arbitrary government'" and one of the most insidious forms of state violence.

The next chapter continues Dayan's focus on punishment as a form of state violence. Here Tom Dumm considers how what he perceives to be "a shift in punishment from time to torture" could signal broader changes in the political culture of the United States and how the new sentencing trends reflect changes in our understandings of the meanings of life and death.

Dumm observes two trends in sentencing that he thinks are related. First, judges are abandoning responsibility for sentencing. This trend is conventionally explained by the influx of sentencing guidelines imposed

Introduction

by other branches of government; however, Dumm sees the shift from judicial judgment to executive decision making to be indicative of "a macro shift in the body politic that has led us to the current state of affairs, where war power and punishment power have been confounded." For Dumm, the shift toward executive decision making indicates "a depoliticization of life" because it displaces our old way of seeing humanity "as a part of what Carl Schmitt has called 'the political,'" and he warns that such a depoliticization of life might lead "to circumstances in which the willingness to die for one's identity as a member of a nation comes to be displaced . . . [in favor of] a hope to live in a state of security," a notion also discussed by Taussig-Rubbo. By supporting "a hidden politics of governmentality," this hope also contributes to the confounding of responsibility for imposing punishment.

The second trend in sentencing that Dumm observes is a shift from sentences that reflect the presumed value of freedom to sentences that emphasize the "primacy of physical pain." Because liberal societies have long identified a sentence of "denial of freedom for a period of time" as the appropriate form of punishment, Dumm suggests that this shift brings us "closer to thinking about embodiment and the meaning of the sentence." Dumm himself argues that the new emphasis on pain, made manifest in the use of torture, confounds the core values of liberal freedom. He also suggests that it reflects a change in our understanding of the meanings of life and death.

To illustrate how a shift in the meaning of the sentence might have been brought about by a shift in our understanding of the meaning of life and death, Dumm examines two aspects of "the contemporary culture of Christian fundamentalist faith." The first pertains to the scientific investigation into the death of Jesus. Dumm finds it paradoxical that "Christians want to know more about Jesus, just not the sort of stuff that is made available to them by statistical and DNA analyses. The knowledge that they do not want is knowledge of the physical body of Jesus, which for Catholic dogma to be accepted, must not be found to exist on earth." Their resistance might also be explained by the second aspect of the contemporary culture of Christian fundamentalist faith that Dumm examines, however. According to Dumm, contemporary Christian fundamentalists understand the meaning of life as "the continuation of time." Dumm claims that this understanding is reflected in the "mythological" notion of death with dignity, which seeks to connect life and death, denying the embarrassing truths of physical death (e.g., the voiding of the bowels and bladder) that undermine "the integrity of the body and the coherence of the self... that is concomitant with the emergence of modern individuality." A modern scientific understanding of death exposes us to all of these embarrassing truths, rendering death undignified and deepening "our desire to evade death's facticity."

The discussion of contemporary Christian fundamentalist culture illustrates how a modern scientific understanding of death can signal an era of decline in rights. As bodies "are the familiar bearers of our rights," the notion of bodily integrity is "closely associated with the evolution of individual rights." Dumm suggests that to avoid the facticity of death, sovereign power exploits the demystification of death, subtly expanding the right to allow or disallow life to include "the power to refuse to allow life to end on its own terms." Despite the fact that "time has become meaningless as a measure of punishment," one might be forced to live and that "mercy in the form of sustaining life becomes a punishment."

In the next chapter, Elizabeth Povinelli examines "the forms, modes, and discourses of lethality in contemporary Australia... in order to understand the dynamic conditions that qualify one kind of lethality as 'state killing' and another as a more amorphous condition of 'letting die.'" She seeks to open "a productive avenue for critically engaging the imaginary and practical relationship of late liberal subjects and institutions to the unequal distribution of life and death in democratic orders."

Povinelli criticizes what she calls "future anterior" modes of understanding life and suffering, claiming that the ethical relationship between citizens in democratic orders "must be radically present tense." In addition, she rejects "the ethics of empathy," calling on those with a good life either to compromise their goods or admit that those goods are more highly valued than ending the suffering of others. Throughout her chapter she focuses on suffering that "is ordinary, chronic, acute, and cruddy rather than catastrophic, eventful, and sublime" to show complicity between the security state and the neoliberal market that "animates contemporary late liberal attitudes toward various forms of living and dying."

Povinelli uses Australia and especially the Australian government's relationship with indigenous communities as a case study. She begins with the contention that the "longstanding and appalling state of indigenous health periodically prompts the question of what, or who, is to blame and,

Introduction

consequentially, what is to be done." This question is often answered, she argues, by pointing to individual people and their behavior rather than the social nature of poverty. This separation between "supra-individual cause" and "the aggregate of individual choice" makes individual persons responsible for "the social causes and social distributions of lethality." As a result, Povinelli notes, "state killing and its public sanction are transfigured into a more amorphous agreement that people are killing themselves." Thus, the Australian government accepts no responsibility for the lethal conditions in the country's indigenous communities. The withdrawal of governmental support was purportedly undertaken to bring indigenous people into the mainstream.

The government portrays the withdrawal of life support in indigenous communities as "a moral good" because "somehow the refusal of [indigenous people's] form of life contributes to the happiness of a majority of citizens." Povinelli sees it differently, however: she argues that this withdrawal is a form of state killing. She wants to make this more subtle, "ordinary" violence visible to us, for the treatment of lethality in indigenous communities as "ordinary" rather than "catastrophic" means that "these kinds of deaths only periodically fix the gaze of national and international publics." Like Dayan, Povinelli argues that these publics are distracted by the creation of "special forms of enemies" that capture the imagination and thus provide "an alibi for the concentration and consolidation of state executive power." The practical and chronic reality of the lethality of indigenous communities cannot compete with the flashy violence of "terrorists" and other areas of interest to the late liberal state.

Povinelli concludes that "any attempt to understand the social imaginaries characterizing lethal conditions within late liberal societies must take into account the two very different forms, modes, and qualities of killing found there: strong and weak state killing." Rather than ignore weak state killing in favor of focusing exclusively on "catastrophic" lethality, she urges us to include weak state killing in our understanding of forms of state lethality by accepting that "no present can be divided in such a way that what I have . . . is not cosubstantial with what you have and do not have."

Antaki and Kirkby continue Povinelli's inquiry into the state's relation to indigenous people, this time in Canada rather than Australia. As do other contributors to this book, they examine the violence implicit in state categorizations of distinct groups of persons with unique relationships to the law. Specifically, they locate the lethality of the state "in 'cognition,' in how the state knows, and hence how it sees and speaks." They look at several pieces of Canadian legislation "to show cognition at work in the attempt to make indigenous peoples legible so as to rewrite them as members of a simplified Indian population." Antaki and Kirkby also see violence in the fact that state recognition is "tied to... submission to Crown sovereignty."

According to Antaki and Kirkby, state recognition engages in "the death of peoples *as* peoples." The state sees statically and simplifies "indigenous peoples into objects of state power, reduces their homelands to territories, and reduces them from peoples to members of a population." Indigenous peoples thus became objects of federal power, "objects amenable to calculation and mastery." This is made evident by the creation of the "legal status of 'Indian'" in the *Indian Act* of 1876.

Subsequent legislation seemed promising in respect to the preservation of indigenous peoples as peoples, specifically Section 35(1) of the *Constitution Act*. Section 35 "seemed to promise both proper sight and honourable speech" as the government came to realize that "to recognize and affirm others is to accept the invitation to see as they see, to allow their sight to affect one's own." Antaki and Kirkby argue, however, that Section 35 actually turned out to be an exercise in state lethality. The problem came with the ambiguity of "reconciliation." Reconciliation between the Canadian state and indigenous peoples was not intended in the sense of facilitating an amenable relationship of mutual respect. Instead, reconciliation included requirements of acquiescence and submission by the indigenous peoples. Antaki and Kirkby conclude that this approach not only threatens to ratify "the dishonorable actions of the past" but also, and more significantly, "justifies their repetition in the future."

The four chapters in Section II focus on the death penalty. When the state executes someone, it concentrates its violence, bringing it fully to bear as a punitive response to allegations of wrongdoing. Here the bloodthirstiness of the state is vividly on display. Here the awe-inspiring moment of sovereign violence is crystallized. Each of the chapters in this part seeks to explain how and why this form of state violence persists.

Peter Brooks begins this inquiry by treating execution as a cultural as well as a state practice. He turns to literature, in particular Victor Hugo's novel *Le Dernier Jour d'un Condamné*, "a novel about the last day of a man sentenced to execution." Brooks argues that the perverse nature of this

Introduction

first-person narration makes us uncomfortable as readers and encourages reflection on whether we are comfortable with capital punishment at all.

The instrument of death about which Hugo writes is the guillotine. "The guillotine," Brooks argues, "is of particular importance, both in Hugo's work and in the French discourse on capital punishment." The instantaneous decapitation "becomes a matter for thought, since the thinking part no longer is attached to the bodily part." Brooks identifies this feature of the guillotine as perhaps "some sinister parodic realization of Cartesian dualism: the thinking self detached from the living self, in an impossible moment of reflection" that serves to intensify the "anguished paradox posed by death sentences of all sorts."

Like Hugo, Brooks questions the death penalty because "it doubles the natural, the inhuman outrage of death with the obscenity of death intentionally imposed by human action." Brooks argues that the state should "refrain from doing nature's cruel work" and that building "a machine for killing one's fellow men is barbarity." Brooks also believes that Hugo's first-person narration is effective in conveying this sentiment because it attaches the reader to the condemned man, forcing us to confront individual feelings rather than allowing us to defer to the sentiments of the society as a whole. Hugo specifically leaves his protagonist as "a kind of faceless, identityless everyman," so that rather than focusing on the nature of his crime or issues of his guilt, the reader must face "one thing only: the consciousness knowing that it will cease to be before the day is over." Brooks therefore argues that in Hugo's novel "it is precisely the impossible ending that matters – the inability to write 'finis.'"

Many deaths, either real or fictional, especially those brought about by state violence, are presented as a means of bringing closure, not only for the person facing death, for whom "life takes on its meaning, becomes transmissible as wisdom, only at the moment of death," but also for the rest of us, who often seek "to understand our lives in more satisfactory and romantic crime-and-retribution ways." Brooks rejects this notion of closure, admiring the lack of completion created by Hugo's first-person narration.

As Brooks sees it, Hugo's abrupt first-person ending "may violate certain conventions of novelistic plausibility but nonetheless quite powerfully provokes a reader's reaction to the state's intentional death dealing." Specifically, the ending forces the reader to confront his or her displeasure with the situation about which Hugo writes: capital punishment.

This hook into the reader's sensibility allows Hugo (and subsequently Brooks) to advance political arguments about the death penalty, namely that "the very emergence of modern civilization requires [the] twilight of the executioner."

Brooks concludes by asking "why Hugo's vision of the end of the executioner hasn't been taken more seriously in the United States," where abolition "now has turned to a piecemeal campaign that may indeed prove effective in reducing the number of executions but will have a very long road to travel." He answers his own question by arguing that the failure of American abolition is directly tied to "a failure in the moral imagination." This is a significant failure, because in Brooks's view the moral imagination is "foundational to ethics: it is only through being able to put ourselves imaginatively in another's place that we can act morally."

Unlike Brooks, Ravit Reichman is skeptical of literature's ability to capture the reality of state violence. She does not condemn or dismiss literature for its limits, however; rather, Reichman focuses on "what this narrative resistance can tell us about our culture's relationship to capital punishment." She begins "with the basic premise that executions today occur behind closed doors" and expands on this notion by suggesting that when the public is forced to imagine state violence rather than see it firsthand, the result is not revulsion but indifference. According to Reichman, it is only "when the curtain does part, as it did in the 2006 execution of Saddam Hussein," that we are truly exposed to "both the horror and the seduction of capital punishment." Reichman argues that "what happens to the juridical and cultural imagination when acts carried out in the public's name take place in private . . . is nothing at all."

To support this claim, in the same way as Brooks, Reichman turns to literature, in this case Albert Camus's *The Stranger*. In the novel, punishment and death unfold "through a steady, deadened listlessness, perhaps the closest thing to narrative inertia." Reichman argues that the source of this inertia is an indifference that results from an inability to imagine an event hidden behind closed doors. Reichman agrees with Camus that once state-sanctioned killing has retreated from the public forum to behind prison walls, it provoked little reaction and began to "fade from consciousness."

Not surprisingly then, Reichman does not find the abrupt end of Hugo's first-person narrated novel as powerful as Brooks does. Instead, she interprets the presentation of the execution as though it "were a mere

Introduction

formality" as a demonstration of "how our culture tolerates its most divisive juridical realities, narrating the modes through which we live with our deepest social ambivalences." Reichman also argues that such a presentation "constitutes a loss, a move away from the political." According to Reichman, "the hush surrounding such public violence, in sharp contrast to the carnivalesque spectacles of the nineteenth century, suggests a connection between the modern death penalty and secrecy." Although executions exist in the mind's eye and support for them circulates among people, they appear only as "distant, surreal images." They are so vague and abstract that the public becomes desensitized to the scandal of the state violence that they represent.

Reichman claims that literature follows suit, refusing to portray the death penalty "as anything other than the impossibility ... of its representation." Existing as it does now as a postscript to the trial, the execution is "cut off from a narrative arc." It is "an event without a story, a nonevent." At best, an execution "fills the social space as form rather than substance." Consequently, focusing on the moment of execution does not aid the abolitionist movement. Public sentiment is unstirred. To communicate the gravity of the death penalty today, something more like Edmund Burke's "idea of the sublime" is required.

The next chapter, by Adam Thurschwell, moves from the domain of literature to political philosophy. Thurschwell argues that there is a disconnect between intellectual debates over capital punishment and "the realities of capital litigation" and that the cause of this disconnect is the fact that "capital punishment has been analyzed as a moral and not a political-philosophical question." By situating capital punishment in moralistic terms, retentionists and abolitionists orient themselves "precisely backward – the most fundamental issues are neither individual nor moral but the profoundly political ones of the constitution and exercise of state sovereignty." Framing the debate about the death penalty in political-philosophical terms rather than moral ones will not necessarily advance the abolitionist cause. Thurschwell instead argues that a shift in the terms of the debate clarifies that the state's right to kill is inherent in the nature of the state and therefore reminds us that to challenge the legitimacy of state violence is to challenge the state itself.

Thurschwell sees state violence as essentially a political issue, because punishment is not merely something that happens to someone, "but also is something that the *state*, as a state, does to someone." Consequently, in his view, "capital punishment ought to be analyzed and evaluated as simply another form of government regulation like any other," in accordance with Foucault's notion of biopolitics and governmentality. Proceeding this way, one can show continuity between the death penalty and other government practices (e.g., those discussed in the chapters by Povinelli and by Antaki and Kirkby) that affect the regulation of life and death. By insisting on the distinctiveness of the death penalty, one unwittingly affirms "a view of the state that makes its power to kill its own citizens its primary and essential attribute."

Thurschwell points out the line of argument that posits a sovereign right to kill its citizens and conscript them to die in its defense. Most important, he shows that "this 'right' is a defining power and not a legal or moral right." According to Thurschwell, the possession of this "right" "implies nothing about the state's legal, ethical, or moral legitimacy or normative entitlement to exercise this power. It is simply the attribute that makes that state 'the state' and not some other entity or institution within civil society."

Thurschwell claims that by recognizing that the power of capital punishment is a defining characteristic of the state itself and therefore purely political, abolitionists can better appreciate the challenge that they face. Specifically, they can better understand how "a complete and total abolition of capital punishment would appear to have to wait on a complete and total transformation in the essential nature of political sovereignty." Given this challenge, the elimination of the death penalty is extremely unlikely, and reform of the practice might be the best that can be accomplished. Nevertheless, regardless of its consequence for abolition, Thurschwell believes that "a philosophical approach to capital punishment that begins from the fundamental questions and categories of the political will bear more fruit, both philosophical and practical, than one that approaches it from a moral perspective."

The last chapter, by Adam Sitze, continues Thurschwell's interest in the development of a political perspective on state killing and on the problems of abolitionism. Sitze claims that abolitionists often pursue their goals in ways that contradict the purpose of the movement, basing their attacks against state violence on problematic premises. He illustrates this claim through a reading of Cesare Beccaria's arguments about capital punishment. According to Sitze, Beccaria "argued that the death of a citizen should be limited to those exceptional situations in which internal enemies threaten

Introduction

the very existence of the *salute pubblica*." Sitze suggests that this argument is not particularly original and that it is therefore surprising that "it should be so widely accepted as abolitionism's primary intellectual origin." We might be even more surprised if we paid closer attention and noticed that the difference between Beccaria's arguments against capital punishment and arguments that advance the same goal is that "Beccaria problematized not only the sovereign right to kill but also the sovereign right to let live."

Sitze argues that Beccaria did this by calling into question "the most theological of all political powers: the sovereign right of clemency." Beccaria claimed that because clemency "is only needed to the degree that punishments are unnecessarily severe," then "clemency would have to be completely excluded (*esclusa*) from any state that finally instituted a predictable and geometrically rigorous system of crimes and punishments." The end goal of this exclusion, according to Beccaria, would be that rather than acting as an exception to law, clemency "would be resplendent in the legal code itself... it would serve as the general norm for a penal law that henceforth would be uniformly mild." Sitze suggests that this argument likely arose from the fact that Beccaria "wrote under conditions in which capital's need for labor power spurred the politicization of life," and thus sovereign power and biopolitics became conjoined because "clemency was desirable not as the attribute through which sovereign power could become most like divine power, but merely as an especially fitting means to the end of preserving the sacred lives of individuals and populations."

In Sitze's view, the heart of Beccaria's argument is that "the more a nation develops out of a state of savagery into civilization, the more its power to punish should be actualized in, through, and as a power *not* to punish." This claim, reinforced by the form of Beccaria's original text, reflects Beccaria's belief, as Sitze puts it, that "biopower modified more than just the sovereign right to kill."

Unfortunately, abolitionists today "not only appeal to but also praise the sovereign right of clemency, as if this right were somehow a self-evident or even sufficient antidote to the right to kill." Sitze disagrees. In his view, "the sovereign's reprieve is the primary juridical basis precisely for *reseizing* the defeated enemy as a slave and for maintaining the slave as a living tool for increasing the wealth of the republic." Although Beccaria exalts the exclusion of clemency as "a radically egalitarian and specifically modern concept of the political," Sitze observes that "this same internal exclusion had viciously inegalitarian implications" and therefore places "a fatal limit on abolitionism's pursuit of its own desired juridical objective." In light of this, Sitze concludes that "the sovereign right to spare life is by no means a self-evident antidote to the sovereign right to kill." In his view, it avoids one form of state violence only to elevate another.

Although the subject areas and theoretical commitments of the essays in this volume vary widely, taken together they suggest that condemning the state's decisions to use lethal force is not a simple matter of demanding that the state engage in only just wars (publicly declared and justified) or abolishing the death penalty. They suggest that even such overt instances of lethal force are more elusive as targets of critique than one might think and, perhaps more to the point, altering such decisions does nothing to change the essential relationship of the state to violence. To change that relationship, we must also attend to the violent state as a state *of mind*, a state of mind that is not just a social or psychological condition but also a moral commitment or a philosophical position.

PART I

ON THE FORMS OF STATE KILLING

2

The Innocuousness of State Lethality in an Age of National Security

Robin Wagner-Pacifici

What is required is thus a sovereignty, a force that is stronger than all the other forces in the world. But if the constitution of this force is, in principle, supposed to represent and protect this world democracy, it in fact betrays and threatens it from the very outset, in an autoimmune fashion, and in a way that is... just as silent as it is unavowable. Silent and unavowable like sovereignty itself.
– Jacques Derrida, *Rogues*

All states are lethal by definition. Max Weber knew this, and in a 1918 speech to law students in Germany, "Politics as a Vocation," he detailed this recognition by way of a definition. Assuring his audience that his lecture would disappoint them, he first announced that politics should be understood as the leadership of a political association, "hence today, of a *state*."[1] Hewing firmly to a sociological point of view, he eliminated the consideration of ends or goals in his definition of a state, because different states historically have had different ends. What defines a state for Weber is its means, and the means specific to all states is the use of physical force. Weber approvingly quotes Leon Trotsky to introduce this sociological definition of the state: "'Every state is founded on force,' said Trotsky at Brest-Litovsk. That is indeed right" (78). Weber then provides two quick definitions of the state. The first defines the state as "a human community that (successfully) claims the monopoly of the legitimate use of physical force within a given territory" (78). The second, following closely, offers "a relation of men dominating men, a relation supported by means of legitimate (i.e. considered to be legitimate) violence" (78).

---

[1] Max Weber, *From Max Weber: Essays in Sociology*, ed. H. H. Gerth and C. Wright Mills. New York: Oxford University Press, 1958, 77; hereafter cited parenthetically by page number.

Physical force is the key in Weber's formulation. According to Weber, the monopoly of force is qualified as legitimate, and its success seems to hinge on this legitimacy. If the "relation of men dominating men" requires legitimacy (which could thus be seen as preconditioning), however, why does legitimacy not have pride of place in the definition as the means specific to the state? Why is legitimacy not the first mover? Clearly, Weber is working out the relationship between means and ends in his definition of the state despite his explicit move to marginalize ends. Legitimacy and its sources inevitably evoke ends of political leadership of states – justifications and obligations from the past (tradition), the future (charisma), or the ongoing present (legality). The identification of violence as the signal means of the state necessarily provokes unease about the (legitimating) relationship to action in the name of the state. In attempting to explain why Weber insinuates the ends of the state into the sociological, means-restricted definition of the state, it might be possible to articulate the reasons why it is so hard to approach the lethality of the state frontally, why political leaders invariably connect state violence to legitimate ends, and why the whole story of the relation of violent means to political ends inevitably founders in conceptual ruptures, repetitions, and tautologies.

This essay critiques the following reports: the George W. Bush administration's *National Security Strategy of the United States of America* (*NSSUSA*) for 2002 and 2006, the 2005 *National Strategy for Victory in Iraq*, and *The 9/11 Commission Report*.[2] All seek to situate and justify state violence in post-9/11 America. I argue that they are all political documents grappling with violence in such a way as to render state violence essentially innocuous. It is an understatement to say that Weber, writing in Germany at the end of World War I, did not view the essential violence of the state as innocuous, but he also did not flinch from his recognition of its necessity – the disappearance of such social institutions that "knew the use of violence" would lead to anarchy. Weber's philosophical struggles focused

---

[2] The White House, *The National Security Strategy of the United States of America*, September 2002, www.whitehouse.gov/nsc/nss.html; National Security Council, *National Strategy for Victory in Iraq*, November 2005, www.whitehouse.gov/infocus/iraq/iraq_strategy_nov2005.html; The White House, *The National Security Strategy of the United States of America*, March 2006, www.whitehouse.gov/nsc/nss/2006/; 9/11 Commission, *The 9/11 Commission Report: Final Report of the National Commission on Terrorist Attacks upon the United States*, authorized ed. New York: W. W. Norton, 2004, available at www.9-11commission.gov (accessed October 23, 2007). Hereafter these documents are cited parenthetically by page number.

The Innocuousness of State Lethality in an Age of National Security

on the impossibility of keeping the violent means and the legitimization ends separate in his sociological definition of the state and the difficulty in developing a sociological vocabulary about these matters that was not normative:

"(i.e. considered to be legitimate)"

A parenthetical word or phrase appears in each of Weber's definitions of the state.[3] In the first, the appearance of "(successfully)" qualifies and buttresses the claim of the monopoly of the use of legitimate physical force. A claim to statehood must obviously be successful to constitute a bona fide state. An ambiguity in meaning presents itself, however: is the claim successful because it is legitimate, appealing appropriately and convincingly to the relevant source of authority, or is the claim successful because those making it do indeed hold the monopoly of physical force? In either case, why is the word *successfully* inserted in parentheses rather than presented uncircumscribed as a full-fledged element of the definition? In the second definition, the parenthetical statement "(i.e. considered to be legitimate)" follows the word *legitimate* and separates that term from the final word, *violence*. Again, the break or pause and qualification in the definition refer to questions of legitimacy. Weber certainly rejects any absolutist idea of legitimacy, having developed his own typology of historically and sociologically variable sources of legitimate authority. He nevertheless feels it necessary to highlight the work of judgment and evaluation in determining the legitimacy of states.

By way of these parentheses, historical contingency and the normative claims of sources of authority threaten to rupture this already compromised sociological definition. For Weber, the state's monopoly of violence defines its sociological existence, but his definition resists collapsing into a version of "might makes right" by the introduction of the concept of legitimacy. This introduction proves problematic, however, because it appears to insinuate "ends" criteria into a "means-only" definition. The parentheses attempt to hold the means (violence) and ends apart, but they succeed only in highlighting the true pathos of the enterprise. As Weber notes toward the end of his speech, "The early Christians knew full well the world is governed by demons and that he who lets himself in for politics,

---

[3] These parentheses do appear in the original German text of the speech.

that is for power and force as means, contracts with diabolical powers and for his action it is not true that good can follow only from good and evil only from evil, but that often the opposite is true" (123).[4]

Weber's definitions of the state and his discussion of politics as a vocation derive from three different contexts: the historical moment of Germany's defeat in World War I, the developing paradigm of sociology as a scientific enterprise, and Weber's own disillusioned monarchical nationalism. The relative weight of each of these contexts varies within his speech. Weber begins with definitions, moves on to case studies of politics in England, Germany, and the United States, and ends with a tentative formulation for a politics with an "ethic of responsibility" that is somehow able to recognize the violent heart of the state and to hold together the contradictions of passion, a sense of responsibility, and a sense of proportion. A strong case can be made for the claim that defeat raises definitional self-consciousness. This is a point that is important for the analysis of the analogue "parenthetical" interloper in this essay, the *National Strategy for Victory in Iraq*. Weber's repeated attempts at defining a state reveal the high stakes that he associated with this term and the impossibility of holding the means and ends apart in doing so.

"Within a given territory... men dominating men"

With their monopoly of legitimate violence, human beings dominate human beings, but they do so only "within a given territory." Once more, this phrase seems to involve a tautology. It also opens a temporal and causal conundrum: "within a given territory" implies a space available and demarcated prior to the achievement of the monopoly of legitimate violence. It must be the case, however, that the territory is fixed only ex post facto as a *function* of the very monopoly of violence that it inscribes.

Which comes first, the monopolized territory of legitimate violence or the legitimate violence that defines the territory? This reflexive relationship of the monopoly of violence and territory becomes particularly

---

[4] In his analysis of the significance of Weber's own breakdown for Weber's sociological project generally, Fredric Jameson connects the modern historical recognition of the division of means and ends with Weber's "heroic cynicism": "In this sense Weber's *Wertfreiheit* is a passionate refusal of the illusions of meaning itself, a repudiation of all philosophies which... seek to persuade us that some teleological movement is immanent in the otherwise chaotic and random agitation of empirical life." Fredric Jameson, "The Vanishing Mediator: Narrative Structure in Max Weber," *New German Critique*, no. 1 (Winter 1974): 52–89, 61.

important when it is implicated in the general theory of sovereign states in an international system of sovereign states. There the paradox touches on the relationship of any given state to the system generally. As international relations scholar Jens Bartleson writes, "For since the state is regarded as historically and ontologically prior to the system of states in the discourse on international politics, the essence of statehood appears to be the necessary condition also of the larger whole, the international system."[5] How is it possible that a sovereign state (e.g., a political-military entity successfully asserting a monopoly of legitimate violence over a given territory) can preexist a system of sovereign states that recognize and define state sovereignty itself? Generations of scholars of sovereignty have grappled with just this dilemma and all of its consequences.[6] Bartleson himself goes on to quote Anthony Giddens, who problematizes this sequential development of states and the state system: "'The sovereignty of the nation-state ... does not precede the development of the European state system, or the transferral of the nation-state to a global plane ... the development of the sovereignty of the modern state from its beginnings depends upon reflexively monitored sets of relations between states'" (46). In any event, the state system seems to divide the world clearly between the domestic spheres of each individual state, over which they have monopoly power, and the international sphere, over which they do not have, in Daniel Philpott's terms, "internal supremacy and external independence."[7] This clear demarcation of world territory has never, in fact, been clear, even granting its questionable conceptual clarity, however.

Refuting the assumption of the monolithic indivisibility of sovereignty, international relations scholars Michael Fowler and Julie Bunck have identified six types of circumstances in which sovereignty is compromised:

1. International legal proceedings
2. Leases of territory in which a weak country relinquishes exclusive rights to its territory to a more powerful country
3. International servitude

---

[5] Jens Bartleson, *A Genealogy of Sovereignty*. Cambridge: Cambridge University Press, 1995, 21; hereafter cited parenthetically by page number.
[6] For a useful review of some recent writings about these dilemmas, see Daniel Philpott, "Usurping the Sovereignty of Sovereignty." *World Politics* 53 (January 2001): 297–324.
[7] Ibid., 316.

4. Foreign military occupation and dictated treaty terms
5. Minority treaties
6. State-to-state political relationships.[8]

These types of circumstances do not occur randomly – they are a function of the historical situation and status of any given sovereign state. Fowler and Bunck note, "Since the international community seems in practice to have adopted a variable approach to sovereignty on numerous occasions, the meaning of the term can indeed differ markedly for a satellite, a superpower, a defeated state, a newly independent nation, and a large, populous superpower."[9]

Of obvious central concern is the deployment of force beyond the borders of the domestic sphere wherein the legitimate monopoly of force exists. Given the definitional criterion of the monopoly of legitimate violence over a given territory, such extraterritorial deployment of violence would appear to be illegitimate on its face, unless the territory beyond can be claimed by and for the state (thus legitimately under the aegis of the monopoly) or unless it is in the service of defending those very borders.[10] As demonstrated by the previous list of actual compromises of state sovereignty, illegitimate deployment of force occurs all the time. Anthropologist Catherine Lutz analyzes this apparent paradox as she considers what she calls the modern imperial project of the United States. Her interest is in the relationships of states to each other within this emerging paradigm, and she refers to the "semi-sovereign status" of such states as South Korea and the Philippines, in which national militaries could be under the command of the U.S. military based there or in which joint military exercises (twenty per year) have taken the place of U.S. military bases.[11]

---

[8] Michael Ross Fowler and Julie Marie Bunck, *Law, Power, and the Sovereign State: The Evolution and Application of the Concept of Sovereignty*. University Park: Pennsylvania State University Press, 1995, 124.

[9] Id.

[10] This situation of defending a state against an attack describes the one exception to the proscription of state violence in the United Nations Charter, Article 51. It identifies an individual or collective right of defense against an armed attack "until the Security Council has taken the measures necessary to maintain international peace and security." United Nations Charter, Chapter 7, "Action with Respect to Threats to the Peace, Breaches of the Peace, and Acts of Aggression," Article 51, June 26, 1945, www.un.org/aboutun/ charter (accessed December 19, 2007).

[11] Catherine Lutz, "Empire Is in the Details," *American Ethnologist* 33.4 (2006): 593–611.

The Innocuousness of State Lethality in an Age of National Security

The apparently pacific arrangements and relationships between states identified by these scholars are often structured as the self-conscious non-deployment of strategically prepositioned deployable forces. A monopoly of force allows a moratorium on the actual use of force. Following Norbert Elias, "When a monopoly of force is formed, pacified social spaces are created which are normally free from acts of violence."[12] Pacified social spaces are thus discovered not only within the acknowledged territory of the state but beyond it as well, in territorial spaces that are thus "pacified" in states of overdetermined sovereignty.

The purposive withholding of violence that *could* be deployed in pacified zones, whether those zones are within the domestic territory of the nation-state or beyond its territorial borders, suggests one inoculating effect of monopolized violence. Here is the irony of monopolies of violence being the *most* capable of withholding violence. The inevitably limited nature of the extent of the monopoly of the nation-state in the international state system, however, mandates constant readiness against the possibility of incursions by others and also seems politically to necessitate the intermittent demonstration of the violence by which it assays its authority. In his analysis of Weber's work on revolution, Randall Collins focuses on the question of the legitimacy of the state and identifies the critical centrality of war: "The source of legitimate power was the fact that people who bind themselves together for war put themselves into a community of fate.... The source of judicial power, the legitimate power to punish individuals in the name of the group, comes from the organization of the community for war."[13] War, with its solidarity claims and compulsions, appears to be an axiomatic element of the state's legitimate monopoly of violence, not just an episodic and contingent variant of the deployment of that violence.

Nevertheless, war must be accounted for or justified if it is to be authorized and legitimized. Weber's discussion of the sources of authority (i.e., tradition, charisma, and rational-legal) names the types of accounts that might be tendered. In any given state, in any given historical case, however, the connection must be made between those sources, their

---

[12] Norbert Elias, *The Civilizing Process*, vol. 2, *Power and Civility*, trans. Edmund Jephcott. New York: Pantheon Books, 1982, 235.

[13] Randall Collins, "Weber and the Sociology of Revolution," *Journal of Classical Sociology* 1.2 (2001): 171–194, 174.

specific mandates, and the actual deployment of violence in specific wars. Thus, a central question remains: how is violence recognized, named, and engaged (by both the parties deploying the violence and those being subjected to it)? In cases of war with other sovereign states, state violence can be operative beyond the acknowledged territorial borders of the state, with its specific *means* riding roughshod over that absence of international ends. The territorial extensiveness of war means that identifying the "given territory" of Weber's definition is more difficult than it might appear. The borders of that territory are more often than not mobile, diffuse, and contested. The deployment of state violence against apparently stateless enemies, such as al-Qaeda, challenges the Weberian formula even further.

The documents under analysis here are situated in the contradictory spaces opened up by Weber's definition, and their burdens are several. They struggle to connect violent means and legitimate state ends, to acknowledge and deny state violence, and to situate and displace the territory of the United States. A serious ethnography of state self-articulation and self-documentation must pose the question of how these documents carry forward these burdens.

Documents of State

The four documents under consideration are similar to each other in some ways and radically different in others. The NSSUSAs of 2002 and 2006 follow a template set in place by the 1986 Goldwater-Nichols Department of Defense Reorganization Act. That act mandated an annual strategy report by the president to Congress (in both a classified and an unclassified form), and every president since has submitted them (although few have done so annually). These reports are to include a comprehensive description and discussion of the following:

1. The worldwide interests, goals, and objectives of the United States that are vital to the national security of the United States.
2. The foreign policy, worldwide commitments, and national defense capabilities of the United States necessary to deter aggression and to implement the national security strategy of the United States.
3. The proposed short-term and long-term uses of the political, economic, military, and other elements of national power of the United

The Innocuousness of State Lethality in an Age of National Security

States to protect or promote the interests and achieve the goals and objectives referred to in paragraph (1).[14]

Innovations in structure have occurred over the years. The 1987 report had two major sections – foreign policy and defense policy – and was focused mainly on the Soviet Union. In 1988, there were separate strategies for different regions of the world. In 1991, regional conflict was identified as the organizing focus for the U.S. military, and U.S. economic health was emphasized as part of national security. The 1997 report was the first to highlight transnational threats and global economic interdependence. The 1998 report took note of domestic terrorism. Even with these innovations and emphases, functions of different administrations, and changing historical circumstances, much of the NSSUSA content is boilerplate. The United States' leadership role in the world is declared and assumed. Other political, military, and economic entities are identified along a continuum (itself subject to its own extensions and contractions) from friend to enemy.[15] Goals are announced, along with opportunities and challenges.

Many scholars have singled out the 2002 NSSUSA for analysis first and foremost for its announcement of a new "preventive war" policy. Commentators have noted the change in the official articulated policy of national defense, with the case being made for a new policy capable of responding to the new threats of terrorism, on the one hand, and "rogue nations" that aim to develop weapons of mass destruction, on the other: "As a matter of common sense and self-defense America will act against such emerging threats *before they are fully formed*" (2; emphasis added). Here a different approach to the 2002 NSSUSA – and to the other documents under investigation – is developed, one focused on its reconstitution of sovereign violence from the "inside." This approach is distinct from legal

---

[14] Don M. Snider and John A. Nagl, "The National Security Strategy: Documenting Strategic Vision," in *U.S. Army War College Guide to Strategy*, ed. Joseph Cerami and James F. Holcomb Jr. Carlisle, PA: Army War College, Institute of Strategic Studies, 2001, 127–142, 127.

[15] Characterizations of other political entities in the NSSUSA reveal a rhetorical-relational map of the world (allies, partners, friends, neighborhoods, and so forth). Carol Greenhouse, in an insightful reading of "legal consciousness" in *King Lear*, notes the residual effects of a model of legality within a unified order of fealty and kinship in the current Bush administration and "the administration's attempt to sustain executive authority through an international order of 'friendship' and the regulation of kinship." Carol Greenhouse, "Lear and Law's Doubles: Identity and Meaning in a Time of Crisis," *Law, Culture, and the Humanities* 2.2 (2006): 239–258, 242.

scholars' analyses of the jurisprudence of preemptive/preventive war and the respective domains of international laws of armed conflict and human rights law, from military scholars' discussions of precedents for preemptive strikes and strategic options, from philosophers' discussions of limit cases of the use of force in conditions of threatened communities, and from ethicists concerned about ethical criteria for just war.[16] Here the focus is on the texts as cultural artifacts of statecraft, understanding their generic strategies, their tonalities, and their rhetorics, because these documents are read through Weber's sociological definition of the state, combining theory with ethnography of the text.

The 2006 *NSSUSA*, although longer than its 2002 predecessor (there were none in the intervening years) and crafted to be a self-conscious intertext with it, received much less attention. There were divergent readings by those who did comment on it. Some noted that it could be read as merely reiterating the reasonableness of the preemptive/preventive war model first declared four years earlier but that it had shifted focus from Iraq to Iran. Others saw a more fundamental shift back to a Clintonian focus on globalization and diplomacy.

The publicizing of sovereignty is directed not just to its own (institutionally) divided self (president and Congress), not just to its collective self (sovereign citizens) but, significantly, to the world. As two U.S. Army War College analysts note, the strategies are sent to many constituencies: "Many of these are foreign, and extensive distributions through the U.S. Information Agency have proven effective at communicating changing U.S. intentions to the governments of many nations *not on our summit agendas*" (emphasis added).[17] Even those nations not on the U.S. summit

---

[16] Alan M. Dershowitz, *Preemption: A Knife That Cuts Both Ways*. New York: W. W. Norton, 2006; Kim Lane Scheppele, "The International State of Emergency: The Challenge for Constitutionalism after September 11" (paper presented at the annual meeting for the American Sociological Association, August 12, 2006, in Montreal); Rosa Ehrenreich Brooks, "War Everywhere: Rights, National Security Law, and the Law of Armed Conflict in the Age of Terror," *University of Pennsylvania Law Review* 153.2 (December 2004): 675–761; Endy Zemenides, "The Doctrine of Preemption: Precedents and Problems," *Officer* 80.3 (2004): 31–33; Franklin Eric Wester, "Preemption and Just War: Considering the Case of Iraq," *Parameters* 34.4 (2004–2005): 20–40; Miriam Sapiro, "Iraq: The Shifting Sands of Preemptive Self-Defense," *American Journal of International Law* 97.3 (2003): 599–605; Michael Walzer, *Arguing about War*. New Haven: Yale University Press, 2004; and Michael Walzer, *Just and Unjust Wars: A Moral Argument with Historical Illustrations*. New York: Basic Books, 1992.

[17] Snider and Nagl, "National Security Strategy," 130.

agendas, those nation-states we barely and rarely recognize, will hear of the U.S. strategy and goals. State power is thus roundly acknowledged in the service of security in the NSSUSA.

In Jacques Derrida's terminology, sovereignty that is forced to share, to communicate its selfhood, is neither monolithic nor indivisible. The language of sharing is a language of (potential or actual) universalization: "As a result sovereignty withdraws from language, which always introduces a sharing that universalizes. As soon as I speak to the other, I submit to the law of giving reason(s), I share a virtually universalizable medium.... The paradox which is always the same is that sovereignty is incompatible with universality even though it is called for by every concept of international, thus universal or universalizable, and thus democratic, law."[18] From this perspective, the NSSUSAs are dangerous documents, as are all documentations of sovereignty, because they undermine the very monopoly that is the ground of their being. For Weber, we should recall, monopoly is constituted of violence that is considered legitimate, thus a violence that has already compromised its own prearticulate adequacy and autonomy. Legitimacy points to an authorizing body or ideal that may contingently refuse to be held hostage by the violence it both legitimates and to which it is subjected. The NSSUSAs seek that legitimate authorization by appealing to "freedom" and "American internationalism," but in so doing they run the risk of losing their sovereignty.

The 9/11 Commission Report was published in 2004 and quickly became a best seller, the product of the work of the 9/11 Commission (formally, the National Commission on Terrorist Attacks upon the United States, established in 2002). The commission unanimously authorized the report, although sections of it were redacted – and some then later restored – by the Bush administration. The commission was bipartisan in its membership, with Republican Thomas Kean as chair and Democrat Lee Hamilton as vice chair. The commission was, however, administered by an executive director, Philip Zelikow, who was a former colleague of Condoleezza Rice and had served in both Bush administrations, most recently on George W. Bush's President's Foreign Intelligence Advisory Board. Zelikow's staff wrote the 567-page report, detailing the events of September 11, along with

---

[18] Jacques Derrida, *Rogues: Two Essays on Reason*, trans. Pascale-Anne Brault and Michael Naas. Stanford, CA: Stanford University Press, 2005, 101.

histories of U.S. intelligence agencies and what the report terms "new terrorism." Strikingly absent is any real discussion of U.S. foreign policy in the post–World War II period.

The *National Strategy for Victory in Iraq* was published by the National Security Council in 2005. Written two and a half years after the initial invasion of Iraq, this document presented itself as articulating "the broad strategy the President set forth in 2003 and provid[ing] an update on our progress as well as the challenges remaining" (1). It was widely disseminated and discussed, as were its key terms: *victory*, *enemy*, and *necessity*. In a certain sense, this document was unprecedented, more a response to a growing opposition to the war in Iraq and to the developing use of words reminiscent of the Vietnam conflict (e.g., *quagmire*) than a set piece of political and military policy reporting like the NSSUSAs.

All four documents, three exclusively products of the executive branch and one a joint effort of the executive and legislative branches, were drafted in the context of the 9/11 crisis. They seek to cauterize the trauma and to announce a strategy whereby the power of the United States is reasserted. They also seek to radically differentiate U.S. power from that of any other sovereign contender. A discourse of strategy (necessarily foregrounded in the *NSSUSA* reports) will announce its means, but as Weber insisted, such a means discourse can never stand on its own in the real world of policy and politics. Means discourses must make contact with ends discourses so that, precisely, the state's sovereign *singularity* can be claimed. The simultaneous and contradictory mandates of acknowledgment and transcendence of violence require the logic of transformation (a process that can never be complete). I argue and shall demonstrate that in these documents state violence is acknowledged but that this violence is simultaneously transformed into something nonviolent, nonlethal, innocuous. How is this attempted? The analysis of the texts of these documents reveals their violence to be innocuous in several ways: U.S. state violence is defensive in nature; it is a function and harbinger of freedom and democracy and is essentially an "ideal type" that is decidedly not the product of a specific, historically contingent "foreign policy." In other words, the legitimate violence of the United States is *universal* in its singularity.[19] Finally, these three claims are presented as a single, self-evident (yet articulated) assumption.

---

[19] I want to argue that this ideal typical quality of singularity as universality is similar to but not quite the same thing as exceptionalism, as understood by Giorgio Agamben and others.

2002 *National Security Strategy*

It is normal for the NSSUSA reports to be accompanied by a letter from the president. The letter is included as a personal message, a communicative moment that demonstrates the traditional and charismatic aspects of the U.S. presidency, before the rational-legal, means-oriented description of strategy. Oddly, however, the actual text of the 2002 report carries forward the generic forms present in President Bush's opening letter, attempting to infuse tradition and charisma into the realm of strategy. These forms reveal the theological underpinnings of such official documents of statecraft. After all, this should not be surprising, given that the ultimate referent is the "community of fate" (in Collins's terms) that is bound together through war by those authorities having, in Weber's terms, "the right to commune with the gods of the city."[20]

Analysts have indeed characterized the discourse of the Bush administration as generally religious in nature, particularly in its articulation of the war on terror. Gordon Chang and Hugh Mehan write: "The plot of the War on Terrorism script contains an eternal tension between good and evil; the scene of the battle, therefore, is not circumscribed by time and place. The scene was transformed from one of civil society to one of national security state in a condition of pure war."[21] Others have discerned a "millennial military state" in the self-presentation of the United States in the 2002 NSSUSA.[22] The claim here, however, is that the very nature of

---

[20] Max Weber, quoted in Collins, "Weber and the Sociology of Revolution," 174.
[21] Gordon C. Chang and Hugh B. Mehan, "Discourse in a Religious Mode: The Bush Administration's Discourse in the War on Terrorism and its Challenges," *Pragmatics* 16.1 (March 2006): 1–23, 7.
[22] Stephen John Hartnett and Laura Ann Stengrim, "War Rhetorics: The *National Security Strategy of the United States* and President Bush's Globalization-through-Benevolent-Empire," *SAQ* 105.1 (Winter 2006): 175–205. Although I agree with Hartnett and Stengrim about the presence of this theme, the analytical perspective taken here seeks to problematize this kind of thematic individuation. In fact, Hartnett and Stengrim discern five overarching themes in the NSSUSA, themes that this essay argues actually resist differentiation:

> First, the NSSUS offers *a doctrine of preemption*, by which the United States claims the right to strike against foes wherever and whenever it feels threatened. Second, the NSSUS proposes *a millennial military state* where waging war is the chief and perpetual function of the federal government. Third, the NSSUS wraps points 1 and 2 in *a promise of benign universalism*, an apparently generous offer to spread U.S. goods, capital, institutions, and values far and wide. Fourth, . . . the NSSUS links U.S. national security, global economic growth, and the fate of foreign governments to their enthusiasm for *evangelical capitalism*. Fifth, the NSSUS makes broad claims about rogue states in a world of evil that . . . hint at

the style of articulating strategy reflects the conundrum of monopolized, legitimized state violence in a Weberian mode. First and foremost, that style consists of repetitions, invocations, and imprecations. Recalling that the 1986 Goldwater-Nichols Act charged these annual reports with articulating the "foreign policy, worldwide commitments and national defense capabilities"[23] of the United States, it is by no means clear that they would take the specific shapes that they have.

Specifically, the incessant repetition of *free*, *freedom*, and *freer* (eighty-five times in this thirty-one-page document; twenty-three times in the first three pages alone) is reminiscent of religious texts with their manifold invocations of and to deities. Freedom seems to be positioned as the first mover and final goal of everything else, although the term as such is never clearly defined. In its adjectival appearances, it invokes free markets and trade, freedom of religion and of politics. There is normative propulsion even in these specified freedoms, with the requisite repetitive invocations: "The concept of 'free trade' arose as a moral principle even before it became a pillar of economics. . . . This is real freedom, the freedom for a person – or a nation – to make a living. To promote free trade, the United States has developed a comprehensive strategy" (18). In its nominal appearances, however, *freedom* is as undefined as it is compelling: "Through our willingness to use force in our own defense and in the defense of others, the United States demonstrates its resolve to maintain a balance of power that favors freedom" (29). Most significant here, however, is *freedom*'s ubiquity in a strategy report. It might appear that freedom itself is being promoted as strategy, yet it is the actual and possible deployment of state violence in response to past, present, and possible future threats that provides the foundational platform for national strategy. Nevertheless, *freedom*'s repetitions make it difficult for a reader to navigate a causal path through the report, as the cloud of *freedom* terms oscillates between signifying means and signifying ends. With the architecture of a prayer book, the NSSUSA keeps returning the reader to the ideal state and goal of freedom in the mode of what Kenneth Burke calls a "God term,"[24] aimed more at communion than at calculation.

---

a form of conflict observers from both Left and Right have called *a clash of civilizations*. (Id., 176)

[23] Snider and Nagl, "National Security Strategy," 127.

[24] Kenneth Burke, *A Grammar of Motives*. Berkeley: University of California Press, 1969, 91.

The Innocuousness of State Lethality in an Age of National Security 39

The designated or chosen actions of the United States are all actions in a defensive rather than aggressive mode, even when these actions involve the use of force: "We will defend the peace by fighting terrorists and tyrants. We will preserve the peace by building good relations among the great powers. We will extend the peace by encouraging free and open societies on every continent" (1).[25] The table of contents presents a similar set of verbs: *champion, strengthen, prevent, expand,* and *develop.* Although certainly activist in tone, none of these verbs implies a rupture or a break of territorial jurisdiction. They engage minimal mobility.

The immediate contrasts established in this document between the United States (with its "conventional superiority") and "failed states," on the one hand, and "rogue states," on the other, suggest a powerful visual metaphor. The discourse of conventional, failed, and rogue states draws from an astronomical model of gravitational fields of celestial objects, each with its proper orbit. Danger comes when states move out of their orbits. These rhetorical and conceptual turns are critical, engaging as they do *indirect recognitions* of the monopoly violence of other sovereign states by way of rejection of the loss of that monopoly by "failed states" and by rejection of the overvaunting of the monopoly by "rogue states." Thus it is immediately noted in the 2002 *NSSUSA,* "America is now threatened less by conquering states than we are by failing ones" (1). Political analyst and President-elect Barack Obama's nominee for U.S. ambassador to the United Nations Susan Rice comments, "Such states can and often do serve as safe havens and staging grounds for terrorist organizations."[26] Absent the monopoly of legitimate physical force within a given territory, Elias's "pacified social spaces" are paradoxically transformed into "safe havens" for the violence of nonstate actors. There is a similar critique of the even more important "rogue states," which "see these weapons [of mass destruction] as their best means of overcoming the conventional superiority of the United States" (15). Analysts of state power and sovereignty, including Derrida, Noam Chomsky, Robert Litwak, and Michael Mann, have problematized

---

[25] The United Nations Charter includes sanctions against aggressive war. Specifically, Article 2 states: "All Members shall refrain in their international relations from the threat or use of force against the territorial integrity or political independence of any state, or in any other manner inconsistent with the Purposes of the United Nations." United Nations Charter, Article 2.

[26] Susan E. Rice, *The New National Security Strategy: Focus on Failed States,* Policy Brief 116. Washington, DC: Brookings Institution, 2003.

the concept of the rogue state.[27] They note that the term was originally applied to countries whose internal domestic policies were abhorrent – for example, Panama under Manuel Noriega, Cambodia under Pol Pot, or Uganda under Idi Amin – but that under Bill Clinton's administration it was applied to states the international behavior of which was deemed erratic, irrational, and dangerous. The new rogue state is isolated and anomalous and has or wants weapons of mass destruction. Of course, being a rogue, these states would inevitably detonate these weapons of mass destruction (rogues not being subject to conventional constraints), likely bringing about the self-destruction of the monopoly of physical force at the very moment that it actualizes its universality. The Bush administration's 2002 *NSSUSA* extends this *rogue* vocabulary and highlights it in the very chapter of the report (Chapter 5, "Prevent Our Enemies from Threatening Us, Our Allies, and Our Friends with Weapons of Mass Destruction") in which the policy of preventive war is first announced.

According to the 2002 *NSSUSA*, all territories should be properly and legitimately monopolized. Territory that is improperly or incompletely covered is ultimately threatening. This universality of coverage is understood to be temporal as well as spatial. Certainly the promotion of "proactive counterproliferation efforts" constitutes an attempt to manage several leaps backward and forward in time. These locutions and policies map the conceptual territory of the appropriate monopoly of legitimate violence. Of note, the appropriate monopoly is sometimes evoked by the term *conventional*, which connotes legitimacy as well as specific kinds of weaponry. This superiority of the United States is conventional because it is understood to be paradigmatic of sovereign statehood, innocuous or non-traumatic, and nuclear without being in the business of mass destruction (despite being the only country to have deployed atomic weapons against civilians in wartime).

Ultimately, the *NSSUSA* can be said to function as a myth, in Claude Lévi-Strauss's terminology – a mediating symbolic structure that is always only provisionally effective in its reiteration. The *NSSUSA* can never be completely and permanently effective, because the contradictions that it

---

[27] Derrida, *Rogues*; Noam Chomsky, *Rogue States: The Rule of Force in World Affairs*. Cambridge, MA: South End Press, 2000; Robert Litwak, *Rogue States and U.S. Foreign Policy: Containment after the Cold War*. Washington, DC: Woodrow Wilson Center Press, 2000; Michael Mann, *Incoherent Empire*. London: Verso, 2003.

The Innocuousness of State Lethality in an Age of National Security 41

attempts to resolve are permanent (the contradictions between means and ends and between singular state sovereignty and the sovereign system).

The 9/11 Commission Report

After significant initial resistance, President Bush convened the special 9/11 Commission in 2002. Releasing its report in 2004, the commission painted a picture of the United States in the late twentieth century in broad strokes. The report/best-selling book itself is a hybrid of several textual genres. It is termed a *historical narrative* by its authors, but at times the report has the structure of a dossier presenting evidence, a chronicle that is diffident on the issue of causality ("Our aim has not been to assign individual blame"; xvi), an exhortation, and a sworn statement (the signatures of the commission members are reproduced on the frontispiece). It cannot settle easily into a single mode of representation. This might be as much a function of its multiple authorship as a function of its ambiguous ultimate charge.[28] It certainly is situated on the site of trauma and seeks to both explain and derive meaning from that trauma. Its joint executive and legislative genesis broadens and pluralizes its own sense of state sovereignty. Despite its very different mandate, however, *The 9/11 Commission Report* shares with the NSSUSAs the assumption of the singular point of view of the nation-state, whose means and ends solicit connection. The report does present a puzzling and contradictory picture of this nation, one that is at once preeminently powerful and strangely inert. The report itself uses the phrase "large and unwieldy" to describe the government agencies that it analyzes. Furthermore, the United States is portrayed as essentially a recipient of actions taken by others, responding to rather than initiating action in the world. There are very few explicit discussions of U.S. foreign policy, even in the historical chapters. Mention *is* made of billions of U.S. dollars supplied to rebel groups in Afghanistan during the Soviet occupation, but that is quickly followed with an assertion by a CIA official, "Bin Ladin and his

---

[28] Ernest May, the historian recruited by Zelikow to help shape the report, formulated a principle of objectivity in writing it, a principle he sought to operationalize through the excision of adjectives and adverbs: "It was also possible to strip away interpretive language, even adjectives and adverbs, so as to assure the reader that we were just reciting the historical facts." Ernest May, "A Memoir of the 9/11 Commission: When Government Writes History," *New Republic*, May 16, 2005, 3–9, 8.

comrades had their own sources of support and training and they received little or no assistance from the United States" (56). Only near the very end (just fifty pages shy of it) does the actual term *foreign policy* appear: "American foreign policy is part of the message" (376). The message being referenced and recommended is that of providing "opportunity to the Arab and Muslim world" (376).

Being thus portrayed as a large and fairly passive organism, the United States is at once immobilized (by its own size, by counterproductive secrecy within and among various intelligence agencies) and yet a site of extraordinary mobility. In recounting the years during which the 9/11 planners were preparing, the report notes that millions of people flew in and out of the United States, crossed borders, received visas, enrolled in schools, and rented apartments. There seems to have been little or no constraint on such movement. Furthermore, the United States is afflicted with confounding technological/strategical, historical, and global disorientations.

Technological misrecognitions and miscalculations necessarily conjure up Vietnam, when a nation of peasants with bicycles defeated a global superpower; however, the conflict in Vietnam is conspicuously missing in the report's historical narrative of the United States in the post–World War II era. Nevertheless, the underestimation of al-Qaeda's capacities reveals the stolid commitment to a calculus of military superiority based on technological sophistication. Describing the response of Clinton administration appointees to Richard Clarke's plan to strike bin Laden's training bases in Afghanistan, the report notes: "Defense Secretary William Cohen told us Bin Ladin's training camps were primitive, built with 'rope ladder'; General Shelton called them 'jungle gym' camps. Neither thought them worthwhile targets for very expensive missiles" (120). The report details myriad technological miscalculations, incongruities, and vicissitudes. Police radios and firefighter radios did not work and could not make contact with each other as the rescue attempts at the World Trade Center proceeded. Civilian airplanes were transformed into weapons by terrorists wielding box cutters. "Conventional" causal reasoning is not effective in this new context.

Historical time is also deceptive. Anachronistic conceptions of the geopolitical world lead to the inability to identify enemies. *The 9/11 Commission Report* takes note of the confusion of the Langley Air Force Base fighter pilots who were scrambled on the morning of September 11, 2001.

The Innocuousness of State Lethality in an Age of National Security

Noting that they were not briefed about the reason that they were scrambled, the lead pilot said: "I reverted to the Russian threat.... I'm thinking cruise missile threat from the sea. You know you look down and see the Pentagon burning and I thought the bastards snuck one by us" (45). Ten years after the dissolution of the Soviet Union, it is striking to hear that a U.S. Air Force pilot's political imaginary takes him back to the major cold war enemy and threat. The difficulty of literally conceiving the end of the era of "mutually assured destruction" and deterrence speaks to more than just organizational lag – it reveals the phenomenological disruption and disorientation of even those centrally involved in national defense.

Spatial disorientation is similarly presented as compromising America's attention and focus. The deictic misrecognitions make things appear to be farther away than in fact they are, with severe consequences: "To us, Afghanistan seemed very far away. To members of al-Qaeda, America seemed very close. In a sense, they were more globalized than we were" (340). Paradoxically, these misrecognitions can also make things seem closer than they actually are, to the point of seeming ubiquitous. The inability of the United States to recognize violent threats that do not take traditional forms raises questions about the locus of the zone of combat. Commenting on the contemporary breakdown of such spatial clarity, Rosa Ehrenreich Brooks writes: "The traditional paradigm of armed conflict assumes that at any given time it will be readily apparent where the armed conflict is taking place and where it is not. To put it another way, the traditional paradigm assumes clear spatial boundaries between zones of war and zones of peace."[29] The dislocated "global microstructures" of terrorist organizations, in Karin Knorr Cetina's terms, can be seen as describing an idiosyncratic variant of the conundrum of monopolized violence and territorial circumference identified earlier.[30]

In the ontologically and epistemologically vexing system of mutually constituting (yet) sovereign states, dangerous voids of attention can allow infiltration and must call forth action. *The 9/11 Commission Report* approaches its conclusion by inverting these voids, flipping them inside

---

[29] Brooks, "War Everywhere," 9.
[30] Karin Knorr Cetina, "Complex Global Microstructures: The New Terrorist Societies," *Theory, Culture, and Society* 22.5 (2005): 213–234.

out by declaring that America is everywhere: "9/11 has taught us that terrorism against American interests 'over there' should be regarded just as we regard terrorism against Americans 'over here.' In this same sense *the American homeland is the planet*" (362; emphasis added). This phrase can be regarded as a rhetorical figure, but it is a logical culminating position given the frustrations of a technologically, historically, and globally confounded superpower sovereign state. There is a seamless move from presenting the late-twentieth-century United States as a large, unwieldy nation-state in a reactive and defensive mode to the post-9/11 declaration that the defensive response can occur anywhere (and can take almost any form), because its monopoly of legitimate violence literally encompasses the globe.

War as a Variation on a Theme of Lethality

Osama bin Laden, in the name of the World Islamic Front, declared a fatwa against America in 1998. *The 9/11 Commission Report* states, "Claiming that America had declared war against God and his messenger, they called for the murder of any American, anywhere on earth, as the 'individual duty for every Muslim who can do it in any country in which it is possible to do it'" (47). Neither President Clinton nor President Bush sought a declaration of war against bin Laden from Congress, even after the 1993 bombing of the World Trade Center, the bombings in 1998 of the American embassies in Kenya and Tanzania, the retaliatory U.S. attacks in 1998 against Afghanistan and the Sudan, and the 2000 attack on the USS *Cole*. Even without a formal acknowledgment of bin Laden's fatwa and a formal declaration of war in response, Clinton was able to call for the missile attacks, and Bush's National Security Council Deputies Committee determined in August 2001 that it was legal for the CIA to assassinate bin Laden were it to have the opportunity because "such strikes would be acts of self-defense that would not violate the ban on assassinations in Executive Order 12333" (212). It is important to identify and analyze the many ways of conceiving of and exercising violent means and the many positions on the continuum reaching from formal declared wars to, on the other end, the axiomatic fact of (unexercised) monopolies of violence within a given territory. The documents under analysis take their shape under the pressure and difficulty of articulating their relevant place along that continuum.

National Strategy for Victory in Iraq

Not especially self-consciously existential in its prose or its mission, the *National Strategy for Victory in Iraq* (2005) is revelatory and exegetical. Its attitude is not one of Weberian tragedy; rather, it digs in with its muscular hermeneutics. In Derrida's terms, the sovereign state that generates the *National Strategy for Victory in Iraq* shares and then takes back. Occurring chronologically between the two *NSSUSA* reports, this document serves as a self-reflective intertext. Coming two and a half years into the occupation of Iraq, the thirty-five-page report responds to the circulating critiques of a war that was revealed to have misrecognized its target in several ways. It is, as noted previously, a response to the emergence of a critical, Vietnam-era discourse of "quagmires." The *National Strategy for Victory in Iraq* actually problematizes and actively reinterprets many of the key terms of state sovereignty and power. Although the word *victory* is prominent in six of the fifteen chapter headings in the table of contents (e.g., "Victory in Iraq Defined," "Victory in Iraq Is a Vital U.S. Interest," and "The Benefits of Victory in Iraq"), it is a word under deconstruction. A certain geopolitical realism also takes over from the incantatory idealism of the 2002 *NSSUSA*: "It is not realistic to expect a fully functioning democracy, able to defeat its enemies and peacefully reconcile generational grievances, to be in place less than three years after Saddam was finally removed from power" (2). *Freedom* disappears from the rhetorical scene and is, in a certain "root metaphor" sense, replaced with the problematic *victory*.

The report goes to great lengths to claim that victory will no longer take its traditional and expected form and that the public might be unable to recognize victory when it arrives: "As the central front in the global war on terror, success in Iraq is an essential element in the long war against the ideology that breeds international terrorism. Unlike past wars, however, victory in Iraq will not come in the form of an enemy's surrender, or be signaled by a single particular event – there will be no Battleship Missouri, no Appomattox" (3). Not only will there be no formal surrender ceremonies or agreements (thus, victory will not be localizable), but victory will also be extended over time – it will not happen all at once. Victory will be defined in "stages" that involve political, security, and economic "tracks." These stages in turn are to be viewed in the short, middle, and long terms. Even these calibrations are indefinite and incalculable, however. The document declares, "We will not put a date certain on when each stage of success will be reached" (12).

As time expands and contracts, so does the enemy. Along with the abandonment of the conventional idea of victory, we find a similar fragmentation of the idea of "the enemy." The enemy is now described as "diffuse and sophisticated" (1). In the same way that victory is no longer a particular state of affairs at a particular moment, the enemy is no longer an identified dedicated opponent (or even a coalition of dedicated opponents). Instead, the *National Strategy for Victory in Iraq* lists many different enemies, including terrorists, rejectionists, Saddamists, insurgents, extremists, criminals, tribes, sects, Shia religious extremists, militias, armed groups, and radicals. Even as the document continues to use the singular form *enemy*, it paints an unclear picture of a whirling mass of enemies with different origins, tactics, and goals, although such things are left to the imagination.

Thus, the *National Strategy for Victory in Iraq* problematizes and reconstitutes *victory* (no longer a dichotomous variable), *time* ("Victory will take time"; 10), *enemy*, and *territory* ("Iraq is the central front in the global war on terror"; 1). Although the traditional terminology of war is not abandoned, even in the face of the unprecedented *forms* of contestation, these terms no longer can be reproduced and recognized automatically. The strategy goes out of its way to defamiliarize the reader/public with these terms.

Finally, although the syntactical proximity of the "war on terror" and "success in Iraq" in the passage quoted previously recapitulates the ubiquitous rhetorical maneuver of connecting 9/11 to Iraq by implying causality from contiguity, the point here is to note the reluctance to abandon altogether the classical terminology of the front. This new front is mobile, expansive, and indeterminate. This new conceptualization of the front also brings into focus the idea that any act of force on the part of the United States is necessitated by reason of defense: "If we retreat from Iraq, the terrorists will pursue us and our allies, expanding the fight to the rest of the region and to our own shores" (6). Once again, space is collapsed as the near and the far make contact.

The *National Strategy for Victory in Iraq* informs the populace that it can no longer recognize victories or enemies and that the vanishing point of the long-term, multitrack war on terror in Iraq preempts the imposition of any deadline. The diffuse and ambiguous conditions of war in Iraq are actually defended by the *National Strategy for Victory in Iraq*, and the concept of freedom is smuggled into the stolid and qualifying prose of the report without actually making much of an appearance. It is not Iraqi freedom that needs invoking but rather American freedom that needs protecting. Victory, then, is the second-order means (the monopoly of physical force is the first-order means) that seeks contact with the ends of freedom, but victory (and thus freedom) can be achieved only asymptotically.

2006 *National Security Strategy*

At nearly fifty pages, the 2006 *NSSUSA* refers to and builds on the foundation of the 2002 *NSSUSA*. It is introduced by another letter, signed by President Bush, with a salutation to "My fellow Americans" (i), unlike his 2002 letter. The first line, one that sets the tone for the forthrightly activist and belligerent report, is "America is at war" (i). War is the context for the security strategy in 2006. With war as the backdrop, *freedom* returns with a vengeance – the term occurs thirteen times on the first two pages – and is accompanied by a drumbeat of *America* (six times on the first page). Ever more tautological in its meaning and action, *freedom* loops around itself in exhortation and admonition: "All *free* nations have a responsibility to stand together for *freedom* because all *free* nations share an interest in *freedom*'s advance" (7; emphasis added). Freedom clearly compels in these strategy documents, and it is inevitably and fatally yoked to violence: "We have also found that the defense of freedom brings us loss and sorrow, because freedom has determined enemies" (i). These associations of freedom and loss, freedom and compulsion, and freedom and "winning the war on terror" highlight an irony of its conceptual deployment. Weber was too keen a social scientist and too practiced a statesman to invoke freedom in his discussion of politics and the state. His dark and tragic sensibility pre-empted considerations of freedom, especially when attempting to prescribe the ideal or typical combination of traits characterizing a good politician (i.e., responsibility, passion, a sense of proportion). Rather than freedom, Weber worried about the relations of consent and coercion in specific forms of authority from which state legitimacy was derived. The irony of the oxymoronic deployment of *freedom* in the 2002 and 2006 *NSSUSA* reports is that its constant, necessary proximity to the violent means of the state actually removes *freedom* from the American ideology of political optimism and draws it into the ambit of Weberian pessimism and gloom.

In a similar vein, the words *policy*, *statecraft*, and *offense* also make self-conscious appearances in the 2006 report. *Offense* is noticeable for its unusual and marked variance from the defense theme that has provided the ontological foundation for the innocuous state violence in the reports. Even though it is embedded in the defensively inclined "Prevent Our Enemies from Threatening Us, Our Allies, and Our Friends with Weapons of Mass Destruction" (Chapter 5, section 4), the chapter contains the following anomalous dictum:

> Both offenses and defenses are necessary to deter state and non-state actors, through denial of the objectives of their attacks and, if necessary, responding with overwhelming force. Safe, credible, and reliable nuclear forces continue to play a critical role. We are strengthening deterrence by developing a New Triad composed of offensive strike systems (both nuclear and improved conventional capabilities); active and passive defenses, including missile defenses; and a responsive infrastructure, all bound together by enhanced command and control, planning, and intelligence systems (22).

The appearance of offensive strike systems and the asserted *necessity* for both offenses and defenses might reveal a sovereignty on the verge of shedding its innocuous skin (although the nuclear forces are still "safe"). This could be the result of an endgame in which the "given territory" resists demarcation, leaving the unhinged violent means to roam the globe.

Possible evidence for this can be found in the deictic qualifications in both Bush administration *NSSUSA* reports about the locus of America; the mobility of the "front"; the spaces of contained, imploded ("failed"), or rogue states; and the ubiquity of terror and terrorists, as these reports seek to map a sovereign state system both over- and underdetermined. "We" must "fight our enemies abroad instead of waiting for them to arrive in our country," "choose leadership over isolationism," and "seek to shape the world" (ii). Furthermore, "The United States can no longer simply rely on deterrence to keep the terrorists at bay or defensive measures to thwart them at the last moment. The fight must be taken to the enemy, to keep them on the run" (8). Sovereignty is and must be on the move as it seeks to contain the unpredictable movements of rogues and terrorists.

Literally contained in an outlined typographical box is a section titled "Afghanistan and Iraq: The Front Lines in the War on Terror" (12). The spaces *of* the report (e.g., the White House, the Capitol, the public sphere), the space constituted *by* the report (e.g., well-governed states, rogue states, stateless terrorists, America, the free world), and the spaces *in* the report all shift in uneasy misalignments. The attempts to keep things separate and yet to control them are ultimately useless, but that goal is wistfully articulated nevertheless: "The goal of our statecraft is to help create a world of democratic, well-governed states that can meet the needs of their citizens and conduct themselves responsibly in the international system. This is the best way to provide enduring security for the American people" (1).

Conclusion

In his historical-sociological ethnography of Los Alamos, Jeffrey Bussolini learned that an exhibit of replicas of the two atomic bombs dropped by the United States at the end of World War II had recently been updated. Whereas the original exhibit had been labeled with a red neon "Weapons" sign, it is now labeled with a clear plastic "Defense" sign.[31] The substitution of the label *defense* for *weapons* should not be surprising; it follows an earlier transformation of the Department of War into the Department of Defense. The stance and concept of *defense* models an innocuous state violence (however destructive in effects), operating only within or at the borders where the internal monopoly of violence might be challenged. That "defense" travels in the air along with the bomb means that "borders" are desituated, and the United States can and should be protected anywhere. The paradigm of defense seems to preclude or at the very least to obviate any need for a military foreign policy in which the violent means of the state operate beyond its own territorial borders or for territorializing purposes. The several contradictions of the international system of sovereign states together with the conundrum of the co-constitution of the monopoly of violence and the territory so monopolized actually end up necessitating a foreign policy precisely to demarcate the (domestic) sovereign sphere. Bartleson explains this in his discussion of "Classical Age" sovereignty,

---

[31] Jeffrey P. Bussolini, "Living with the Bomb: Technological Existence in Los Alamos" (paper presented at the meeting for the American Sociological Association, August 2006, in Montreal).

but it can be argued that it still holds true in the modern era: "Without a 'foreign policy' there can be nothing domestic, since the former has as its task precisely to define the latter by domesticating what initially was foreign to it, buried in the depths of its violent prehistory and inserted as a state of nature in its contractual justification."[32] Violence on the road to monopolization is always prehistory, from the point of view of the state, because it is always violence that has not been legitimized – yet. State violence confronts the dilemma of simultaneous acknowledgment of a (*successfully*) achieved monopoly and the necessity for its continual reiteration. In the context of a sovereign superpower that achieves its legitimacy by a democratic disavowal of conquest, empire, and territorial expansionism, there are obviously dangers in connecting those ends of democracy and freedom too intimately to the violent means and to becoming the only singular state with the asserted legitimacy to defend a territory outside of which there is no longer anything foreign.

[32] Bartleson, *Genealogy of Sovereignty*, 180.

3

Oedipal Sovereignty and the War in Iraq

Jeremy Arnold

You know, of course, that one does not count the dead in the same way from one corner of the globe to another.[1] — Jacques Derrida

That the dead are not always counted in the same way because the dead do not count in the same way is manifest in the United States' invasion of Iraq in 2003. Justifications for the invasion, proffered from various positions on both the right and the left, reveal through their absence the dead bodies of those who are not and perhaps cannot be counted. What the invasion of Iraq has also revealed is a paradoxical aspect of sovereign power, an effect of sovereignty that traditional juridical accounts of sovereign power cannot explain: *sovereignty is the cause of the very problems it claims the right to solve*. The invasion of Iraq *produced* a specific space of violence that did not preexist the invasion, and since that time the United States has continued to claim the right to rid the space that it has created of the violence within. Far from being a war of defense and being not quite a war of aggression or territorial conquest, the invasion of Iraq was carried out in the name of the sovereign right to protect against a violence that did not in fact exist, and a threat that many justifiably claimed would never materialize. Even

[1] Giovanna Borradori, *Philosophy in a Time of Terror: Dialogues with Jürgen Habermas and Jacques Derrida*. Chicago: University of Chicago Press, 2003, p. 92. At the outset, I would like to add that the relationship of what I am saying about sovereignty bears intimate connections with what Derrida calls "autoimmunitary" processes, for example, a process in which the "defenses and all the forms of what is called, with two equally problematic words, the 'war on terrorism' work to regenerate, in the short or long term, the causes of the evil they claim to eradicate" (*Philosophy in a Time of Terror*, p. 100). At this moment, Derrida seems to indicate the 'cause' of such processes as emerging from a logic of repression both psychoanalytic and political. As I shall argue, Oedipal sovereignty emerges from a knowledge of death that would reveal an unbreakable limit for the political such that security can be achieved.

if one takes into account the strategic interests of the United States in the Middle East – oil, the protection of Israel, the containment of Iraq – this only supports the claim that the United States produced a space of violence that it also claims the right to end.

The idea that sovereign power claims the right to use violence is not new, but the possibility that sovereign power is *productive* of the political problem it is erected or employed to solve is absent from the juridical theories of sovereignty in Hobbes or Carl Schmitt, for example. In such theories, sovereignty is a response, and a necessary one to a prepolitical violence, a violence that threatens before the institution of sovereignty, and that the sovereign is instituted to repel.[2] Rather than turn to the traditional theorists of sovereignty, I argue that it is Oedipus, as portrayed in Sophocles' Theban trilogy, who gives us the best representation of the paradox of sovereignty, in which it is the cause of and solution to the problem of the political. Oedipus saves Thebes from the plague endangering the city by answering the riddle of the Sphinx, yet in the very moment that he saves the city, he also dooms it, bringing a new plague upon it. In other words, Oedipus saves and dooms at the same time; he is at the same moment the cause of and solution to the problem of the political. *Oedipal sovereignty*, as I call it, bears an intimate relationship with Sophocles' interpretation of human finitude, specifically the figure of death. The meaning of death and the knowledge death that provides are crucial to the success of the sovereign. How death is counted, in other words, is crucial to understanding the structure of Oedipal sovereignty.

The first half of this essay offers a close reading of Sophocles' Theban trilogy, to lay out the structure of Oedipal sovereignty, looking at the relationship between death and sovereignty and how Oedipal sovereignty differs from the theories of Hobbes and Schmitt. The second half of the discussion returns to the war in Iraq, to bring Oedipal sovereignty to bear upon the invasion. First, I briefly try to show in more detail how the invasion mirrors the logic of Oedipal sovereignty and then argue, once again attending to the relationship of death and sovereignty, that most

---

[2] In fact, I would argue that within the theories of Hobbes and Schmitt one can see, in different ways, the very paradox I am trying to explain. Of course, this is not the space to make such an argument.

justifications for the war in Iraq obscure the dead bodies, which cannot be counted because they do not count. Worse, those justifications that offer a "liberal-humanitarian" rationale for invasion, based on the universality of human/liberal rights, do count Iraqi bodies, but only as a part of a *calculus* in which certain bodies can be *sacrificed* for the greater end of liberation. Finally, I claim that Oedipal sovereignty helps us to criticize more deeply the logic of means and ends that makes some bodies unaccounted for, because Oedipal sovereignty shows us that the ends of sovereign power, however good, are in inherent conflict with the means to achieve those ends, however instrumentally rational the choice of means might be.

Oedipal Sovereignty

Death

Oedipus the King and *Oedipus at Colonus* are stories of and about birth and death, of the misfortune and suffering that birth brings as well as the comfort and security that death promises. The central moments of tragic plots, as Aristotle classified them, of astonishment and recognition, reversal and suffering, circle around the disclosure of Oedipus' birth; in the wake of his own self-disclosure, Oedipus blinds himself and eventually dies a willing exile from Thebes and citizen of Athens in *Oedipus at Colonus*.[3] For this reason, Heidegger writes of *Oedipus the King* that "the way from the radiant beginning to the gruesome end is one struggle between appearance (concealment and distortion) and unconcealment (being)."[4] The revelations that occur in the plays, however, reveal not only the person named Oedipus. What is at issue is not simply that we can never know *a* or *our* or *Oedipus'* birth or death; what Sophocles exposes is the *meaning* of birth and death, birth and death as figures of human finitude. One can see Oedipus as a condensed image of two pieces of tragic wisdom that help to clarify the meaning of human finitude as Sophocles understood it. The first, famously recalled by Nietzsche and Hannah Arendt among others, is the assertion of the Chorus in *Oedipus at Colonus* that "Not

[3] Aristotle, *Poetics*, trans. Malcolm Heath. London: Penguin Books, 1996, 52a2–52b13.
[4] Martin Heidegger, *Introduction to Metaphysics*, trans. Ralph Mannheim. New Haven: Yale University Press, 1987, 106.

to be born is best of all;/when life is there, the second best/to go hence where you came,/with the best speed you may."[5] Second, of the many figural meanings of death, a key interpretation is found in the last line of *Oedipus the King*: "Count no mortal happy till/he has passed the final limit of his life secure from pain."[6] These are, of course, statements inspired by Oedipus' misfortune and suffering, but they are not meant to leave the audience happily complacent, glad simply not to be Oedipus. Oedipus' existence and the figures of birth and death that convey that existence in Sophocles' poetry are interpretations of human finitude in general and not merely the particular character named Oedipus.

Broadly speaking, the figure of death signifies – unlike the birth that opens us to suffering, instability, and unrest – *security*. Many of the references to death in the plays treat it as a stable resting point. It is the limit beyond which humans can finally secure their happiness;[7] it is also the best option for humans, either to never be or to die quickly. It is further, as Oedipus tells Antigone, the "single word that overthrows/all tasks of work."[8] Most important, death is the inescapable, the most certain and known thing for finite men. In other words, *death is a limit on human existence that cannot be transgressed*. Death as the inescapable limit appears fully in the famous choral ode to the wonders of humans in *Antigone*. The ode describes human beings as a wonder, as strange, for they cross the sea, till the earth, yoke the horse, devise medicines, build shelters; in short, the human "wears away the Earth." None of the human being's powers can stop death, however, because "He has a way against everything,/and he faces nothing that is to come/without contrivance./Only Against death/can he call on no means of escape;"[9] Despite the human power of wearying the Earth, human beings are, as mortals, helpless in the face of death. The idea of death as an inescapable limit, a limit that cannot be transgressed or undone, becomes more apparent if we follow Heidegger in seeing the tragic hero/sovereign as *das Unheimlische*, insofar as he "departs from his customary, familiar limits, because he is the violent one, who, tending toward the strange in the sense of the overpowering, surpasses the limit

---

[5] *Oedipus at Colonus*, 1410–1413.
[6] *Oedipus the King*, 1529.
[7] *Oedipus*, 1529.
[8] Ibid., 1837–1838.
[9] *Antigone*, 392–397.

Oedipal Sovereignty and the War in Iraq

of the familiar [das Heimische]."[10] Human beings *are* those beings who constantly undo limits and transgress the familiar, yet death is that limit that cannot be transgressed. As Heidegger puts it, "all violence shatters against one thing. That is death. It is an end beyond all consummation, a limit beyond all limits."[11]

The image of security in its relationship to death comes starkly into relief in the Messenger's speech to the Chorus, delivering the news of Haemon's suicide, near the end of *Antigone*:

> You who live by the house of Cadmus and Amphion,
> hear me. *There is no condition of man's life*
> *that stands secure.* As such I would not
> praise it or blame. It is chance that sets upright;
> it is chance that brings down the lucky and the unlucky,
> each in his turn. *For men, that belong to death,*
> *there is no prophet of established things.*[12]

Human life is constantly in a state of insecurity because *humans belong to death*.[13] In this belonging, two things come to the forefront: on the one hand, human life is beyond normative evaluation because nothing is stable enough to have a value justifiably attached to it. On the other hand, chance reigns from the vantage point of mortal beings; that is, *for humans*, there is no prophet of established things, but there are, after all, established things, because it is Fate that establishes the course of human lives. If this is a piece of tragic wisdom, the message is that the problem is not merely that humans do not know or control their world; the problem is that humans, in a certain sense of the Messenger's "men, who belong to death," *do not belong to life*. Human existence is not the property of life but of death, and if this is true, then birth exiles the human into a land of suffering and insecurity. Conversely, death is a homecoming into the peacefulness of

---

[10] Introduction to Metaphysics, p. 151.
[11] Id., p. 158. If one takes Heidegger's reading of *Antigone* back to the account of death in *Being and Time*, one can see how death is that distinctive end of Dasein that throws Dasein back on itself, shattering it from its customary and familiar attachments to the reigning norms of the everyday and frees it for its authenticity, its "departure" from the customary. That would take us far afield, however.
[12] *Antigone*, 1226–1232, italics added.
[13] A similar sentiment is expressed by Dillon: "Mortal being, the condition of the condition known as tragic, is tragic not because we die or because we are fated and miserable, therefore, but because being temporal we live by virtue of death"; *Politics of Security*, 141.

nonbeing. We find our security and our freedom from suffering in death, and thus life becomes a wandering through a time in which "nothing very great/comes to the life of mortal man/without ruin to accompany it."[14] As the Messenger tells us, no condition of any human's life stands secure, except of course for death, which as we have seen, is that limit that is inescapable and assured. Death is the most secure thing in human existence, the limit to be counted on in an insecure and unstable world.

If human beings belong to a death figured as a place of security and the cessation of suffering, what does this have to do with the relation between death and sovereignty? The link between death and sovereignty is pronounced in Oedipus' death scene in *Oedipus at Colonus*. Oedipus dies on sacred ground, a place where the Goddesses of Earth and Darkness rule, as well as the founding place of Athens. It is also, Oedipus says, "a place of hospitality for strangers."[15] Oedipus, the failed, deposed sovereign, implores Theseus, himself formerly an exile, to let him die in that spot, guaranteeing Theseus that his hospitality ensures Athens' eternal security. Theseus agrees and is asked to view the death itself, something that is barred to the other characters in the play as well as the play's audience. Whatever was said and whatever was seen to ensure the success of Athens remains with the sovereigns and not with the citizenry, Oedipus' own family, or the audience of the play.

For this reason, at least one difficulty in understanding the link between death and sovereignty is due to the ban on the image of Oedipus' death, the scene of which is the "politically most important place in the play."[16] Because of this ban, we simply do not know what Oedipus conveys to Theseus. Only blind Oedipus, who shows Theseus "the way without a hand to guide me to the place where I must die" can, paradoxically, see his own death scene, except of course for Theseus. The ban and the reasons for it is proclaimed in Oedipus' command that Theseus must

> describe this to no man, ever,
> neither where it is hidden nor in what region,
> *that doing so may make you a defense*
> *beyond the worth of many shields, or many neighbors' help.*

---

[14] *Antigone*, 664–666.
[15] *Colonus*, 103.
[16] Charles Segal, *Tragedy and Civilization: An Interpretation of Sophocles*. Cambridge: Harvard University Press, 1981, 371.

Oedipal Sovereignty and the War in Iraq

> The things within this ban, not to be uttered,
> Yourself shall learn, when you come there alone,
> *For I shall not declare them to anyone*
> *Of these citizens, nor to my daughters*, dear though I hold them.
> *Keep them yourself always, and when you come*
> *To the end of life reveal them only*
> to him that is nearest to you, and he in turn to his successor.[17]

The only report we get of the death scene comes from a messenger, relaying the news to the chorus that "when we departed,/in a few moments we looked back and saw that/Oedipus, yes, Oedipus was no longer there,/but the king by himself, holding his hand/before his face, to shade his eyes, as though/some deadly terror had appeared to him/that sight could not endure."[18] In Oedipus' death, as we learn, the security of Athens is guaranteed so long as the site of that death and the truth of it are kept secret. The bearers of that secret must remain those in power: the sovereigns. There is, then, a connection between death – its meaning, its experience, and what it teaches – and sovereignty. Could it be that death – the figure of security – and sovereignty – the political structure in charge of achieving that security *in life* – go hand in hand? In understanding death, sovereignty would understand that which humans essentially belong to, that which affords humans security against a life that brings, more often than not, misery and suffering, and, finally, that limit of human life that cannot be transgressed, limits being central to the organization of the polis. Bernard Knox argues that the dying Oedipus "assumes the attributes of divinity [knowledge, certainty and justice] once again, but this time he is made equal to the gods."[19] If that is so – if Oedipus has become, in the sacred and hidden space of death, the equal of a god – then Theseus is given access to a specific knowledge, certainty, and justice that no man is allowed to experience save the sovereign. Following Knox, we might say that Theseus views a singular death, one that occurs at the border between mortality and immortality, humanity and divinity, a death that provides insight into human finitude at the limits of that finitude. In other words, it is a moment when mortality can be witnessed as such, at the precise instant the mortal

---

[17] *Colonus*, 1737–1748, emphases added.
[18] Id., 1869–1875.
[19] *The Heroic Temper*, 147.

human transforms/disappears into the immortal divine. If we are all barred from the experience of our own death, and if we cannot experience the other's death *as* that other but only as a witness, then human finitude itself never comes into view. We are always a moment too soon or too late. If Knox is right, then Theseus is capable of seeing the totality of the mortal precisely because Oedipus's death marks the transition between finitude and what lies beyond it. This is a very special knowledge.

The practice of sovereignty must include this knowledge of death and maintain that knowledge as its own to secure the best possible life. In understanding human beings and everything they create as destined for ruin, the goal of sovereignty is to prevent that tendency toward ruination from spreading, breaking all boundaries, polluting everything, and destroying life. That which prevents the breaking of boundaries are limits upheld, however, and that which is immune to ruination is death. Death is, for mortal men, the unbreakable limit, the limit that none can surpass, *the* figure and foundation of security. Death never dies, and death is never transgressed. Michael Dillon misses this point when he claims that tragedy is not concerned "to specify what particular indispensable limit has to be met in order for social order to be established and maintained; as Hobbes does paradigmatically for modern politics . . . in his insistence that the fear of violent death at the hands of other men is the fundamental constraint which compels men to establish the social contract."[20] Dillon is absolutely correct to name Hobbes, but death *is* the single indispensable limit that Sophocles offers for security in political life, however different from Hobbes Sophocles' interpretation of death might be. Death brings us into contact with what is proper to finite humans, the experience of human finitude that reveals something *about* human finitude. Taken from the perspective of a finite sovereign, there can be no knowledge, no prophet of birth and of life and established things because life is unstable and Fate inescapable. Stable death, on the other hand, does afford a kind of knowledge that can keep the body politic secure.

The need for sovereignty and for security in life, however, compels us to ask why we should bother, given that the best is to never be born or to die quickly. The answer to this seeming contradiction is that, as we saw, life is neither to be praised nor blamed. For all of the suffering that life entails,

[20] *Politics of Security*, 149.

nowhere is life judged as valueless; on the contrary, life, as the Messenger claims, is inimical to valuation. Human life, in exile from its proper place in death, is neither good nor bad. Tragedy, even if has been read to posit a kind of resignation, certainly does not *demand* suicide; the suicides that occur in the Theban plays, from Jocasta to Antigone, are not blamed or praised either. What remains in life is something inimical to death: joy and happiness. Happiness, secure only in death, is not for the dead; death secures the end of suffering, and thus a life is to be *judged* happy only when it has ended, because only then can one say "it was happy" and not "so far, so good." A life without joy is, in the same speech of the Messenger cited previously, not life at all, because "when a man forfeits joy/I do not count his life as life, but only/a life trapped in a corpse."[21] Life without happiness and joy is not life, but happiness and joy make sense only in the context of misery and suffering. The sovereign's role is to make a space within life where happiness and joy are possible by minimizing misery and suffering.

The politics of security as found in the Theban plays foregrounds death as the access to a knowledge that will save the body politic and give the living the best chance for joy and happiness. This knowledge is, for reasons we have seen, never given directly in the play, although we have seen that such knowledge concerns the limit that is death. By looking at the structure of sovereignty in the plays, however, some portions of it can be discovered.

The Structure of Oedipal Sovereignty

One entrance into the structure of sovereignty is to look at what exactly sovereigns do, what they are there for, and why they and not others must perform the tasks charged to them. Foucault offers us an important clue to understanding the practice of sovereignty as found in tragedy. He argues that the purpose of tragedy

> is to show the ceremony in shreds, the moment when the sovereign, the possessor of public might, is gradually broken down into a man of passion, a man of anger, a man of vengeance, a man of love, incest, and so on. In tragedy, the problem is whether or not starting from this

---

[21] *Antigone*, 1238–1240.

decomposition of the sovereign into a man of passion, the sovereign-king can be reborn and recomposed: the death and resurrection of the body of the king in the heart of the monarch.[22]

Tragedy records, one might say, the excess of sovereign*ty* over the sovereign, the unchanging structure of rule and order within which the individual ruler succumbs to his personal failings by surpassing limits and is then replaced by the next sovereign, who repeats the cycle. Foucault's point is analogous to my central claim, that sovereignty is the *cause of* and *solution to* the problem of the political. Insofar as the decomposition of the sovereign into a man of passion is the origin of the political ills that infect the body politic, the sovereign causes the very problems that he is required to solve. It is this particular pattern that we must examine more closely.

A remarkable feature of many tragedies, including *Oedipus the King*, is that the action begins in the middle of cycles of degeneration and regeneration, the details of which come out in the course of the play; however, the beginning of the play is nearly always a point of degeneration. In Aeschylus' *Oresteian Trilogy*, *Agamemnon* begins, akin to *Hamlet*, with a watchman on guard, waiting to hear news of the war in Troy. The events leading up to that war are a series of terrible deeds: Paris stealing Helen, Atreus feeding his brother's children to him, Agamemnon sacrificing his own daughter to win the war against Troy. In the first place, then, *the sovereign is the cause of these terrible deeds*. Similarly, in *Oedipus the King*, the play begins with the Priest imploring Oedipus to save the city once again from the blight on it; little does Oedipus know at the time that he is the cause of the blight. *Sovereignty begins and ends with its ability or inability to drive out a fundamental pollution*, to solve the problems that sovereign excess has created. As the Priest tells Oedipus: "So, let us never speak about your reign/as of a time when first our feet were set/secure on high, but later fell to ruin."[23] The pollutions that sovereignty confronts and causes appear to originate with the sovereigns themselves.[24]

---

[22] Michel Foucault, *Society Must Be Defended*, trans. David Macey. New York: Picador, 2003, 176.

[23] *Oedipus the King*, 48–50.

[24] For a brief account of the possible historical origin of the plague in Oedipus, as well as a (very) general overview of the historical context of Sophocles' plays, see *Oedipus Tyrannus*, 9–11, and

Perhaps the knowledge that sovereigns possess and the reason for the pollutions that sovereigns both cause and are asked to solve stem, as the Nietzsche of *The Birth of Tragedy* argues, from the Dionysian impulse. The Dionysian is primarily the knowledge of and the longing to be immersed in the ultimate oneness of existence, "the desire to tear asunder the veil of Maya, to sink back into the original oneness of nature."[25] The veil of Maya, on the other hand, corresponds to Apollonian individuation, the desire to make forms and images out of the stuff of existence. In this Apollonian mood, the Oneness is demarcated, limited; the Apollonian *forms* those limits that the Dionysian impulse constantly compels us to destroy to reassert the unity of existence. The sovereign/hero is that individual who, having seen into the abyss of existence the truth that all is One and that individuation is "natural" but unreal, breaks through that nature by unnatural acts. Nietzsche writes of Oedipus as the "liberator of his mother" and that "wherever soothsaying and magical powers have broken the spell of present and future, the rigid law of individuation, the magic circle of nature, extreme unnaturalness – in this case incest – is the necessary antecedent."[26] The pollutions that sovereignty causes and fixes arise, on this view, from Dionysian wisdom, the excessive knowledge of the terror and joy of abundant Being. In short, something like the joyous Truth of existence is revealed to the sovereign and to the sovereign alone, and, knowing the Truth, he or she cannot fail but to commit acts that destroy all limits, be these parricide, incest, feeding a child to his father, or stealing a wife: the tragic sovereign is a "slayer of distinctions."[27] Succumbing to the Dionysian is what Foucault calls the decomposition of the sovereign into a man of passion. It is at this point, where the sovereign is de-individuated into the One, that those limits that sustain the political order are undone and exposed as dreams and images and the pollution that endangers the security of the body politic comes to be. After all, the

---

of course, Thucydides, *History of the Peloponnesian War*, trans. Rex Warner. London: Penguin Books, 1972, 247–255.

[25] Friedrich Nietzsche, "The Birth of Tragedy" in *The Birth of Tragedy & The Genealogy of Morals*, trans. Francis Golffing. New York: Anchor Books, 1956, 27. The oneness of nature, however, is not an ordered totality; it is an abundant, chaotic, contradictory, strife-ridden oneness. The unity of nature that the Dionysian seizes on lacks form, that is, lacks individuation; it does not lack a kind of primordial difference, a difference in itself.

[26] Id., 61.

[27] Rene Girard, *Violence and the Sacred*, trans. Patrick Gregory. Baltimore: Johns Hopkins University Press, 1977, 74.

limits of the political, like the limits that bar incest, cannibalism, and patricide, are themselves, as limits, Apollonian in inspiration. *Knowledge of Being destroys the boundaries and limits that sustain political order.*

If Foucault is right, then tragedy does not stop at the dissolution of the sovereign into the One; there is also an attempt to show the rebirth of a sovereign. If the Dionysian knowledge of and immersion into the One destroys the sovereign and endangers the polis, then I would argue that it is the knowledge of death, a knowledge of the untransgressable limit, that restores sovereignty, and with the restoration of sovereignty, the restoration of security. It is this knowledge of death that Oedipus teaches to Theseus to ensure that Athens will be secure forever. If death is the limit par excellence, then a knowledge of death is a knowledge of limits, boundaries, and demarcations. The very nature of that knowledge is – as the ban on the image of Oedipus' death attests – that it itself constructs a limit: the limit between sovereign and subject, ruler and ruled, the passage of which will endanger the polis. Recall Oedipus' list of those who cannot know what Theseus knows: the citizens, his own daughters, and, by implication, the audience. The first and most important demarcation emerging from the knowledge of death given to Theseus is the boundary between sovereign and subject that itself must be maintained lest security once again be jeopardized. Theseus learns the lesson well, as he rejects Antigone's desire to see her father's grave, telling her that it is not lawful because "He/has forbidden approach to the place,/nor may any voice invoke/the sacred tomb where he lies./He said, if I truly did this,/I should have forever a land unharmed."[28]

The answer to what sovereigns do and why they do it is that it is the sovereign who has a knowledge that all limits are finally dreamlike, opposed to the One, and at the same time, the sovereign has the knowledge that political order depends on those dreamlike limits. On the one hand, the joy (and terror) of Being in its excess leads to the destruction of all limits and to the most terrible of acts, to misery, and to suffering; on the other hand, without that joy, life really is not the best at all. In fact, it is not life at all, but life trapped in a corpse. The price of power, of being the sovereign and understanding the essence of the political, appears to be the inevitable destruction of the polis. If, as Nietzsche claims, Greek tragedy is

[28] *Colonus*, 2004–2008.

an "Apollonian embodiment of Dionysiac insights and powers," then from the perspective of sovereignty and political thought, Greek tragedy is the story of what the proper role of sovereignty is: to create those political forms, boundaries, and limits within which the joy of life can be experienced without destroying those limits. Charles Segal seems to concur, because

> the hero... enacts paradigmatically the place of man on the axis between god and beast, between the divine order and the threat of chaos or meaninglessness. The two axes intersect at the points of man's uniquely human creations: the city, the house, ritual, law, justice, language. It is just these creations and the structures on which they rest that the hero calls into question, threatens, and paradoxically affirms.[29]

In the questioning, threatening, and overcoming of the bounded, limited spaces of human civilization, there is not, as Segal notes, a *negation* of those limits or boundaries but an *affirmation*. The affirmation is paradoxical because only in destroying such limits do they come to light as necessary. This paradox is the other message of Greek tragedy: the final and complete reconciliation of the Apollonian and the Dionysian, limit and transgression, is *impossible*. The very thing that sovereignty aims to achieve through a knowledge of death – the possibility of a joyous finite life – is the same thing that sovereignty destroys with its knowledge of Being. The sovereigns have access to a dangerous knowledge: they know that the boundaries and limits of the polis, however necessary to achieve security in an insecure world, are nonetheless themselves insecure, mere human artifacts.

Oedipal Sovereignty, Hobbes, and Schmitt

I have claimed that Sophocles provides us, in the figure of Oedipus, with a crucial aspect of sovereignty: the sovereign is the cause of and solution to the problem of the political. To better understand the importance and usefulness of this definition, it might be best to compare Oedipal sovereignty to two other accounts of sovereign power that themselves emphasize the relationship of sovereignty and the political to death: sovereignty as elaborated in Thomas Hobbes and Carl Schmitt.

[29] *Tragedy and Civilization*, 9.

Hobbes does not provide a succinct definition of sovereignty, although in the Introduction to *Leviathan* he calls the sovereign the "artificial soul" of the body politic.[30] More telling, however, is the list of faculties and powers of the sovereign that forms the subject of Chapter XVII of *Leviathan*. Such rights include freedom from prosecution, freedom from being put to death, the right to judge what is necessary for peace and security, the right to censor ideas, the right to make and interpret laws, and others (twelve in total). The essence of sovereign right is, in short, the right *to judge* and to enforce one's judgments. Similarly, in *De Cive*, Hobbes argues that the sovereign not only has power of the sword but also the power to judge, for "all judgment, therefore, in a city, belongs to him who hath the swords; that is, to him who hath the supreme authority."[31] The centralization of all judgment in the sovereign is necessary because the basic problem of the state of war is the problem of multiple competing judges, each with the right to be a judge in his own case (which is another way of stating the Right Nature, the right to do anything that one judges to be conducive to preserving life). In instituting the sovereign, people authorize one person to be judge over all. If it is correct to see Hobbesian sovereignty as, in essence, the right to judge and to enforce one's judgments, then one can quickly see how different Oedipal sovereignty is, not only in its content but in the "kind" of insight that Sophocles gives us.

Hobbes' account of sovereignty is a description of rights and powers, that is, an account of sovereign power that tells us what sovereignty is, what sovereigns are set up to do, how they should best carry out their rights and duties, and what makes sovereignty legitimate. Oedipal sovereignty, by contrast, does not tell us exactly what sovereignty is or even what sovereigns have the right to do. Oedipal sovereignty describes the *structure* of sovereignty, that is, how sovereignty works, what its effects are, what becomes of those who bear sovereign power, what becomes of those under the rule of sovereigns – generally speaking, what we can expect from sovereignty in human existence. To see the distinction better, note what Hobbes tells us at the end of *Leviathan*, in "A Review and Conclusion," where Hobbes' summarizes his accomplishments:

---

[30] Thomas Hobbes, *Leviathan*. New York: Norton, 1997, Introduction.
[31] Thomas Hobbes, "De Cive," in *Man and Citizen*, ed. Bernard Gert. Indianapolis: Hackett, 1991, Chap. VI, §8.

> And thus I have brought to an end my Discourse of Civil and Ecclesiastical Government, occasioned by the disorders of the present time, without partiality, without application, and without other designe, then to set before men's eyes the mutuall Relation between Protection and Obedience; of which the condition of Human Nature, and the Laws Divine, (both Naturall and Positive) require an inviolable observation... And in this hope I return to my interrupted Speculation of Bodies Naturall....[32]

Apparently, the job is done; politics and sovereignty have been described, and now back to nature. Oedipal sovereignty tells us what happens next, now that the sovereign has been instituted. More precisely, it tells us what happens at the very same time that order is secured, namely that disorder is bound to erupt as the result of sovereignty. The reason for this disorder is not, to be sure, that any particular sovereign fails to adequately enact his or her rights and make good on his or her duties; it is the nature of sovereignty that sovereign right is in *inherent conflict* with sovereign duty. Sovereigns, we might say, following Nietzsche, simply know too much; they cannot but destroy that which they are supposed to preserve.

From a different perspective, it is precisely this last point, that sovereigns "know too much," that one can see mirrored in Carl Schmitt's definition of sovereignty as "he who decides on the exception."[33] This definition of sovereignty posits the sovereign as both "outside the normally valid legal system" while "nevertheless belong[ing] to it."[34] The sovereign's liminal position between the legal system and what lies outside it allows it to make the decision on the exception, a decision that suspends the normal legal order for the purpose of the state's self-preservation.[35] One can sketch a topography of the paradoxical position of Oedipus, a map in which his unique position allows him paradoxically to affirm the boundaries and limits of the polis at the same time that he calls into question and threatens them. The Schmittian sovereign equally stands in such a paradoxical place, from which he can suspend the normal legal order at the same time that such a suspension affirms the state that is under threat.

---

[32] Leviathan, "A Review and Conclusion."
[33] Carl Schmitt, *Political Theology*, trans. George Schwab. Chicago: University of Chicago Press, 2005, p. 5.
[34] *Political Theology*, p. 7.
[35] Id., p. 12.

In spite of these similarities, Oedipal sovereignty does not take the same form as the definition we find in Schmitt. Schmitt's definition, which opens *Political Theology*, sounds as if it were a response to an unasked question: who is sovereign, or perhaps, how do we know or recognize who is sovereign? Unlike Hobbes' description of the institution, rights, and duties of sovereignty, Schmitt begins as if sovereignty were a concept and institution that we no longer know or are in danger of forgetting. Much as in *Concept of the Political*, Schmitt's concern is that the forces of modernity – especially liberalism – are threatening not only the existence but also our own recognition of sovereignty or the political. In telling us how we recognize the sovereign (he or she who decides on the exception) or the political (the decision on the friend/enemy), as well as his tacit normative appeal to the preservation of both sovereignty and the political, Schmitt's concern is to give us, as it were, the criterial and perceptual means to recognize and see something that modernity has occluded.

Oedipal sovereignty does not tell us who is sovereign or how we know who is sovereign, nor does it tell us that sovereignty is something that we should either preserve or destroy. Rather, vis-à-vis Schmitt, one might say that it sounds a warning to sovereigns: "Beware!" This is in effect what Teiresias, the blind prophet who appears in *Oedipus the King* and *Antigone*, tells both Oedipus and Creon. In both cases, Oedipus and Creon ignore the warning, ignore the advice to be cautious and open minded, and tragedy results. What Schmittian sovereignty does not recognize is, as it were, the existential situation of the sovereign as he or she stands between the law and the suspension of law, the position of the one who knows that "authority proves that to produce law it need not be based on law."[36] The knowledge that law does not require law to be law, that in effect the legal order is not something grounded in nature or divine revelation but only on human decree and authority, is a knowledge that the limits of the law are mere limits, mere constructions grounded in human decision: mere Apollonian dreams. To be the one with this knowledge – this sovereign knowledge – might lead us to imagine what would happen to the person with that knowledge. Oedipal sovereignty suggests that the one with that knowledge is bound to destroy what he or she aims to preserve, driven, as were Oedipus and Creon, by a heedlessness toward the all-too-human limits of the law and the polis. Only a knowledge of human limits – of

---

[36] Id., p. 13.

death – can prevent the sovereign from destroying that which he or she aims to preserve. Lacking such knowledge, banned from knowing what Thesesus knows, Oedipal sovereignty in all of its contradictoriness remains.

In providing a structural and "psychological" account of sovereignty, Oedipal sovereignty teaches us something new, something we simply cannot find in Bodin or Hobbes, Rousseau or Schmitt. Driven to define sovereignty, to ground its rights and duties, to argue for its necessity, the classical theorists of sovereignty lose a vision of what sovereign power does: sovereignty preserves and destroys in the same act. The knowledge of death that Theseus is given – found in Sophocles' last play, written just before the fall of Athens – is, for us, banned. The balance to be found between the Dionysian knowledge that destroys and the Apollonian impulse that limits and forms is not to be found in the plays themselves. What is suggested, as I have been arguing, is that death is what sovereigns must know, yet the implication in the ban on Oedipus' death scene is that a knowledge of death, and thus a knowledge of that which will eternally secure the body politic, is a knowledge that none of us and no individual sovereign can be privy to. The deeper implication of Oedipal sovereignty is that it could be precisely birth and death – the figures of human finitude – that we must interrogate if we are to contest the concept and practice of sovereignty.

Oedipal Sovereignty and the War in Iraq

The Contradictions of Sovereignty

Accurate counts of the number of civilian deaths resulting from the war in Iraq are difficult to verify and are controversial for that reason. The Iraq Body Count project, basing its findings on press reports cross-referenced against at least two sources, puts the figure, as of February 4, 2008, at somewhere between 81,020 and 88,466.[37] Epidemiologists from The Johns Hopkins University, however, conducting mortality rate studies, have estimated that from 2003 to 2006 as many as 654,965 civilians might have died (although the number could be significantly lower), 91.8 percent of which deaths were caused by violence.[38] The number of refugees who have left Iraq as of late July 2007 has risen to 2 million; there are another

---

[37] http://iraqbodycount.org.
[38] http://www.jhsph.edu/publichealthnews/press_releases/2006/burnham_iraq_2006.html.

2 million who have been internally displaced.[39] These numbers alone suggest that somewhere between 4 million and 4.5 million Iraqi civilians – from a prewar population of 27 million, or around 15 percent of the civilian population – have been killed or displaced. Obviously, the number of civilians adversely affected in one way or another by the invasion of Iraq must be higher. Even if one takes the lowest mortality figure – approximately 70,000 deaths – and adds the number of internal and external refugees and then compares this to the equivalent effect on American society (population 301,000,000 as of July 2007), it would mean that were the war in Iraq to happen in the United States, approximately 45,000,000 people would have been affected.[40]

At the same time that Iraqis are being killed and displaced, some reports suggest that the invasion of Iraq has increased the number of terrorists who have taken the war as a catalyst to act against American power. The summarized judgments of the 2007 *National Intelligence Estimate* includes the claim that

> the spread of radical – especially Salafi – Internet sites, increasingly aggressive anti-US rhetoric and actions, and the growing number of radical, self-generating cells in Western countries indicate that the radical and violent segment of the West's Muslim population is expanding, including in the United States. The arrest and prosecution by US law enforcement of a small number of violent Islamic extremists inside the United States – who are becoming more connected ideologically, virtually, and/or in a physical sense to the global extremist movement – points to the possibility that others may become sufficiently radicalized that they will view the use of violence here as legitimate.[41]

A 2006 *National Intelligence Estimate* proved controversial insofar as it suggested that the Iraq war itself was one among many factors increasing

---

[39] http://web.amnesty.org/library/Index/ENGMDE140362007.

[40] A colleague of mine, Jairus Grove, pointed out to me that one can trace the effects of American violence in Iraq farther than the beginning of the Iraq invasion, back to the sanctions imposed by the United States and others in the 1990s. The basis of this claim is that the distinction between actual killing and "letting die," between the violence of war and the "passive" violence of sanctions is a distinction in need of criticism. I agree with Grove, but to analyze the sanctions regime imposed on Iraq is beyond the scope of this essay. Suffice it to say that the numbers of Iraqi deaths are much higher if one takes Grove's point.

[41] http://www.dni.gov/press_releases/20070717_release.pdf.

the number of terrorists around the world.[42] Robert Kagan, writing in *The Washington Post*, rightly questioned what it means to say that Iraq has increased the terrorism threat.[43] What does seem clear, however, is that the war has, beyond the violence present in preinvasion Iraq, *produced* a specific space of violence that did not exist before the Iraqi invasion. The space of violence produced by the invasion includes the targeted and "accidental" killings of Iraqis by the United States and its coalition forces, violence between Iraqis, dislocation, and, if not directly, then tangentially the current tension and violence between Kurds in Northern Iraq and Turkey. The Bush administration itself claims to have produced this space insofar as it has justified the war by claiming it is better to fight the terrorists *over there* then to fight them here at home (America certainly, but in Europe or Asia?). Thus, if the war has only possibly (or probably) produced or at least helped to produce a greater number of combatants, it has most certainly produced a space of violence that simply did not exist before the invasion.

The structure of the war in Iraq, begun in the name of the sovereign right to protect the body politic and continued in the name of protecting the lives of Americans, follows the logic of Oedipal sovereignty. In the name of securing the body politic, the United States has produced a situation of insecurity both for its citizens (more terrorists are emerging) and, more disastrously, in Iraq (where millions of civilians are affected). Unlike Oedipus, however, who does not invade a foreign country, the Iraq war has brought sovereign-produced violence not only to the citizens of the United States but also to another nation-state. The global reach of sovereign power, however "international" the Peloponnesus might have been, is something that the Greeks could not have fathomed, nor could they have predicted the current effectiveness and force of sovereign violence.

Liberal-Humanitarian Justifications for the War in Iraq

Beyond the formal resemblance between Oedipal sovereignty and the invasion of Iraq, Oedipal sovereignty can help us to contest various rationales for the invasion. Justifications for the war have come from both the right

---

[42] http://select.nytimes.com/search/restricted/article?res=F40716F635550C778EDDA00894DE404482.
[43] http://www.washingtonpost.com/wp-dyn/content/article/2006/09/25/AR2006092500912.html.

and the left. For example, Robert Kagan and William Kristol argued in 2004 that the war "would have come eventually because of the trajectory that Saddam was on" and that although "we [i.e., the United States] are paying a real price in blood and treasure in Iraq, the price of the liberation of Iraq has been worth it."[44] For Kristol and Kagan, it is not solely the desire to spread democracy that justified the invasion; it was the failure of the containment strategies in the 12 years after the first Gulf War that demanded military action. Note the lacuna, however: neither the blood of Iraqis nor the treasure of Iraq (whether we construe this in terms of money or the cultural treasure of the National Museum) are mentioned as a counterweight to the "right reasons" for the "right war." Charles Krauthammer offers a more measured foreign policy position (aligned against the position of Kristol and Kagan) that he calls "Democratic Realism," which justifies intervention if humanitarian aims and democratic hopes are connected to "geopolitical necessity."[45] The necessity that entailed invading Iraq as part of a larger war on terror was both strategic and an "existential threat," namely a struggle "over existence and identity" that, according to Krauthammer, is the nature of the threat from radical Islamic movements.[46] Missing from Krauthammer's position is the question: what of the dead bodies that appear not because they constituted the threat but merely because they once lived in the vicinity of the threat? There are also justifications (there are, of course, many justifications) for the invasion that rely on the ideal of universal liberal rights, of humanitarianism, and of a commitment to expanding access to liberal human rights that those in Western democracies now enjoy, a view to be considered more fully in a moment. What unites the justifications for the invasion, whether these justifications spring from a desire to reshape the world in America's image, to counter an existential threat, or to enforce the universality of human rights, is a consistent lack of attention to the violence that falls and has fallen on so many Iraqi bodies in the course of the war. Why do these bodies not count?

The liberal view, what Thomas Cushman calls a "liberal-humanitarian" justification for invading Iraq, is worth considering in more depth precisely

---

[44] Robert Kagan and William Kristol, "The Right War for the Right Reasons," in *The Right War? The Conservative Debate on Iraq*, ed. Gary Rosen. Cambridge: Cambridge University Press, 2005, pp. 32–35.
[45] Charles Krauthammer, "In Defense of Democratic Realism" in *The Right War?*, p. 192.
[46] Id., p. 189.

Oedipal Sovereignty and the War in Iraq

because it puts to the side strategic interests in the name of the universality of rights (including, one supposes, the right to life) – that is, he offers normative justifications for invasion – and thus would seem to open itself to criticism from a position that asks about the deaths required to liberate the survivors. The crux of this justification is that "there are situations in which ethical imperatives trump laws, especially if those laws are unjust."[47] Cushman's position challenges the priority of the rule of international law as a justifiable criticism of the war in Iraq because, as he summarizes his position: "one of the strong ethical arguments for the humanitarian intervention argument lies in considering the consequences of the war.... One precondition for accepting a humanitarian case for the war is the acceptance of a certain kind of consequentialist ethics that judges actions based on their outcomes rather than the intentions and motivations of the actors."[48] I turn to his introduction to a series of essays on the war in Iraq because he usefully summarizes the main questions and preliminary answers to the issues that his volume raises.

Cushman asks a question of those who oppose the war in Iraq: "What would you say to the Iraqi person who asked you one year later why you stood against our liberation?" – a question to which he claims to have received no answer. This lack of response, according to Cushman, is due to the uncomfortable position of the antiwar protestor, whose answer "would mean that the average Iraqi who desired liberation from Saddam would still be subject to his terror, enslaved to tyranny, and denied the basic human rights that liberals purportedly cherish as central to their own existences."[49] Cushman poses an important question, one that highlights the difficulties of thinking through the situation produced by the invasion. Cushman presses us to see that in a situation in which governmental violence has and is being brought to bear on Iraqi bodies, the pull on others to put an end to that violence is strong, even if violence itself must be employed. Cushman also returns us to the universality inherent in claims to the rights of humans, because he argues that those who believe in the fundament of liberal rights ought to extend those rights to those who are denied them.

---

[47] Thomas Cushman, ed., *A Matter of Principle: Humanitarian Arguments for War in Iraq.* Berkeley, University of California Press, 2005, p. 8.
[48] Id., p. 9.
[49] Id., pp. 12–13.

Of course, the Iraqi questioner whom Cushman constructs has two defining features: he is "liberated" and *alive*. One could equally ask, in response to Cushman, what he would say to those 4 million Iraqis who have become refugees, without a home, without a polis to guarantee those human rights that, as Hannah Arendt has shown, are the rights of citizens and not of human beings.[50] Equally, one might ask (if one could) of those Iraqis who have died: "Was your life *worth* the liberation of those who managed and are managing to live?" This is not to deny that some, perhaps many, revivified Iraqis might say that the end of their lives was worth the liberation of others. This alternative question instead reveals something latent in Cushman's moral justification for the war: the questions of *worth*, of *value*, of *exchangeability*, of *economy*, and in a specific sense, of *sacrifice*, are silently invoked. Some deaths, it appears, are *justified* by the achievement of a moral end. They are sacrifices in the sense that the deaths of some Iraqis acquire a *meaning*, a raison d'être, insofar as these dead had to die for the purpose of liberating others. Is that so? What is implicit in the claim that some will or must sacrifice either their lives or their homes in order to achieve a moral end? Furthermore, what grants any sovereign agent – especially if that sovereign represents another people or, more ambiguously, secular-liberal "civilization" – the right or duty to end certain lives in order to pursue a moral end?

Lurking beneath Cushman's liberal-humanitarian justifications is a certain *calculus*, a calculation: some lives are "worth" more than others; the lives of those who are liberated are worth more than the dead bodies that appear in the process of liberation.[51] We might say, following Derrida, that some bodies count and are to be counted differently from other bodies. Not only Iraqi lives, but the lives of U.S. soldiers are a part of the calculation. Soldiers (sometimes) know what they are getting into; how can we expect the dead to rise and tell us whether their lives were indeed exchangeable for what they will never experience, no matter how morally superior such a future might be? Cushman breezily claims that "a basic principle of

---

[50] Hannah Arendt, *The Origins of Totalitarianism*. San Diego: Harvest Books, 1994, pp. 267–305.
[51] A detailed, moving, and convincing discussion of the problems surrounding mourning in post-9/11 America, including the politics of who can be mourned and which lives are capable of (or worthy of) being mourned can be found in the essay "Violence, Mourning, Politics" in Judith Butler, *Precarious Life: The Powers of Mourning and Violence*. London: Verso, 2006, pp. 19–49.

sociological reasoning is that social outcomes are seldom the product of the motivations or intentions of actors. In this respect, the outcomes of the war in terms of social dislocation, factionalism, and resistance were unanticipated negative consequences of the war. In similar fashion, however, the victory of the Iraqi people over Saddam must be seen as a positive consequence from the standpoint of moral principles of human rights."[52] Whether the negative consequences of invasion were – or should have been – unanticipated, the argument that Saddam's removal is a positive consequence of the war that "all other critiques must be made in light of" is a red herring, simply another formulation of the rhetorically powerful but intellectually bankrupt question; namely, isn't the world better off without Saddam Hussein in power? Removing a tyrant is, I agree, a positive consequence, yet Cushman once again ignores the calculation that he implies in his reference to the negative consequences of the invasion. *His* position forces us to ask: *How much* social dislocation, factionalism, resistance, and death is justified by the removal of a tyrant? The apparently unambiguous positive moral consequence of removing Saddam must, to reverse Cushman, be seen in the light of 4 million refugees and perhaps 600,000 dead bodies. What legitimates this calculation, this valuation of singular human beings against an abstraction (or perhaps one day, a reality), a liberal-democratic state? Oedipal sovereignty, as I have outlined it, does not *directly* help us to address these questions, but it does offer us a different standpoint from which to assess the invasion: not the standpoint of the "moral principles of human rights," but the standpoint of the relationship between sovereign power and the meaning of death.

In attending to the latent calculation inherent in Cushman's position, it is important to begin asking how the figure of death, specifically the figures of dead bodies, is understood in the construction of his position. The figure of death in Sophocles was understood in connection to the idea of security and as that limit that, because it cannot be transgressed, is the limit productive of security. In Cushman's list of negative consequences of the invasion, Iraqi deaths are not even listed. If we ourselves add these dead bodies to the list of negative consequences, then we might say that "between these victims," to take out of context a passage from Rene Girard's *Violence and the Sacred*, "and the community [in this case, we who are citizens of

---

[52] Id., p. 9.

an invading country] a crucial social link is missing, so they can be exposed to violence without fear of reprisal."[53] I point to this passage not to argue that Iraqi bodies are sacrifices in Girard's sense of surrogate bodies that are the object of a violence intended to deflect the cycle of violent vengeance but rather to focus on the idea that a "crucial link" is missing, such that these bodies can be exposed to violence without in themselves counting. Rather than deflecting a cycle of revenge, such dead bodies are countable (even when they are unaccounted for) only as "negative consequences," as if death, in Cushman's position, is to be understood only as a *consequence* of the invasion, either positive (I will presume that Saddam's death is a positive consequence or at best an indifferent consequence) or negative. In other words, death – like factionalism, resistance, and social dislocation – is an *effect* of invasion. However, there are positive consequences, such as liberation. Dead bodies do not count and are not to be counted any differently than other consequences, such as resistance, dislocation, and liberation. Which is to say that Cushman's position bars the possibility of counting *a* dead body, taking account of the singularity of a once-living human being.

The crucial link that is missing in Cushman's position – the link between the one who justifies the invasion from the standpoint of human rights and the dead Iraqi body – is, ironically enough for a position committed to humanitarianism, the human being in its singularity, the dead body that can no longer bear human rights because it can no longer claim the right to life that grounds the other human rights. A dead body does not matter because it is dead. From the standpoint of the universality of rights, *a* dead body no longer counts, is not countable as such, because only what is potentially universal in that body counts, and a dead body is, almost by definition, excluded from the universal.[54] Which is not to say that Cushman's position entails an indifference to death. Rather, Cushman's standpoint precludes understanding death as a singular phenomenon, as something that happens, even in mass killing, to each singular being in their singularity (I return to the idea of singularity later). Presumably, there

---

[53] Rene Girard, *Violence and the Sacred*, trans. Patrick Gregory. Baltimore: Johns Hopkins University Press, 1977, p. 13.

[54] In other words, the dead body cannot make a claim to a right, but it also cannot receive a human right, because its humanity, from the standpoint of human rights, lay in the universal aspect of its life and not its death, which can only be its own. The dead body cannot vocalize a claim and thus cannot voice a collective claim to human rights. The dead body is silent and thus excluded from the universal.

is within Cushman's position a threshold beyond which dead Iraqi bodies become, in their generality as a mass, a negative consequence, but who decides that threshold point? Death, figured as what happens to some bodies, becomes only one variable in a calculation designed to test the net result of invasion.

Oedipal sovereignty, in directing our attention to the link between sovereign power and the meaning of death, helps us to understand and criticize a crucial presupposition in the liberal-humanitarian justification for the invasion of Iraq. To adopt the standpoint of Oedipal sovereignty, in a "methodological" sense, allows us to question not only the philosophical grounds for human rights claims but also the relationship of the one who speaks and acts in the name of human rights to the dead bodies that might appear as a result of humanitarian intervention. I have argued that Cushman's justification for the invasion of Iraq can understand those dead bodies only from a standpoint that discounts their singularity and thus can count such bodies only as a general consequence functionally equivalent to, if evaluatively distinct from, liberation, dislocation, factionalism, and resistance. To understand these dead bodies differently might be crucial to challenging sovereign power. I will return to this issue later, but I would now like to turn to another distinct but related aspect of Oedipal sovereignty that can help us to criticize not only Cushman's position but more broadly any justification of sovereign power: the relationship of means to ends.

Oedipal Sovereignty and Instrumental Rationality

Lives have been destroyed to protect life; homes have been destroyed to secure a homeland; the removal of one tyrant has produced conditions in which several tyrants have emerged. This is Oedipal sovereignty in practice. Attention to Oedipal sovereignty helps to challenge moral positions such as Cushman's because it too tends to look at effects rather than intentions. I argued previously that rather than identifying philosophical grounds for sovereign power, Sophocles points us to the effects of sovereign power and how those effects undermine the very ends of sovereignty. Oedipal sovereignty ignores the supposed reasons and justifications for what sovereigns do, focusing instead on the paradoxical consequence of sovereign action regardless of intention. For this reason, those who argue, as Cushman does, for a consequentialist justification of liberal-humanitarian intervention in Iraq must respond to Sophocles' insight.

In a broader sense, what becomes of justifications for using sovereign power to achieve various ends if Oedipal sovereignty is correct? This question can be taken in two ways. First, the question implies a criticism of the *instrumental effectiveness* of sovereign power. If sovereignty causes that which it is supposed to solve, then it is obviously the wrong means to achieve any of its ends. Second, the question asks whether justifications of sovereignty make sense *at all* insofar as, to put it in Hobbesian language, sovereign right is in conflict with sovereign duty. I believe that the first problem, that of the instrumental effectiveness of sovereignty, is fairly straightforward. The invasion of Iraq has shown that at best the results of the invasion are difficult to assess, precisely because the idea of a calculation such as Cushman's cannot ascribe, without inherent arbitrariness, the relative values of liberation, resistance, death, factionalism, and dislocation. Thus, I would like to focus on the second problem, the idea that Oedipal sovereignty suggests that the ends of sovereign power, whatever they might be, are in inherent contradiction with the means of sovereign power, whatever they might be.

Oedipus himself represents what might be the limit point of instrumental rationality, the point at which such rationality, even when executed perfectly, fails to achieve its ends. Oedipus is confronted with a problem: to save the city of Thebes from the curse of the Sphinx, he must answer a riddle. The end of his action is clear – saving Thebes from a curse – and more than that, saving the city is, I assume, unquestionably a good, moral, and worthwhile end. The means to this end is equally clear: answer the riddle correctly. There is no question of other means, other tasks that can be performed. Oedipus and the Sphinx present us with a situation in which the end is good and the means to that end is both known and achievable, and in fact, Oedipus succeeds. He nonetheless dooms Thebes in the very act of saving it. He dooms it, of course, because he himself is the bearer of a plague, of a troubled and troubling identity that he does not truly know. As J. Peter Euben points out, "Oedipus' unique intellectual ability is commensurate on the familial level with his acts of patricide and incest" such that "each riddle has an answer that is a further riddle; each victory obscures the defeat within it."[55] The perfect execution of instrumental

---

[55] J. Peter Euben, *The Tragedy of Political Theory: The Road Not Taken*. Princeton: Princeton University Press, 1990, p. 113.

reason is undermined by a lack of knowledge that is not of the order of instrumental rationality.

Broadly speaking, it is not solely a lack of knowledge that, according to Oedipal sovereignty, is to blame for the consequences of the invasion. Oedipal sovereignty emphasizes something beyond the inability of the United States government to plan carefully for postinvasion Iraq. Much of the criticism directed toward the war, partially inspired by the Bush administration's response to Hurricane Katrina, emphasizes the *incompetence* of the U.S. government. The almost unthinkable failure of the Pentagon and the Bush government generally to understand the history, ethnic diversity, and culture of Iraq, and the effects of such ignorance on the civil war that has emerged in the wake of the collapse of the Iraqi government, is ably demonstrated in recent journalistic accounts of both the buildup to the war and its aftermath.[56] Although the degree to which the administration of the war and the occupation have been bungled might be unique, the fact that wars turn out quite differently from how they were planned is not. Criticizing the competency of the Bush administration in prosecuting the Iraq War is essential but insufficient. Criticism that focuses on competency tends to obscure the questionability not only of the stated ends of the Iraq invasion but also of the entire logic of means–ends rationality in the context of sovereignty. If there is a paradox in sovereign power that manifests itself as the simultaneous achievement and undermining of the goals of sovereignty, then there is no such thing as *an* end of sovereign action. *Any particular end of sovereignty includes its opposite within it.*[57] By this I do

---

[56] See, for example, Michael R. Gordon and General Bernard E. Trainor, *Cobra II*. New York: Pantheon Books, 2006 and Peter W. Galbraith, *The End of Iraq*. New York: Simon & Schuster, 2006.

[57] I should qualify this claim or in fact the claim of the entire essay insofar as conversations with George Oppel, Dick Flathman, and Bill Connolly have all alerted me to what might be called the "formalism" of my position as well as its "absolutism." In various ways, it has been brought to my attention that sovereignty can be plural and appear in several different places in the body politic; that the sovereign state in modern democracies have their own "checks" (e.g., a relatively independent civil service); and that, as is the case, I certainly do endorse some forms of state power (e.g., I believe that here in America, health care should be universally guaranteed by the state). How then, can I account for these difficulties and my own support of certain state actions if I thought that no end of sovereignty could be anything but mixed and self-annihilative? Derrida alerts us to the same point: "We are always led back to the same aporia: how to decide between, on the one hand, the positive and salutary role played by the 'state' form (the sovereignty of the nation-state) and, thus, by democratic citizenship in providing protection against certain kinds of international violence (the market, the concentration of world capital, as well as 'terrorist' violence and the proliferations of weapons) and, on the other

not mean, for example, that the end of establishing a democracy in Iraq is in contradiction to the end of securing access to oil (although that might be the case). Rather, Oedipus puts into question the purity of any end, the possibility that achieving an end would not also bring about the achievement of that which undermines the end. To this extent, competency is a nonissue, because it is less a result of incompetence than of an inherent contradiction that is responsible for the failures in the Iraq invasion.

It is also important to emphasize once again that it is not Oedipus' *intentions* that are to be blamed for his saving and dooming Thebes at the same time. Analogously, the problem with the invasion of Iraq is not only the questionable intentions of the Bush administration, the fact that they might have lied to the country about their true reasons for going to war. The problem is that the end of sovereign power is at the same time moral *and* immoral, life *and* death, liberation *and* new forms of tyranny. Oedipus lets us see that there is no such thing as "collateral damage," as if the death that sovereign violence brings is a function of the dirty means used to carry out pure moral ends. On the contrary, I have been arguing that sovereignty, as Oedipal, has an inherent contradiction, an inherent tendency to cause what it must solve, to save and doom in the same act,

---

hand, the negative or limiting effects of a state whose sovereignty remains a theological legacy, a state that closes its borders, excludes or represses noncitizens, and so forth" (*Philosophy in a Time of Terror*, p. 124). One possibility, suggested to me by Daniel Levine is that we can distinguish between "true" acts of sovereignty and administration. Sovereign acts are rare; administration occurs all the time. Although I am sympathetic to this idea, it might lend itself to neglecting the biopolitical point, which would be that sovereignty in modernity suffuses administration as much as it decides on the enemy and on the suspension of the legal order (sovereignty as a power over *life* and death). Conversely, I do not wish to pluralize as it were the concept of sovereignty, to make it a concept under which all sorts of actions fall. For better or worse, I agree with Schmitt that sovereignty is that political concept that puts power and authority in a single political position, the sovereign. In other words, the concept of sovereignty implies unity, whether the unity of a single ruler or the unity of a people (as in Rousseau). As for the civil service, events in America have shown that, whatever the outcries of bureaucrats have been against the incompetence of the Bush Administration, they have proved incapable or unwilling of subverting the policy directives given to them. After all, Eichmann was a civil servant, and his very "neutrality" vis-à-vis the state helped only to better enact the Final Solution. The more difficult point is my endorsement of the state's securing certain basic living conditions for citizens (i.e., a home, health care, education). All I can say to this point is that as long as the political institutions that we have are what they are, we should press as much as possible on the state to provide for the betterment of the basic living conditions of citizens (and, I all too naively hope, noncitizens). It is a bio-political risk, but what is the better option right now?

Oedipal Sovereignty and the War in Iraq

and thus the end of sovereign power, what it aims to achieve, can never be security or insecurity, but must be both.

If Oedipal sovereignty offers us a new insight into the effects of sovereign power, then we must ask: *Why* does sovereignty cause what it aims to solve? If it is not a question of better intentions, better means, better knowledge, or morally superior ends, then what are we to draw from Oedipus that can help us to understand the invasion of Iraq and sovereign power more broadly? I hesitate here; I am not sure what to say. I want to say: *something intervenes*. For Oedipus it is Fate, a nonhuman power at work in the world that intervenes in the actions of human beings, unsettling their plans and undermining even the most perfectly rational actions. This idea of fate is analogous to the idea of the eventfulness of the world, of the world as a place in which the new surges into being and thus of the world as beyond the power of human mastery. I do not want to deny that the eventfulness of the world plays a role in undermining sovereign power; however, eventfulness not only undermines sovereignty; it also undermines (or aids) any being. What I would like to suggest, specifically in response to liberal-humanitarian justifications of the invasion of Iraq, is that what intervenes in the deployment of sovereign violence is *singularity*. By singularity I do not mean the idea of the individual as a bearer of rights, a formed personality, or an isolatable atom among other atoms. Rather, here is Jean-Luc Nancy, expressing the singularity of all beings in *Being Singular Plural*:

> As English [and French] allows us to say, other beings are curious (or bizarre) to me because they give me access to the origin; they allow me to touch it; they leave me before it, leave me before its turning, which is concealed each time. Whether an other is another person, animal, plant, or star, *it is above all the glaring presence of a place and moment of absolute origin, irrefutable, offered as such and vanishing in its passing*. This occurs in the face of a newborn child, a face encountered by chance on the street, an insect, a shark, a pebble... but if one really wants to understand it, it not a matter of making all these curious presences equal.[58]

---

[58] Jean-Luc Nancy, *Being Singular Plural*, trans. Robert D. Richardson and Anne E. O'Byrne. Stanford: Stanford University Press, 2000, p. 20, italics added.

For Nancy, each being is singular insofar as it is an absolute origin, that is, insofar as each being is inassimilable because it exists *each* time (each being is marked by the singularity of the moment in which it comes to presence) in *each* space (each body is what it is because of the spatial relations that help to constitute it), and presents a unique body. The "place and moment" of each singular being are irrefutable precisely because they are inassimilable, because they cannot be captured by and reduced to a general concept or thought. I would like to add to Nancy's list a dead Iraqi body, the singular existence that that body is, and the life to which it testifies. What I would like to suggest is that the singularity of the dead Iraqi body is that which renders the sovereign invasion of Iraq Oedipal and thus exposes the contradiction of sovereign power.

To better explain this point, let us return to Oedipus. What we might glean from Sophocles' dramatization of sovereignty is that the something that intervenes has to do with the meaning of human finitude, of death, with whatever Theseus was given to understand and we, all of us, are banned from knowing. This something is captured in the image of Theseus before the dying Oedipus, holding his hands before his face, shading his eyes as if some deadly terror had revealed itself to him, a sight that no human being could endure. We are left to imagine what the deadly terror might be. Perhaps it is the transformation of a human into a god (as I argued earlier). Perhaps it is the disappearance of a human into the underworld, or perhaps, and I would like to dwell on this possibility, it is simply the dead body of a man who was himself a victim of the sovereignty of the gods, or of Fate, of a power or powers superior to him. This is a body that we are not allowed to see, or to count, as if the only thing that guarantees the security of Athens forever is the sovereign power to hide the dead body, to control the meaning of its death, to foreclose the revelation that a singular being has been killed.

This practice of hiding the body seems to be at work in the justifications for the war in Iraq. It is not, of course, that we do not hear about dead Iraqi bodies or sometimes see them on television; rather, what the justifications and often enough the discourse of the Bush administration occlude is the idea that there might be something incalculable, inassimilable, unequal in the singular dead body. Cushman's calculation, for example, can assess death only by making each body equal, simply a dead body, an effect of invasion. If the dead body is inassimilable – more precisely, if we ought

Oedipal Sovereignty and the War in Iraq

to relate ourselves to the dead body in its singularity – then the *ends* of the invasion in Iraq, whether those ends are liberation, democracy, protecting the United States, finding weapons of mass destruction (WMD), or securing oil supplies, must also include the singular dead body. The dead body is not a *means* to achieve other ends – that would assimilate the dead body, make it part of an instrumental calculation – but is *itself* an end of sovereignty. The appearance of a dead body, whichever one's theory of sovereignty might be and whichever one's justification for the war in Iraq, has never been an end of sovereignty but the very thing sovereignty aims to avoid and the problem sovereignty is instituted to solve. Even Damiens' tortured and dead body, the regicide whose spectacular execution opens Foucault's *Discipline and Punish*, is not an end of sovereign power, that which sovereignty was instituted to do, but the revenge taken by sovereign power on the body of one who injured it, a restoration of sovereignty "by manifesting it at its most spectacular."[59] The sovereign right to kill or let live was not and never could be a duty to kill as an end in itself, nor could the appearance of dead bodies be one raison d'être of sovereignty. Hence the need to hide the body, to control its meaning by making it a sacrifice or part of the birth pangs of History or by simply ignoring its appearance. These various ways of hiding the body are expressions and repressions of what Nancy calls our *curiosity* toward the singularity of the dead body. Sovereignty seems to work – that is, seems to be noncontradictory – only insofar as it follows Oedipus's command to Theseus and hides the singular dead body by making it equal to other dead bodies, making all these bodies sacrifices, obscuring the singular existence that the dead body is and the singular life to which it testifies.

The contradiction that Oedipal sovereignty exposes might result from the fact that the sovereign right to kill, the right over death (whether it be killing or letting die), when enacted, is immediately confronted by a singular dead body, a body that can be assimilated to the logic of sovereignty only by hiding it, whether literally or at the level of the meaning of the body's death. The logic of sovereignty – in which killing is a means to achieve the cessation of killing – is undermined by the inassimilability of the singular dead body. To link ourselves to the dead body, to remain

---

[59] Michel Foucault, *Discipline and Punish*, trans. Alan Sheridan. New York: Vintage Books, 1995, p. 48.

curious about it, to let the body confront and challenge us, to contest the meaning of the dead body, and to disobey Oedipus' command might be necessary if we are to challenge Oedipal sovereignty.

If we begin our criticism of the war in Iraq and more broadly of sovereignty by beginning with the singular dead body, then we might be able to contest the occlusion of the body or the meaning that sovereignty tries to give to that body. If we start with the claim that sovereignty kills not as a means but as one of its ends and thus in contradiction with the reason for its institution, then we might be able to formulate deeper challenges to sovereign power. If we add to these starting points the problem of the meaning of human finitude and of how we understand the figures of birth and death – and do so through an ethical and political relationship to the singularity of beings – then we might be also be able to infuse our appeals to nonsovereign forms of power with possibilities of being in the world that emerge from affects other than fear and resentment over the limits of human mastery. Sovereign power does not work, but something else might.

4

Sacrifice and Sovereignty

Mateo Taussig-Rubbo*

They made the ultimate sacrifice and they are missed by their friends and families and their clients. – The Red Zone (Web site for private military contractors)[1]

Sacrifice seeks to establish a desired connection between two initially separate domains. – Claude Lévi-Strauss, *The Savage Mind*

In recent years, sacrifice is often discussed as the act that U.S. citizens have not been asked to perform. Although many of our highest officials declare that this is a time of war, the complete giving of the self – or its taking by the government – that had come to characterize total war of the twentieth century is absent. Sacrifice instead appears as a tactic that America's adversaries employ when they martyr themselves.[2] Even so, sacrifice and sacralization are visible at sites like Ground Zero in New York and in the public reception of the deaths of U.S. soldiers in war, and we can still detect republican currents by which sacrifice and citizenship are mutually constitutive, however attenuated or partisan these links might seem.[3]

One reason to focus on sacrifice is that it can be a register of the government's dependence on the citizenry. Especially in the context of

---

* Associate Professor, University at Buffalo Law School, State University of New York.
[1] The Red Zone military contractor Web site, accessed Mar. 31, 2006, http://psd-eod.typepad.com/dont_worrywell_protect_yo/2005/06/index.html.
[2] Talal Asad, *On Suicide Bombing*. New York: Columbia University Press, 2007, 43–45, 51. Asad acknowledges and criticizes the use of sacrifice as a widespread analytic to describe suicide bombing.
[3] For discussion of "sacralization" at Ground Zero see Mateo Taussig-Rubbo, "Sacred Property: Searching for Value in the Rubble of 9/11," at SSRN http://papers.ssrn.com/sol3/papers.cfm?abstract_id=1269533.

war, in which citizens kill and are killed on behalf of the government, the logic and rhetoric of sacrifice can function as a form of accountability. It serves to ground a claim that a loss was of (or should have been) of great significance. At the same time, because this accountability can verge on the ephemeral, in many instances it might seem like little more than a cynical screen for an underlying ability to demand or accept an offering without giving compensation. What at one moment might look like a transcendent act of sacrifice can at another come to seem like a purely pointless and banal loss.

From the point of view of the citizen, the reasons to want to avoid sacrifice are understandable, but it is also important to realize that the government that avoids asking for sacrifice is in some sense declaring its autonomy from the citizenry. Put another way, we have seen again and again in U.S. history that citizens who can frame their losses as sacrifices often gain a claim on the government and a means of showing that they are part of the popular sovereign, "We the People." Seen in this light, a turn away from sacrifice in the U.S. political and legal order constitutes a recalibration of relations between citizen and government that runs parallel to the state of exception and governmental sovereignty. These developments share a common theme: the independence of the government from the citizenry in one case and the legal order in the other.

Rather than examine sacrifice as a category that pertains only to the barbaric other – such as the suicide bomber – I assume that it has been central to the critical moments of founding, maintenance, and transformation of the U.S. political and legal order. I do not undertake a deconstruction of social contract theory, in which the preservation of the individual's life is the purpose of the covenant, or liberal political thought, for which death is nothing but negation, as unable to account for the actual place of sacrifice in our political order. Paul Kahn, in his book *Putting Liberalism in Its Place*, has already done this in a profound way; he has urged that that sacrifice and sovereignty must be considered together and that sacrifice and not contract is the most accurate way of framing the political relationship as it has been experienced.[4] I take as a point of departure that the U.S. government pursues not only a monopoly of violence but also a monopoly

---

[4] Paul Kahn, *Putting Liberalism in Its Place*. Princeton, NJ: Princeton University Press, 2005, Ch. 5; see also Danielle Allen, *Talking to Strangers: Anxieties of Citizenship Since* Brown v. Board of Education. Chicago: University of Chicago Press, 2004, 39.

Sacrifice and Sovereignty

of sacrifice – that is, control over sacralized, transcendent loss. In using a vocabulary that has Christian (not to mention Jewish and Islamic) resonances, I do not mean to address the question of whether the state is actually a church, nor do I propose to examine the reception of religious meanings and forms by the political order in the founding moments of political modernity, when sovereignty is redistributed from divine king to the sacralized but ephemeral People. Rather, I seek to explore a form of meaning of action that can be detected in a variety of present-day settings, putting to the side the question of whether they are "religious" and/or part of a "political theology"[5] and draw instead on what the secular state has designated as religious for what seem to be suggestive analogies (and presumably homologies).

Having made these assumptions, what I actually explore in this essay are efforts by officials, through law and policy, to *avoid* sacralization and sacrifice, to unbundle the sacred and the state. More specifically, I describe a state that uses legal form to attempt to construe certain deaths as sacrificial and others as banal and meaningless in relation to a given audience. I then explore some of the difficulties that these attempts encounter as nonstate actors employ and advance their own conceptions of sacrifice and meaningful loss. In sum, I (1) suppose that the sovereign (either the popular or the state sovereign and without specifying the relation between these two and the government) is a sacralized entity and that sacrifice is central to the citizen's relation to the sovereign; (2) look at the attempts that officials make to avoid this reality; and (3) describe nonstate actors reasserting the importance of sacrifice and the sacred, but now as a form of action and a resource that they command.

My first case study construes the emergence of the private military contractor in recent decades as an effort to displace or outsource sacrifice and avoid engaging with the rich tradition that designates soldiers as participating in sacrifice. This attempt at desacralization, an attempt to render certain deaths banal for a national audience, has encountered difficulties.

---

[5] For discussions of these themes see Talal Asad, *Formations of the Secular: Christianity, Islam, Modernity*. Stanford: Stanford University Press, 2003, Ch. 1; Michael Taussig, *The Magic of the State*. New York: Routledge, 1997; Winnifred Sullivan, *The Impossibility of Religious Freedom* (Princeton: Princeton University Press, 2005); Carl Schmitt, *Political Theology: Four Chapters on the Concept of Sovereignty*, trans. George Schawb. Cambridge, MA: MIT Press, [1922] 2006.

I consider the U.S. reception of the spectacular televised killing and desecration of four contractors in Fallujah in 2004, where actors who had contracted their security services to the private sector became reconceived as sacralized citizens, their bodies a visible site for the idea of the nation. In a second case study, I look at instances in which U.S. officials try to "privatize" sacrifice by placing it in a gendered framework or making it a "family matter," and the corresponding attempts of nonstate actors to manipulate their private status. In a third case study, I turn to what might be seen as sacrificial action by those deemed the enemies of the United States, focusing on hunger strikes by detainees in Guantánamo Bay, Cuba. Detainees' attempts to turn themselves into martyrs – this is how military officials and some detainees describe what they are doing – are blocked by a counter-sacrificial policy by officials, including force-feeding and increased secrecy.

Each of these cases concerns a legal form and policy – whether it is contract and exclusion from military law in the case of contractors, the privatization of a mother's sacrifice, or exclusion from normal law in Guantánamo – and the ways in which the meaning attributed to violence and loss can attempt to overcome those classifications. My aim is not to discuss comprehensively the theories of sacrifice; instead, I wish to point out some important dynamics that merit more thorough investigation.

One theme that runs throughout this essay is the relation of sacrifice to law and ritual. Ritual sacrifice often marks the sacrifice practiced by others as alien for moderns, Christians, and post-Christians, for whom sacrifice (if the category makes any sense at all) must be a sincere and heartfelt giving of the self, not a formalistic and economistic act and not a giving of a substitute in place of the self.[6] My examples are ones in which sacrificial

---

[6] Many interpreters of our dominant religious traditions insist, like theorists of modern disenchantment, that ours is a postsacrificial era. For instance, many commentators describe archaic shifts internal to the sacred Book from sacrifice to law in the Jewish case, or from sacrifice to love in the Christian. Christ's "sacrifice" is a paradigm case where the body of an individual is human, divine, and a stand-in for all "mankind," yet it is described as the *last* sacrifice, the sacrifice of sacrifice. See Jean-Luc Nancy, "The Unsacrificeable," *Yale French Studies*, 79: 20–38, 24 (1991); *see also* Jill Robbins, "Sacrifice," ed. Mark Talyor, *Critical Terms for Religious Studies*. Chicago: University of Chicago Press, 1998, 288. ("Both the figure of Christ and Socrates propose a transfiguration and a transcendence of sacrifice. They determine it as autosacrifice, namely, not only as sacrifice of the self that is willed and desired, but also, it will be shown, self-sacrifice on its way to becoming the very sacrifice of sacrifice. They determine it by a repetition of the old sacrifice that reveals an entirely new content, as when

meaning appears in places where it is officially excluded, where it is more improvisational and post hoc than ritually or legally permitted.

In my second epigraph, I quote anthropologist Claude Lévi-Strauss. Levi-Strauss derided sacrifice as nonsensical because it confounded classification by asserting a connection between ordinarily separate categories – such as individual person and god or cucumber and ox in a famous anthropological example.[7] It blurred distinctions and hence, for the great structuralist, meaning itself. Those moments of merging between different entities, the sacrificer and his or her god, surely can help to ground authority. The technique of sacrifice, however, is not invariably tied to law and ritual, nor is the monopoly by officials ensured – it can be taken up by a variety of unauthorized actors. It is the potential nonsense of sacrifice, when in the hands of nonstate actors, that is especially interesting in our current moment. The schemes of significance and insignificance that law and policy designate (the soldier's death is a sacred presence of the sovereign; the contractor's, banal) can be challenged by other actors. From the perspective of the *ex ante* scheme, these assertions are indeed nonsense, but *ex post*, in some of my examples, we can see that the structure of legal and policy classification can begin to shift, or that officials will have to take special action to preserve the *status quo*.

Finally, I must mention Giorgio Agamben's much-discussed conception of sovereign power as that which can take life without the action being considered a sacrifice (or a homicide).[8] Each of my examples could be read as supporting Agamben's conception as a description of the government's ideal world, because it appears that sacrifice is the form of action and meaning that officials generally attempt to displace. I would locate Agamben's formulation not as describing a transcendent truth of modern sovereignty but as one tentative effort to constitute actors whose death

---

the New Testament understands itself as the revelation of what was concealed in the Old. Both claim to have acceded to the truth, hitherto concealed, of sacrifice. That is why, in the West, the movement of going beyond, or the transcendence of sacrifice, is foundational.") *See also* Jonathan Sheehan, "The Altars of the Idols: Religion, Sacrifice and the Early Modern Polity," *Journal of the History of Ideas*, 67, 4: 649–674 (2006).

[7] Claude Lévi-Strauss, *The Savage Mind*. Chicago: University of Chicago Press, 1966, 224–228.

[8] Giorgio Agamben, *Homo Sacer: Sovereign Power and Bare Life*, trans. Daniel Heller-Roazen. Stanford: Stanford University Press, 1998, 83. Agamben writes that the "*sovereign sphere is the sphere in which it is permitted to kill without committing homicide and without celebrating a sacrifice, and sacred life* [homo sacer] – *that is life which may be killed but not sacrificed – is the life that has been captured in this sphere.*" (Italics in original.)

is not a sacrifice (or a homicide). Although the main thrust of this piece is the enormous difficulty that this encounters, the examples I have selected are those in which we can detect an effort by the United States to be a sovereign in Agamben's sense, to chart the course carefully between two forms of liability: the designation of a killing as a sacrifice or as a homicide.

Outsourcing Sacrifice and Private Military Contractors[9]

While stopped in traffic, several armed Iraqi insurgents walked up behind these two unarmored vehicles and repeatedly shot these four Americans at point blank range, dragged them from their vehicles, beat, burned and disfigured them and desecrated their remains.[10]   – Plaintiff's Complaint, *Nordan v. Blackwater*

[A mercenary is] motivated to take part in the hostilities essentially by the desire for private gain... material compensation substantially in excess of that promised or paid to combatants...[11]   – Geneva Convention, Protocol 1

This section examines one important example of the difficulties entailed in creating a group of unsacrificeable subjects. This came early in the U.S. war in Iraq, in March 2004, when four armed Blackwater contractors were ambushed and then grotesquely and spectacularly killed, dismembered, and immolated by hundreds of Iraqis in Fallujah. For many U.S. officials and media commentators, these acts of "desecration," as many called them, re-nationalized what had been privatized, and the deaths were conceived by many as sacrifices on behalf of the United States. How are we to think about this overcoming of the official insignificance attributed to the contractors' deaths?

A Web site for private military contractors speaks of contractors whose deaths were an "ultimate sacrifice" and "is dedicated to the men who gave their lives so 'the client' would be safe."[12] In the military context,

---

[9] This section is drawn from Mateo Taussig-Rubbo, "Outsourcing Sacrifice: The Labor of Private Military Contractors," *Yale Journal of Law & Humanities* (forthcoming) (posted on SSRN http://papers.ssrn.com/sol3/papers.cfm?abstract_id=1157399).

[10] Plaintiff's Complaint, *Nordan v. Blackwater*, North Carolina, Wake County Superior Court, 7 No. 05-CVS-000173 (filed Jan. 5, 2005) [hereinafter Complaint].

[11] Protocol Additional to the Geneva Conventions of Aug. 12 1949 and Relating to the Protection of Victims of International Armed Conflict (Protocol 1), Art. 47.

[12] The Red Zone, *supra* note 1.

we typically think of sacrifice as something that the soldier does for the nation or state at least if we recall Lincoln at Gettysburg, when he speaks of the "consecration" of the battlefield by those who "gave their lives that [the] nation might live."[13] As the military contractor quote might suggest, however, the matter of who can sacrifice for whom is complicated: the nation is not the only purported recipient of this form of offering.

Indeed, killing by and the killing of armed private military contractors in Iraq has drawn attention to their ill-defined legal and cultural position. Are these contractors and their employers subject to Iraqi law, U.S. military or criminal law, state tort law, or international law? Can they kill with impunity? Can they be killed with impunity? By this I mean not whether an Iraqi who kills a contractor would be immune from prosecution but whether the killing of a contractor implicates the U.S. government in the same way that the killing of a U.S. soldier does – that is, as a sacrifice for the nation that officials and the public are expected to recognize, count, and honor. Are the contractors, in sum, unable to commit murder and ineligible for sacrifice? Do the legal form of contract and the policy of privatization serve to immunize and dissociate the United States from these forms of liability for those who act on its behalf?

Before addressing these questions, it is important to note that in the United States, sacrifice and citizenship have long been seen as mutually constitutive: to forgo one is to disaggregate an ancient coupling. In his notorious pre-Civil War opinion in *Dred Scott v. Sandford*,[14] Chief Justice Taney evoked this tradition to buttress his position that African Americans were aliens, not citizens, referring to their exclusion from state militias. He cited the laws of New Hampshire as one example according to which

> No one was permitted to be enrolled in the militia of the State, but free white citizens.... Nothing could more strongly mark the entire repudiation of the African race. The alien is excluded, because, being born in a foreign country, he cannot be a member of the community until he is naturalized. But why are the African race, born in the State, not permitted to share in one of the highest duties of the citizen? The answer is obvious; he is not, by the institutions and laws of the State,

[13] Abraham Lincoln, Gettysburg Address (Nov. 19, 1863), in 7 *Collected Works of Abraham Lincoln*, ed., Roy P. Basler. New Brunswick, NJ: Rutgers University Press, 1953.

[14] *Dred Scott v. Sandford*, 60 U.S. 393, 415 (1856).

numbered among its people. He forms no part of the sovereignty of the State, and is not therefore called on to uphold and defend it.

Although Taney's decision was rejected by the Civil War Amendments, the assumption of the passage cited was not. Indeed, this same structure is at the heart of Lincoln's Gettysburg Address and Emancipation Proclamation – except that the "state" that is receiving the sacrifice is now the United States, not its member states.[15] Those excluded from military service have understandably claimed that they are losing out on accessing the particular prestige accorded to it,[16] whereas those who serve but are not accorded full citizenship rights have found that their exclusion can be challenged as violating the mutually constitutive nature of sacrifice and citizenship.

Although this traditional citizen/sacrifice coupling is still visible, it is also easy to see it as anemic – whether it has become weak because of a "Vietnam gap" between the military and the rest of the population, the end of conscription under President Nixon, or some other reason, such as a diminished need for active mass participation in warfare. Many of the clichés about and diagnoses of American society after World War II suggest that America is a hedonistic, self-centered, consumer society and that the traditional relationship of citizenship to military service is disintegrating.[17] One commentator notes "a central paradox of present-day American militarism. Even as U.S. policy in recent decades has become progressively militarized, so too has the Vietnam-induced gap separating the U.S. military from society persisted and perhaps even widened."[18]

---

[15] Abraham Lincoln, Gettysburg Address (Nov. 19, 1863), in 7 *Collected Works of Abraham Lincoln*, ed., Roy P. Basler. New Brunswick, NJ: Rutgers University Press, 1953; Abraham Lincoln, The Emancipation Proclamation (Jan. 1, 1863), *available at* www.archives.gov/exhibits/featured_documents/emancipation_ proclamation/transcript.htm.

[16] Elaine Scarry, "War and the Social Contract: Nuclear Policy, Distribution, and the Right to Bear Arms," 139 *University of Pennsylvania Law Review*, 1257, 1308 (1991). Scarry notes: "The logic of that coupling [civil rights and military obligations] is clear: from the earliest moments of the republic to the most recent, the concept of the civil franchise has been inseparable from the record of military participation."

[17] Lizbeth Cohen, *A Consumers' Republic: The Politics of Mass Consumption in Postwar America*. New York: Knopf, 2003.

[18] Andrew J. Bacevich, *The New American Militarism: How Americans Are Seduced by War*. New York: Oxford University Press, 2005, 28. Bacevich writes at 27: "For the generations that fought the Civil War and the world wars, and even those who served in the 1950s and 1960s, citizenship and military service remained intimately linked. Indeed, those to whom this obligation to serve did not apply – including at various times the poor, people of color, and women – were thereby

Sacrifice and Sovereignty

Thus, the picture today is complicated. The roles of those giving and receiving sacrifices for the nation are not clearly defined. We can see sacrifice invoked both as an inclusive practice and as an unfairly distributed burden. Having said that, it remains the case that the soldier's sacrifice remains, in U.S. public culture, remarkably sacrosanct, even though (or because) military service is now voluntary and enlistment is openly promoted as providing educational and other benefits. Officials are expected to honor the deaths of soldiers, and their failure to do so is easily turned into a scandal.

It is in relation to this structure, by which soldiers are recognized for their sacrifice, that I wish to locate the private military contractor. There are many reasons to think that contractors' deaths are not sacrifices, most obviously because they are motivated by private gain, not national service. Thus it may be said that they are mercenaries whose deaths do not resonate with a broader national audience.[19] Contractors are not included in the overall troop figures, even though at present in Iraq they are almost at parity.[20] Their deaths are not included in the daily body count of soldiers (by one estimate they have been killed at a rate one fourth that of U.S. soldiers), nor are they given medals, pensions, or public honor.[21]

---

marked as ineligible for full citizenship... In our own time, all of that has changed... There is a simple explanation for this fact. As with so many other aspects of life in contemporary America, military service has become strictly a matter of individual choice."

[19] For an argument that contractors should often be seen as mercenaries, see Zoe Salzman, "Private Military Contractors and the Taint of Mercenary Reputation," *New York University Journal of International Law & Policy* (2008) 40: 874–891. Protocol I provides that mercenaries "shall not have the right to be a combatant or prisoner of war." Protocol I, art. 47(1). It defines a mercenary as "one who (a) is specially recruited locally or abroad in order to fight in an armed conflict; (b) does, in fact, take a direct part in the hostilities; (c) is motivated to take part in the hostilities essentially by the desire for private gain and, in fact, is promised, by or on behalf of a Party to the conflict, material compensation substantially in excess of that promised or paid to combatants of similar ranks and functions in the armed forces of that Party; (d) is neither a national of a Party to the conflict nor a resident of territory controlled by a Party to the conflict; (e) is not a member of the armed forces of a Party to the conflict; and (f) has not been sent by a State which is not a Party to the conflict on official duty as a member of its armed forces."

[20] John M. Broder and James Risen, "Contractor Deaths in Iraq Soar to Record," *The New York Times*, May 19, 2007 (noting that almost "300 companies from the United States and around the world supply workers who are a shadow force in Iraq almost as large as the uniformed military.... about 126,000 men and women working for contractors serve alongside about 150,000 American troops, the Pentagon has reported").

[21] Ibid. (estimating that 917 contractors had been killed in Iraq). Only a small portion of the total number of contractors are armed – but of that smaller group, there might be mortality rates higher than those of soldiers. Moreover, because the deaths of non-U.S. citizen contractors

(In fact, individual contractors have accepted medals from the United States, including Bronze Stars and Purple Hearts, in recognition of their service. When it was discovered that the recipients were contractors, however, the medals were retracted.[22]) To emphasize their exclusion from sacrificial logics, we need only point out that there is a Tomb of the Unknown Soldier but none for the Unknown Contractor.[23]

We might infer that for the U.S. government and the American public more generally, the contractor's death is neither offered nor received as a "sacrifice." This sense is strengthened when we reflect on the intellectual pedigree that surrounds the turn to private military contractors, that is, ideas associated with privatization, outsourcing, or neoliberalism. These lines of thought and argument are, to say the least, skeptical of public spiritedness as a firm ground on which to build government policy, and for which the very notion of sacrifice might be analytically impossible or morally abhorrent, because sacrifice entails a giving of the inalienable self.[24]

Contractor firms got their first significant entrée into U.S. foreign policy under President Clinton, who did not want to pay the political cost of sending 9,000 reservists to the Balkans. It has been under President George W. Bush (and Vice President Dick Cheney, former head of contracting giant Halliburton) that the move to contractors has accelerated exponentially.[25]

---

are not, under U.S. Department of Labor rules, required to be reported, there may be underreporting of that category. See Thomas E. Ricks, *Fiasco: The American Military Adventure in Iraq*. New York: Penguin, 2007, 370–371.

[22] Renae Merle, "Contract Workers Are War's Forgotten: Iraq Deaths Create Subculture of Loss," *Washington Post*, July 31, 2004. A1; *see also* Ariana Eunjung Cha and Renae Merle, "Line Increasingly Blurred between Soldiers and Civilian Contractors," *The Washington Post*, May 13, 2004 (the Pentagon mistakenly awarded honors to contractors).

[23] To adapt Benedict Anderson's observation. Anderson, in insisting on the national nature of Tombs to the Unknown Soldiers, writes: "The cultural significance of such monuments becomes even clearer if one tries to imagine, say, a Tomb of the Unknown Marxist or a cenotaph for fallen Liberals. Is a sense of absurdity unavoidable?" Benedict Anderson, *Imagined Communities: Reflections on the Origin and Spread of Nationalism*. New York: Verso 1991, 10.

[24] See, for example, Milton Friedman's complaint about President Kennedy's famous line from his inaugural address – "Ask not what your country can do for you, ask what you can do for your country." Friedman objected: "The organismic, 'what you can do for your country' implies that government is the master or deity, the citizen the servant or votary." Milton Friedman (with the assistance of Rose Friedman), *Capitalism and Freedom*. Chicago: University of Chicago Press, 1962, 1.

[25] Peter Singer, *Corporate Warriors: The Rise of the Privatized Military Industry*. Ithaca: Cornell University Press, 2003, 6, 208–209.

Sacrifice and Sovereignty

I want to suggest that the turn to the military contractor represents an attempt by officials to designate, by law and policy, a class of persons whose deaths will be banal and insignificant to a national audience. Their existence and relation to the body politic is one of contract, not sacrifice.

As mentioned, among contractors another position can be detected. For the contractors themselves, as well as for their employers and their families, their deaths might indeed be described as "sacrifices" for the company. A journalist recounts that Blackwater has created something of a mini-Arlington at its corporate headquarters: a "memorial rock garden on their compound in Moyock, NC, where each contractor that has been killed while serving the company is given a stone with their name engraved on it."[26] The use of contractors can thus be called an *outsourcing* of sacrifice – sacrifice takes place, but the significance is removed from the purview of the government and the public and is contained within the private sphere of the family and the company. This view rejects the assumption that sacrifice can exist only for the nation, that the state monopolizes not only legitimate violence, as Max Weber urged, but sacrifice as well.[27]

A third and more startling view, which can be detected in the reception and classification of deaths of U.S. citizen contractors (there are but a few examples of it extending to noncitizens[28]) by the United States, is that the contractors' deaths not only are sacrifices for the employer but also sacrifices to and for the United States. This view, which President Bush has expressed, owes much to the attack on the contractors in Fallujah.[29] The sacrifice is still "outsourced" in the sense that it is not performed by

---

[26] Bill Sizemore, "Suit Against Blackwater Over Contractor Goes to Arbitration," *The Virginia-Pilot*, May 20, 2007.

[27] Max Weber, *Politics as a Vocation*, in *From Max Weber: Essays in Sociology*, eds., H. H. Gerth and C. Wright Mills, trans. 1958), 78 ("[A] state is a human community that (successfully) claims the monopoly of the legitimate use of physical force.").

[28] One example of the recognition of the sacrifices of noncitizen contractors may be seen in 2008 when five Fijian contractors who died in Iraq were awarded the Defense of Freedom medal, the medal specially created to honor the civilian victims of 9/11 at the Pentagon. The U.S. Embassy representative explained to the *Fiji Times* that "the ceremony was to honour the five men who bravely laid down their lives as part of an international effort to fight terrorism and create freedom." See Monica Singh, *Local War Casualties Get Medals*, Fiji Times Online, August 15, 2008, at www.fijitimes.com/story.aspx?id=97870.

[29] President Bush, commenting on investigations into Blackwater for shooting civilians in September 2007, said, "I will be anxious to see the analysis of their performance," and "There's a lot of studying going on, both inside Iraq and out, as to whether or not people violated rules of engagement. I will tell you, though, that a firm like Blackwater provides a valuable service. They protect people's lives, and I appreciate the sacrifice and the service that the Blackwater

people wearing the marks of the sovereign – the uniform or the flag – but it is not outsourced in the sense that the deaths are seen, recognized, and honored by the United States, albeit in an *ad hoc* and after the fact manner. The state, nation, or public returns as the recipient of the sacrifice, rejecting the opposition between monetary self-interest and national service.

One event that challenged the initial policy move of desacralization was the grotesque and spectacular killing of four Blackwater contractors in March 2004 in Fallujah. Although these contractors had contracted their security services to the private sector, they became reconceived as sacralized citizens, their bodies a visible site for the idea of the nation. The contractors had each entered into an independent contractor service agreement with Blackwater, and they were to provide security and logistical support to ESS Support Services Worldwide, which in turn had contracted with Kellog, Brown & Root, which further had contracted with the U.S. Army.[30]

On March 30, the four contractors were sent on a mission to escort three ESS kitchen supply trucks to a military base. Without maps, with no familiarity of the area, and with no logistical support, the convoy got lost, and on the second day all four were killed. Blackwater's account of the attack emphasized that the contractors were targeted as Americans: "The ESS truck drivers – all third country nationals – were intentionally spared and left to escape... The ambush, apparently, was only intended to kill the Americans."[31]

Amid great public excitement and drawing a crowd numbering in the hundreds, the contractors were dragged through the streets behind a vehicle, torn limb from limb, and immolated. Finally, portions of two of the contractors' bodies were hung on a bridge over the Euphrates River. Denunciations of the United States and the burning of the American flag accompanied the attack. Videotaped and disseminated to media outlets,

---

employees have made." See Associated Press, *Blackwater Will Probably Leave Iraq, Officials Say*. Oct. 17, 2007. *Available at* www.msnbc.msn.com/id/21352794.

[30] In the Complaint filed by the Estates of the contract workers, at 7–10, the contractual structure is described.

[31] Blackwater emphasized that the cause of the incident was betrayal by Iraqi forces, not its own incompetence. "Blackwater's Response to 'Majority Staff Report' on 'Private Military Contractors in Iraq: An Examination of Blackwater's Actions in Fallujah." Not dated or signed; released in Oct. 2007 at 3.

Sacrifice and Sovereignty

the event dominated the print and television news in the United States,[32] conjuring an atmospherics entirely different from the "shock and awe" phase of the war.

Immediately after the attacks, officials and mainstream media commentators in the United States compared the deaths to those of the U.S. Army Rangers killed and desecrated in Somalia during the Clinton presidency. The fear of a repeat performance, the "Mogadishu effect," was no doubt important to officials who had subsequently made timely extraction of injured soldiers pivotal to their protocols – recognizing that the body of the soldier was an invaluable canvas on which to work.[33] What is remarkable, given our assumption that the contractor is ineligible for sacrifice, is the ease with which the contractors were assimilated to a consecrated status.[34]

Four days later, at the direction of the White House and the Secretary of Defense, military officials on the ground were ordered to invade the city, over the objections of on-site commanders.[35] Even though military officials were extremely critical of the fact that while the contractors represented the United States to Iraqis, they (the military) had very little control over the contractors, and despite envy and animosity between ordinary soldiers and contractors, the Marines named the bridge where the bodies were hung "Blackwater Bridge." The U.S. siege of the city lead to approximately 800 Iraqi civilian deaths.[36] The insurgents managed to hold the city, which

---

[32] Images of the attack ran on the front page of *The New York Times*, *USA Today*, and *The Washington Post*. The publication of the gruesome images was itself a topic of debate.

[33] Gwynne Dyer, "The Fallujah Effect," *Pittsburgh Post-Gazette*, Apr. 4, 2004 ("In the mid-90s there used to be something called the 'Mogadishu line' which the U.S. military were never supposed to cross. Rounding up from the 18 U.S. soldiers who were killed in one day in Mogadishu in 1993, it was a doctrine which stated that the U.S. armed forces should undertake no overseas mission that was likely to cause the deaths of more than 20 American soldiers except when vital national interests were involved.").

[34] William Kristol, "After Fallujah," *The Weekly Standard*, Apr. 12, 2004 ("The similarity struck everyone right away: Mogadishu, October 3, 1993; Fallujah, March 31, 2004. But we cannot permit these two outrages to be similar in their effect." According to Kristol, Mogadishu had led to the U.S. withdrawal from Somalia and to genocide in Rwanda. To "properly honor[] the sacrifice of those who died on March 31 in Fallujah" the U.S. should "deepen" its "commitment to victory" and act aggressively against hostile residents).

[35] Ricks, *Fiasco*, 332–333.

[36] Jeremy Scahill, *Blackwater: The Rise of the World's Most Powerful Mercenary Army*. New York: Nation Books, 2007, 143.

itself marked a major turning point, showing that the United States could be fought to a standstill.[37]

From what we know of the perspective of the attackers, the event is full of sacrificial thematics and evinces a complex global exchange. According to one account, some participants declared that "With our blood and our souls, we will sacrifice for Islam," and one resident compared the contractors bodies, dangling from the bridge, to "slaughtered sheep" – one archetypal sacrificial victim.[38] Nir Rosen described the attacks as part of a standardized routine: "There is a word for this sort of thing. In Iraqi dialect, the Arabic word *sahl*, which literally means dragging a body down the street, has grown to mean any sort of public massacre."[39] In another report, the Brigades of Martyr Ahmed Yassin claimed authorship of the attack, describing it as "a gift from the people of Fallujah to the people of Palestine and the family of Sheikh Ahmed Yassin who was assassinated by the criminal Zionists."[40]

The sacrificial status of the *victims* (as contrasted with the perpetrators) of terrorist and insurgent violence has received little attention, although Arjun Appadurai has described the genre of the videotaped beheading of kidnapping victims, starting with that of journalist Daniel Pearl, as a "public sacrifice."[41] Whether the Iraqis were making a conscious reference to their own traditions of sacrifice in their mode of killing the contractors, for the American officials the attackers released the latent sacrificial potential of the contractors as American citizens. To make an analogy to the law of business organizations, the attack pierced the veil of contractual intermediaries, making visible for Americans the displaced tie between themselves and the contractors.

---

[37] Ricks, *Fiasco*: 344.
[38] Scahill, *Blackwater*, 103.
[39] Nir Rosen, "Home Rule," July 5, 2004, *The New Yorker*.
[40] John Lee Anderson, "Letter from Baghdad," *The New Yorker*, May 3, 2004, p. 63.
[41] Arjun Appadurai, *Fear of Small Numbers*. Durham: Duke University Press, 2006, 12. See Faisal Devji, *Landscapes of the Jihad: Militancy, Morality, Modernity*. Ithaca: Cornell University Press, 2005, 96. Devji writes: "Indeed, there is a sense in which even the jihad's enemies – or victims – come to participate in the rites of martyrdom by dying alongside its suicide bombers in spectacular set-pieces like the attacks of 9/11. This may explain why supporters of the jihad are forever drawing parallels between its own dead and those of its enemies, because both coalesce in a community of martyrdom made possible by the virtual intimacy of the media, which allows each party to exchange words and deeds with the other."

If we ask what went wrong with the effort of the United States to displace sacrificial meaning, we must turn to the attackers' specific framing of their assault as one on the United States. As important as the communications infrastructure of a hand-held video recorder and distribution was – and it was clearly essential – we should not let a focus on the technology overshadow the content of what was communicated and which message was received. To understand these, we must have recourse to American popular sovereignty, which, as Kahn puts it, "tells us that we – each of us – are the popular sovereign, that our bodies constitute its body."[42] It was precisely this location of sovereignty in the body of the individual citizen that is credited for the restriction of mercenary activity by the United States through neutrality laws shortly after the revolution. This distribution of sovereignty made it increasingly difficult for states to deny responsibility for or identification with the violence employed by their citizens abroad – be that mercenary, filibuster, privateer, or pirate violence. Doing so was "inconsistent with view that sovereignty came not from God through the monarch but from man or the citizen himself. With the individual citizen as the ostensible source of sovereignty, the state could no longer disclaim responsibility for his violent activities in the international system."[43] In destroying the contractors' bodies, the Fallujah attackers simultaneously gave them back to the United States as citizens. To avoid sacrifice more successfully, policy makers should not employ U.S. citizens, and yet doing so would bolster claims that the contractors are mercenaries.

The notion of sacrifice does not entirely grasp the provocative quality of the action in Fallujah – although the literal meaning of the word *sacrifice*, to "make sacred," seems on point so far as the reception by the United States is concerned. After all, the attack was aimed at someone else's sacred character; it was a "desecration." Desecration, however, entails destroying something *already* sacred – as in the cases of "Koran desecration" or in the proposed constitutional amendment banning the "desecration" of the

---

[42] Kahn, *Putting Liberalism in Its Place*, 246.
[43] Janice Thomson, *Mercenaries, Pirates and Sovereigns; State-Building and Extraterritorial Violence in Early Modern Europe*. Princeton: Princeton University Press, 1994, 148. Thomson describes the controversy over mercenaries who sold their labor on the international market as posing the question of whether the mercenary was "a market actor, pursuing private ends through the sale of his labor? Or was he a political actor for whose actions his home state could be held accountable?" (55).

U.S. flag. Given that one of the attractions of military contract workers is that they are not located as sacred characters – unlike the soldier in the armed forces, whose death is officially a national loss – the reception of the event entailed a resacralization (seeing the contractors as citizens, as belonging to the sovereign).[44] Not only did the Fallujah killing bring added scrutiny to the contractor sector, it also helped to legitimate it. Like soldiers, contractors could have national meanings inscribed on their bodies. The Fallujah case showed that the dichotomy between the contractor and sacrifice could be transcended: relations could be both contractual and sacrificial.

Sacrifice is often described as action contained within ritual and legal formats and is thus formalized and institutionalized. In this incident it emerges as an assertion, a claim that cuts across the legal order advanced by the United States. The designation of "sacrifice" is essentially retrospective. Compared with sacrifice that is contained by the state, exemplified by war memorials, this is unexpected and entrepreneurial.

Despite the moment of consecration and the assimilation of the contractors to the high status enjoyed by the victims of the attack in Somalia, the event did not, of course, *legally* transform killed contractors into killed soldiers. The families of the Fallujah contractors, remaining legally in the domain of contract and tort law, brought a fraud and wrongful death suit against Blackwater in North Carolina state court. Blackwater has vigorously sought to avoid facing a group of local jurors, which might award a large punitive damages award. The soldier, compensated with recognition for "sacrifice" – honor, medals, and other benefits of the regulatory state, is generally excluded from state and federal courts. (This exclusion is but a part of the overall transformation of the soldier's status to something closer to a possession of the United States. Whereas the contractor can quit, the soldier who leaves can, under certain circumstances, be

---

[44] For an examination of the importance of negation in creating the sacred, see Michael Taussig, *Defacement: Public Secrecy and the Labor of the Negative*. Stanford: Stanford University Press, 1999, 13. Taussig writes: "Around me there is no sacrifice, nor much passion for sacred things. The disenchantment of the world still seems to me a largely accomplished fact. What exists now is perhaps best thought of as a new amalgam of enchantment and disenchantment, the sacred existing in muted but powerful forms, especially – and this is my central preoccupation – in its negative form as desecration." I would suggest that there remain in U.S. political culture official sites of the sacred – the Constitution and other manifestations of the popular sovereign – even in the absence of "desecration."

killed for desertion. The soldier's enlistment contract is akin to what Max Weber described as a "status contract," which is what some courts call it as well.)[45]

Despite its founder Erik Prince's claim, to want to be the military services version of Federal Express, Blackwater's response to the litigation reveals that in some respects the company does *not* want to be a private actor.[46] Blackwater has argued that because war is essentially a federal function, the claim should not be reviewed by state courts and attempted to shift the litigation from the everyday world of contract and tort – in which one might expect a private actor – into another register, that of sovereignty and the sovereign's immunity from suit.[47] Two traditions intersect: one (derived from popular sovereignty) that allows Americans to see themselves in the bodies of fellow citizens, to see "America" when they see the contractors' bodies, and another (the tradition of state sovereignty) by which the state is itself a sovereign and immune from suit.

For two years Blackwater pushed these various claims unsuccessfully, finally seeking review from the U.S. Supreme Court with the assistance of Kenneth Starr.[48] Blackwater finally derailed the case by invoking the binding arbitration clause in the contract – in April 2007, a federal court sent the matter to arbitration, which takes place in private and does not offer punitive damages.[49] (The inclusion of binding arbitration clauses in employment and independent contractor contracts is itself related to the broader currents of privatization, with its valorization of nonpublic fora.[50])

---

[45] See, for example, *In re Grimely*, 137 U.S. 147, 151–152 (1890) (describing enlistment contracts as "special because they bring about a change in status, from civilian to soldier, just like marriage contracts change a man's status to husband and the woman's status to wife"); see also *Qualls v. Rumsfeld*, 357 F.Supp.2d 274 (D.D.C. 2005) (denying motion for preliminary injunction by serviceman claiming that government's "stop-loss" policy which involuntarily extended his service in Iraq was a breach of contract included provision for such extension).

[46] *Nordan v. Blackwater Security Consulting*, LLC, 382 F.Supp.2d 801 (E.D.N.C. 2005).

[47] *Nordan*, 382 F.Supp.2d *at* 807.

[48] *Cert. denied, Blackwater Sec. Consulting, LLC v. Nordan*, 127 S. Ct. 1381 (2007). John M. Broder and James Risen, "Blackwater Mounts a Defense with Top Talent," *The New York Times*, Nov. 1, 2007.

[49] Order, Apr. 20, 2007, Judge Fox, U.S. District Court, N.C. 2:06-CV-49-F.

[50] Clyde Summers, "Mandatory Arbitration: Privatizing Public Rights, Compelling the Unwilling to Arbitrate," 6 *University of Pennsylvania Journal of Labor and Employment* (2004) "The effect of the these contracts has been to privatize justice, substituting privately constructed arbitration for publicly established courts."

The Fallujah event also reached Congress when the Republican Party lost its majority in the 2006 midterm elections and Congressman Waxman began to hold hearings on the contractor industry, and Blackwater in particular. In these hearings Prince, the head of Blackwater, emphatically rejected the mercenary label. He referred to the contractors as "veterans" (which many of them are) and to Blackwater as a place where they reenlist: "Military contractors, comprised largely of military veterans 're-enlisting' through the private sector like the four Americans killed in Fallujah, fill vital gaps in the all-volunteer force."[51] This marvelous locution – "'re-enlisting' through the private sector" – captures well the novel space of outsourced sacrifice as both private and sacrificial. Blackwater officials also offered testimony from a State Department official: "We will always remember their courage, commitment, and ultimate sacrifice for their country."[52]

In our understanding of sacrifice as "outsourced" yet still sacrifice for a national audience, we run into a fundamental question. Is sacrifice a giving of the self, or can it can be the giving of a substitute?[53] In many of the classic stories of sacrifice, there is a substitution of the sacrificial victim at the last minute (the ram in place of Isaac, a hind in place of Iphigenia), although this (some commentators say) is transcended with the self-sacrifice of Jesus or that of Socrates. The contractor case seems to teeter on just this divide, between a giving of the self and the giving of the substitute. In this emergent conception of outsourced sacrifice, does the American public perceive the loss of the contractor as a giving of itself, as seems to be the case with the soldier? If not, then we might think of the contractor as more closely tied to the substitution version of sacrifice – more the ram than Isaac. The significance of this, politically speaking, is that the loss of the contractor will not serve as a check on officials' willingness to have them die.

---

[51] "Blackwater's Response to 'Majority Staff Report' on 'Private Military Contractors in Iraq: An Examination of Blackwater's Actions in Fallujah.'" Not dated or signed; released in Oct. 2007 *at* 10.

[52] Statement of Andrew Howell, Esq., General Counsel, Blackwater USA for the Committee on Oversight and Government Reform, Feb. 7, 2007 *at* 2 quoting Sean McCormick. Indeed, the State Department had become increasingly close with and reliant on Blackwater since it hired the company to provide for the security of much of its personnel around the world.

[53] 2 *Genesis* 12–15; Maurice Bloch, *Prey into Hunter: The Politics of Religious Experience*. New York: Cambridge University Press, 1992, 30.

Sacrifice and Sovereignty

In a more recent scandal involving Blackwater, contractors shot and killed 17 Iraqi civilians in Baghdad in 2007. As with the contractors' deaths, the deaths of the civilians at first appeared to push against the legal structure that the United States (and the now sovereign Iraqi state) has designated for them as insignificant. In this case, the repressed category is not sacrifice but homicide. Months after the Fallujah attacks and just before leaving Iraq and transferring sovereignty from the Coalition Provisional Authority to Iraq, Paul Bremer issued Order 17, giving the contractors (Blackwater had been guarding Bremer) immunity from prosecution under Iraqi law,[54] implicitly designating those killed by the contractors as "not murdered." Numerous legal reforms are currently proposed that seek to increase accountability of the contractors and establish more adequate structures of oversight and control. In late 2006, a defense spending bill, with very little notice, placed contractors under military law, the Uniform Code of Military Justice – but doubts have been raised about exercising military jurisdiction over civilians.[55] Most recently, Iraq (through the 2008 Status of Forces Agreement with the U.S. and fueled by anger at the killing of civilians in Baghdad by Blackwater) asserted jurisdiction over contractors.[56] And back in the U.S., in late 2008, several of the Blackwater workers involved in the Baghdad shooting have been indicted for manslaughter.[57] Overall, the contractors are increasingly subject to various forms of civil and military jurisdiction in the U.S. and Iraq but there remains much uncertainty.

What policy discussions have *not* focused on is the other side of liability – the "sacrificial" liability of the U.S. government. There have been

---

[54] Coalition Provisional Authority Order Number 17 (Revised), Status of the Coalition Provisional Authority, MNF-Iraq, Certain Missions and Personnel in Iraq, at www.cpa-iraq.org/regulations/20040627_CPAORD_17_Status_of_Coalition__Rev__with_Annex_A.pdf (Section 4.3 "Contractors shall be immune from Iraqi legal process with respect to acts performed by them pursuant to the terms and conditions of a Contract or any sub-contract thereto").

[55] National Defense Authorization Act for Fiscal Year 2007, Pub. L. No. 109–364, §552, 120 Stat. 2083, 2217 (amending 10 U.S.C. § 802(a)(10)).

[56] Agreement Between The United States Of America and The Republic Of Iraq On The Withdrawal Of The United States Forces From Iraq And The Organization Of The Activities During Their Temporary Presence In Iraq, Art. 12(2), November 17, 2008, at www.whitehouse.gov/infocus/iraq/SE_SOFA.pdf.

[57] United States v. Slough et. al., Indictment, filed Dec. 4, 2008, CR-08–360 (D.C.D.C); see Ginger Thompson and James Risen, *5 Guards Face U.S. Charges in Iraq Deaths*, The New York Times, December 6, 2008.

no proposals to bury contractors at Arlington National Cemetery or to insert them into the politically costly structures of honor and recognition that played an important role in the rise of the industry in the first instance. If contractors are to act on behalf of the sovereign – which, if they are to kill and be killed in the interests of the United States, they are – perhaps they should bear the marks of the sovereign as well. Of course, this could generate other problems, because to designate an actors' suffering as a sacrifice for the nation is to grant a particular form of prestige and power.

The Family and the Sovereign

The concept of sacrifice gives a particular kind of meaning to death, suffering, and violence, and it also seems to generate what we might think of as sacrificial "energy."[58] This sacrificial energy can be used to mobilize patriotic sentiment, but it is not always easy to manipulate. I argued in the last section that, in an attempt to avoid the potential misdirection of that sacrificial energy against the state, the U.S. government uses private military contractors to distance the sacrificial action from its potential association with the state. In that case, the attempt was not entirely successful, and this section describes a few parallel ways in which the idea of sacrifice is negotiated – ways in which U.S. officials try to privatize (and thereby neutralize) sacrificial energy that they cannot control and nonstate actors attempt to remobilize that energy. Whereas in the contractor case, the United States uses the legal form of contract to privatize sacrifice, the examples in this section show a different kind of privatization: here, we can see an attempt to privatize sacrifice either by calling on gendered understandings of sacrifice or by arguing that it is primarily in the private sphere of the family that death has meaning. Much as in the contractor case, however, the sacrifice theme cannot be so easily contained.

One reason that this sacrificial energy is so volatile is that several different conceptions of sacrifice circulate simultaneously in U.S. public culture. As a result, who sacrifices for whom is not always entirely clear, and the ambiguity means that the idea of sacrifice can be deployed by people in many different spheres. I will outline a few of these different conceptions

---

[58] See Henri Hubert and Marcel Mauss, *Sacrifice: Its Nature and Function*, trans. W. D. Halls, Foreword by E. E. Evans-Pritchard. Chicago: University of Chicago Press, [1898] 1981, 12.

Sacrifice and Sovereignty

of sacrifice and, using the examples of Jessica Lynch and Cindy Sheehan, discuss how these conceptualizations are manipulated both consciously and unconsciously by actors who are trying to claim, or to avoid, the various meanings that death and suffering can generate.

Two of the most frequently invoked constructions of sacrifice seem entirely at odds with one another: on the one hand, we have an individualistic and egalitarian conception of sacrifice (in which sacrifice for one's country can actually ground a claim to equal rights). On the other is a gendered division of sacrificial labor in which the primary sacrificial role is taken by men. This gendered conception in turn sets up a particular relationship of sacrifice and the family. I will discuss some of the permutations of that relationship later.

Nancy Jay has elaborated on the gendered conception of sacrifice. She describes sacrifice as a way in which men become the creators of life and the social order. It frees men of the "consequences of being born a woman ... and at the same time integrate[s] the pure and eternal patrilineage."[59] Lincoln's Gettysburg Address, with its invocation of the "bringing forth" and "conception" of the "nation" by "our fathers," the death of soldiers so that the "nation might live," and the "new birth of freedom" that their sacrifice allows, illustrates the point.[60] Through military sacrifice, men give birth to themselves and to society; they become part of and create the nation; they encompass the duality of male and female. The female obverse of this conception, captured in the notion of republican motherhood, is that women sacrifice as mothers, giving their children to the state.[61] The "family," associated with the female-gendered private realm, thus has a shifting position with respect to sacrifice. If in some conceptions, the family gives up its sons for the state; in others, the state goes to war to protect the family – a parallel narrative to one in which men go to war to protect women.

An individualistic conception of sacrifice, which draws on the revolutionary effects of the women's and civil rights movements of the 1960s

---

[59] Nancy Jay, *Throughout Your Generations Forever: Sacrifice, Religion and Paternity*. Chicago: University of Chicago Press, 1992, 40.
[60] Abraham Lincoln, Gettysburg Address (Nov. 19, 1863), in 7 *Collected Works of Abraham Lincoln*, ed., Roy P. Basler. New Brunswick, NJ: Rutgers University Press, 1953.
[61] Jean Bethke Elshtain, "Sovereignty, Identity, Sacrifice," in M. Ringrose and A. J. Lerner, eds., *Reimagining the Nation*. Philadelphia: Open Press, 1993.

and 1970s, seems to have made some headway against the gendered conception. In this construction, sacrificial eligibility follows legal and social notions of equality and individualism. Women and racial minorities have asserted equality claims to serve in the military, and service in the military has grounded equality claims. As a citizen, each person can participate in sacrificial dynamics, and those who participate in sacrifice have a claim to equal citizenship.[62]

If, however, we focus on the shared vulnerability entailed by the existence of nuclear weapons as a kind of conscription to a military conflict, we see the matter differently. The post-WWII era emerges as one in which all Americans are grasped by the potential for sacrificial death, albeit a passive sort. In the Cold War nuclear age, for example, each citizen was told that he or she could be incinerated without a moment's notice. In this more passive idea of sacrifice, of *being* sacrificed, the threat of nuclear war represents the entire citizenry's availability for sacrifice. This is Paul Kahn's conception of the matter:

> Nuclear weapons are a constant reminder that the state's interests come first and last, that all individuals – citizens and noncitizens alike – may be sacrificed to the primacy of the sovereign state. These weapons rest implicitly on a policy of conscription that extends to every citizen – and even beyond – for which no exemptions are granted.[63]

In the current war on terror, we can see a similarly passive conception of sacrifice: the conflict apparently does not require a full military and economic mobilization. Citizens learn to equate attacks on a small percentage of their number as an attack on the United States.

The combination, then, of a developing notion of individual rights and an imagined shared apocalypse, challenges a conception of society as composed of distinct groups and offers a view in which each body can instantiate the sovereign regardless of race, gender, or even nationality. Differentiated conceptions of sacrifice have not disappeared, however; within the military, soldiers can see themselves as sacrificing not for the

---

[62] See Judith Shklar, *American Citizenship: the Quest for Inclusion*. Cambridge, MA: Harvard University Press, 1991.

[63] Paul Kahn, "Nuclear Weapons and the Rule of Law," 31 *New York University Journal of International Law and Policy*, 349, 355, 1999.

Sacrifice and Sovereignty

country but rather for their unit, their "band of brothers." We might also think of an older conception of military sacrifice, as formulated by Samuel Huntington, in which a "monastic" military sacrifices for a corrupt civilian population;[64] or a more contemporary version, in which the hardworking residents of the "heartland" sacrifice for blue-state elites.[65] While Senator Obama, on the campaign trail in 2008, invoked death for the U.S. as a powerful demonstration of unity: soldiers "have fought together and bled together and some died together under the same proud flag. They have not served a Red America or a Blue America – they have served the United States of America."[66] In this section, the focus is on the shifting sacrificial politics of gender and the family, but the range of conceptualizations is worth referencing as tribute to its potential for meaningful manipulation and mobilization.

The story of Jessica Lynch can be seen as a case in which the sacrifice concept was extensively manipulated. Originally a "heroic" story that seemed to speak to a gender-neutral notion of military service and sacrifice, it ultimately suggests that the gendered conception of sacrifice remains significant. A 19-year-old serving in Iraq in late March 2003, the early days of the U.S. invasion, Private Jessica Lynch was part of a supply convoy that lost its way and came under attack. She fought off her attackers, firing until she ran out of bullets and was injured, captured, and, according to some accounts (but not Lynch's), raped.[67] A week later, a daring and videotaped rescue mission brought her home. Lynch's story saturated the news, appearing on the cover of national magazines as a "female Rambo" and an "American hero."

Lynch's presence on the battlefield should have served to undercut the gendered conception of sacrifice – how can men be sacrificing to protect

---

[64] See, for example, Samuel P. Huntington, *The Soldier and the State: The Theory and Politics of Civil-Military Relations.* Cambridge, MA: Harvard University Press, 1964, 465–466. Huntington describes West Point as a Sparta in a the "midst of Babylon." He continues: "Yet today America can learn more from West Point than West Point from America.... If the civilians permit the soldiers to adhere to the military standard, the nations themselves may eventually find redemption and security in making that standard their own."

[65] Robert D. Kaplan, *Imperial Grunts: The American Military on the Ground.* New York: Random House, 2005, 259–260.

[66] Mark Z. Barabak and Richard B. Schmitt, *Barack Obama has Advantage of Big Bucks, a Big Name: Colin Powell,* Oct. 20, 2008, L.A. Times.

[67] Véronique Pin-Fat and Maria Stern, "The Scripting of Private Jessica Lynch: Biopolitics, Gender and 'Feminization' of the U.S. Military," *Alternatives,* 30: 25–53, 2005.

women if women are dying beside them? As though in answer to this question, the Lynch story turned into one in which she was the victim, rescued by men; it focused on her return to civilian life, in which she hoped to become a nurturer, a kindergarten teacher.[68] Lynch was carefully reinscribed as female in the traditional genre of womanhood in peril, the captive narrative.[69] In addition, the facts behind the heroic version of Lynch's story began to unravel: Lynch insisted that she hadn't fired a shot, because her weapon was jammed; the Iraqi doctors, it turned out, had been professional and caring, and the rescue itself actually encountered little resistance. Lynch rejected the rendition of herself as a hero: "That wasn't me. I'm not about to take credit for something I didn't do.... I'm just a survivor." She complained to Diane Sawyer that the Pentagon "used me to symbolize all this stuff."[70]

Lynch's story simultaneously belies a generalized aversion to sacrifice and demonstrates several ways in which the sacrifice narrative was first gendered and ultimately undercut. Indeed, the U.S. relation to sacrifice is not simply one of avoidance: sacrifice has been used rhetorically to strengthen patriotic and nationalistic conceptions of the state. There are also numerous ways in which U.S. officials attempt to contain, ignore, avoid, or displace sacrificial energy, however. Thus, even while Lynch was being proclaimed a hero at the center of a media frenzy, the eleven U.S. soldiers who died in the same attack (one of whom was a mother) were not mentioned. The silence around their deaths is reflected in many other attempts to minimize the visibility of soldier sacrifice and – through elisions of different conceptualizations of sacrifice – to displace sacrifice into the same "private" realm where Jessica Lynch's story ultimately ended.

The ban on photos of returning caskets of U.S. soldiers arriving at the Dover Air Force Base in Delaware is one such attempt and begins to demonstrate how the relationship of sacrifice and family can be manipulated. According to President Bush's spokesperson, the policy (implemented in 1991 by then Secretary of Defense Dick Cheney) served to protect the "privacy" of the affected families, even though there are no

---

[68] Id.
[69] Id.
[70] Quoted in David Kirkpatrick, "Jessica Lynch Criticizes Accounts of Her Ordeal," *The New York Times*, Nov. 7, 2003.

Sacrifice and Sovereignty

identifying marks on the caskets.[71] A Pentagon official explained that the Dover base is "a tarmac, not a parade ground."[72] This is not the reception that we expect for the return of "heroic" soldiers, but in the context of an increasingly unpopular war, the potential political danger posed by these consecrated persons is palpable. The energy released by the dead, in this context, is channelled by officials into "privacy," yet privacy seems imposed, in a preemptive effort to forestall the sense that the families could publicly utilize the energy released from sacrifice. Not only is the press barred from the base, so too are the deceased soldiers' families, those whose "privacy" is being protected.[73]

This is an intriguing privatization and one that reflects not only the particularities of the war in Iraq but also (and more interestingly) turns to the private sphere and the family to explain loss on behalf of the state. From this view, the purpose of the political community is seen as the preservation of private and family life – the private becomes the core public value, as bemoaned by Hannah Arendt.[74] This need not result in a liberal interest group conception of the political sphere, however, because the family is also a site full of sacrificial rhetoric that can be deployed to transcend the private.

For officials, granting such prominent place to the private sphere and the family carries its own risks, because there is no guarantee that families will not make public use of their now exalted "private" position, as exhibited by the families of those killed in the 9/11 attacks. Those families were able to force an independent investigation into the attacks,[75] even as the president

---

[71] A settlement in a suit against the Pentagon brought under the Freedom of Information Act has succeeded in releasing some of the images, but the ban on the press remains. Ralph Begleiter, who worked for the release of the images saw it as "significant victory for the honor of those who have made the ultimate sacrifice in war for their country, as well as for their families, for all service personnel and for the American people." John Files, "Pentagon Agrees to Issue Photos of Coffins of Iraq War Dead," *The New York Times*, Aug. 5, 2005.

[72] Lt. Col. Barry Venable, Defense Department Spokesman, quoted in Rebecca Carr, "Pentagon Denies Mother's Plea for Photo," in *Times Argus* Mar. 24, 2005.

[73] John Files, "Pentagon Agrees to Issue Photos of Coffins of Iraq War Dead," *The New York Times*, Aug. 5, 2005. "The Pentagon issued a statement, saying, 'As with all information, including images, the Department of Defense has an obligation and a responsibility to strike a balance between our strong desire to be as transparent as possible and the legitimate concerns to protect the privacy of military families and as necessary, operational security.'"

[74] See Hannah Arendt, "Public and Private," in *The Human Condition*. Chicago: University of Chicago Press, 1958.

[75] See Jonathan Simon, "*Parrhesiastic* Accountability: Investigatory Commissions and Executive Power in an Age of Terror," 114 *Yale Law Journal*, 1419 (2005).

successfully channelled the energy and fear generated by the attacks in the directions that he wished. To examine the potential implications of an emphasis on the family and the private sphere, I conclude this section by examining the widely publicized story of Cindy Sheehan, the 48-year-old mother of U.S. Marine Casey Sheehan, who was killed in Iraq in April 2004, a few days after the contractors in Fallujah.

Cindy Sheehan staged a vigil outside President Bush's Texas ranch during his summer holiday.[76] She demanded that the president meet with her so that she could question him about the war, which at that point had claimed more than 1,800 U.S. soldiers' lives (a number that, as usual, did not include contractors or Iraqi civilians killed). Claiming the power of sacrifice that she had made as a mother, she urged Bush to withdraw all U.S. troops from Iraq. Sheehan had met with the president during one of the many closed-door sessions he held with the families of soldiers killed in the war, but she took offense at his jovial attitude, his refusal to say her son's name, and at the fact that he referred to her as "Mom."[77] Her protest rejected the president's description of grief as private or, more precisely, mobilized her private suffering in the public domain.

Sheehan became both a focal point for antiwar demonstrators and a target for some of the president's supporters who accused her of aiding the enemy in the "global war."[78] Sympathetic commentators dubbed Sheehan's outpost outside the president's ranch "Camp Casey," in honor of the dead son, but when she and her supporters placed small wooden crosses on the roadside outside Bush's ranch – one for each U.S. soldier killed – other parents of the deceased soldiers objected to the mobilization of *their* children's deaths in the service of an antiwar protest. Competing concepts of sacrifice were used either to support or reject her claim to protest. A conservative commentator wrote that Sheehan's "loss of a son does not give her particular standing with respect to analyzing the nature of this conflict or the consequences of abandoning the fight."[79]

---

[76] MacNeil Lehrer Newshour, Aug. 16, 2005, "Cindy Sheehan's Protest," transcript *at* www.pbs.org/newshour/bb/military/july-dec05/sheehan_8–16.html.

[77] Richard W. Stevenson, "Of the Many Deaths in Iraq, One Mother's Loss Becomes a Problem for the President," *The New York Times*, Aug. 8, 2005.

[78] Frank Gaffney, guest on MacNeil Lehrer Newshour and columnist for the *Washington Times*. Aug. 16, 2005, "Cindy Sheehan's Protest," *at* www.pbs.org/newshour/bb/military/july-dec05/sheehan_8–16.html.

[79] Frank Gaffney, "Poster Child for Surrender," *Washington Times*, Aug. 16, 2005. Frank Rich, "The Swift Boating of Cindy Sheehan," *The New York Times*, Aug. 21, 2005, summarized: "True to form, the attack on Cindy Sheehan surfaced early on Fox News, where she was immediately

Sacrifice and Sovereignty

Indeed, the various ideas of sacrifice can easily become blurred: Was Sheehan mobilizing her son's sacrifice, or was she speaking of her own sacrifice as a mother? Was hers a private or a public loss? Was it an individual or a collective loss? Some claimed that her effort to bring her loss into the public, to nationalize and publicize it, was a means of exploiting her private position. Others wrote that she was either a dupe of larger forces opposing the President, or disqualified as an innocent victim because her political activism against the war made her a partisan.

As Sheehan's protest gained momentum and support – including paid television advertisements in Texas and a national tour – the White House countered with its own war mother, Tammy Pruett, whose husband and four sons had served (but not died) in Iraq. President Bush praised the family in a public address: "America lives in freedom because of families like the Pruetts."[80] Sheehan's supporters pointed out, and Ms. Pruett conceded that, as Pruett had not lost anyone in the war, she should not be compared with those who had.[81] One parent declared that Sheehan "better not be presenting herself as the voice of all the fallen."[82] A tour under the banner of "You Don't Speak for US, Cindy" began in Sheehan's hometown and made its way to Bush's ranch. On the other side of the debate, candles were lit across the United States in more than 1,600 antiwar protests.[83] The father of a soldier killed in Iraq objected: "The lady's not honoring her son's sacrifice, because we don't have a draft, and he went and signed his name on the dotted line."[84] In other words, because Sheehan's son's action was voluntary and was a sacrifice that he himself had authored, her complaint was really with him.

Again, several ideas about sacrifice are simultaneously present, and different formulations lead to drastically different conclusions about official and individual responsibility. If Sheehan thought that her son's death was

---

labeled a 'crackpot' by Fred Barnes. The right-wing blogosphere quickly spread tales of her divorce, her angry Republican in-laws, her supposed political flip-flops, her incendiary sloganeering and her association with known ticket-stub-carrying attendees of 'Fahrenheit 9/11.' Rush Limbaugh declared that Ms. Sheehan's "story is nothing more than forged documents – there's nothing about it that's real."

[80] Elizabeth Bumiller, "In the Struggle over the Iraq War, Women Are on the Front Line," *The New York Times*, Aug. 29, 2005.
[81] Id.
[82] Abby Goodnough, "In War Debate, Parents of Fallen Are United Only In Grief," *The New York Times*, Aug. 27, 2005.
[83] Paul Harris, "Mother Tips Balance against Bush," Aug. 21, 2005, *The Observer*.
[84] Id.

a waste, then perhaps officials are responsible for his death having been a meaningless death – rather than a sacrifice, the death starts to look more like a homicide. Her claim that it *was* a meaningless death also raises questions about the purported purpose of the war. As another mother of a dead soldier said, "I read that she questioned whether her son died for a noble cause, and I totally disagree with her on that.... Her son died for the most noble cause: human rights."[85] In this formulation, official responsibility is intermingled with a more "universal" cause. Casey Sheehan did not sacrifice for the American popular sovereign so much as for human rights or, instead, the two are intermingled. Contemporary advertisements for the army portray the delivery of freedom to the oppressed and sustenance to the needy. Indeed, this version of U.S. military action as oriented less to the destruction of an enemy than the expansion of universal rights is increasingly visible.[86] It speaks to a transcendent imperial project in which the U.S. is willing to sacrifice to save others and to provide the basic public good of global security. In its strongest form, which perfectly inverts narratives of the U.S. as an exploitative empire, the globe is seen as covered in the blood of Americans who have died for others. As former presidential candidate John McCain urged: "But the fact is, America is the greatest force for good in the history of the world. My friends, we have gone to all four corners of the Earth and shed American blood in defense, usually, of somebody else's freedom and our own."[87] In the same vein, President Bush, when asked on 60 *Minutes* whether he owed an apology to the people of Iraq, responded that, on the contrary, "the Iraqi people owe the American people a huge debt of gratitide" and most Iraqis "understand that we've endured a great sacrifice to help them."[88]

What unites the examples of the contractors and Sheehan is that it is nonstate actors who are advocating for greater recognition of sacrifice and consecration, while officials seem unnerved by the unpredictability and political danger inherent in doing so. This posture of officials is,

---

[85] Id.
[86] Although, as Ann Stoler remarks, it would be a mistake to see American empire as unique in imagining itself as beneficent and committed to universal values. Ann Laura Stoler, "Degrees of Imperial Sovereignty," 18, 1: *Public Culture*, 125–146, 133 (2006).
[87] Transcript of Second McCain–Obama Debate, *at* www.cnn.com/2008/POLITICS/10/07/presidential.debate.transcript.
[88] Transcript of President Bush in an interview with Scott Pelley on 60 *Minutes*, January 14, 2007, *at* www.cbsnews.com/stories/2007/01/14/60minutes/main2359119_page2.shtml.

Sacrifice and Sovereignty

presumably, grounded in the specifics of the Iraq conflict and in the particular examples that I have selected. Even so, some more general patterns can be discerned. Calling a death a sacrifice can be a sort of accountability, because the designation means that a death was for some higher purpose, which is a claim that can then be tested. If the death seems to meet that test, then the "sacrifice" label can serve to protect officials from the anger directed at them. If it fails, then the term *sacrifice* sets out the basis of a complaint – that what should have been meaningful was not.

Sacrifice and the Detainee

"They have no regard for human life."[89]
— U.S. Navy Rear Admiral Harry Harris in response to detainee suicides at Guantánamo Bay, Cuba

[t]ake some of my blood... take pieces of my death shrouds... take some of my remains... take pictures of my dead body when I am placed in my grave, lonely... – Suicide letter of Jumah al-Dossari, Guantánamo Bay detainee

Sacrifice, as I have discussed it so far, has been tied to a "giving of the self" – either a person gives of him- or herself for the sake of the community or a community gives of itself for the sake of its members. This emphasis on the self and the community makes sense, given that I am discussing sacrifice in the context of citizenship in a regime grounded in popular sovereignty. In this section, however, I want to ask a different – if related – question: Can the suffering of those considered to be "enemies," the detainees held at Guantánamo Bay, Cuba, be seen as sacrificial?

Suicide in custodial settings has often had a sacrificial dimension. The deaths of hunger-striking members of the Irish Republican Army in the 1980s are well-known examples of suicides that were construed as sacrificial.[90] Prisoners described their self-imposed death as a gift to

---

[89] "Guantanamo Inmates Commit Suicide," June 11, 2006, *Aljazeera.net News Global*, at www.english.aljazeera.net/english/Templates/GeneralArticle.aspx.

[90] Unlike the United States, the United Kingdom has recognized the mentally competent prisoners' right to refuse medical care. Sec'y of State v. Robb, [1995] Fam. 127. See Alan Feldman, *Formations of Violence: The Narrative of the Body and Political Terror in Northern Ireland.* Chicago: University of Chicago Press, 1991, 247. In the United States, while there is a right to refuse unwanted medical treatment, there is no right to assisted suicide. *Washington v. Glucksberg*, 521 U.S. 702, 728 (1997). The fact of custody renders detainee conduct "assisted,"

larger cause. In such cases, death becomes a path to transcendence. At Guantánamo, however, where suicides, attempted suicides, and hunger strikes have been an ongoing part of daily life in recent years, the sacrificial component is much less clear. We have little information about how detainees frame their conduct, and the United States has sought whenever possible to prevent detainee suicide.

In a sense, the sacrificial dimension here is present in its negation, a denial of sacrifice that we see both in Giorgio Agamben's explicit equation of Guantánamo detainees with *homo sacer*, he who cannot be sacrificed, and in U.S. officials' emphasis on "preserving life" (or preventing potentially meaningful deaths).[91] I want to explore here the different meanings given to the detainees' suffering, using the sacrifice theme more loosely as a way to open up questions about the communicative potential of death.

By way of background, it should be noted that the U.S. posture at the detention center has evolved over time. Sometimes Guantánamo is described in easily comprehensible terms – as a site for intelligence gathering, removing combatants from the field of battle, or holding trials.[92] Although it is a highly secretive location about which the public is told very little, Guantánamo has also served as a theatre in which the United States performs its domination over its enemies, a feature of the camp that was most obvious in the initial images released by the Pentagon, of stooped and hooded detainees.[93] Some formulations present the prison as a site of beneficence, where detainees are treated more humanely than they deserve; others see it as a place of justice, where they are subjected to

---

turning the state's act of omission into one of commission. The detainee's interest in privacy is less than that the state's interest in "preserving life." One court wrote regarding a hunger-striking prisoner: "We cannot condemn fasting – Gandhi taught us about its force – as a way to secure change. But prison officials must do their best to preserve [the prisoner's] Life." *White v. Narick*, 170 W. Va. 195, 292 S.E.2d 54 (W. Va. 1982) (convicted murderer serving a life sentence protesting prison conditions). For a discussion of U.S. case-law of force-feeding of hunger strikers in custodial settings, see Mara Silver, *Testing Cruzan: Prisoners and the Constitutional Question of Self-Starvation*, 58 Stanford Law Review, 631 (2005).

[91] Giorgio Agamben, *State of Exception*, trans. Kenin Attell. Chicago: University of Chicago Press, 2005, 3–4.

[92] These are the elements that Joseph Margulies, who represented many of the Guantánamo detainees, offers to describe what the prison was "originally intended" to provide. Joseph Margulies, *Guantánamo and the Abuse of Presidential Power*. New York: Simon & Schuster, 2006, 4.

[93] See Stephen Holmes, *The Matador's Cape: America's Reckless Response to Terror*. New York: Cambridge University Press, 2007, 280. Holmes interprets one appeal of torture to its defenders as stemming from the fact that it flouts all restrictions.

Sacrifice and Sovereignty

the harsh treatment and interrogation that they deserve. Finally, the fact that the camp is seen as an exception from U.S. civilian and military law is a debated but important facet – although the Bush administration would insist in any formal legal proceeding that it was acting legally, tacitly and rhetorically transgressing "law" in its public statements was an important way of signalling commitment to (American) "life."[94]

It is possible to plot two parallel and sometimes intersecting challenges to the unchecked executive control initially asserted at Guantánamo: the legal struggle to bring the detainees' case before the Supreme Court, and the detainees' bodily struggle through the use of suicide and hunger strikes. Although Guantánamo was beset with protests from at least 2003, the most detailed information available concerns two hunger strikes in 2005.

Attorneys for the detainees reported that between 100 and 200 detainees had undertaken a hunger strike in July 2005;[95] it was called off when camp officials agreed to improve conditions and accelerate access to legal procedures. In the statements of detainees and their advocates (drawn principally from litigation discussed at greater length later), this hunger strike serves as a founding moment for the political society of the camp. In a variation of Hobbes' parable adapted to the custodial setting, everyman lowered his sword from his own neck. A report on the hunger strikes

---

[94] The rejection by top Bush and Cheney advisors of "acting extralegally" is the perhaps most interesting part of Jack Goldsmith's account of his brief tenure as head of the Office of Legal Counsel. Advisors such as Alberto Gonzales and David Addington, according to Goldsmith, rejected what Goldsmith calls the "Locke-Jefferson" paradigm: where the executive would take legally questionable steps (in Locke's language, exercise prerogative) when absolutely necessary but would then "throw himself on the mercy of Congress and the people so that they could decide whether the emergency was severe enough to warrant extralegal action." By contrast, because of the "hyper-legalization of warfare," according to Goldsmith, this model was "off the table." "The President had to do what he had to do to protect the country. And the lawyers had to find some way to make what he did legal." Jack Goldsmith, *The Terror Presidency: Law and Judgment Inside the Bush Administration*. New York: Norton, 2007, 83, 81. It is hoped that the term *sacrifice* is not stretched too much to think that it is relevant here: that the official who knowingly makes him- or herself a criminal for the common good sacrifices him- or herself for it. S/he hopes that the sacrifice will be necessary, that they will be forgiven. This seems to be the civil disobedience model of prerogative power that Judge Posner has described. Richard Posner, *Not a Suicide Pact: The Constitution in a Time of National Emergency*. New York: Oxford University Press, 2006, 152–155. It is a favorite motif of the television series *24* that government agent Jack Bauer invariably has to break the law to defuse the latest terrorist plot but then offers himself up for judgment once the crisis has passed. By comparison, Goldsmith's account puts the rejection of this offering of the self for judgment at the heart of what was asked of the Office of Legal Counsel.

[95] Charlie Savage, "46 Guantánamo Detainees Join Hunger Strike," *The Boston Globe*, Dec. 30, 2005.

at Guantánamo by the Center for Constitutional Rights summarizes the quasi-contractual nature of this founding moment:

> The breadth and severity of the June/July 2005 Hunger Strike forced the DoD [Department of Defense] to permit the creation of prisoners' representative committee and to negotiate with prison officials concerning the protestors' demands. Based upon U.S. promises to bring the detention center into compliance with the Geneva Conventions, the June/July 2005 Hunger Strike ended on July 28, 2005.[96]

The detainees, acting in concert, gained a form of government and won "promises" that the officials would follow international law.

It was a short-lived peace, however: on August 8, 2005, another mass hunger strike was initiated and continued throughout the year.[97] Detainee Yousef al-Shehri explained to his attorneys that

> [A]fter the first strike, they gave us promises. They said we will respect you and your religion and we will give you your rights. They promised me I would be freed. They promised many detainees they would be released. We waited but they did not deliver. Instead they disrespected us and our religion, they threw the Koran on the floor and stripped us naked.[98]

The agreement between detainees and jailors had not included the interrogators, who, according to detainee Al-Azmi, proved its undoing because they were "opposed improving the conditions at Guantánamo...."[99] When the detainees began a second hunger strike, however, the DoD was ready for them, having ordered twenty-five "Emergency Restraint Chairs" – the advertisement for which described them as "Like a Padded Cell 'on Wheels'" – from an Iowa company.[100] A detainee from Yemen, Emad Hassan, described the chairs:

---

[96] Center for Constitutional Rights, "The Guantánamo Prisoner Hunger Strikes and Protest: February 2002–August 2005," Sept. 8, 2005, p. 12.

[97] Charlie Savage, "46 Guantánamo Detainees Join Hunger Strike," *The Boston Globe*, Dec. 30, 2005.

[98] Statement made Oct. 1 2005 *in* Supplemental Declaration by Julia Tarver, Esq., filed Oct. 13, 2005, *Al-Joudi et. al. v. Bush*, Civ. 05-0301 *at* 6–7.

[99] Quoted in Declaration of Thomas B. Wilner, filed Oct. 14, 2005, Al Odah v. United States, Civ. 02-0828.

[100] Tim Golden, "Tough U.S. Steps in Hunger Strike at Camp in Cuba," *The New York Times*, Feb. 9, 2006.

Sacrifice and Sovereignty

The head is immobilized by a strap so it can't be moved, their hands are cuffed to the chair and the legs are shackled... They ask, 'are you going to eat or not?' and if not, they insert the tube. People have been urinating and defecating on themselves in the feedings and vomiting and bleeding.[101]

Medical organizations and the United Nations criticized the policy of force-feeding, but U.S. officials were prepared to exploit the potential irony of the situation. When the U.N. Commission on Human Rights concluded that "some of the methods used for force feeding definitely amounted to torture,"[102] the United States responded that "it is bewildering to the United States Government that its practice of preserving the life and health of detainees is roundly condemned by the Special Rapporteurs and is presented as a violation of their human rights and of medical ethics."[103] Faced with criticism from the medical community,[104] a Pentagon spokesman responded that, "the policy of the department... is to support the preservation of life by appropriate clinical means and to do that in a humane manner."[105] In response to the medics' observation that the World Medical Association prohibits force-feeding of prisoners, the Pentagon replied that "Professional organization declarations by doctors, lawyers, dentists, etc., are not international treaties, and therefore are not binding and not applicable to sovereign nation-states."[106]

Attorneys, concerned about their clients' well-being, petitioned a federal judge to allow access to their clients' medical files and notice of when their clients were to be force-fed.[107] The government contended that its policies – force-feeding in particular – ensured that "no detainee's life

---

[101] Quoted in Eric Schmitt and Tim Golden, "Force-Feeding At Guantánamo Is Now Acknowledged," *The New York Times*, Feb. 22, 2006.
[102] United Nations Economic and Social Council, Commission on Human Rights, "Situation of Detainees at Guantánamo Bay," Feb. 15, 2006.
[103] Letter Jan. 31, 2006 addressed to Office of the High Commissioner for Human Rights from Kevin Edward Moley, Ambassador, Permanent Representative of the United States of America to the United Nations and Other International Organizations in Geneva, *cited in id.*, Annex II.
[104] In a letter signed by over 250 doctors and published in the British medical journal *The Lancet*. "Forcefeeding and Restraint of Guantanamo Bay Hunger Strikers," (2006) 367: 811.
[105] Will Dunhan, "US Defends Guantánamo Force-feeding," *Reuters News Agency*, Mar. 10, 2006.
[106] Id.
[107] *Al-Joudi v. Bush*, 406 F.Supp.2d 13 (D.D.C. 2005) (J. Kessler).

or health will be endangered" and thus there is no chance of irreparable injury from the hunger strike, noting that "no one has died."[108] The attorneys did not raise their clients' right to deny medical treatment, what we might construe as a right to sacrifice; rather, they expressed concern about their clients' condition. Al-Shehri's lawyer, for example, noted that "his psychological and mental condition is commensurate with his rapidly failing health,"[109] and another attorney wrote of Mr. Al-Azmi that he "looked like the pictures one sees of starving people in the Sudan."[110] In addition, some of the attorneys positioned themselves as opposed to the hunger strike, as advocates for life over what they apparently saw only as self-destruction:

> [w]e tried to encourage him to end his hunger strike, telling him that we believed that there had been positive developments before the courts and that we hoped he would be granted a hearing soon. Mr. Daihani told us that he had no faith in the U.S. courts. We had brought him a pizza from the local Subway on the base, which he refused to eat.... He said the only control he has at Guantánamo is over what he eats, and that he will not eat again until he is released or charged and tried so that he can defend himself and prove his innocence.[111]

In its October 2005 decision, the court accepted the attorneys' rendition of the detainees' vulnerability and found that although the detainees did "not lack legal competence as children do, they are indeed vulnerable to further physical deterioration, and possibly death, by virtue of their custodial status at Guantánamo and weakened physical condition."[112] A preliminary injunction is typically entered to stop one party from harming another; in this instance, the simple-minded reading would be that the detainees requested an injunction against their own behavior. But because

---

[108] Transcript of hearing *at* 43 *cited* in *Al-Joudi v. Bush*, 406 F.Supp.2d 13, 20 (D.D.C. 2005).
[109] Supplemental Declaration by Julia Tarver, Esq., filed Oct. 13, 2005, Al-Joudi et al., v. Bush, Civ. 05–0301 *at* 6.
[110] Declaration of Thomas B. Wilner, filed Oct. 14, 2005, Al Odah v. United States, Civ. 02–0828, *at* 10.
[111] Id., *at* 3.
[112] *Al-Joudi*, 406 F.Supp.2d at 20.

the detainees were in custody, their actions could not be attributed to them in any simple way:

> [T]he Court is cognizant of the fact that Petitioners have voluntarily decided to participate in the hunger strike. Petitioners claim, however, that their voluntary participation is, in fact, a desperate protest against what they perceive as a long, potentially indefinite, confinement without final adjudication of their status. The legal analysis of irreparable harm must focus not on the cause of the injury, but rather the degree and imminence of the harm that will result if the court does not issue emergency relief.[113]

The court solved the puzzle of the self-inflicted injury by disaggregating the injury from its cause. Of note, other federal courts faced with the same claim have refused to do this and rather have seen the harm as self-inflicted and hence as not warranting a preliminary injunction.[114] This disagreement seems quite fundamental: Who really is the cause of the hunger strike?

The court ordered that the detainees' attorneys be given 24-hour notice of force-feeding of their clients and that for those who were force-fed, their medical records be provided to their attorneys. This would allow the attorneys to "counsel [the detainees] in order to persuade them to stay alive," an obvious requirement if they are "to present their claims to the

---

[113] Id.

[114] See Al Odah v. U.S. 406 F.Supp.2d 37, 44 (D.D.C. 2005). "The Court cannot agree that any risk of death that Petitioner faces is solely 'due to the government's improper and substandard force-feeding treatment.' Petitioner has eliminated an important causal link in his analysis – the fact that Petitioner himself is participating in a hunger strike. Without passing judgment on the motives behind Petitioner's participation in the hunger strike, the Court finds that Petitioner, causally, is first and foremost at risk of death of his own accord. Thus the proper question for the Court to consider in determining whether or not to grant Petitioner's request for an injunction forcing Respondents to provide medical reports and access to medical records is whether failure to access such documents will cause irreparable injury above and beyond the state that Petitioner is already in. . . . [T]he Court concludes that on this record, irreparable injury in this case is caused not by Respondents' treatment of Petitioner but by Petitioner's own actions." See also El-Banna v. Bush, 394 F.Supp.2d 76, 78 (D.D.C. 2005), which presented another issue: the detainees claimed that they were imminent danger because "Guantanamo Bay medical personnel stated that if a hunger-striking detainee provided written authorization, medical personnel would refrain from using heroic means to preserve the striking detainees' health and, ultimately, life." When officials assured the court that this was not the case, that they would provide involuntary care, the court determined that there was no imminent danger that warranted a preliminary injunction.

Court..."[115] The court situated its preliminary injunction as deriving from the "privilege of litigation" that the Supreme Court had extended to the Guantánamo detainees in *Rasul v. Bush*.[116]

The court did not confront the issue (which the attorneys had not raised) of whether the detainees had a right to take their own lives.[117] Thus, this decision from a federal trial court, although a small and a relatively insignificant episode in the struggle at Guantánamo, indicates that opposition to detainee suicide is the default position. The military rhetoric focused on the "preservation of life," and neither the court nor the detainee advocates consider an affirmative case for the detainees' right to commit suicide. What then constitutes the difference in the positions of the military, the advocates, and the court? I want to suggest that the difference lies partly in the fact that the military is keenly aware of the possibility that detainee deaths might be construed as deeply meaningful, whereas the detainees' attorneys emphasized the detainees' helplessness. Following the logic presented by the military officials, we might see the hunger strike as a form of powerful action retained by detainees until officials instituted force-feeding. While he or she has some control over his or her own body, the detainee retains some small domain of what Georges Bataille understands as sovereignty, as "life beyond utility," life opposed to servility, or the ability to destroy a surplus. Harming oneself, then, is a means of claiming sovereignty in this sense because it asserts that one has something to destroy (or to "give," in sacrificial terms).[118]

In June 2006, three detainees succeeded in committing suicide, hanging themselves with bedsheets,[119] notwithstanding the fact that since February officials had been reading to detainees passages from the Koran forbidding suicide.[120] The detainees left suicide notes, but officials have refused to

---

[115] *Al-Joudi* at 22.
[116] *Rasul v. Bush*, 542 U.S. 466 (2004).
[117] One reason for this is that the right to petition for habeas corpus, which underlay the attorney's claims, concerns access to the courts and challenges to the fact of detention, not its conditions.
[118] Georges Bataille, *The Accursed Share: An Essay on General Economy*, trans. Robert Hurley. New York: Zone Books, Vol. 3, 197. Bataille explains that "[t]he sovereignty I speak of has little to do with the sovereignty of States, as international law defines it. I speak in general of an aspect that is opposed to the servile and the subordinate."
[119] *See* Mark Denbeaux and Joshua W. Denbeaux, "June 10th Suicides at Guantánamo: Government Words and Deeds Compared," August 21, 2006 *at* www.law.shu.edu/news/guantanamo_report_june_suicides_8_21_06.pdf.
[120] David S. Cloud and Neil A. Lewis, "Prisoners' Ruse Is Inquiry Focus at Guantánamo," *The New York Times*, June 12, 2006. Sgt. Sara Wood, "Three Guantanamo Bay Detainees Die of

Sacrifice and Sovereignty

release them. One reaction to the suicides saw them as cover-ups for murder. The father of one detainee expressed skepticism that his son had killed himself,[121] and a Saudi state-sponsored human rights group wrote that the lack of oversight at the camp made it "easy to pin the crime on the prisoners...."[122] Former detainees who knew the deceased also scorned the claim that the deaths were suicides and speculated that it was more likely that the guards killed them during one of the regular and violent cell extractions.[123] The released detainees drew a firm line between hunger strikes and suicide and did not entertain the notion that suicide could have been an honorable act. It was "offensive" "to suggest that [one of the deceased] would stoop to the level of taking his own life."[124] Advocates for the detainees in the United States, in contrast to military officials, saw the fault as laying with the United States for having "pushed" the detainees "on the road to death" by creating "despair."[125]

The military articulated two points: its own love of life and the aggressive nature of the suicides. One DoD official framed the United States' interest: "we are always concerned when someone takes his own life, because as Americans we value life even if it is the life of the violent terrorist captured waging war against our country."[126] Military officials also described the suicides as acts of war against the United States. U.S. Navy Rear Admiral Harry Harris said that the detainees "have no regard for human life." He continued, "Neither ours nor their own. I believe this was not an act of desperation but an act of asymmetric warfare waged against us."[127]

Apparent Suicide," *American Forces Press Service*, U.S. Department of Defense, June 10, 2006, *at* www.defenselink.mil/news/newsarticle.aspx?id=16080.

[121] "Family Disputes Guantanamo Suicide" June 14, 2006, *Aljazeera.net News Global*, accessed July 7, 2006 *at* http://english.aljazeera.net/english/Templates/GeneralArticle.aspx.

[122] Mufleh al-Qahtani, Deputy Director, Saudi Human Rights group, quoted in "Guantanamo Inmates Commit Suicide," June 11, 2006, *Aljazeera.net News Global*, *at* www.english.aljazeera.net/english/Templates/GeneralArticle.aspx.

[123] Statement by Tarek Dergoul and Statement of June 13, 2006 by British citizens formerly held at Guantánamo Bay, www.libertysecurity.org/article994.html and at www.cageprisoners.com.

[124] Id.

[125] Barbara Olshansky of the Center for Constitutional Rights, quoted in "Guantanamo Inmates Commit Suicide," June 11, 2006, *Aljazeera.net News Global*, *at* www.english.aljazeera.net/english/Templates/GeneralArticle.aspx.

[126] Cully Stimson, U.S. Deputy Assistant Secretary of Defense, quoted in "Dead Detainee Was to Be Freed," June 12, 2006, *BBC News*, accessed June 21, 2006 *at* http://news.bbc.co.uk/2/hi/americas/5070514.stm.

[127] Rear Adm. Harry Harris quoted in "Guantanamo Suicides 'not PR move,'" *BBC News*, June 12, 2006, *at* www.newsvote.bbbc.co.uk.

Harris also referenced what he called the "mystical" belief among detainees that three of their number had to die for the rest to go free.[128] Suicide, understood as intended to shame the United States internationally, undermine its morale, and attack its commitment to "life," is seen a manipulative technique, which thus positions force-feeding as a responsive tactic. The sacrifice theme is present here in its "evil" iteration – in references to the extremism of those who are willing to martyr themselves to harm America. The use of the term *asymmetric* suggests that the United States does not engage in such practices, but the very fact that, of all the interpreters of the suicides (including detainees), the U.S. officials come closest to seeing the detainees' act as a sacrifice – as lives offered to further a meaningful cause – suggests that they are highly attuned to sacrificial dynamics. The United States' "commitment to life," then, is perhaps more accurately framed as a demand that the state monopolize death. In this case, the suicide of the detainee harms the United States not only in public and international opinion but also in its ability to command sacrifice.

The officials attempt to neutralize the meaningful potential of suicide by naming the act as aggressive, as though by this designation they can combat the effectiveness of the technique. Indeed, the DoD has elaborated an entire vocabulary that emphasizes the communicative and manipulative nature of detainee conduct. No longer content with the broad brush of "suicide attempt," since 2003 officials speak of "hanging gestures" and "manipulative self-injurious behavior" to describe a variety of acts, including some suicide attempts.[129] Only those acts in which officials discerned a sincere intention to commit suicide are designated suicide attempts.[130]

---

[128] James Risen and Tim Golden, "3 Prisoners Commit Suicide at Guantanamo," *The New York Times*, June 11, 2006. Tim Golden writes that Col. Mike Bumgarner, warden of Guantánamo Bay at the time of the hunger strike, told him that a Saudi detainee, Shaker Aamer, told Baumgarner that "several of the detainees had had a 'vision,' in which three of them had to die for the rest to be freed." Tim Golden, "The Battle for Guantánamo," *The New York Times Magazine*, Sept. 17, 2006.

[129] Associated Press, "23 Detainees Attempted Suicide in Protest at Base, Military Says," *The New York Times*, Jan. 25, 2005.

[130] Mark Denbeaux and Joshua W. Denbeaux, "Report on the Guantanamo Detainees during Detention: Data from Department of Defense Records," Seton Hall Public Law Research Paper No. 916789, July 10, 2006, at SSRN: www.ssrn.com/abstract=916789, p. 14 ("According to Capt. Edmondson, this category includes acts of self-harm in which 'the individual's state of mind is such that they did not sincerely want to end their own life,' but instead was intended to obtain release or better treatment").

Sacrifice and Sovereignty

Although it is the U.S. officials who seem most attuned to sacrificial possibilities, they are also the ones most determined to impede and disguise them.

Agamben has compared the detainees in the U.S. war on terror to the victims of the Nazi concentration camps.[131] Those in the camps were, like *homo sacer*, people who could be killed but not sacrificed. He chides Georges Bataille for emphasizing the "prestige" that can be generated through sacrifice, claiming that he "immediately exchanges the political body of the sacred man, which can be killed but not sacrificed and which is inscribed in the logic of exception, for the prestige of the sacrificial body, which is defined instead in the logic of transgression."[132] Agamben's comparison to the Nazis seems legalistic and formalistic in that it does not address obvious substantive differences. My case study highlights one other issue: the nature of the U.S. interest in the body of the detainee. The U.S. response to hunger strikes suggests that there is indeed for the United States a "prestige of the sacrificial body," a potential that must be blocked and prevented. What Agamben describes, then, is what the United States attempts to enact: a situation in which the detainee is excluded from sacrifice. An enormous effort seems directed toward this exclusion, even when there is little evidence that the detainees or other audiences see their conduct in such terms. One of the interesting things about this case is that none of the actors is able to claim the significance of the deaths authoritatively, in a manner that silences the others. If I speak of sacrifice, it is largely because of the energy expended in *denying* that meaning.

Ultimately, however, is it appropriate to talk about sacrifice in this situation? On the one hand, the detainees' custodial status raises questions about their relationship to the United States (are they a part of the sovereign or not). On the other, it is unclear whether the form of communication that they are engaged in is truly accessing a form of sacred or transcendent

---

[131] Agamben, *State of Exception*, trans. Kenin Attell. Chicago: University of Chicago Press. Agamben writes of President Bush's November 13, 2001 military order authorizing the indefinite detention of noncitizens suspected of terrorist involvement: "Neither prisoners nor persons accused, but simply 'detainees,' they are the object of pure de facto rule ... since it is entirely removed from the law and from judicial oversight." He then engages in what seems to be excessive formalism: "The only thing to which it could possibly be compared is the legal situation of the Jews in the Nazi *Lager* [camps], who, along with their citizenship, had lost every legal identity, but at least retained their identity as Jews" (3–4; italics and parenthesis in original).

[132] Agamben, *Homo Sacer*, at 113.

meaning or whether it is a more exchange-oriented sense of the word; that is, are the detainees "giving" themselves to the United States? Actually, the question of "giving" is a conundrum of sacrifice noted in many of the religious examples: how can one give to an entity that already owns the thing given? (If all of creation belongs to God, how can we give to that entity what God already possesses? The United States certainly seems to take the position that the life of the detainee belongs to it.) What is critical to the detainee transaction is the dual assertion of taking and giving in the same act of destruction. Destruction claims ownership at the same time as it alienates that claim. This combination links and separates the parties, the detainees, their captors, and the courts.

This understanding of the place of destruction in sacrifice as derivative from the fact that the giver does not really "own" the thing given suggests one reason why in everyday speech in a liberal society we can "sacrifice" something by alienating our interest in it but need not destroy it. Liberal theory supposes the self-owning person and thereby avoids the confusion of ownership that the religious (and sovereign) examples of sacrifice address.[133] If humans, not God (or the sovereign state), are the owners of creation, sacrifice need not involve the two-step process of destruction and then alienation.

The detainee makes no claim that asserts membership in the popular sovereign, yet a part of the United States is offered up to itself: if, as the officials say, the United States is committed above all to "life," then the detainee is able to access this core value for which this sovereign says that it stands. Indeed, the detainee implicitly recognizes this claim to his or her life by the United States; the action presumes that the state has an interest in his or her life. Of course, this "life" that the United States stands for

---

[133] Even classic liberal texts resist an absolute commitment to self-ownership. See, for example, John Locke, *The Second Treatise of Government*. New York: Macmillan, [1690] 1952, Ch. II, 6 ("for men being all the workmanship of one omnipotent, and infinitely wise maker; all the servants of one sovereign master, sent into the world by his order, and about his business; *they are his property*, whose workmanship they are, made to last during his, not one another's pleasure: and being furnished with like faculties, sharing all in one community of nature, there cannot be supposed any such subordination among us, that may authorize us to destroy one another, as if we were made for one another's uses, as the inferior ranks of creatures are for ours. Every one, as he is bound to preserve himself, and not to quit his station wilfully..."; emphasis added).

Sacrifice and Sovereignty

refers to a variety of things: human life in general, American lives, or the life of the state itself over and above any particular human lives.

After the successful suicides and the resulting media interest, officials expressed their new countersacrificial posture, as I would deem it, in architectural form. Plans to provide less restrictive housing for the remaining detainees were replaced with a supermaximum security facility – the building-sized version of the restraint chairs used for hunger strikers. Moreover, in June 2006 the government imported a new group of fourteen "high-value" detainees to Guantánamo, at least one of whom has more obligingly played the role the government has seemed to assume all along.[134] When Khalid Sheikh Mohammed, recognized by many as the planner of the 9/11 attacks, recently demanded of his Guantánamo tribunal that he be put to death since "I'm looking to be martyr for long time,"[135] the officials might have sensed that they were finally dealing with someone who spoke their language.

A final glimpse into the context of the hunger strikes, suicide attempts, and other forms of protest by detainees can be found in an October 2005 letter by one detainee, Jumah al-Dossari, to his New York attorney and translator, explaining his suicide.[136] In the letter, a two-page document declassified by the Pentagon, which I first encountered on the Center for Constitutional Rights Web site, Dossari apologizes to his attorney and interpreter for performing his suicide in their presence: "I feel very sorry for forcing you to see . . . It might be the first time in your life . . . to see a human being who suffered too much . . . dying in front of your eyes . . . I know it is an awful and horrible scene." He explains: "[t]here was no other alternative to make our voice heard by the world from the depths of the detention centers except this way in order for the world to reexamine its standing [. . .]." Dossari's attorney surmised that he required

---

[134] President Bush, quoted in Jonathan Karl, "'High-Value' Detainee's Transferred to Guantanamo," *ABC News, at* www.abcnews.go.com/International/story?id=2400470.

[135] Quoted in William Glaberson, "Arraigned, 9/11 Defendants Talk of Martyrdom," June 6, 2008, *The New York Times.* See Mateo Taussig-Rubbo, "The Unsacrificeable Subject?" in Austin Sarat and Karl Shoemaker, eds., *Who Deserves to Die? Constructing the Executable Subject.* Amherst, MA: University of Massachusetts Press (forthcoming 2009) Ch. 1.

[136] The letter is available www.ccr-ny.org/v2/legal/september_11th/docsjumaa_English.pdf. Ellipses are in original document. It is not apparent from the English translation whether it was redacted.

their audience "so that the military could not cover it up and his death would not be anonymous."[137] Dossari envisages that his "soul is leaving my body to rise to its creator," and he asks that his attorney and interpreter

> [t]ake some of my blood... take pieces of my death shrouds... take some of my remains... take pictures of my dead body when I am placed in my grave, lonely... send it to the world... to the judges... to people with live consciences... make them carry the burden of guilt in front of the world for this soul that was wasted with no guilt it has ever done...

Dossari asks to be turned into a sacred relic, that his blood, shroud, remains, and photos of his body be circulated throughout the world. In a stream of images running parallel to the illicit photographs of victims from Abu Ghraib wherein U.S. soldiers recorded their own theatre with detainee bodies, Dossari establishes himself as the director of his own performance, one intended to "burden" anyone with a "conscience."

Dossari's death did not take place as he had envisaged, however: his attorney, whom Dossari intended to serve as his witness, discovered Dossari in a bathroom hanging from the ceiling by his neck, while a pool of blood formed on the floor beneath him. The attorney interfered in the rite and summoned the authorities. Dossari's life was saved, his ritual preempted, and no photos circulated showing his gruesome state.[138] On the other hand, Dossari's efforts were not unnoticed: his attorney has recounted the dramatic story numerous times in media outlets. Dossari's letter has been widely distributed, is included in a book of poems from Guantánamo, and is recited on YouTube.[139]

Conclusion

The types of action that are recognized as sacrificial are, necessarily, controlled and fraught. In a world with much pain, states attempt to draw out

[137] Quoted in Josh White, "Suicidal Guantánamo Inmate Moved out of Isolation," *The Washington Post*, Dec. 17, 2005.
[138] Josh White, "Guantanamo Desperation Seen in Suicide Attempts: One Incident Was During Lawyer's Visit," *The Washington Post*, Nov. 1, 2005; see also Margolis, *Guantánamo*, 212–214 (describing that "Jumah tried to kill himself again, this time by attempting to reopen the gash he had made a month earlier").
[139] Mark Falkoff, ed., *Poems from Guantánamo: The Detainees Speak*. Iowa City: University of Iowa Press (2007); YouTube reading *at* http://youtube.com/watch?v=6qtakOxnfoo&feature=user.

some portion as sacrificial, as invoking larger meanings that involve the collectivity. A series of divides and explanatory devices assist in deciding whose suffering is to be recognized and the type of recognition granted. I have not addressed two of the most powerful constructs that channel how our legal and social order frames suffering: the accident and a statistical conception of events. Both divert attention from human and divine agency as explanatory frameworks for understanding misfortune. There is nothing inherently "accidental" about accidents, however, as Guido Calabresi pointed out long ago. They arise from an implicit or explicit policy choices to accept certain losses.[140]

This chapter has explored legal and policy forms that organize suffering as meaningful and meaningless for the U.S. public – whether it is the use of private military contractors, a description of the soldiers' sacrifice as private and belonging to the family, or the exclusion of detainees from the normal legal order. These are interesting cases because the effort to construct these losses as insignificant seems difficult and in some cases runs contrary to extremely deep national traditions.

In the examples that I have explored, designations that officials have established are challenged. In the military contractor context, a policy of subcontracting and privatization seems overwhelmed by the spectacle of the attack on the contractors who are then resacralized. The state's attempt to unbundle itself from sacred meanings is not entirely successful. My account of the privatization, this time to the family sphere, of a soldier's death, is challenged by Cindy Sheehan's ability to take the role of a grieving mother, privately comforted by the president for her son's death, into the public sphere. Her actions, linked to widespread underlying doubts about the meaningfulness of the Iraq war and the disproportion between its justification and her son's death, opened up the question whether his death was sacred or banal. My detainee example shows the struggle between the United States trying to hold onto a framework of exclusion from ordinary law and the efforts of the prisoners to claim a position for normal treatment. Judging by the response of authorities, the detainees were not mistaken about the potential efficacy of their acts.

---

[140] Guido Calabresi, "The Decision for Accidents: An Approach to Nonfault Allocation of Costs," 78 *Harvard Law Review*, 713 (1965); see also John Fabian Witt, *The Accidental Republic: Crippled Workingmen, Destitute Widows, and the Remaking of American Law*. Cambridge, MA: Harvard University Press (2004).

In each of these cases, the event potentially exceeds the capacity of the legal and cultural framework to contain the deep meaning that these actors (and their audiences) find in destruction. Although this potential is palpable, it is not necessarily realized. The detainees' efforts are met with the policy of force-feeding and the construction of a maximum-security detention facility. The legal position of the contractors has been changing rapidly as of this writing, and this can be traced in part to the Blackwater scandal. It is hard to point to a specific legal or policy change stemming from Cindy Sheehan's efforts, but she did mobilize antiwar sentiment.

A focus on sacrifice draws attention to a form of meaningful loss and violence that seems hard to grasp with other terms. We could adopt another vocabulary – of grotesque violence against contractors, of an outraged mother, of a desperate detainee – but this would leave unexamined the various transactional forms in each case. We could consider another register of meaningful loss. Criminal liability, for instance, also appears in each of my examples. Just as sacrifice was a form of meaning that came in and out of focus in each case, so was homicide.

We have encountered recent attempts to hide and privatize various forms of loss and violence. The examples presented in this chapter suggest some of the difficulty entailed in constructing the character whose suffering is meaningless. It could be then that we see in these instances a portrait of the United States attempting to shed the liability that is implied by recognizing a loss as a sacrifice.

5

Due Process and Lethal Confinement

Colin Dayan

> Even when it comes to "being a guerilla," a label alone does not render a person susceptible to execution or other criminal punishment.
> – Justice Anthony Stevens, in response to Justice Clarence Thomas's dissent in *Hamdan v. Rumsfeld*

> How simple would be the tasks of constitutional adjudication and of law generally if specific problems could be solved by inspection of the labels pasted on them!
> – Chief Justice Earl Warren, *Trop v. Dulles*

New World Security

As the White House of George W. Bush continues to incarcerate the innocent in Guantánamo Bay, to rewrite international law, and to use techniques that are cruel, inhuman, and degrading, we read complaints about an administration outside the law, secret CIA sites that are lawless, and "war prisons" that create a legal vacuum for more than 30,000 detainees in U.S. military prisons in Iraq, Afghanistan, and Guantánamo Bay. Being outside legality might not be the point, however. Before the "global war on terror" and the export of local prison practice to a network of overseas prisons, numerous U.S. Supreme Court decisions in dialogue with prison correctional policy had already retooled the incidence of civil death for the

---

Versions of this essay were presented at the University of California at Santa Barbara for the colloquium "Torture and the Future: Perspectives from the Humanities," May 18, 2007; at the inaugural of the Vanderbilt History Seminar, January 28, 2008; at the Institute for the Humanities, University of Illinois, Chicago, on February 27, 2008; and at "From the Plantation to the Prison: Incarceration and U.S. Culture," Yale University, April 12, 2008. For assistance in research and editing and for genuine support, I thank Julie J. Miller.

incarcerated. Not only has this limited the reach of Eighth Amendment jurisprudence but also it has redefined the substance of the due process clause.

To the extent that the probable cause and due process protections of the Constitution are ignored and abolished in the wake of the war on terror, the directive achieving such ends is illegal by any post–Magna Carta standard. Legal boundaries are being equated with the legitimacy of the government's goals, with the ends being used to justify the means. The extremism of current practices of punishment in the United States – anomalous in the rest of the so-called civilized world, even before September 11 – derives not only from a colonial legal history that disabled the slave while inventing the legal person but also from the extremely legalistic nature of the American system in general. In this context, the supralegal negation of civil existence remains to be deciphered.[1]

What kind of world would we find ourselves in if too much law were the problem, if legal interpretation took place, in Robert Cover's words, not only "in a field of pain and death," but also supplied the terms for rethinking the meaning of *human*?[2] The White House lawyers have displayed a preoccupation with legality and a delicacy about legal proprieties, the result of which has been to facilitate a state of official and pragmatic lawlessness. What is remarkable now as we observe the extension of legal reasoning into appreciably unprecedented domains is how historically bound is law's ability to invent persons who yet remain in a negative relation to law.

In the United States, the undoing of personhood has a lengthy history, whether in creating slaves as *persons in law* and criminals as *dead in law*, or the perpetual re-creation of the rightless entity, who has, in Hannah Arendt's inimitable words, lost the "right to have rights."[3] What is the

---

[1] For a bracing discussion of the hyperlegality of contemporary practices of detention and the justifications of torture that accompany them, see Nasser Hussain, "Beyond Norm and Exception: Guantánamo," 33: *Critical Inquiry*, 734–753 (2007).

[2] Robert Cover, "Violence and the Word," in *Narrative, Violence, and the Law: The Essays of Robert Cover*, ed. Martha Minow, Michael Ryan, and Austin Sarat. Ann Arbor: University of Michigan Press, 1993, 203.

[3] Hannah Arendt, *The Origins of Totalitarianism*. 1951; New York: Schocken Books, 2004, 376, 379. In *Trop v. Dulles* (1958), Chief Justice Earl Warren echoed Arendt in articulating how the loss of citizenship and the loss of status that accompanied it were cruel and unusual punishment in violation of the Eighth Amendment. Emphasizing the mental suffering and anguish of such deprivation, he argued that although there is "no physical mistreatment, no primitive torture," there is "instead the total destruction of the individual's status in organized society," since the individual person has "lost the right to have rights." *Trop v. Dulles*, 356 U.S. 86, 101–102 (1958).

wreckage left behind by the machinations of law, the remnants that sustain a purified image of liberty or freedom? Law is the subject of this chapter, the protagonist of its plot. Instead of atrocities being a departure from legal thinking, I would rather see them as the residue or accretions of past points of law that can absolve and even transcend violations of the rule of law. What is it, then, about these law words that allows for the aberration, the tweaking, and the deformation?

In *Democracy in America*, Alexis de Tocqueville tried to explain how oppression could operate in a society of equals. What, he wondered, could be the key to a domination so novel that old words like *despotism* and *tyranny* do not fit? The ominous leeway in the interpretation of American legal rules – from slave codes, to prison cases, to the memos regarding torture of George W. Bush's administration – has led to the redefining of persons in law: the stateless, the civilly dead, and the disposable. The redefinition – the creation of new classes of condemned – sustains a violence that goes beyond the mere logic of punishment.[4]

If This Language Becomes Law

On September 21, 2006, the Bush administration and congressional Republicans (led by "rebels" John McCain, John Warner, and Lindsey Graham) reached a compromise or accord on the detainee bill. The Military Commissions Act (MCA), passed by Congress on September 28, 2006 (signed into law by President Bush on October 17, 2006), was a direct response to the Supreme Court decision in *Hamdan v. Rumsfeld* (2006). *Hamdan* ruled that the courts retained jurisdiction over pending cases and that the military commissions had been improperly established by the president without congressional authorization. The Court argued that these commissions were unauthorized by federal statute and violated international law. A critical part of the majority opinion by Justice John Paul Stevens with a concurring opinion by Justice Anthony Kennedy focused on Common Article 3 of the Geneva Conventions of August 12, 1949, which the Court held applies to the Guantánamo detainees and is enforceable in federal court. The decision emphasized the Common Article 3 requirement of a

---

[4] For earlier studies of the legal history of civil death, incarceration, and negative personhood, see Colin Dayan, "Legal Slaves and Civil Bodies," *Materializing Democracy*. Durham, NC: Duke University Press, 2002, 53–94; Colin Dayan, "Legal Terrors," *Representations* (Fall 2005): 42–80; and Colin Dayan, *The Story of Cruel and Unusual*. Cambridge, MA: MIT Press, 2007.

"regularly constituted court affording all the judicial guarantees which are recognized as indispensable by civilized peoples."[5] Although not explicitly mentioned in *Hamdan*, Article 3 also prohibits "outrages upon personal dignity" and provides for treatment (conditions of detention as well as interrogation procedures) that is not "humiliating and degrading."[6]

Although Bush had argued in 2002 that Common Article 3 did not apply to al-Qaeda, once the Supreme Court had rejected that argument in *Rasul v. Bush* (2004), Bush's focus in 2005 was on the article's "ambiguity." Which kind of legal clarity can be used to signify license to torture, however?[7] What Bush has called "alternative sets of procedures" (and *The New York Times* "Bush's shadow penal system") is not illegal.[8] The new acceptance of torture is rather a sign of increased social rationalism, a hyperlegality that institutes judicial novelties that the law itself was designed to prohibit.

The MCA not only authorized Bush's military commissions but also provided that "no court, justice, or judge shall have jurisdiction to hear or consider an application for a writ of habeas corpus filed by or on behalf of an alien detained by the United States who has been determined by the United States to have been properly detained as an enemy combatant or is awaiting such determination."[9] Tried before new military

---

[5] *Hamdan v. Rumsfeld*, 126 S. Ct. 2749, 2795–2796 (2006).

[6] Note that although much has been made of the difference between the legislation proposed by President Bush and that of the so-called rebels on the Senate Armed Services Committee, the section of the MCA on detainee treatment is the same, except for the replacement of the prohibition of "serious violations of Common Article 3" with the prohibition and definition of "grave breaches of Common Article 3." U.S. Military Commissions Act of 2006, Pub. L. No. 109–366, 120 Stat. 2600, 2632, 2635 (October 17, 2006); hereafter cited as MCA. Neither addressed outrages on personal dignity or humiliating and degrading treatment. This silence confirms the continued refusal to recognize degradation, whether we turn to McCain's "torture ban" in the Detainee Treatment Act of 2005, to the continued reservation to Article 16 of the U.N. Convention against Torture, or to the perpetual White House attack on the "vagueness" attached to any concern with dignity or degradation, the intangible aspects of personhood that manifest no physical injury.

[7] Jeremy Waldron warns against the effort to clarify the meaning of torture on a continuum of brutality: "There are some scales one really should not be on, and with respect to which one really does not have a legitimate interest in knowing precisely how far along the scale one is permitted to go." Jeremy Waldron, "Torture and Positive Law: Jurisprudence for the White House," *Columbia Law Review* 105 (October 2005): 1701.

[8] George W. Bush, "President Discusses Creation of Military Commissions to Try Suspected Terrorists," White House, September 6, 2006, www.whitehouse.gov/news/releases/2006/09/20060906-3.html; and "Rushing off a Cliff," editorial, *The New York Times*, September 28, 2006.

[9] MCA, section 7, subsection (a) (1) at 2636.

tribunals, terrorist suspects will not be told who their accusers are or how they came to make their accusations. Documents containing the accusations can be redacted in order to hide the names of accusers. Incriminating statements can be introduced through hearsay testimony, and the defendants will not be able to confront the witnesses against them. In eliminating the constitutional right of habeas corpus, the act strips all courts of jurisdiction to hear hundreds of cases now challenging the arbitrary detention, torture, and abuse of prisoners detained by the federal government. The jurisdiction-stripping subsection applies to "all cases, without exception, pending on or after the date of the enactment of this Act which relate to any aspect of the detention, transfer, treatment, trial, or conditions of detention of an alien detained by the United States since September 11, 2001."[10] The MCA also alters the U.S. criminal code to ban "serious and non-transitory mental harm (which need not be prolonged)."[11] The act thus guarantees terrorist masterminds charged with war crimes an array of procedural protections but bars hundreds of minor figures and people who say they are innocent bystanders from access to the courts to challenge their potentially lifelong detentions.[12]

On April 19, 2007, the U.S. Department of Justice asked the U.S. District Court for the District of Columbia to dismiss the Guantánamo Bay detainees' habeas corpus cases pending before it. The action followed the decision by the U.S. Court of Appeals for the D.C. Circuit in February against the detainees in *Boumediene v. Bush* (2007) and *Al Odah v. United States* (2007). The court upheld the constitutionality of the MCA and directed that all such cases be dismissed for lack of jurisdiction. Then, having initially denied certiorari, the U.S. Supreme Court – in its first reversal in 60 years – announced that it would hear the consolidated *Al Odah* and *Boumediene* cases. On December 5, 2007, the Court heard oral arguments in *Boumediene*, the third time in the history of the Guantánamo detention camp that the Court considered whether foreign citizens imprisoned

---

[10] MCA, section 7, subsection (b) at 2636.
[11] MCA, section 3, chapter 47A, subchapter 7 at 2628 and section 6 at 2635.
[12] In an editorial, *The New York Times* condemned the Military Commissions Act of 2006 not only for prohibiting claims of habeas corpus but also for expanding "the definition of illegal enemy combatant" so that Bush can designate *any* person as an illegal combatant, outside the protection of all customary rules of law. "Guilty until Confirmed Guilty," editorial, *The New York Times*, October 15, 2006.

indefinitely as enemy combatants can claim constitutional entitlement to habeas corpus.

Status

In *The Origins of Totalitarianism*, Arendt describes what happens to those "out of legality altogether" or "outside the scope of all tangible law."[13] "In her catalog of the deprived – the refugee, the stateless, the Jew made rightless before being exterminated, and the Negro 'in a white community'"[14] – Arendt distinguishes their legal status from that of the criminal. Not only do these entities lie outside the legal definition of persons, but they also seem to occupy a space of incapacitation outside the claims of legality. What is the legal effect of a label such as "illegal enemy combatant"? The dispossessed person seems to exist nowhere. As Arendt claims, "The calamity of the rightless... is not that they are not equal before the law, but that no law exists for them."[15]

In the current war on terror, the disappeared ghost detainees in Iraq, Afghanistan, the military base on Diego Garcia (an Indian Ocean island that the United States leases from Britain), and numerous CIA secret prisons or "black sites" inhabit a spectral world that has no political boundaries, where even geographical boundaries do not necessarily separate state from state and nation from nation. This anonymity or generality is also the source of lethal distinctiveness for those caught up in the grip of the new classificatory procedures, however. Labeling and the range and gradations of ever-new categories of exclusion construct new persons in law. This legal, all-too-legalistic background is relied on by lawyers and other officials in the White House, the Department of Justice, and the Department of Defense.

Due Process

In *Hamdi v. Rumsfeld* (2004), the Supreme Court ruled that Fifth Amendment due process guarantees give citizens held in the United States as enemy combatants the right to contest their detention. The question before the Court, according to Sandra Day O'Connor, was "not whether Congress

---

[13] Arendt, *Origins of Totalitarianism*, 373, 371, 383.
[14] Dayan, "Legal Terrors," 70.
[15] Arendt, *Origins of Totalitarianism*, 375.

Due Process and Lethal Confinement

had authorized the President to detain enemy combatants, but whether the President's exercise of that power to detain American citizens without serious judicial review violates the Constitution's Fifth Amendment, which says that no person may be deprived of liberty without 'due process of law.'"[16] The Fifth and Fourteenth Amendments prohibit the government from depriving anyone of "life, liberty, or property, without due process of law." The due process clause in the Fourteenth Amendment mimics the same clause in the Fifth Amendment, and therefore the meaning of that clause in the latter controls the meaning in the former. In antebellum law, federally sponsored deprivation of an enslaved person's fundamental liberties never stopped because of the requirements of due process.[17] The label "terrorists," according to the White House lawyers' reasoning, can suspend the requirement of due process without in any way touching or harming the core of constitutional and judicially ascertained principles of liberty and justice.

Derived from Magna Carta, the writ of habeas corpus guarantees that persons cannot be imprisoned or restrained in their liberty without due process of law: "No free man shall be taken, imprisoned, disseised, outlawed, banished, or in any way destroyed, nor will we proceed against or prosecute him, except by the lawful judgment of his peers and by the law of the land."[18] What most troubled Justice David Souter as he heard oral arguments in *Hamdan v. Rumsfeld* on March 28, 2006, was the suspension of the writ, if Congress removed from the federal courts the jurisdiction to hear habeas petitions from detainees. When Solicitor General Paul D. Clement tried to exclude enemy combatants outside the United States from the writ, Souter interrupted: "The writ is the writ.... There are not two writs of habeas corpus for some cases and for other cases."[19] The imperatives of this antiterror administration demand such a doubling function, or duplicitous procedure of law, however. In the new politically oriented legal persecution, which erases the vital tension between morality and law,

---

[16] Sandra Day O'Connor, quoted in Ronald Dworkin, "What the Court Really Said," *New York Review of Books*, August 12, 2004.

[17] For an acute analysis of the double uses of the word *due* in both the fugitive slave clause and the Bill of Rights, see Andrew Hymen's "The Little Word 'Due,'" *Akron Law Review*, 38.1 (2004–2005): 1–51.

[18] Magna Carta, chapter 39. See A. Dick Howard, *The Road from Runnymede: Magna Carta and Constitutionalism in America*. Charlottesville: University of Virginia Press, 388.

[19] Supreme Court of the United States, *Hamdan v. Rumsfeld*, oral argument transcript, 59, lines 3–7, www.supremecourtus.gov/oral_arguments/argument_transcripts/05-184.pdf (accessed on January 24, 2008).

both the formal law of evidence and the possibilities for legal appeal are being wiped out.

No concept has been as central to constitutional law as due process. The substance of the Bill of Rights applies to the states through the due process clause, because these rights are "fundamental" and articulate "principles of liberty and justice which lie at the base of all our civil and political institutions."[20] In the current war on terror and the Bush administration's treatment of suspected terrorists, no concept is more threatened than due process. The cases that pertain to due process – when it is due and how much – are crucial to the lives of those restrained in their liberty.[21]

The legal-minded discourse of the war on terror, so rhetorically powerful, helps us to trace how the moral imagination can become fundamentally a legal imagination, to paraphrase the gist of R. W. Kostal's remarkable *A Jurisprudence of Power: Victorian Empire and the Rule of Law*.[22] Guantánamo, black sites or secret prisons, and other detention centers throughout the world are not exactly regions in legal limbo. It all depends on which law you are discussing.

Due process and its slippery, difficult-to-define nature can be traced back to *Dred Scott v. Sandford* (1856) and the *Slaughter-House Cases* (1873).[23] Its antebellum history demonstrates how deeply the law counted on a philosophy of personhood in its delineation of the status or type of the slave or criminal. In *Dred Scott*, Chief Justice Roger Taney stripped federal courts of jurisdiction over suits brought by blacks whose ancestors were imported into the United States and sold as slaves. Thus, no matter where Scott finds himself, he is condemned never to be free of the status

---

[20] *Powell v. Alabama*, 287 U.S. 45, 67 (1932).
[21] The idea that prisoners retain certain due process liberty rights even after they have been incarcerated was not clearly articulated until *Wolff v. McDonnell* (418 U.S. 539, 556 [1974]).
[22] R. W. Kostal, *A Jurisprudence of Power: Victorian Empire and the Rule of Law*. Oxford: Oxford University Press, 2006.
[23] Robert Bork claims that the concept of substantive due process originated in Chief Justice Taney's decision that no state can have a law making slavery illegal because the right to own slaves is protected by the due process clause; therefore, the Missouri Compromise's ban on slavery in some of the territories deprived slave owners of property without due process of law. Robert Bork, *The Tempting of America: The Political Seduction of the Law*. New York: Free Press, 1990, 93. Three years after Bork's *Tempting of America*, Ronald Dworkin made a moral argument central to the application of the due process clause: "The Supreme Court early decided that this clause was not to be understood as simply procedural, but that it imposed substantive limits on what government could do no matter what procedures it followed." Ronald Dworkin, *Life's Dominion*. New York: Vintage Books, 1993, 127.

Due Process and Lethal Confinement

that consigns him to degradation in the eyes of the law. Although Taney's ruling was reversed soon enough, first by the Civil Rights Act of 1866 and then more conclusively by the Fourteenth Amendment, which passed Congress the same year and was ratified in 1868. Radical Reconstruction failed in the Supreme Court in a series of decisions from the 1870s to the end of the century.

In *Slaughter-House*, the Court construed the privileges or immunities clause of the Fourteenth Amendment – "No State shall make or enforce any law which shall abridge the privileges or immunities of citizens of the United States" – so narrowly as to render it a practical nullity. In so doing, it rejected the notion that the clause incorporated Bill of Rights freedoms against the states. This rejection and the limitation of the privileges or immunities clause led to the Court's frequently relying on the Fourteenth Amendment's due process clause as a significant source of substantive rights: the "fundamental liberty interest" or "unenumerated right" offshoot of substantive due process.[24]

The most obvious meaning of the due process clause of the Fourteenth Amendment is that a state has to use sufficiently fair and just legal procedures whenever it is going to use legal means to take away a person's life, freedom, or possessions. In the prison context, any transfer or treatment for disciplinary proceedings generally expects certain procedures necessary to satisfy the minimum requirements of procedural due process: advance written notice of the alleged violation, a written statement of evidence, and the ability to call witnesses. Civil rights and legal capacities are often rationalized as dispensable for those held under close, special, or secure management, however. As early as 1976, Justice Byron White, in *Meachum v. Fano*, set the stage for prison transfer that allowed no redress:

> Massachusetts prison officials have the discretion to transfer prisoners for any number of reasons. Their discretion is not limited to instances of serious misconduct.... Whatever expectation the prisoner may have in remaining at a particular prison so long as he behaves himself,

---

[24] Substantive due process is a tricky and contentious issue. See John Harrison, "Substantive Due Process and the Constitutional Text," *Virginia Law Review* 83 (April 1997): 493–557; and especially Peter J. Rubin, "Square Pegs and Round Holes: Substantive Due Process, Procedural Due Process, and the Bill of Rights," *Columbia Law Review* 103.4 (2003): 833–85. Rubin gives a detailed analysis of the status of substantive due process. According to him, there are two aspects to substantive due process claims: one pertains to fundamental rights, the other to irrational or conscience-shocking governmental action.

it is too ephemeral and insubstantial to trigger procedural due process protections as long as prison officials have discretion to transfer him for whatever reason or for no reason at all.[25]

According to the Court, "confinement" – no matter where or why – "in any of the state's institutions" is considered "within the normal limits or range of custody, which the conviction has authorized the state to impose."[26] Even if harm comes to the prisoner in being transferred – and some transfers amount to a death sentence – transfer is part of imprisonment and thus implicates neither a liberty interest nor any grievous loss. Commenting on *Meachum*, a deputy warden in Arizona explained to me, "Due process doesn't mean anything when it comes to transfer. We can move him whenever we like."[27]

In his dissent, Justice Stevens stressed that liberty and custody are not mutually exclusive concepts. He emphasized the "residuum of constitutionally protected liberty" possessed by a person, even within prison walls. Appealing to ethical tradition and the substance of liberty and custody as being mutually adaptable, Stevens concluded his argument by pitting "prison regulations" against "protected liberty interests." He reminded the Court that if what the state allows becomes the yardstick for liberty, thereby erasing claims to dignity and worth, then the inmate "is really little more than the slave described in the 19th century cases."[28]

Atypical and Significant

It was Chief Justice William Rehnquist's decision in *Sandin v. Conner* on June 19, 1995, that not only redefined the constitutional limits of confinement but set the stage for legally ordaining the supermax (i.e., supermaximum security) prison as an administrative, not a disciplinary, necessity. Focusing on the nature of the hardship imposed – and not on

---

[25] *Meachum v. Fano*, 427 U.S. 215, 228 (1976).
[26] Ibid. at 225.
[27] Interview with deputy warden by author, Arizona State Prison Complex, Tucson, August 10, 1995. The name is withheld by mutual agreement.
[28] *Meachum*, 427 U.S. at 232–233. Dissenting in *Slaughter-House*, Justice Stephen J. Field in his interpretation of the first clause of the Fourteenth Amendment created "citizens of the United States," making their citizenship "dependent upon the place of their birth, or the fact of their adoption, and not upon the constitution or laws of any state, or the condition of their ancestry." *Slaughter-House Cases*, 83 U.S. 36, 38 (1873).

Due Process and Lethal Confinement

the language of the state prison's regulations (as in *Hewitt v. Helms*, 1983) – Rehnquist gutted the meaning of solitary confinement.[29]

In August 1987, a correctional officer subjected DeMont Conner, who was serving a sentence of 30 years to life at a maximum-security prison in Hawaii, to a strip search, including an inspection of his rectal area for contraband. During the search, Conner used profanity and made sarcastic statements to the guard. Several days later, the prison gave Conner written notice that he had been charged with "high misconduct" for physically interfering with correctional functions and with "low moderate misconduct" for using obscene language and harassing a prison guard (*Sandin*, 475).

At the disciplinary hearing, the adjustment committee found Conner guilty of all charges and sentenced him to 30 days of disciplinary segregation in solitary confinement. Prior to the administrator's finding that the high misconduct charge was inappropriate and his expunging the guilty charge from Conner's record, Conner had instituted a civil rights action against the adjustment committee chairperson and other prison officials in the U.S. District Court for the District of Hawaii. His amended complaint alleged, among other claims, that the committee's refusal to allow him to call witnesses deprived him of adequate procedural due process.

The district court granted the defendant's motion for summary judgment. On appeal, the Ninth Circuit Court reversed the decision, concluding that Hawaii's prison regulations created a liberty interest in avoiding disciplinary segregation and remanded the case to determine whether Conner had in fact received sufficient due process. The Supreme Court agreed to hear the case and "reexamine the circumstances under which state prison regulations afford inmates a liberty interest protected by the Due Process Clause" (*Sandin*, 474).

The Supreme Court had previously stated in dictum that solitary confinement is a "major change in conditions of confinement"[30] that should be governed by the same procedures as deprivation of statutory good time (*Wolff v. McDonnell*, 1974), and the lower federal courts had almost universally adopted this view. In a five-to-four decision, the majority in *Sandin* rejected it and claimed that Conner's punitive confinement

---

[29] *Sandin v. Conner*, 515 U.S. 472 (1995); hereafter cited parenthetically by page number as *Sandin*.

[30] *Wolff*, 418 U.S. at 572 n. 19.

"did not present the type of *atypical, significant deprivation* in which a State might conceivably create a liberty interest" (*Sandin*, 486; emphasis added).

Acknowledging that states may create liberty interests protected by due process, Rehnquist explained that these "will generally be limited to freedom from restraint which, while not exceeding the sentence in such an unexpected manner as to give rise to protection by the Due Process Clause of its own force, . . . nonetheless imposes atypical and significant hardship on the inmate in relation to the ordinary incidents of prison life" (*Sandin*, 484). What are these "ordinary incidents"? An extension of the hands-off reasoning of *Meachum*, *Sandin* explained that prison litigation is qualitatively different from other due process litigation, because the inmate's deprivation must be judged against prison security. The "residuum of liberty" recognized in *Wolff* as remaining even within the walls of the prison is no longer as important as the maintaining of order. Dispensing with the usual grievous loss test, the majority instead judged that Conner's sentence to disciplinary segregation was not atypical because it was "within the range of confinement to be normally expected for one serving an indeterminate term of 30 years to life" (*Sandin*, 487).

Deprivation and containment are the basis of the Court's holding. Although it might appear that the Court set limits to brutality, its curious logic makes a fiction of protection. Rehnquist gives inmates a new bottom line in terms of conditions of confinement: *restraint*, with the certainty that new hardships calling for due process will have to be ever more extreme to get the attention of the courts. What the Court accomplished by putting "atypical and significant" in league with "ordinary" is to level the distinction, to make it difficult to prove when the due process clause should kick in: how atypical must something be to be extraordinary?[31]

---

[31] As early as *Hewitt*, Rehnquist had begun to skirt the requirements of due process. In a subtle maneuver, he removed the distinction between administrative custody and punitive isolation – "the two types of confinement are substantially identical" – except in one particular: "Unlike disciplinary confinement the stigma of wrongdoing or misconduct does not attach to administrative segregation." Arguing that the inmate's "private interest" is not very consequential, he concluded, "He was merely transferred from one extremely restricted environment to an even more confined situation." *Hewitt v. Helms*, 459 U.S. 460, 464 n. 1, 473 (1983). Imagine that: if you use a different name, you can remove the stigma and treat an inmate who is not guilty of misconduct the same as an inmate who is.

The Court reasoned that disciplinary confinement, "with insignificant exceptions," was similar in "duration and degree" to administrative segregation and protective custody (*Sandin*, 486). Thirty days in the special housing unit of Halawa Correctional Facility in Hawaii, the Court concluded, is not "a major disruption in his environment" (*Sandin*, 486).[32] How typical, however, are 23-hour lockdown and Conner's removal from the general population, without the possibility of presenting witnesses in his defense?

Justice Ruth Bader Ginsburg, joined by Stevens, dissented, concluding that Conner had a liberty interest in avoiding disciplinary confinement, which, unlike administrative confinement, stigmatized him and adversely affected his parole prospects. The practical meaning of "atypical and significant hardship" is far from clear. "What design lies beneath these key words? The Court ventures no examples, leaving consumers of the Court's work at sea, unable to fathom what would constitute an 'atypical, significant deprivation,'... and yet not trigger protection under the Due Process Clause directly" (*Sandin*, 490 n. 2).

Echoing arguments made by Justices Brennan, Marshall, and Stevens in dissents to other due process cases that had severely narrowed the applicability of procedural rights for prisoners, Ginsburg viewed the due process clause itself, rather than state prison regulations, as the source of the prisoner's protected liberty interest. In his dissent in *Meachum*, Stevens writes: "I had thought it self-evident that all men were endowed by their Creator with liberty as one of the cardinal inalienable rights. It is that basic freedom which the Due Process Clause protects, rather than the particular rights or privileges conferred by specific laws or regulations."[33]

In contemporary uses or misuses of due process in the global war on terror, what qualifies as ordinary? What does *atypical* or *significant* mean

---

[32] In *Wolff*, the Court had expressed willingness to apply the same procedural safeguards afforded to deprivations of good-time credits to discipline imposed through solitary confinement, categorizing solitary as a "major change in the conditions of confinement." *Wolff*, 418 U.S. at 572 n. 19. Conner expressed his shock at finding that the *Wolff* analysis no longer held: "Their erroneous decision is clear because they never even discussed the fact that the law that existed at the time I filed my claim had supported me 100% because from the very beginning I used (it) as a basis to file my claims: *Toussaint v. McCarthy, Hewitt v. Helms*, and *Wolff v. McDonnell*." DeMont Conner, personal correspondence with author, June 17, 1999.

[33] *Meachum*, 427 U.S. at 230.

not only in the prison context but also in the elaborate legal justifications for the uses of terror in the current jurisprudence of the White House – justifications critical to the radical substitution of penal for civil life?[34]

Koch v. Lewis

For three years, from 1996 to 1998, I had access to Special Management Unit II (SMU II) in Florence, Arizona, a high-tech, state-of-the-art prison, even harsher than the well-known Pelican Bay in California. I was helmeted, vested, and warned about paper darts, urine, and feces thrown out of cells by prisoners. I had been prompted to try out leather shackles made by the Humane Restraint Company. It seemed unlikely that I would be threatened by inmates, because the cells where "the worst of the worst" were locked down for 23 hours a day – without human contact except for the violent cell extractions – had doors covered with thick steel plates perforated with small ventilation holes, described by one officer as "irregular Swiss cheese."[35] Nothing ever happened to me. I walked down the corridors on impeccably clean floors. There was no paint on the concrete walls. The light seemed too bright, forcing me to blink uneasily. Although the corridors had skylights, the cells had no windows. Nothing inside the cells could be moved or removed. There was nothing inside except a poured concrete bed, a stainless steel mirror, a sink, and a toilet.

According to Terry Stewart, director of the Arizona Department of Corrections until 2000 (in 2003, Stewart accompanied three other corrections professionals to reform prisons in Iraq, including the security and operations of Abu Ghraib), SMU II is "the most secure super-maximum security prison in the United States."[36] Alleged gang members are locked down under the most draconian rules in the history of the contemporary prison. This locale – a model for other special housing or special treatment units in

---

[34] In his critique of Richard Posner's *Not a Suicide Pact: The Constitution in a Time of National Emergency*, David Cole, the most acute analyst of the erosion of constitutional freedoms in the war on terror, focuses on due process – especially Harlan's dissent in *Poe v. Ullman* – to demonstrate just how shocking is the ease with which Posner summarily dismisses principles of liberty, equality, and dignity in the quest for national security. David Cole, "How to Skip the Constitution," *New York Review of Books*, November 16, 2006.

[35] Anthony Zellenek, interview with author, Department of Corrections, Phoenix, Arizona, June 1996.

[36] Stewart deposition, *Koch v. Lewis*, November 13, 2000.

Due Process and Lethal Confinement

the United States – was built for those inmates called security threat groups (STGs, meaning gangs), special needs groups (meaning psychologically disabled), or assaultive (meaning never divulged).

The process by which such words are specified, by which their technical meaning is determined, remains curious and illogical. Whereas disruptive inmates who threaten or injure inmates or staff, repeatedly try to escape, or possess contraband are often placed in the supermax, inmates who are merely perceived to be threats (whether based on gang, political, or religious associations) end up in indefinite solitary confinement. Most of these segregation decisions are based only on alleged status of gang affiliation, not on evidence of an actual infraction of prison rules. In other words, something assumed to be criminal intent is not based on criminal action: "a prisoner who commits a violent crime in prison could receive less harsh punishment and enjoy greater procedural protection than a prisoner who is a gang affiliate but who has not committed a crime."[37]

The severe sensory deprivation and enforced idleness of the supermax have been condemned since the 1980s by the United Nations Committee against Torture, Human Rights Watch, Amnesty International, the American Civil Liberties Union, and the Center for Constitutional Rights. The U.N. Convention against Torture (May 2006) and the U.N. Human Rights Committee (July 2006) documented in detail the psychic violence endured by supermax prisoners. Labels demarcating those identified as threats to the secure and efficient operations of prisons carry with them the unwholesome possibility that solitary confinement can extend indefinitely, that 23-hour lockdown status cannot be judged a constitutional violation, and that the absence of training programs, vocational training, education, personal property, and even human contact is nothing but the expected element of confinement when administrative security is the primary goal.

In the precedent-setting decision *Koch v. Lewis* (2001), Senior Judge James B. Moran of the U.S. District Court ruled that Mark Koch's five and a half years in SMU II, with no end in sight, gave rise to a protected

---

[37] Scott N. Tachiki, "Indeterminate Sentences in Supermax Prisons Based upon Alleged Gang Affiliations: A Reexamination of Procedural Protection and a Proposal for Greater Procedural Requirements," *California Law Review* 83.4 (July 1995): 1117–1148. His analysis of the constitutional shortcomings of due process protections in *Madrid v. Gomez* (1993), the notorious Pelican Bay case, is especially relevant to the new penology based on status.

liberty interest under the "atypical and significant" clause of *Sandin*.[38] Koch was locked in his cell for 165 of the 168 hours in a week. His three weekly hours out of his cell were spent in shackles, and during those three hours, he had only eight minutes to shower and shave. For the three hours a week out of his cell, Koch walked 20 feet down the hall in one direction for a shower and 10 feet down the hall in another direction to an empty exercise room (12 feet by 20 feet), also known as the "dog pen," a high-walled cage with a mesh screening overhead. The light was always on, although it was sometimes dimmed. When Koch appeared in district court in Phoenix, he had not seen the horizon or the night sky for more than five years.

SMU II is singular among control units in that it arbitrarily includes inmates on death row. None had exhibited threatening behavior. They had lived in a regular maximum-security wing without any serious infraction of rules. The psychic stress experienced by death-row inmates is now compounded by the psychological deterioration of indefinite solitary confinement. As one inmate wrote to me, "We are dead twice over, killed in our mind and tortured as we await the death of our bodies." At the time of Koch's case, SMU II housed 620 inmates, including those on death row. "They are treated worse than individuals with the Ebola virus," forensic psychiatrist Jack Potts, MD, wrote in a report to the court on Koch's behalf. "There is an unequivocal toll on individuals placed in such isolation."[39]

After years of analyzing the effects of supermaxes on inmates' mental health, Harvard psychiatrist, Stuart Grassian, MD, defined the environment as "strikingly toxic." What he has called a *supermax syndrome* includes such symptoms as hallucinations, paranoia, and amnesia. Inmates have difficulty remaining alert, thinking, concentrating, and remembering owing to prolonged sensory deprivation.[40] During a *60 Minutes* episode on

---

[38] The "saga" of Koch's "epic journeys," as described by Moran, is contained in *Koch v. Lewis*, 96 F. Supp.2d 949 (D. Ariz. 2000); *Koch v. Lewis*, 216 F. Supp.2d 994 (D. Ariz. 2001) (hereafter cited parenthetically by page number as *Koch*); and *Koch v. Lewis*, 2001 WL 1944737 (D. Ariz. 2001). For a discussion of STG classification, due process, and Koch's case, see Maximilienne Bishop, "Supermax Prisons: Increasing Security or Permitting Persecution?" *Arizona Law Review* 47 (2005): 480–491, which came to my attention after the completion of this essay.

[39] Personal communication with author, June 1999. The name is withheld by mutual agreement. Jack Potts's words communicated in an e-mail message from Daniel Pochoda to the author, July 20, 2003.

[40] Dr. Stuart Grassian, *Lee v. Coughlin*, 26 F. Supp.2d 615, 637 (1998).

California's Pelican Bay, Grassian complained, "In some ways it feels to me ludicrous that we have these debates about capital punishment when what happens in Pelican Bay's Special Management Unit is a form of punishment that's far more egregious."[41]

In seeking legal representation for injunctive relief from detention, Koch chronicled the arbitrary detention that followed his classification as an STG member. Writing about Arizona's SMU II in 2000, a year before the probable cause and due process protections of the Constitution were repealed in the wake of the global war on terror, Koch gives some insight in his appeal into the legal incapacitation suffered by those detained offshore at Guantánamo:

> I have been validated as a member of the Aryan Brotherhood, after three previous hearings that cleared me of gang activity. My validation is based on nothing that I did. Instead, it is based on the simple fact that other inmates possessed my name after I have been a jail house lawyer, approved legal assistant and representative – educated by the Arizona Department of Corrections for over ten years.... Due process has been violated in every manner possible. The most frequent claims are denial of witnesses and denial of access to alleged evidence.... I was denied all my witnesses and denied the opportunity to see any evidence by the blanket reasoning of "confidential."[42]

Koch had been the subject of fourteen state and court opinions over 20 years of litigation. Most of his allegations involved matters that preceded his first STG hearing and transfer to SMU II.[43] When lead counsel Daniel Pochoda and Timothy Eckstein of Osborn Maledon in Phoenix took on Koch's civil rights litigation in 2000, they were able to take numerous

---

[41] Mike Wallace, "California's High Tech Maximum Security Prison Accused of Torture and Mental Abuse," 60 *Minutes*, September 12, 1993.

[42] Mark Koch, personal e-mail correspondence with author, July 2003.

[43] After the case, Pochoda explained to me that the ruling created "new law" and could be far reaching if other inmates in similar confinement joined in a class action lawsuit. In *Wilkinson v. Austin* (2005), at the same time that the Supreme Court heard *Rasul v. Bush*, the Court had the chance to decide against supermax confinement. Instead, although the Court found the prisoners to have a due process liberty interest in avoiding supermax placement, it upheld the written policy that includes annual review of such placement as comporting with due process. Most significantly, there is no substantive limitation on prison officials' ability to put prisoners in supermaxes in the first place. In *The Law Is a White Dog* (Princeton University Press, forthcoming), I analyze this case at length, along with *Beard v. Banks* (2006), a First Amendment case. See Colin Dayan, "Words behind Bars," *Boston Review* (November/December 2007), www.bostonreview.net/BR32.6/dayan.php (accessed January 30, 2008).

depositions and to submit a second amended complaint with primary focus on the two STG validations and solitary confinement. They dropped many of the original incidents and some defendants. Because the procedural due process deficiencies of the first STG hearing had been repaired and the necessary procedures instituted in 1998, the plaintiff's lawyers decided to streamline the case, drop all issues before 1995, and identify a substantive due process claim.[44]

According to Pochoda, the reliance on substantive and not procedural due process was absolutely necessary:

> You can have all the procedures in the world to prove that x is true, but if there is no connection between x being true and the actions taken in connection with that assumption, you've got a substantive due process violation. It's as if the officials had said, "If he's got red hair, then we're going to put him in SMU." If x leads to y, then there's got to be some rational connection between x and y. Otherwise, it's absolutely arbitrary.

In other words, there is no rational, reasonable, demonstrable connection between Koch's allegedly being a member of the Aryan Brotherhood and his being put in lockdown in SMU II. Pochoda explains, "A finding of imminent danger based on gang membership alone is an abstraction without foundation."[45]

The vague contours of "substantive due process" give a broader interpretation of the clause, one that protects basic substantive rights, as well as the right to due process. Perhaps the most influential substantive due process opinion is still Justice Marshall Harlan II's dissent in *Poe v. Ullman*

---

[44] Substantive due process is the fundamental constitutional legal theory on which the *Griswold*, *Roe*, and *Casey* privacy rights are based. "Substantive" rights are those general rights, unlike basic procedural rights, that give the person the power to possess or do certain things, regardless of the government's desire. See John Harrison, "Substantive Due Process and the Constitutional Text," *Virginia Law Review* 83.3 (April 1997): 493–558. It is important to distinguish between economic due process, an entirely discredited doctrine that held from *Lochner v. New York* (1905) through *West Coast Hotel v. Parrish* (1937), and the basis for substantive law more broadly, as derived from Harlan in *Mugler v. Kansas* (1887). In words reminiscent of his attack on "sterile formalism" in his dissent in the *Civil Rights Cases* (1883), he wrote the oft-repeated words: "The courts are not bound by mere forms, nor are they to be misled by mere pretences. They are at liberty – indeed, are under a solemn duty – to look at the substance of things, whenever they enter upon the inquiry whether the legislature has transcended the limits of its authority." *Mugler v. Kansas*, 123 U.S. 623, 661 (1887).

[45] Daniel Pochoda, telephone interview with author, July 2003.

Due Process and Lethal Confinement 145

(1961), in which he lays out the nature of the liberty guaranteed by the due process clause, which

> ... cannot be found in or limited by the precise terms of the specific guarantees elsewhere provided in the Constitution. This "liberty" is not a series of isolated points pricked out in terms of the taking of property; the freedom of speech, press, and religion; the right to keep and bear arms; the freedom from unreasonable searches and seizures; and so on. It is a rational continuum which, broadly speaking, includes a freedom from all substantial arbitrary impositions and purposeless restraints, and which also recognizes, what a reasonable and sensitive judgment must, that certain interests require particularly careful scrutiny of the state needs asserted to justify their abridgment.[46]

We can rationalize *Koch* within the existing and ordinarily accepted adjudication of substantive due process by considering the irrationality or arbitrariness of his STG classification, as well as the particularly harsh and oppressive conditions of confinement in SMU II. Substantive due process holds that the due process clauses of the Fifth and Fourteenth Amendments guarantee not only that appropriate and just procedures (or processes) be used whenever the government or the state is punishing a person or otherwise taking away a person's life, freedom, or property but also that a person cannot be so deprived without appropriate justification, regardless of the procedures used to do the taking.

Considering the severe conditions of Koch's confinement and the duration of the deprivation at issue, the court found that Koch's solitary confinement violated his right to due process under the Fourteenth Amendment, which is applicable to states, because there was no evidence that Koch had committed any overt act to warrant such action. The claim that he was a member of the Aryan Brotherhood was not sufficient. Substantive due process required that the evidence used should bear a logical relation to the specific deprivations. "The labeling of plaintiff Mark Koch as a gang member does not itself create legal concerns. Rather, it is the placement in SMU-II as a result of this alleged association that is constitutionally significant."[47]

---

[46] *Poe v. Ullman*, 367 U.S. 497, 543 (1961) (John Harlan dissenting). Cited in Rubin, "Square Pegs and Round Holes," 862–863.
[47] Plaintiff's Post-Trial Brief and Request for Injunctive Relief (June 15, 2001), *Koch v. Lewis*, No. CIV90-1872-PHX-ROS (JBM), 19.

Judge Moran explained in the middle of the trial: "We are not talking about punishment for misconduct; we are talking about incarceration because of status and subsequent indefinite confinement in SMU." He questioned what the Arizona Department of Corrections called "a basic and irrebuttable presumption" that "status=risk": "We are not unmindful of the danger posed by prison gangs... but we do not agree with the defendant's conclusion that indefinite segregation in SMU II based on status alone passes constitutional muster" (*Koch*, 1005–1007). In other words, according to Moran, Koch "cannot constitutionally be held indefinitely in virtual isolation because of his status and not because of any overt conduct."[48] Unless there is overt misconduct, gang status alone does not justify the "extreme nature of the deprivation at issue here" (*Koch*, 1004).

What had Koch done to be certified as a member of the Aryan Brotherhood STG? In 1996, when Koch was notified that he had been identified as an STG member, he was validated at a hearing but received little or no details of the charges against him. Then, in 1998, he was revalidated under new procedures instituted by the Arizona Department of Corrections. The evidence was tenuous at best: a 1981 photograph of Koch posing with alleged STG members at a rodeo, incident reports noting that he had been seen associating with known members, and purported membership lists that identified Koch as an STG member.

Moran noted that Koch's "legal practice has been remarkable" (*Koch*, 996 n. 3). Over a period of 20 years, Koch had helped other prisoners understand their convictions and file suits. According to his testimony, retaliation by correctional officers consisted of numerous attacks on his person and his property and transfers to harsher units. Because of Koch's assumed gang involvement, the only way out of SMU II was to debrief (i.e., name names of gang members) and renounce, but how could he debrief if, as he continued to argue, he was not a gang member? Falsely accused, he would be condemned to serve out his time indefinitely because he knew of nothing to tell and therefore could not effectively debrief. Furthermore, because debriefers are targeted for death by gang members, Koch would have had to be sent to another restrictive segregated facility, protective custody in SMU I. Anyone suspected of gang affiliation, whether that person debriefs or not, is thus condemned to what amounts to solitary confinement for the rest of his or her life.

---

[48] *Koch*, WL 1944737 at 3.

Due Process and Lethal Confinement

Debriefing, as Koch later explained to me, is "a fixed process designed to generate false numbers and . . . to justify massive ADOC [Arizona Department of Corrections] spending and create your 'scapegoat' labels so the ADOC can impose whatever dictatorial controls they can throw in under the umbrella of 'security.'" Disgruntled or bored inmates or those seeking vengeance help the interrogators to artificially inflate the gang membership roll. "They take out a list of names and ask, starting in alphabetical order, if 'this guy' is a member or not. If you answer 'yes,' then they want any information you have (or can create) on this individual. You see, by first providing the suspect's name they have sealed someone's fate. After a few positive answers they have an entire list of what they declare to be 'CONFIRMED STG MEMBERS.'"[49]

Only in Arizona, Moran stated, are gang members held in these facilities without the prospect of returning to the general population and without any chance of reclassification for good behavior. Arizona's restriction on the return of inactive gang members to lower custody units, Moran noted, "is apparently unique.... A policy preference is not without constitutional limitations. It would certainly ease the burdens of a correctional system if all prisoners were executed or perpetually chained to a wall, but no one, we believe, would suggest that such a system would pass constitutional muster."[50]

After hearing evidence of SMU conditions and the psychological harm faced by inmates, the court found not only a significant liberty deprivation but also that the very practice of sending inmates to supermaxes based on status alone – with no charges or evidence of misconduct – violated due process. The court concluded that there must be some evidence to justify

---

[49] Mark Koch, personal e-mail correspondence with author, July 2003.
[50] *Koch*, WL 1944737 at 2. Terry Stewart, who succeeded Sam Lewis as director of the Arizona Department of Corrections in 1995, changed the rules of supermax confinement for alleged gang members. Department Order 806 rescinded the active/inactive provision, which allowed validated STG members to demonstrate that they were no longer active gang members and therefore eligible for transfer out of SMU II. According to Stewart, "blood in/blood out" was the rule: once a gang member, always a gang member. "Once you've 'blooded in' to a gang, you are like a loaded weapon to that gang." Deposition of Terry Stewart, Florence, Arizona, November 14, 2000. It is no accident that Stewart, the harshest of directors in the history of the Arizona prison system, who initiated death-row chain gangs, what he called "humane restraint," the indefinite confinement of SMU II, cell extractions with unmuzzled German Shepherd dogs, and the cover-up of rape by correctional officers, was chosen, along with three other corrections professionals, to reform the prison system in Iraq in the summer of 2003. By the time he left, he had directed the training, security, and operations of Abu Ghraib.

placing Koch in SMU II for an indefinite (and very likely permanent) term.

The harsh logic of supermax detention and its reliance on arbitrary deprivations based on status attests to the magnitude of what is happening at Guantánamo. The STG label in U.S. prisons has been extended to anyone thought to threaten national security, even to the point of extending criminal jurisdiction over foreigners in foreign countries. Although the Supreme Court has ruled against military commissions (in *Hamdan*), decided that Guantánamo is legally within the jurisdiction of the United States (in *Rasul*), and will determine whether alternative procedures for habeas corpus (e.g., combatant status review tribunals) are adequate (in *Boumediene*), virtually lifelong supermax detention for alleged STGs in our domestic prisons continues to be judged constitutional. What began as the labeling of gangs as "predators" or the "worst of the worst" has been extended to "illegal enemy combatants," "security detainees," or "terrorists." The future of lethal incarceration seems assured.

William Blackstone warned in his *Commentaries on the Laws of England* that execution and confiscation of property without accusation or trial signaled a despotism so extreme as to herald "the alarm of tyranny throughout the whole kingdom." He added, however, that even these practices were not as serious an attack on personal liberty as secret forms of imprisonment. The "confinement of the person, by secretly hurrying him to gaol, where his sufferings are unknown or forgotten" because it is "less public" and "less striking" is, he wrote, "therefore a more dangerous engine of arbitrary government."[51] Captured on battlefields, pulled from beds at midnight, grabbed off streets as suspected insurgents, tens of thousands have passed through U.S. detention, the majority in Iraq. Secret prisons, unknown in number and location, remain available for future detainees now that Bush has (as he claims) "emptied" the CIA sites. In Iraq, the U.S. Army oversees more than 30,000 prisoners in supermaxes at Camp Cropper near Baghdad airport, Camp Bucca in the southern desert, and Fort Suse in the Kurdish north.

The ever more inclusive propensities of labels such as "threat" or "terrorist" can subsume all kinds of people, especially the low-level detainees sold

---

[51] William Blackstone, *Commentaries on the Laws of England*. Chicago: University of Chicago Press, 1979.

Due Process and Lethal Confinement

into custody by bounty hunters. Suspects considered the most dangerous probably have the most rights, whereas others do not have the ability to challenge their imprisonment. At Guantánamo Bay, where only 10 of the nearly 300 inmates have been charged with crimes, a new, $38 million supermax, called Camp 6, stands in stark contrast to the cages that housed detainees when they began arriving in January 2002. Although the military claimed that Camp 6 housed terrorists such as Khalid Sheikh Mohammed and the thirteen other recent transfers from CIA detention, officials have now confirmed that the alleged "high-value detainees" are actually being held in Camp 7, "run by a special unit code-named Task Force Platinum." The camp is off-limits to media and even to military defense lawyers.[52] The innocent, more than the guilty, are fated to remain confined with no end in sight.

[52] See Carol Rosenberg, "'Platinum' Captives in Off-Limits Camp," *Miami Herald*, February 7, 2008.

6

From Time to Torture
The Hellish Future of the Criminal Sentence

Thomas L. Dumm

> If this God of the Christians were *proved* to us to exist, we should know even less how to believe in him.   – Nietzsche, *The Anti-Christ*

The word *sentence* defines both what is written here – "an expressed thought" – and the punishment meted out by a judge to someone who has committed a crime – "a pronounced judgment." If we focus our attention on the common root of the two meanings of the word derived from its etymology – old French, from the Latin *sentential*, a way of thinking, opinion, sentiment (prob. for *sentientia* < *sentiens*, prp. of *sentire*, to feel, see *sense*) – and then trace the connection between the word *sense* and the word *send* – the complications multiply. *Sense* refers both to the five senses through which the brain receives all external stimuli and the faculty of common perception. We all, more or less, have the ability to "make sense" of experience. Any judgment entails the use of the senses and the exercise of sense. Sentencing fundamentally involves sensing, and sensing in turn involves making sense.

I begin by directing attention to these tangled roots, because the judgment that has shaped the development and employment of criminal sentences in the form of imprisonment over time is intimately connected to the shifting meaning of sense and sensibility, as framed by a history of embodiment. That history is, as Michel Foucault demonstrated, coterminous with what can be thought of as the history of bio-politics and its relationship to governmentality.[1]

---

[1] See especially Foucault, *Security, Territory, Population: lectures at the College de France, 1978* (New York Palgrave, 2007), trans. Graham Burchell, and *The Birth of Biopolitics: Lectures at the College de France, 1979*, trans. Graham Burtchell. New York: Palgrave, 2008.

The current problematic status of criminal judgment in the United States, associated at an important level with what Jonathan Simon has identified as an abandonment by judges of the responsibility to sentence,[2] has been attended by a new migration in the capacity to sentence that has divorced sentencing from sense. Decisions concerning punishment are issued through demographic formulae developed by executive branch policy makers, in keeping with the demands of a government of population. As Simon and many others have noted, the establishment of sentencing guidelines and mandatory minimum sentencing laws have contributed significantly to the contemporary phenomenon of "mass" imprisonment. The effects of this shift have been well documented by Simon and others, but I think there is something more at work here as well, suggested by Simon but not developed in the way I hope to develop it in this chapter.

We might note the paradoxical idea of judges abandoning the responsibility to sentence. Sentencing, as Simon notes, has historically been a core function of the judge, an intrinsic element of judgment, but the shift to judgment by executive, not judicial, power in the United States suggests a macro shift in the body politic that has led us to the current state of affairs, in which war power and punishment power have been confounded (Simon, 264–266). What Simon does not pursue is how this new incarnation of a very old sovereign power, supposedly dispersed by the constitutional system of checks and balances, might contribute to yet another new investment in the body of what Foucault once called "the least condemned man."[3]

The establishment of the sentence as the denial of freedom for a period of time has been long noted as the appropriate form of punishment in liberal societies, which by definition value freedom above all. It would follow that a shift away from liberal freedom as a core value of a society ought to mean that there is also a shift in the evaluation of what the meaning of time without freedom consists of as well. One looks in vain for such a discussion among most liberals, who remain attached to working out the niceties of Rawlsian contractualism.[4]

---

[2] Jonathan Simon, *Governing Through Crime*. New York: Oxford University Press, 2007, 139–140.
[3] Foucault, *Discipline and Punish: The Birth of the Prison*. New York: Pantheon, 1977, trans. Ian Sheridan, 31.
[4] In that regard, see the Rawlsian-inspired essay on punishment by Corey Brettschneider, "The Rights of the Guilty: Punishment and Political Legitimacy," 35.2: *Political Theory*, 175–199 (2007), and the subsequent exchange, between Brettschneider and Frank Lovett, in 35.6: *Political Theory*, 806–815 (2007).

We come closer to thinking about embodiment and the meaning of the sentence in discussions concerning torture, because torture as punishment shifts the focus from the primacy of psychic pain of punishment as denial of freedom to the primacy of physical pain through the infliction of directed pain on the body. In current political context, however, the focus on the legitimacy or illegitimacy of torture does not, for the most part, ask us to attend to the meaning of punishment in this sense. Whether, for example, the rise in executive acceptance of torture to elicit testimony by held suspects can be shown as a sign of a shift in the meaning of the sentence is dubious, because it does not touch on the idea of torture as punishment but only as an instrument of interrogation.[5] This lack of discussion is no doubt a result of the prohibition on cruel and unusual punishment, a prohibition that leads us to conclude that in a liberal polity, torture cannot be made into a form of punishment. As Colin Dayan comes close to suggesting in the concluding pages of her brief history of the Eighth Amendment, an examination of both the amendment's origin – as a restraint on the *degree* of physical punishments, such as whippings, that were permissible by slave owners – and of the amendment's severely diminished applicability to the practical effects of conditions in prisons as a result of recent Supreme Court decisions (effects that by any common-sense standard are tortuous in effect if not clearly in intent), makes it possible for us to imagine how, under the right political circumstances, which this country has come close to experiencing, torture could be resurrected as a form of punishment in the United States. Whether such a polity could subsequently claim to be liberal and whether the American polity can even now be described as liberal could be doubtful.[6]

The question I wish to pose concerns how such a shift in punishment from time to torture might reflect other shifts in American political culture. How to frame the question of the sentence in terms that permit us to consider relevant questions concerning culture presents some difficulties. One place to begin might be to look to a cultural tradition that discusses embodiment and the sentence from yet another perspective. Western understandings of embodiment have been strongly influenced by

---

[5] On this question see David Luban, "Liberalism, Torture, and the Ticking Bomb," in *The Torture Debate in America*, edited by Karen Greenberg. New York: Cambridge University Press, 2006, 35–83. I address Luban's argument at greater length later.

[6] See, for example, Sheldon Wolin, *America, Inc.* Princeton: Princeton University Press, 2008.

theological and more specifically Christian thoughts about the meaning of life, the question of secular and sacred time, and the issue of judgment.[7] In what follows, I want to trace one thread of the contemporary shift in judgment through what I think is a contemporary dilemma of Christian faith. To be clear, I am not interested in theological argument as much as I am in the late Christian experience of the potential loss of faith itself and how Christians resist that loss. By rethinking the question of torture as punishment through the perspective of what we might call the contemporary culture of Christian fundamentalist faith, I hope to highlight how the shift that has occurred in our understanding of the meaning of life – a shift deeply connected to the emergence of the biopolitics of security – has the potential to transfigure the meaning of the sentence dramatically.

Jesus Is Dead

The headline on page A10 of *The New York Times* for February 27, 2007 read "Crypt Held Bodies of Jesus And His Family, Film Says." James Cameron, maker of the films *Titanic* and *The Terminator*, made a documentary film for the Discovery Channel that presents evidence that Jesus and Mary Magdalene were married, had a son named Judah, and that they and Mary and Joseph, and Mary's brother Matthew were all placed in the same burial crypt, in six inscribed burial boxes, or ossuaries. The inscriptions on the boxes are of their names, and although such names were common in the day (as common as Tom, Dick, and Harry said one of the team), a statistician determined that the odds of coincidence – that another grouping of such names could have occurred as coincidence – was at least 1 in 600 and possibly as high as 1 in 1 million. The evidence for the marriage of Mary Magdalene and Jesus is the fact that the residues of mitochondrial DNA found in their boxes showed that they were not closely related. "'A lot of conservative, orthodox and moderate Christians are going to be upset by the recklessness of this,' said Ben Witherington, a Bible scholar at Asbury Theological seminary in Wilmore, KY. 'Of course,

---

[7] For a trenchant and compelling reading of judgment in capital sentencing based on a a reading of Nietzsche's history of an error, see Jennifer Culbert, *Dead Certainty: The Death Penalty and the Problem of Judgment*. Stanford: Stanford University Press, 2008. I am deeply indebted to this work for clarifying some of the important issues surrounding the relationship of judgment to the history of truth.

we want to know more about Jesus, but please don't insult our intelligence by giving us this sort of stuff. It's going to get a lot of Christians with their knickers in a knot unnecessarily.'"

We could say that what we have before us is just another example of the two competing paradigms for understanding the meaning of Jesus and his life – on the one hand, the scientific, and on the other, the theological. The penetration of ancient life by use of the techniques of contemporary scientific technology is certainly not unprecedented. The Shroud of Turin has been subject to carbon dating, the search for Noah's ark has been the subject of archeological investigation, and even the plagues of Egypt have been scrutinized by forensic archeologists, to set the dates of the flight of the Jews and provide natural explanations for storms of toads and swarms of locusts. One could also point toward other schools of thought, for example, twentieth-century psychoanalysis, which in the body of Freud's work especially (aside from providing a new explanation for belief in God, in *The Future of an Illusion*) presents evidence about the identity of Moses that both explains the power of monotheism as an idea and undermines the Biblical tale of Moses's identity as a Jew (in *Moses and Monotheism*).

There is something else at work here that is worth noting, however. Namely the very investigation into the death of Jesus and that of his mother, Mary, calls into question two core tenets of Catholicism, as they are embodied in the dogmas first and foremost: from the fourth century, the resurrection of Jesus and his ascent into heaven and, from the nineteenth century onward, of the assumption of Mary, body and soul, into heaven.[8] The residue of genetic material is all that is left, because, as the article states, "There are no bones left, because the religious custom in Israel is to bury archeological remains in a cemetery." We therefore have the destruction of evidence of the mortality of Jesus and Mary as a consequence of official Israeli respect for the Jewish tradition of burying remains. This could be considered an irony.

A striking feature of the comment of the theologian from Kentucky is his insistence that Christians want to know more about Jesus, and just not

---

[8] For a critical discussion of the establishment of the resurrection as an article of Christian faith, see William E. Connolly, *Capitalism and Christianity, American Style*. Durham: Duke University Press, 2008, Chapter 5. On the establishment of the Assumption as an article of faith in the nineteenth century, and more generally on the cult of Mary, see Marina Warner, *Alone of All Her Sex: The Myth and the Cult of the Virgin Mary*. New York: Alfred Knopf, 1976.

the sort of "stuff" that is made available to them by statistical and DNA analyses. The knowledge that they do not want is knowledge of the physical body of Jesus, which for Catholic dogma to be accepted must not be found to exist on Earth. The power of science to piece together evidence that favors the dissenting body of early Christian writing – what are known as the *Gnostic Gospels* – undermines the orthodoxy concerning the form of godliness that Christ's body took when the authors of the conventions of Catholicism first allied themselves with the powers of empire. There is something more than this, however; there is a sense of offense, at the blasphemy, at what must be considered a violation of not only the body of Christ but also the humanity of Christ that is also under attack. In short, the intervention of modern science into the ancient scene of death seems to deny that death its dignity.

Dignity, worthiness, value, and the comportment of the self in a way that emphasizes the integrity of the body and the coherence of the self has a history. It is associated perhaps most closely with the history of manners and what I have elsewhere labeled as the migration of sovereignty, a migration that is concomitant with the emergence of modern individuality.[9] One of the great ironies of the current controversy about Jesus is the superimposition of our contemporary understandings of the autonomous self back to the body of the single person in history who might have been most responsible for the eventual emergence of that very self, but whose historical circumstance and trajectory of life were nothing like what we humans now experience. In opening Jesus to our contemporary sense of autonomy, we must cross back through the medieval to the ancient sense of self, to make claims for Jesus and the value of His life that are incommensurate with the time when he walked the Earth but that are all too relevant to our contemporary sense of what constitutes our dignity.

So the question becomes the following: What knowledge do these Christians want? It is our presumed knowledge of the meaning of life and death that shapes our postures toward it. For Christian believers, the problem with probing Jesus's DNA is that it risks reducing his life to the biological, when for the modern believer the core meaning of his life lies precisely in his simultaneous defiance of and submission to the biological. Jesus was born

---

[9] See Dumm, *Michel Foucault and the Politics of Freedom*. Washington, DC: Rowman and Littlefield, second edition, 2002, Chapter 2.

of man to redeem us. Jesus died for our sins to give us an opportunity for eternal life. An alternative theology to orthodox Catholicism would have emphasized the humanity of Jesus. Indeed, that is what the excluded books of the New Testament did, establishing an alternative relation of Jesus's life to his death, one that did not emphasize the eternal but the temporal, placing an ethos of responsibility on the world as the center of life. In fact, the book of Phillip, which is mentioned in the article as providing the name of Mary Magdalene, describes the marriage of Jesus and establishes Mary Magdalene as an apostle. Sometimes it appears as though the history of Protestantism is no more than a series of attempts to return to this sense of the humanity of Jesus, although even here something is evaded.

I wish to argue, perhaps perversely, that death is now more undignified than it once was. In fact, death is so undignified that as our history of manners has advanced, our shame over the circumstances of death has also intensified, in turn deepening our desire to evade death's facticity.[10] In what follows, I shall explain why I think death is undignified and then try to illuminate the problem by referring to the case of Terri Schiavo. From the Schiavo case I derive a generalization about the meaning of a sentence based on the understandings of the human that have been contested in the wake of the struggle over her neomorphic status. This struggle, a political struggle, seems to confirm the worst fears of Giorgio Agamben about what he calls the zone of indistinction between life and death and yet provides grounds for rethinking the terms of life so that the question of the sentence becomes more closely associated with the meaning of life than ever before.

Death and (In-)Dignity

"Man is an obligate aerobe." So said Hippocrates, and so it is.[11] We depend on air, oxygen more specifically, and dying is finally no more and no less than the end of oxygenation of the organs of the body, whether through trauma, disease, or contamination. What happens to the body is not pretty

---

[10] A classic investigation into the American avoidance of the facticity of death is Jessica Mitford, *The American Way of Death*. New York: Simon & Schuster, 1963. In another register, see Norman O. Brown, *Life against Death*. Middletown: Wesleyan University Press, 1959, especially Chapter 16, "The Resurrection of the Body."

[11] I am dependent on Sherwin Nuland, *How We Die: Reflections on Life's Final Chapter*. New York: Knopf, 1994, for much, although not all, of what follows in this section about what happens to the body at death.

and is indeed ugly, aesthetically repulsive. This base process undermines the posture that allows for dignity. In fact, Nuland suggests: "I have not often seen much dignity in the process by which we die... The quest to achieve true dignity fails when our bodies fail"(xvii). Death is undignified because it is the ultimate loss of bodily integrity. The process of death involves the failure of organs, either suddenly or gradually, and as they fail strange things happen. For heart attack victims, eyes bulge as the heart fibrillates, and then turn glassy and blank. The elevated acidity of the blood of a suddenly dead person causes the voice box to contract, creating a rasping, whooping sound known as the "death rattle." Heart failure leads to brain failure, and the intervening minutes between the stoppage of the heart and death of brain often results in the release of the sphincter muscles and the ureter, leading to a voiding of bowels and bladder.

In slower deaths, for example those associated with congestive heart failure or the encroachment of lung cancer, the gradual shutdown of organs as the blood backs up because of inefficiencies of the heart–lung system results in a slow starvation, first of the extremities, which swell with excess fluid, and then those organs that are the most "blood rich" as environments, the kidneys, liver, and pancreas. These organs begin to fail, intensifying the levels of toxins in the blood, which contributes as well to further edema, more fluid settling in the limbs and in the lungs themselves. The dying person therefore begins to drown. This itself is a complicated process, because in response to the lack of oxygen, the body produces adrenalin, increasing the heart rate and making the person restless. At the same time that panic develops in the dying person, he or she becomes increasingly confused. Lack of oxygen to the brain results in the dying person's suffering disorientation, aphasia, hallucinations, and sometimes blindness. All of these events usually occur while the person is also in severe pain. As death approaches, the person's heart pumps harder and harder with less and less effect, eventually goes into fibrillation, and then stops. Brain death ensues shortly after.

Dying occurs in a variety of contexts. One of the struggles that we have as living beings is to comprehend the process of dying in such a way as to make it available to us as something other than as a thing in itself. This contextualizing of death leads to its mythologizing, and the mythologies are not necessarily true or false to the experience – they are instead one step removed from the actual dying. The physiological impact of dying is profound and harsh; rarely is there such a thing as an easy death, which is basically what Nuland wants us to remember as his message. Any meaning that we might try to extract from death, including the idea of dignified death, is something that is necessarily attached to histories of power, identity, and affective connections to each other. None of these attachments is necessary; they are perhaps the most contingent elements of human existence.

Does this necessarily mean that death is undignified? Simply put, if we can comprehend that death is the disintegration of the body through the loss of oxygen to its tissues, then we can claim that, to the extent that dignity is synonymous with or even closely related to bodily integrity, dying is by definition undignified. Bodily integrity itself is something that has a complex history, however, closely associated with the evolution of individual rights. It is also associated with a history of manners, the emergence of disciplined and docile bodies, bodies that are simultaneously understood to be ends in themselves, in the sense that they are the familiar bearers of our rights, and utilitarian, as the useful bodies of modern political economy.

If there is a decline in dignity, it might be a sign that we are entering an era of postdiscipline and a concomitant decline in rights, a time when the usefulness of disciplined bodies for the needs of the political economy might be called into question, when the metastasizing prisons have less to do with discipline and more to do with disposing of surplus bodies. Many who have studied the current system of criminal punishment in the United States see this development with dismay, because of the cruelties that it has imposed on millions of our fellow citizens. This development might also offer us a clue about how death and dignity might become unraveled from each other and, in turn, that eventually might tell us something about what sentencing means in an era when the meaning of life itself has shifted its basic registry.

Let us return to the moment of death itself. From an existential perspective, Alphonso Lingis has written of the gradual withdrawal from the world of those who are dying, their functions fading, vacating a space to be filled by others. The time of dying, he emphasizes, is like no other time. "Dying takes time; it extends a strange time that undermines the time one anticipates, a time without a future, without possibilities, where there is nothing to do but endure the presence of time. What is impending is absolutely out of reach...."[12] As one gets closer to death, the world begins to fall away and becomes less intelligible. Even as the dying person withdraws from the world, he or she becomes more intelligible to him- or herself, because of becoming closer to experiencing what is beyond experience, not simply unknown, but something that could be said to be epistemologically incoherent, something beyond the pairing of known and unknown. Lingis teaches that we withdraw *from* the world and *into* the world as death approaches. This falling from and into the world could be called the loss of self, except that it is the most self-aware, most personal, and most individuating moment of life, in which we become a member of the community of those who have nothing in common. "The shadow of death circumscribes, in the unending array of possibilities that are possible for anyone, what alone is possible for me" (169).

Lingis writes as the last sentence of his book on this community of nothingness, "The grief, when the other has been taken and no medication or comfort were possible, understands that one has to grieve" (179). The nothing that grief teaches is this, that one has to grieve what is taken – not from me or from you, only taken. The caregiver, who is soon to be the griever, goes toward the dying person to touch that person while that person is still touchable and while that person is still capable of the comfort that a touch might bring, while that person is still alive. "The touch of consolation is not itself a medication or protection; it is a solicitude that has no idea of what to do or how to escape.... The touch of consolation is an accompaniment, by one mortal and susceptible to suffering, of the other as he sinks into the time that goes nowhere, not even into nothingness" (178). When that person is gone we grieve, but we no longer touch the person, because as Lingis knows, the lost one is no longer touchable.

Was that person ever touched? How can any one of us know the answer to such a question? To experience the untouchable character of the death of someone whom we have touched and who has touched us is to experience the death of that person as an inverted form of birth. That which we imagine as a part of us is separate now; the separation is occasioned by the sinking

---

[12] Lingis, *The Community of Those Who Have Nothing in Common*. Bloomington and Indianapolis: University of Indiana Press, 1994, 173–174. Subsequent references are in the text. I develop this argument as well in Chapter Four, "Grieving," in Thomas L. Dumm, *Loneliness as a Way of Life*. Cambridge: Harvard University Press, 2008.

into nowhere of the other. For Lingis the imperative is found in the ethics of our responsible attention to the other in suffering and enjoyment. We might experience an enjoyment that is a consequence of how we embrace the imperative, how we trust ourselves, or how we notice the other. So often our lives turn around in moments when we are unaware of what we are doing. In this sense, more of life is retrospective than not. Shame comes to us when we reflect backward and see our failure to look forward. If the conditions of our possibility are known to us only retrospectively, then we are surely lost and not to be found again. To die out of nature, to enjoy ourselves, is to think forward, prospectively, to imagine what Emerson once evoked as a new way of being and to hail the prospect of a new yet unapproachable America. The final prospect for everyone, and for those yet unborn, is still the experience that leads us to nothingness.

This experience of nothingness is unintelligible, no matter how close we come to thinking of it. This is a key reason that we have developed the idea of death with dignity. This idea connects dying with living; it is an artifice that establishes a continuity between life and death. No matter how discontinuous those states might be in their sheer facticity – in the sense that dying is not living – the artifice also establishes a connection to the dead for those of us who still live. When we are under the pressure of new knowledge, it becomes less possible to deny that falsehood, and a recalibration of our mythologies of dying needs to be undertaken. The new mythology, what we might call a post-Heideggerian mythology, seems to have a profound effect on what we think of and how we come to execute sentences, because sentences are currently closely tied to our understanding of the meaning of life as the continuation of time, and life in turn is closely associated with this way of thinking about the experience of death as an ending of time.

The new mythology also is an abandonment of an older way of imagining our humanity as a part of what Carl Schmitt has called "the political." For Schmitt, the claim of the political is related deeply to our understanding of the meaningfulness of death. As Tracy Strong notes in his foreword to a recent English translation of *The Concept of the Political*, "To claim [that inquiry into the political was an inquiry in the "order of human things"] was to claim that the possibility of dying for what one was was the final determining quality of the human. Schmitt's existential Hobbesianism thus saw moral claims as implicitly denying the finality of death in favor of an abstract universalism in which human beings were not particularly involved in what they were."[13] The danger, as Schmitt seemed to see it, is that a depoliticization of life would lead to circumstances in which the willingness to die for one's identity as a member of a nation comes to be displaced, through a more acute awareness of our fear of dying, to a hope to live in a state of security. Such a state of security seems to abandon explicit claims of state sovereignty, but abandonment only disguises and never vanquishes sovereign power. Abandonment rather leads to a hidden politics of governmentality, in which the mutual interpenetration of state and society implicitly politicizes all questions of life and death.[14] As Schmitt puts it,

> The equation state = politics becomes erroneous and deceptive at exactly the moment when state and society penetrate each other. What had been up to that point affairs of state become thereby social matters, and, vice versa, what had been purely social matters become affairs of state – as must necessarily occur in a democratically organized unit. Heretofore ostensibly neutral domains – religion, culture, education, the economy – then cease to be neutral in the sense that they do not pertain to state and to politics. As a polemical concept against such neutralizations and depoliticizations of important domains appears the total state, which potentially embraces every domain. The results in the identity of state and society. In such a state, therefore, everything is at least potentially political, and in referring to the state it is no longer possible to assert for it a specifically political purpose.[15]

If we examine the particular interpenetration of the state and religion as represented by the case of Terri Schiavo, we might be able to see how this struggle concerning the meaning of death, once contained within a more limited realm of "the political," extends throughout all relationships of state and society. A concomitant shift in the meaning of the "sentence" then reveals itself.

---

[13] Tracy Strong, "Forward," in Carl Schmitt, ed., *The Concept of the Political*, expanded edition, trans. and intro. George Schwab, with notes by Leo Strauss. Chicago: University of Chicago Press, 2007, xvii.
[14] Foucault, *Territory, Security, Population*, 211.
[15] Schmitt, 22.

Terri Schiavo's Death

Terri Schiavo's death on March 31, 2005 elicited this comment from President George Bush: "I urge all who honor Terri Schiavo to continue to work to build a culture of life where all Americans are welcomed and valued and protected, especially those who live at the mercy of others.... In cases where there are serious doubts and questions, the presumption should be in the favor of life. The most solemn duty of the American president is to protect the American people. Since September 11th, 2001, we've taken bold and vigorous steps to prevent further attacks and overcome emerging threats."[16] In linking national security to the culture of life, Bush seems to enact with some precision Michel Foucault's description of modern political regimes, which emphasize the deep continuities between bio-power and national security, as well as Schmitt's characterization of the shift in the relationship of citizen to state, such that the interpenetration of state and society leads to a conflation of religion, culture, security, and state power.

In his comment, Bush is echoed by James Dobson, who, in a letter appealing for funds to lobby Congress sent to hundreds of thousands of supporters following the death of Schiavo, linked her death both to support for gay marriage and opposition to the death penalty for minors by what he termed an antidemocratic, judicial tyranny.[17] One might imagine that there is a significant question concerning the politics of life in the form of an Agambenian enactment of the zone of indistinction between the human and the nonhuman that leads him to see the modern nomos as being that of a camp. I want to suggest something else, however, to go behind Agamben to his other source (the first being Foucault), and briefly think of both Schiavo and the search for the body of Jesus as examples of the power of the Christian ethos of life as it is refracted through the secularization of society. I suggest that Arendt's understanding of the priority of life itself in the modern era, leavened by a more acute sense of the polymorphous power of social embarrassment, explains much of the intensely felt reaction to the dying Schiavo by latter-day Christian politicians.

---

[16] My citations to much of the Schiavo material is taken from the Web site abstractappeal.com, which has an extensive Schiavo archive. I am also relying, in this draft, on unpublished essay by Ruth Miller, Assistant Professor of History at UMASS, Boston, entitled, "On Freedom and Feeding Tubes: Reviving Terry Schiavo and Trying Saddam Hussein."

[17] See James Dobson, "Life, Death and Judicial Tyranny," at FocusontheFamily.com.

In section 44 of *The Human Condition*, Arendt argues the following:

> The reason why life asserted itself as the ultimate point of reference in the modern age and has remained the highest good of modern society is that the modern reversal [that of *animal laborans* over *homo faber*] operated within the fabric of a Christian society whose fundamental belief in the sacredness of life has survived, and has even remained completely unshaken by, secularization and the general decline of the Christian faith.... It is precisely individual life which now came to occupy the position once held by the "life" of the body politic, and Paul's statement that "death is the wages of sin" since life is meant to last forever, echoes Cicero's statement that death is the reward of sins committed by political communities which were built to last for eternity... life on earth may be only the first and the most miserable stage of eternal life; it still is life, and without this life that will be terminated in death, there cannot be eternal life (314–316).

This deep claim that the life philosophy of Christianity persists through the secularization of the world does not originate with Arendt, and she acknowledges the work of Max Weber throughout her ruminations. It is quite interesting to note, however, that the general decline of Christianity that she describes, although it might have reflected a mid-twentieth-century view of European political life, was not even then true of the circumstances of the United States in the decade in which she wrote this work, prior to what we might call the fundamentalist revival. It is certainly is not true for the circumstances of the contemporary world, which has seen an enormous resurgence of fundamentalist religious belief worldwide. It could be that this revival is simply a reaction formation in a group psychological sense, a response to the ongoing event of the death of God. This would account for some of the virulence with which the supporters of Terry Schiavo advanced their case, going so far as to pass laws through Congress to continue her on life-support systems.

Nonetheless, there is more than reaction at this level that attends the struggle over the body of Terry Schiavo. She continued to live precisely as a consequence of the technological advances of modern medicine, as a result of one of the most distinguishing features of modern life, modern science. A silent irony of all discussions of life itself is its relationship to the technological sublime – that is, the science (fictional) aesthetic that allows us to imagine life as immortal, those advances of biology and physics that have enabled us to penetrate, in one particular sense, the mystery of life itself. This was supposed to be God's territory: now it is the domain of humankind. Christians, rather than being struck by this paradox of knowledge, or an appreciation of the powerful claims concerning synthetic immortality posed by the existence of the aesthetic itself, plow onward, supporting life in all of its guises.

If life is all, however, why is it so bad that we are intimately involved in these processes that sustain and allow it? Arendt's usual response is that modern science has contributed to the domination of labor and made more difficult the possibilities for action. What might be called the Christian inability to appreciate the aesthetic aspect of the life-sustaining techniques that are a part modern science is also shared by Arendt, who in the end sees modern science as participating in a disastrous undermining of the possibility of political action through the determinacy of cause and effect. This position is an all-too-common reduction of scientific knowledge but enjoys a predictable currency in an era of technologically produced disasters. As Connolly has convincingly shown in his recent writings, however, the idea that scientific knowledge is deterministic at the level that perhaps neurologists are working is simply mistaken. The mistake, however, has consequences in the life of the culture.[18]

Those Christians who wanted the life of Terry Schiavo to be sustained indefinitely by means of advanced medical technologies saw in the withdrawal of her support systems an act of murder, in the form of a disallowance of life. Their embrace of science at this level – its resulting support for life in this instance – and their silence on the withdrawal or denial of other supports for the evasion of death for others through stem cell research, or less controversially, the development of HIV-AIDS medications and prevention tools (i.e., condoms, which could save lives) are impossible to reconcile with their faith in a Christian God who rules over nature. This is bad faith, in the form of cherry-picking, and because it is a bad-faith gesture that informs the support for Terri Schiavo against her husband, it accounts for some but not all of the vociferousness of their attempt to intervene in her dying.

It might be an uncomfortable truth, but Terri Schiavo's life condition was itself undignified. All of the attempts by those who wished her life to

---

[18] See William E. Connolly, *Neuropolitics*. Minneapolis: University of Minnesota Press, 2005.

be sustained to emphasize her humanity came across as pathetic, precisely because she palpably demonstrated her lack of awareness on every occasion that her awareness was insisted on. They would say she smiled when she grimaced, or that her eyes were following a balloon when her eyes were rolling back in her head, or that there was brain activity when she was lacking higher brain function. Each emphasis only demonstrated what was not there. The very failure of her embodied self to *be* turned her supposed supporters' argument into a grotesque parody.

They persisted, however. They insulted her husband, accused judges of acts of murder, physically tried to force themselves into the hostel where she lay dying to give her water (which she would have been unable to swallow), insisting that this was an attempt to save her life. The truth is that her dying was to be one of those rare ones, lacking in the terrible pain and base violence that accompanies most of us as we go away. Most of her suffering had already occurred when she collapsed so many years before.

Schiavo's autopsy revealed what every reputable neurologist had already testified to in court, that her brain had been devastatingly injured from oxygen deprivation on the evening that she suffered her heart attack. At the insistence of the governor of Florida, she was also examined to determine whether there were signs of physical abuse against her. (There was an unverified rumor, spread through Internet gossip, that her husband had choked her to death.) No signs of such abuse were found. Of course, the autopsy report failed to satisfy those who insisted that new evidence might be found.

The insistence on the examination of the body of Terri Schiavo could be contrasted with the twenty-first-century posthumous struggle over the body of Jesus, which conservative Christians insist must be left alone. In both cases there is a doubt that runs deep below the surface of belief. Schiavo's life was to be sustained because it is a sin to allow someone to die, even or especially when that person wants to die. This is called suicide, and because, according to Christian doctrine, our lives belong to God, the worst thing that one can do is to end one's own life. It is the deepest defiance of God's will. Schiavo had to be made a victim of others so that she would not be accused of this sin, and yet it was also the case that a deep cruelty at the heart of Christianity risked exposure here. The very sovereignty of God when coupled to the power of modern medical science creates a new nightmare for the faithful, the sustaining of life when it is no longer a meaningful life, the nihilism of the meat puppet. This danger is especially great for those who are most dogmatic in their belief; hence we witness the intensity of their struggle.

To penetrate the body of Jesus with the tools of modern science creates the risk not of reanimating him but of the opposite, providing him with a final death certificate. He would not only be merely dead but truly most sincerely dead, and with that death the meaninglessness of the life philosophy of Christianity would be revealed in all of its nihilism.

The New Sentence

We might contrast the cruelty of the exercise in keeping Terri Schiavo alive with the force-feedings that have been exercised at Guantánamo Bay (and that follow on a tradition of force-feeding, going back at least to the British treatment of IRA prisoners in Northern Ireland or the suffragettes of the early twentieth century).[19] The power to sustain or disallow life is in the hands of those who run the prison. Force-feeding a prisoner who refuses to eat is a painful process for the prisoner, a tube inserted down the throat against one's will, the accompanying confinement, strapped to a cot under continuous surveillance. At its core, however, force-feeding is an exercise of the sovereign right to allow or disallow life, only in this case and perhaps in more and more future cases, put negatively, as the power to refuse to allow life to end on its own terms. In this strange state of affairs, the bio-political power to allow and sustain life comes to be the bio-political power to force one to live. Mercy in the form of sustaining life therefore becomes a punishment.

To imagine sustaining life as a form of torture links the experience of the unconvicted prisoners of Guantánamo with the convicted prisoners inhabiting the supermaximum prisons of the United States. The tortuous aspect of the form of punishment associated with supermax units is well documented.[20] The more ordinary prison experience associated with the increasingly constrained reach of the Eighth Amendment is also well known. The elision of temporality and confinement with torture does not yet suggest that torture itself is what convicted criminals are sentenced to suffer; instead, what is entailed in torture is a withdrawal of law itself.

---

[19] See "Guantanamo Force-Feeding Tactics Are Called Torture," by Josh White, *The Washington Post*, Wednesday, March 1, 2006, p. A08.

[20] Op. cit., Dayan, 54–56, with references to the relevant literature on 96–97.

Such a situation is anticipated in the classic Harlan Ellison science fiction short story, "I Have No Mouth, and I Must Scream."[21] In this story, a nuclear war world conducted through the use of computers comes to an end when one of those computers achieves self-awareness, proceeds to absorb the other computers into itself, and launches an all-out and successful attack on the human race, carefully saving the lives of only five humans beings, doing so for its own sadistic pleasure, torturing them but also sustaining them. The prisoners keep trying to kill themselves to be relieved of this torment, but the computer keeps them alive. They are virtually immortal, but their immortality is a terrible one.

As is often the case with science fiction, this story anticipates a contemporary technological development – the advent of virtual immortality through the union of machine and body.[22] Of course, the future is never what it is expected to become, and futurists make such predictions as inspirational devices for those working in the bowels of artificial intelligence laboratories at MIT as much as they do because they are convinced that the new Utopia is around the corner. This aspiration itself tells us something, however. In presenting the idea that life persists into an indefinite but vastly extended future, the futurist also presents two implicitly correlative ideas: first, that time has become meaningless as a measure of punishment, and second, that death becomes a much more absolute sentence than it is when the idea of immortality is still associated with religious faith. The first idea, of course, is a result of imagined capacity of the machine/body fusion to repair itself continuously, upgrading and replacing its constituent parts. The second is a more subtle result of what we might call the "Schiavo affect." A consequence of the Christian desire to keep ourselves alive as long as we can becomes secularized in an era when we may be able to live as virtual immortals. We become the gods that we once thought that we would join in the afterlife.

In another sense, the legal situation of torture might be thought of as inhabiting an Agambenian zone of indistinction. The withdrawal of the law, the reduction of life to mere life, and the sustaining of that life in neomorphic forms are all associated with stripping bodies of their personhood. As Dayan points out in an earlier essay, however, the status of the person in

---

[21] First published in the magazine *IF: Worlds of Science Fiction*, March, 1967, this story went on to win the 1968 Hugo Award for best science fiction story.
[22] See Ray Kurtzweil, *The Singularity Is Near: When Humans Transcend Biology*. New York: Penguin, 2005.

prison, even in civil death, does not entail a total effacement of personhood as much as personhood's shadowy redeployment in a postslavery context.[23]

It remains to be seen what the constituent elements of such a personhood might be. Given the potential decoupling of the relationship of time to punishment suggested by the Schiavo case, the forced feeding of prisoners who wish to die, the ongoing willingness of the United States government to allow the torturing of those whom they suspect of being terrorists, and a culture that is becoming increasingly familiar with the secular goal of a virtual immortality, we might already have reached a threshold. Dayan notes the comment of Rear Admiral Harry Harris, camp commander at Guantánamo, after the suicide deaths of three prisoners there. "I believe this was not an act of desperation, but an act of asymmetrical warfare waged against us."[24] She suggests that the admiral, despite the obscenity of his remark, might have understood something, that these prisoners were fighting against the updating or the recrudescence of an older form of punishment, the cruelties of the old form returning to us in an ironically "humane" form.

One might think of the prisoners who killed themselves as inhabiting the same psychological space as those fictional survivors described in "I Have No Mouth, and I Must Scream." In the face of such hellishness, who will be the first liberal humanist to suggest that there must be a more moderate way, that a carefully measured degree of pain – a limb amputated here, a branding there, the imposition of a series of electric shocks, confinement in the dark for a regulated period – might be the humane reform needed by our current standards of sentencing? Which would be worse, the argument might go: an endless time in prison in which we know that we are unable to control the pain suffered by this convict or a calibrated, limited, potent, and physically painful mortification of that convict's body, followed by his or her quick release back into society, debt paid, no pretense at rehabilitation made but no further misery?

---

[23] Dayan, "Held in the Body of the State: Prisons and the Law," in Austin Sarat and Thomas R. Kerans, eds., *History, Memory, and the Law*. Ann Arbor: University of Michigan Press, 1999, 229–232.

[24] Op. cit., Dayan, *The History of Cruel and Unusual*, 92.

7

The Child in the Broom Closet
States of Killing and Letting Die

Elizabeth A. Povinelli

The Child in the Broom Closet

Ursula Le Guin's "The Ones Who Walk Away from Omelas" tells the tale of a city, Omelas, where the happiness and well-being of its inhabitants depend on a small child being constrained to and humiliated in a small, putrid broom closet.[1] It is critical to Le Guin's fiction-based ethical wager that Omelas's happiness is not ideological in Louis Althusser's sense nor is it naive. It is experientially unmediated, materially substantive, and morally desirable. This happiness is what every average Joe and moral philosopher would wish for, but it nevertheless depends on a child's being constrained and humiliated in a cramped space and on this being known by all Omelas inhabitants. Some actually visit the child's fetid chamber. Some have merely heard of it since they were children themselves. Every member of Omelas, however, must assume some relationship among his or her present personal happiness, the present happiness of the millions inhabiting Omelas, and the present suffering of one small human being. Some offer facile excuses for preferring their happiness to the child's. At this point, they reason, the child is "too degraded and imbecile to know any real joy."[2] She is so destroyed and so used to her destitution that liberating her would do more harm than good. Others face the true paradox. For them "their tears at the bitter injustice dry when they begin to perceive the terrible justice of reality, and to accept it."[3] Others leave Omelas but not

---
[1] For the Jamesian influence, see Linda Simon, "William James's Lost Souls in Ursula Le Guin's Utopia," *Philosophy and Literature* 28.1 (April 2004): 89–102.
[2] Ursula Le Guin, "The Ones Who Walk Away from Omelas," in *The Norton Anthology of Short Fiction*, ed. R. V. Cassill. New York: W. W. Norton, 2006, 862–866, 866.
[3] Ibid.

en masse. They leave one by one: "The place they go is a place even less imaginable to most of us than the city of happiness. I cannot describe it at all. It is possible that it does not exist. But they seem to know where they are going, the ones who walk away from Omelas."[4]

"The Ones Who Walk Away from Omelas" was conceived as a fictional counterpoint to William James's "The Moral Philosopher and the Moral Life" and more broadly to the moral philosophy of American pragmatism, of which James was a leading voice.[5] James begins his essay with the position that "there can be no final truth in ethics any more than in physics, until the last man has had his experience and said his say."[6] This ethical position was deeply influenced by the semiotic musings of James's colleague Charles Sanders Peirce. More specifically, James borrows Peirce's understanding of the temporal and modal structure of the "final interpretant" and applies it to the question of ethical truth. For Peirce, the interpretant is a sign that establishes a relationship between two other signs – Paul de Man's act of critical reading.[7] Ethical readings of the kind that interested James have a specific temporal and modal structure: the future anterior. They are the "toward which the actual," as the sum total of all interpretants, "tends."[8] It is what will have been the ultimate truth, good, and justice, after every last human has had his or her experience and say.

Le Guin disagrees with this account of time, possible worlds, and ethics. Why she disagrees opens a productive avenue for critically engaging the imaginary and practical relationship of late liberal subjects and institutions to the unequal distribution of life and death in democratic orders. Le Guin's alternative ethics depends on altering three ways in which liberal subjects normally encounter the social time, meaning, and scale of suffering and lethality. First, as opposed to those who would read ethics from

---

[4] Id.
[5] See Louis Menand, *The Metaphysical Club: A Story of Ideas in America.* New York: Farrar, Straus, & Giroux, 2002.
[6] William James, "The Moral Philosopher and Moral Life," in *The Will to Believe and Other Essays in Popular Philosophy.* Cambridge, MA: Harvard University Press, 1979, 141.
[7] Paul de Man, *Allegories of Reading: Figural Language in Rousseau, Nietzsche, Rilke, and Proust.* New Haven, CT: Yale University Press, 1982.
[8] Charles Sanders Peirce, "Letter to Lady Welby," in *Semiotic and Significs: The Correspondence between Charles S. Peirce and Lady Victoria Welby,* ed. Charles S. Hardwick and James Cook. Bloomington: Indiana University Press, 1977, 110–111.

the perspective of ends, Le Guin insists that because there is no horizon in which this child could be incorporated into the material and emotional good of the city without that good being compromised, the ethical nature of the relationship between the residents of Omelas and the child in the broom closet cannot be deferred to some future anterior perspective – what will have been the meaning of this suffering from the perspective of a future interpreter we cannot as of yet know. As a result, the ethical relationship that links the citizens of Omelas to the child in the broom closet must be radically present tense. Second, any goods generated from the kind of misery found there must be seen as socially cosubstantial as well as temporally nontransferable. My happiness is substantially within her unhappiness; my corporeal well-being is part of a larger mode of embodiment in which her corporeal misery is a vital organ. As a result, the ethical imperative is not to put oneself in the child's place, nor is it to experience the anxiety of potentially being put in her place. Le Guin rejects the ethics of empathy. Instead, the ethical imperative is to know that your own good life is already in her broom closet, and as a result, either you must compromise on the goods to which you have grown accustomed (and grown accustomed to thinking of as "yours") or admit that these goods are more important to you than her suffering. To be sure, Le Guin seems to provide readers an exit from this grim worldview. Some residents, although only one by one, walk away from Omelas. Why does she allow them to do so? Perhaps Le Guin could not bear the claustrophobic character of her ethical statement, but perhaps the world into which they walk compromises the good – and the goods – to liberate the child. Finally, the nature of the suffering that interests Le Guin is ordinary, chronic, acute, and cruddy rather than catastrophic, eventful, and sublime. Every so often the child in the broom closet is given a kick, but for the most part her misery is a quieter form of abjection, despair, and impoverishment. There is nothing spectacular to report. Nothing happens that rises to the level of an event. Life drifts into a form of death that can be certified as due to "natural causes." As a result, any ethical impulse dependent on a certain kind of event and eventfulness flounders in these closets.

This essay is not a critical reading of Le Guin's story; even less is it an extended reflection on American pragmatics. Instead, in this essay I examine the forms, modes, and discourses of lethality in contemporary

Australia, focusing first on the contemporary carnal conditions of indigenous life and second on recent state security measures said to be a reaction to the post-9/11 world. I do so to understand the dynamic conditions that qualify one kind of lethality as "state killing" and another as a more amorphous condition, of "letting die." I do so to understand how present-tense modes of living and dying are transformed into future anterior modes of the proper life. My argument is that a specific catachresis between the security state and the neoliberal market – between the sovereign state and bio-political state – animates contemporary late liberal attitudes toward various forms of living and dying that so interested Le Guin. What makes this catachresis interesting theoretically, as well as socially, is that it comprises qualities of state practice at one and the same time apprehensible by a Schmittian model of the sovereign state and by a Foucauldian model of the bio-political state.

Australia is a good example of how this catachresis is unfolding in late liberal societies. As will become clear, Australian forms of governmentality have strong institutional and discursive ties to the U.S. neoconservative movement. Former prime minister John Howard advocated state powers that would enhance the government's ability to designate friends and enemies and to declare special legal statuses for enemies that would cast them outside normal democratic principles and procedures. At the same time, Howard's government advanced the bio-political regime of the neoliberal global market ever more deeply into the recesses of the social order, producing and distributing divisible forms of life, qualities, vitalities, and borders as well as their agencies and powers. The market does this not through the kinds of spectacular events that the sovereign state causes, references, and defends against, but through the kinds of events the visibilities of which are so dispersed into the background conditions of ordinary life that to refer to them as "events" seems strange and awkward. It is my contention here that if we want to understand state killing in contemporary late liberal societies, then we need to look at how this dynamic intersection of the security state and the neoliberal market – the sovereign state and bio-political state – helps to secure a specific "imaginary" about the agencies of life and death, making the content of different kinds of ethical statements and actions practical or impractical, self-evidently true or absurd, coherent or incoherent, sane or mad.

In the Broom Closets

Late liberal societies hardly lack the kinds of dingy broom closets that so interested Le Guin. No less than the citizens of Omelas, members of these societies are fully aware of the existence of such situations in their polis and make decisions about the relation between them and their own well-being. These fetid spaces are often the occasion for public hand-wringing, outrage, and scandal. In Australia, for example, indigenous rural and urban communities are open broom closets of poverty, disease, and despair. Since 1969, one year after the federal government was given the power to legislate on behalf of indigenous Australians, the commonwealth government listed health as one of four domains for indigenous development. In 1976, the commonwealth government commissioned the House of Representatives Standing Committee on Aboriginal Affairs to conduct a review of Aboriginal health. It released its report in 1979, the contents of which were so scandalous that the commonwealth government started a $50 million five-year Aboriginal Public Health Improvement Program in response. The program, administered by the Department of Aboriginal Affairs, focused in particular on inadequate water, sewerage, and power systems in rural Aboriginal communities.[9] Unfortunately, the crisis in indigenous health has continued to make front-page headlines, periodically prompting the organization of special inquests and parliamentary committees at the federal and state levels and the reorganization of government agencies responsible for indigenous health, education, and welfare. This long-standing and appalling state of indigenous health periodically prompts the question of what, or who, is to blame and consequently what is to be done.

It is a somewhat arbitrary decision to begin the history of the lethal conditions of indigenous worlds in 1969. Since colonization, British administrators, the Australian state, and a variety of domestic and international publics have asked and answered the questions of what and who is to blame

---

[9] Summarized from Australian Indigenous HealthInfoNet, "Indigenous Health Policy Timelines," www.healthinfonet.ecu.edu.au/html/html_programs/programs_policy/ programs_policies_timelines.htm (accessed December 27, 2007). See also Ian Anderson, "The National Aboriginal Health Strategy," in *Health Policy in Australia*, ed. Heather Gardner. Melbourne: Oxford University Press, 1997, 119–135.

for the fetid state of indigenous life. Prior to the federal government's listing health as one of four critical domains in indigenous affairs, not merely indigenous health but the rapid loss of indigenous life was discussed, explained, and managed in terms of a series of historically fluctuating accounts of the causes and cures of social pathology. In the early years of Australian federation, the lethal conditions of indigenous life were justified in social Darwinian terms. "Full-blooded" indigenous subjects would be allowed to live a somewhat traditional life as they faded into human evolutionary history, whereas "mixed bloods" would be slowly interbred with the white population until all traces of cultural and genetic difference disappeared. From the perspective of a future world, in which indigenous people would be museum pieces, the immediate suffering of living people will have made ethical sense. But is this temporal location of the ethical end of indigenous suffering and death unique to social Darwinism? Is the ethical truth of the fetid conditions of indigenous life still apprehended through the future anterior – a form of future in which this misery would have been redeemed?

Contemporary answers to the question of who or what is to blame for the appalling conditions of Aboriginal health pivot between discourses and imaginaries of the social and individual causes of poverty. The Australian Institute of Health and Welfare, a bureaucratic arm of the federal government, reports a "relationship" between "socio-economic status and health... with people at the lowest socio-economic levels experiencing the highest rates of illness and death."[10] In Australia, indigenous people are the poorest of the poor. Not surprisingly, therefore, between 1996 and 2001, the life expectancy at birth was estimated at 59 years for indigenous men and 65 years for indigenous women, well below the 77 years for all Australian men and 82 years for all Australian women between 1998 and 2000.[11] Although the Australian Bureau of Statistics reports that "after adjusting for age differences between the populations, Indigenous Australians were

---

[10] Aboriginal and Torres Strait Islander Health and Welfare Unit, "Socio-Economic Context of Indigenous Health," Australian Institute of Health and Welfare, www.aihw.gov.au/indigenous/health/socio_economic_context_of_indigenous_health.cfm (accessed December 27, 2007). See also Yin Paradies, "A Systematic Review of Empirical Research on Self-Reported Racism and Health," *International Journal of Epidemiology* 35 (2006): 888–901, http://ije.oxfordjournals.org/cgi/content/abstract/dylo56v1.

[11] Australian Institute of Health and Welfare, *The Health and Welfare of Australia's Aboriginal and Torres Strait Islander Peoples*. Canberra: Government Printer, 2005.

twice as likely to report their health as fair or poor as non-Indigenous Australians," the bureau also notes that the statistics that they compiled are "likely to be underestimates of the true rates of illness in the Indigenous population because of the under-identification of Aboriginal and Torres Strait Islander people in these data collections."[12]

The statistics are dramatic, but the diseases are not. The typical illnesses that afflict indigenous people are chronic and endemic, infectious and cumulative, but not spectacular and catastrophic. They are the illnesses of the poor, typically staphylococcal and streptococcal infections, parasites such as scabies and giardia, circulatory diseases, diabetes, respiratory diseases, musculoskeletal conditions, kidney disease, eye and ear problems, and mental and behavioral disorders. It can be hard to see these illnesses in their normal physical state. Their effects on mortality are usually slow and corrosive, with one thing leading to another. For instance, the chronic nature of group A streptococcal infections contributes to diseases of the circulatory system for indigenous men and women, leading to hospitalization rates two to three times those for nonindigenous men and women. The risk of septicemia from chronic staphylococcal infections – which are common and for the most part untreated – in rural communities is constant. Even in indigenous communities with functional health clinics, the treatment of cruddy health moves through the international divisions of race. For example, in the indigenous communities where I live and work, health care policies stipulate that "sores" – which might be streptococcal or staphylococcal infections but in any case are never cultured – are treated only if a person has more than six on his or her body at any one time, even though in many cases the sores are necrotic and cellulitic.

In other words, the agent of infection might be pathogenic, but the vector of infection is related to socioeconomic factors – who you are and where, how, and with whom you live.[13] As a result, the answer to the question of what or who is to blame for the stubborn persistence of indigenous ill health can be quickly attached to contemporary accounts

---

[12] Aboriginal and Torres Strait Islander Health and Welfare Unit, "Health," Australian Institute of Health and Welfare, www.aihw.gov.au/indigenous/health/index.cfm (accessed December 27, 2007).

[13] See Jon Altman and Boyd Hunter, "Indigenous Poverty," in *Australian Poverty: Then and Now*, ed. Ruth Fincher and John Nieuwenhuysen. Melbourne: Melbourne University Press, 1998, 238–257.

of the causes and cures of poverty and especially to what is considered a social, as opposed to an individual, vector. After more than a decade of conservative leadership under Howard, Australia has witnessed a distinct shift from a strong social welfare state to a form of neoliberalism and its concomitant economic and dominant discourses of privatization and the individualization of wealth, value, and destiny. During his government, Howard pushed through the privatization of state holdings, including the airlines, telecommunications, and health care; rolled back social welfare; assaulted the trade union movement; and shifted the source of public care from the state to the private individual person and family.[14]

Given that discourses of poverty, ill health, and social pathology are increasingly saturated, especially at the state and business levels, by the logic of the neoliberal market, it should come as no surprise that the Australian Institute of Health and Welfare tempers any argument that poverty causes ill health with a bureaucratic proviso: "Socio-economic status does not alone explain the variations in health status that exist between groups in society."[15] According to this argument, to understand health status one must look beyond socioeconomic status to individual risk and "behavioral" practices. Socioeconomic status is not a risk factor for ill health, according to the institute. The sentence "poverty is a risk to your health" is not sensible within its language game because risks are restricted to the potentially harmful behaviors that a person chooses. Behaviors that put one at risk are associated with individual choice: immunization, smoking, diet and exercise, and high blood pressure. However we critically read this discursive separation of the social nature of poverty and the individual nature of behavior – and we should, I think, do so – it would still seem to create and conserve an explanatory space that links poverty to some supraindividual cause, a phenomenon not reducible to the aggregate of individual choice. For some reason, this separation transforms the social causes and social distributions of lethality into the responsibility of the individual person or his or her culture. State killing and its public sanction are transfigured into

---

[14] For instance, having finally gained control of both houses of Parliament in 2004, Howard radically transformed labor relations by introducing Australian Workplace Agreements. These individual agreements made between employer and employee replaced the "awards" system, in which pay packages were negotiated among the federal government, industry, and the trade union movement.

[15] Aboriginal and Torres Strait Islander Health and Welfare Unit, "Health."

a more amorphous agreement that people are killing themselves. Indeed, separating the socioeconomics of poverty and the behavioral choices of individual people seems to make it much more difficult to understand the state's withdrawal as a form of state killing. How does this transformation take place?

Sweeping out the Broom Closet

To understand how this separation sinks into various social worlds in such a way that those who suffer most from the socioeconomics of poverty take the most responsibility for this suffering, we need to move more closely into the nitty-gritty of everyday social life within the broom closets of late liberal states. Take, for example, an interaction between a young indigenous man in his late thirties and his family. The young indigenous man's social profile is typical of most people his age living in the community. Despite the horrific nature of the following account, if you met him, you would often see him in good spirits. This young man characterizes himself as an alcoholic. Like everyone in his family, he has had "sores" (staphylococcal and streptococcal infections) on and off since he was a child, bearing the scars on his body. He has high blood pressure but does not take his medication regularly. He was hospitalized for congestive heart failure, while his mother was in her last stages of oral cancer. His father died of a stroke when he was in his teens. His mother's youngest brother died years before of kidney failure associated with septicemia. His younger brother has a congenital heart condition. Three weeks after he was released from the hospital, his eldest sister was taken to the hospital with septicemia. The treatment resulted in massive congestive heart failure. Although told by doctors and family to stop drinking, this young man started drinking within a week of his release from the hospital. Furthermore, what would perhaps be more surprising to the sensibilities of many Australians, he demanded that his family members drive him to a local shop to buy alcohol with the money he had saved during his hospitalization. When family members refused, he angrily told them he could do what he wanted with his body. He knew the risks, and they were his to take. How he gambled with his life was his business. These were his words: *risk, gamble, my body*. Only the future could say whether he won or lost his gamble and was right or wrong in his approach to this world of misery.

Forty years his senior, his aunt vehemently disagreed not only with his account of the location of his risk but also with the underlying logic of his social imaginary. To his statement that his body was his alone, she replied, "No, that is not your body; that is my body. When you die, my body will suffer and die."[16] When she referred to her physical risk, this woman was not simply referring to a generalizable empathic form of grief. She was not saying, "I will mourn you as a person." Her brother was this young man's father. Thus, she and he share "one body": They are both *murumuru* (long yam), an ancestral being from which they both substantively descend as surely as an average nonindigenous Australian believes that he or she shares the genetic substance of his or her mother and father. In other words, the woman was attempting to mobilize a discourse of socially cosubstantial corporeality against her nephew's social imaginary of individuated bodies engaged in private wagers. His language of privatized loss, and its incumbent discourse of individual risk, was not met by the risk of another private loss but by an appeal to a cosubstantial distribution of life, health, and social being – a position much closer to that of Le Guin than to that of the young man.

The state and businesses do not greet these social imaginaries of lethality, individuality, and responsibility in the same way. They amplify and channel the nephew's rather than the aunt's social imaginary into agencies of social life in such a way that the one is sensible, practical, and productive, whereas the other is insensible, impractical, and sterile. By the time the aunt makes her argument, the language game of individual risk has already organized social, economic, and political life increasingly around the neoliberal view of her nephew – that bodies and values are poker chips in individual games of chance and that the social is an impediment to the production of value. This view has social ramifications that are especially hard on the poor. As Craig Calhoun concisely puts it, privatizing risk makes "individuals bear the brunt of hardships that are predictable in the statistical aggregate without effective mechanisms to share the burden, let alone reduce the risk."[17] Privatizing risk creates and fosters a language game in which the social is practiced as nothing more than an aggregate

---

[16] Conversation with author, at Belyuen, Australia, August 2005.
[17] Craig Calhoun, "The Privatization of Risk," *Public Culture* 18.2 (2006): 257–263. See also Tom Baker and Jonathan Simon, eds., *Embracing Risk: The Changing Culture of Insurance and Responsibility*. Chicago: University of Chicago Press, 2002.

The Child in the Broom Closet

of individuated risk calculators working according to mathematically predictable econometric models. I am not in you. You are not in me. We are merely playing the same game of chance, the truth of which lies not here and now between us but there and then in who wins and who loses. No one is killing me. I am killing myself. Maybe... we shall see... the future will tell.

"Are you killing yourself, yes, you are, and we will no longer help you do so." This is the answer that the current federal government gives in response to the question of what or who is to be held accountable for the lethal conditions in indigenous communities. Cultural and social logics of exactly the sort articulated by the aunt are, according to Howard, an impediment to the maintenance of a unified social fabric and to the fostering of an entrepreneurial spirit among indigenous people. Indeed, they are said to be the cause of poverty, along with long-standing federal and state commitments to indigenous social welfare. When indigenous people stop seeing their social worlds from the perspective of local cultural sense or from state-backed social welfare, then they will emerge from poverty and with this emergence they can gain the health that all other Australians have.

Then, then, then... local men and women are quite familiar with the temporal ethics of this future anterior. Needless to say, it is the aunt who is sober and the nephew who is not; the aunt is outside the logic of life as a set of privatized risks, but the nephew is not. Nevertheless, as an "incentive" to indigenous people to take up the nephew's position, Howard committed his government to withdrawing federal economic support from rural indigenous communities as part of the "mainstreaming" of indigenous people and policy. Is this withdrawal, seen throughout late liberal worlds, a form of state killing? Howard would say clearly not. In his corner are many indigenous men and women. Noel Pearson, an Aboriginal activist, has famously and forcefully argued that state welfare, when applied to indigenous peoples, is a technique of numbing indigenous and nonindigenous people to the radical state of dysfunction in Aboriginal communities.[18] For Pearson, indigenous subjects are so destroyed and so used to their destitution that only liberating them from a failed social welfare net and

---

[18] For a different approach to indigenous poverty, see Peggy Brock, *Outback Ghettos*. New York: Cambridge University Press, 1993.

local social imaginaries can save them. In the future, according to Howard, Pearson, and others, the young man's stultifying life will be shown to have been the vigorous beginning of a new day for indigenous welfare. The evidence will not be in for quite some time, of course.

What if we do not accept that the social welfare net and local social imaginaries are not working in some general way but only in a specific way? Why are they not seen to be working? What is not working? Take, for example, the local policies in many indigenous communities of not treating staphylococcal and streptococcal infections until a person has at least six active infections on his or her body. I have received several reasons why this policy is in place in poor indigenous communities. One reason is that health officials have to assess the risk of creating a drug-resistant form of staphylococci or streptococci as opposed to the value of clearing a person of infection; therefore, this reasoning goes, because indigenous persons living in indigenous communities are constantly reexposed to staphylococci and streptococci, their bodies should be allowed to fight off the infection until antibiotics are absolutely necessary. This risk analysis might make sense if it were not for the fact that these infections are rarely if ever cultured and that their treatment has not changed over the course of the last 20 years. When I first began living in indigenous communities in north Australia 22 years ago, amoxicillin or penicillin would quickly cure the infections that I had. Presently, doctors in indigenous communities continue to administer such medication, whereas doctors in the United States prescribe amoxicillin clavulanate (Augmentin). On amoxicillin clavulanate, my infections receded within a week. On amoxicillin or penicillin, they can persist for months and then reemerge – the same is true for my indigenous friends in Australia. How much would it cost to culture the various sores infesting indigenous Australians? How much to treat them with the proper antibiotics?

These questions need not be asked or answered when we are dreaming of future worlds in which no one has these sores or these life expectancies even as others are never impeded in their quest to accumulate as much wealth as possible. The actual cost-benefit analysis occurring, however, is not the balance between the risk of untreated staphylococci or streptococci versus the risk of developing a drug-resistant form, but the risk of untreated staphylococci or streptococci within certain populations and the cost of investing in poverty-stricken communities for the short or long term. The presupposition underlying the treatment of infections in indigenous communities is that the communities themselves will remain fetid. Within a neoliberal state, any social investment that does not have a clear end – a projected moment when input value (i.e., money, services, care) can be replaced by output value – is not merely economically suspect but morally suspect, no matter what the life-enhancing nature of the investment is. One example is a quite effective program on rural indigenous communities, the Community Development Employment Project (CDEP).

CDEP is an indigenous-specific work plan that was established in 1977 and run by the Aboriginal and Torres Strait Islander Commission until the Howard government dissolved the latter in 2005. As Jon Altman and M. C. Gray note, CDEP has been described as "a labor market program, an alternative income support scheme and a community development scheme," but whatever it is, CDEP has raised the personal income of rural indigenous men and women.[19] This basic fact, that a state-run social program increased the quality of life for the most disadvantaged, was judged a failure, however, because it did not project its own end – the movement of indigenous workers out of the program and into the market. As a result, the Howard government radically cut back positions available in the program and increased the reporting requirements for receiving social welfare. The young indigenous man whom I mentioned earlier was denied a position on CDEP because of cutbacks to the program. To be sure, when CDEP was a more robust alternative, he moved in and out of it. Even this use of the program, however, increased the gross numbers of days that he did not drink. Why is the cancellation of this support of life not seen as a form of state killing – a form of the death sentence? On the contrary, withdrawing this life support is considered a moral good. Somehow the refusal of this form of life contributes to the happiness of a majority of citizens, even though their own mortality and economic well-being have continued to increase regardless of the presence or absence of CDEP.

We should not be surprised by this way of assessing failed forms of state welfare. After all, the neoliberal weak state and strong market do not produce and distribute life, its qualities, vitalities, and borders, evenly or

---

[19] See the 2002 analysis of Jon Altman and Matthew Cameron Gray, "The Effects of the CDEP Scheme on the Economic Status of Indigenous Australians: Some Analyses Using the 1996 Census," http://129.3.20.41/eps/lab/papers/0408/0408003.pdf (accessed December 27, 2007).

equitably, nor do all forms of lethality produce the same qualities, visibilities, and intensities as others. Lethality is apprehended and perceived and is discussed, explained, and managed in terms of historically fluctuating accounts of agency, eventfulness, sociality, and normality. Even tsunamis, earthquakes, and hurricanes that generate terrific waves of empathy and generate moral capital for those who demonstrate outrage leave in their wake a nonplussed public. When the waters recede and the ground stops shaking, empathy also evaporates, as ethical sense settles back into doxic accounts of poverty and its causes and consequences. Cost reemerges as a central issue for how to calculate who can or should be protected, relocated, cared for. Here we see how prescient Le Guin's suspicion of the ethics of empathy is. Empathy asks us to put ourselves in someone else's shoes. What would it be like to be them? What would it be like to be in this tidal wave, that fetid broom closet, or that cultural condition? This very act – this ethical gesture – initiates a separation between you and me, however. I am not substantially the result of your tsunami or your staphylococci. As a result, to give to you can end up seeming like a taking away from me, because mine seems to be mine. Never has Le Guin's basic point that all goods are generated in a system of distributed misery seemed so hard to fathom, so impractical, and yet so close to liberal reality.

Captive Audiences

I would be surprised if most Australian citizens would confuse their mode of happiness with the mode of happiness of the fictional citizens of Omelas. Although they share some of the same characteristics, the broom closets perforating Australia do not work the same magic on Australians as they do on the citizens of Omelas. Things are not that good. The middle class is being squeezed as a new gap emerges between rich and poor. There are mortgages to worry about and new individual labor contracts to negotiate. In Le Guin's imaginary society, nothing but a robust happiness acts as a comparative backdrop to the everyday abuse of the small child. This is not so in Oz, however. True, like the fetid space in Omelas, indigenous communities are often cruddy, corrosive, and uneventful. An agentless slow death characterizes their mode of lethality: quiet deaths, slow deaths, rotting worlds. The everyday drifts toward death: one more drink, one more sore; a bad cold, bad food; a small pain in the chest. Unlike Omelas, however, these kinds of deaths only periodically fix the gaze of national and international publics. When they do, they do not do so in a way that unambiguously concretizes their ultimate or immediate cause, agent, and effect. Who is killing these people? What is killing them? Answers must yield to the complexity of an entire system. How might a subject within late liberal society dream of something decisive, clear, or sublime?

Late liberal subjects do not have to be lulled to sleep to see deathscapes with much clearer borders, agencies, and intensities. In contrast to cruddy, cumulative, and chronic lethality are special forms of enemies and spectacular forms of death that capture and rivet the imagination of late liberal societies and act as an alibi for the concentration and consolidation of state executive power. Certain kinds of enemies, events, and history are seen as having a spectacular, even sublime, quality: they cut time into a present-tense decisive ideological struggles and demand that exceptional measures be taken. Those within late liberal societies seeking to increase state surveillance powers cite these decisive kinds of enemies and devastating images of airplanes, nightclubs, and towers exploding and spewing forth singed and dismembered bodies. The lethal state of indigenous life hardly competes with the society of the terrorist spectacle: bodies in hoods, in naked piles, attached to real or fake electrodes. Bodies disappear only to reappear with drill marks. These forms of violence seem to oppose and stand outside of the everyday uneventful forms of misery and dying that characterize indigenous life. These new terrorist forms of death are spectacular in outward form. In appearing to be spectacular, they seem to create the ontological necessity to respond ethically – a demand that we take sides – and citizens and their governments do.

The Howard government cited both the bombing of Bali nightclubs and an omnipresent invisible domestic and international terrorist threat when it sought to modify the Crimes Act 1914. Passed in 2005, amendments to the Crimes Act gave the Australian Security Intelligence Organization the power to detain any person for up to seven days without charge if he or she is suspected on "reasonable grounds" of being involved in any terrorist activity. During this time, detainees are prohibited from exercising their rights to have a lawyer present, to silence, and to protect themselves against self-incrimination.[20] Although Australia does not have a declaration of rights

---

[20] Australian Anti-Terrorism Act, no. 2 (Cth.), 2005.

that enshrines freedom of speech in general, the High Court of Australia found a specific implied right of freedom of political speech in the 1992 *Australian Capital Television v. Commonwealth*.[21] It is exactly this more circumscribed right that the amendments to the Crimes Act assaulted. What has especially worried free speech advocates is the definition of terrorist activity under the "advocacy" clause. There a terrorist is defined as anyone who advocates the "doing" of a terrorist act, including praising "the doing of a terrorist act in circumstances where there is a risk that such praise might have the effect of leading a person" to commit "a terrorist act" or "advocates the doing of a terrorist act (whether or not a terrorist act has occurred or will occur)."[22]

These carceral forms of state power, premised on actual and potential spectacularly catastrophic mass deaths, incited mass protests and engaged public and private consciences. In November 2005, in major cities throughout Australia, thousands of people marched against the new crime amendments. The news media highlighted, and in some instances violated, the far-reaching scope of the new terrorist laws. Beyond the specific crime amendments, these protests were aimed at what many left/progressives saw as the Howard government's forging an uncritical alliance with the Bush administration that compromised fundamental Australian principles of social and personal justice. For example, although Australia has a long history of strongly opposing the death penalty domestically and internationally, since the Bali bombings of October 2002 there has been a significant silence about the death penalty for "terrorists." Although no troops are stationed in indigenous communities shooting at armed and unarmed resistance to the lethal state of indigenous life, police have faced a number of indigenous riots in places such as Red Hook, Palm Island, and, most recently, Aurukun, after alleged police abuse and murder. The Howard government has stationed Australian troops in foreign nation-states as part of a humanitarian effort. For example, troops entered East Timor putatively to stop the carnage that erupted as Indonesia withdrew; however, critics argued that after decades of refusing to intervene against Indonesian atrocities in the region, the government was merely attempting to gain strategic control over the Sunrise Oil Field. Likewise, critics saw the Australian

---

[21] *Australian Capital Television Pty. Ltd. and Ors v. Commonwealth*, (1992) 117 CLR 106.
[22] Australian Anti-Terrorism Act, no. 2 (Cth.), 2005, schedule 1, section 9.

intervention in the Solomon Islands as compromised by the government's refusal to publicly renounce a first-strike policy in the Asian Pacific and its continual references to the Islamic fundamentalist infiltration of the Pacific through Southeast Asia.

There is serious debate about why Howard, whose government predated the U.S. Supreme Court appointment of George W. Bush in 2000 by four years, made such a firm commitment to the international unilateralism of the U.S. neoconservative movement. Some have argued that Howard is a "true believer," whose political thinking ultimately derives from Milton Friedman's school of laissez-faire capitalism developed at the University of Chicago during the same time that Leo Strauss taught there.[23] As a result, so this story goes, Howard's foreign policy could be easily adapted to the Straussian neoconservativism of the current Bush administration with its deep resonant ties to Carl Schmitt's theories of political theology. Others have insisted that Howard is an extraordinarily skilled modern prince, astutely morphing his party's message to fit shifting public anxieties about the location of economic, social, and political threats and never letting belief get too much in the way of securing and holding power. Whether believing or not, Howard's allegiance to the liberal democratic parliamentary system seems shaky, if not outright hostile, to some of his critics. Ian Duncanson argued that the Howard government reflected a "kind of Peronism" in which the separation of powers, foundational to liberal democracies, was replaced by elections in which "victories become empty mandates to pursue previously undisclosed or hitherto non-existent policies" and by "opportunistic opinion polls" in which "majority opinions act as plebiscites on single issues."[24] Indeed, Howard's refusal in the mid- to late-1990s to countenance even a hint of contemporary national responsibility for past historical wrongs carried out against the indigenous population foreshadowed rather than reflected the U.S. neoconservative disdain for guilt-saturated liberalism.

For whichever reason, this strong state rhetoric continually foregrounds and creates spectacular scenes of killing. Two examples suffice. One occurred in late August 2001 as the U.N. World Conference against Racism

---

[23] Robert Garran, *True Believer: John Howard, George Bush, and the American Alliance*. Sydney: Allen & Unwin, 2004.

[24] Ian Duncanson, "The Peronist and the Ghost in the State of Australia," *Law/Text/Culture* 8 (2004): 107, 111.

in Durban, South Africa, was under way. The Norwegian *Tampa* picked up some 433 asylum seekers who found themselves trapped on a sinking ship as they traveled from Indonesia to Australia. The asylum seekers were mainly Afghani people fleeing the Taliban. The *Tampa* sought to drop off its unintended passengers on Christmas Island. On August 27, Howard declared that the asylum seekers would not be allowed into Australia or Australian territory, including Christmas Island. Instead, Howard pushed ahead with the so-called Pacific solution, the use of economic incentives to entice the near-bankrupt state of Nauru to establish a detention center for asylum seekers attempting to enter Australia. As many have noted, Nauru agreed to set up these detention camps in exchange for Australian foreign aid after its material resources had been exhausted by a history of British and Australian extractive capital. Still more shocking was Howard's stance on the "children overboard" controversy. It was alleged that some families threw their children overboard to force the government's hand. Howard figured this decision as a sign of the barbarous cunning of these asylum seekers.[25] Prior to the establishment of the security state in Guantánamo Bay (which, as we know, swept up the Australian David Hicks), Howard was testing how far the international community was willing to go to stop what he and his government readily admitted were potentially permanent detention camps. These camps were just, argued Howard, because they were good for Australian nationalism. Very quickly, international human rights groups at the Durban conference, as well as members of the United Nations, denounced the Pacific solution as a violation of the U.N. refugee convention.[26] How could they not, if for no other reason than, as in the post-9/11 U.S. mantra that the government must protect "the homeland,"[27] Howard's "Pacific solution" had shocking resonances with fascist rhetorics of World War II?

It is important to note that mandatory detention has been part of the migration policy of Australia since 1992, and that it was a Labour government that removed the 273-day limit on mandatory detention. In other

---

[25] John Warhurst, "The Australian Federal Election of 10 November 2001," *Australian Journal of Political Science* 37 (2002): 153.

[26] For example, see Amnesty International, "MV Tampa and the Pacific Solution Fact Sheet 07," www.amnesty.com.au/refugees/ref-facto7.html (accessed November 10, 2007; site no longer working).

[27] See "Dissent from the Homeland," special issue, *SAQ* 101.2 (Spring 2002).

The Child in the Broom Closet

words, it is not simply the neoconservative movement that is responsible for the fetid conditions in detention camps on Nauru and Manus Island and on Australian soil such as at the Woomera Immigration Reception and Processing Centre. As early as 1998, Amnesty International cited the mandatory detention of adults and children as a violation of human rights, noting that the U.N. Human Rights Committee had found Australia in violation of the International Covenant on Civil and Political Rights. In the eight years that followed, various U.N. committees and commissions have investigated the conditions of detention camps in Australia. In July 2002, a delegation from the office of the U.N. High Commissioner for Human Rights stated that the camps were "offensive to human dignity."[28] Later that same year, the U.N. Working Group on Arbitrary Detention characterized this detention regime as bordering on the extrajudicial because of its "automatic and indiscriminate character, its potentially indefinite duration and the absence of juridical control of the legality of detention."[29]

The Howard government steadfastly refused the recommendations of Amnesty International, the U.N. Human Rights Council, the U.N. Working Group on Arbitrary Detention, and other human rights advocates, arguing that the detention policies were lawful because they had been written into law under the Migration Act since 1992. There is no humanitarian exemption if the government lawfully states the exemption of certain humans from humanitarian conditions. The Australian High Court has agreed, finding in favor of the government in two cases decided in 2004. In *Behrooz and Ors v. Secretary of the Department of Immigration and Multicultural and Indigenous Affairs*, the High Court found that the inhumane conditions of the detention camps did not annul their legality.[30] In *Al-Kateb v. Godwin*, the High Court found that unsuccessful asylum seekers could be held indefinitely in these same fetid camps if they could not

---

[28] The press widely reported this comment, made by Prafullachandra Natwarlal Bhagwati, special advisor for Asia and the Pacific and UN envoy to the UN Human Rights Commission, after his visit to the Woomera Detention Facility in 2002 and the Howard government's immediate reaction. See "Australia Rejects UN Criticism on Camps," BBC, August 1, 2002, http://news.bbc.co.uk/2/hi/asia-pacific/2165661.stm (accessed April 12, 2005).

[29] See Amnesty International, "Mandatory Detention Fact Sheet 2002," www.amnesty.org.au/resources/fact_sheets/refugees/mandatory_detention_of_asylum_seekers_-_fact_sheet (accessed November 10, 2007; site no longer working).

[30] *Behrooz and Ors v. Secretary of the Department of Immigration and Multicultural and Indigenous Affairs*, (2004) HCA 36, 125–132.

be returned to another country.[31] Hunger strikes, mouths sewn shut, the absence of physical and mental health facilities: the law easily survives the inhuman conditions that it creates, fosters, and inhabits. It was only after the 2006 discovery of two seriously mentally ill Australian citizens mistakenly confined in these camps – one of whom claimed, as part of a psychotic delusion, that she was German – that the Howard government reversed state policy. Mandatory detention was abolished, and asylum seekers can now challenge their confinement.

A second example of the kinds and modes of eventfulness characterizing the strong state and riveting public response occurred in July 2006 as Israel began a sustained attack on Lebanon. Devastation to southern Lebanon and Beirut was massive, as was the humanitarian crisis. The news media showed extensive footage of refugees streaming down roads as Israeli jets bombed nearby, refusing to guarantee civilians safe passage. Various states organized the evacuation of their national citizens from Lebanon, hiring cruise liners and freighters and making room on military vessels. The Australian government's effort to hire a vessel to evacuate its citizens was continually stymied, however. Members of the large Lebanese community in Australia accused the government of abandoning its citizens and, according to some, doing so because of its support of the Israeli offensive. Strongly protesting any suggestion that it was in any way slow to respond, the federal government insisted that the real cause of the crisis was the weak Lebanese state. As the crisis dragged on amid images of bodily and material carnage, members of the conservative public added another culprit to the weak Lebanese state: they openly questioned how much public finance should be spent on evacuating people who were dual citizens and spent most of their time in Lebanon. Were these "real" Australians? Did they not choose to put themselves in harm's way? The federal government vigorously denied that these kinds of questions affected its actions, insisting that the problem was purely logistical. Other state and public events leading up to the war, however, provided a fertile discursive ground for suspicions of a new virile form of racial discrimination in Australia: the government passage of new security laws in 2005, said to address domestic and international Islamic terrorism; the public race riots in Cronulla in 2005; and the ongoing public debate about the loyalty of Muslim clerics

---

[31] *Al-Kateb v. Godwin*, (2004) HCA 37, 241.

The Child in the Broom Closet

and immigrants, especially Sheikh Feiz Mohammad, who now resides in his ancestral village in north Lebanon. On July 22, 2006, 20,000 people marched in Sydney against the Israeli attack of Lebanon and the government's attack on Muslim civil rights.

No Exit

Any attempt to understand the social imaginaries characterizing lethal conditions within late liberal societies must take into account the two very different forms, modes, and qualities of killing found there: strong and weak state killing and the modes and forms of agency, causality, and eventfulness on which they rely. I began this essay by noting that from the perspective of state security, we are witnessing the emergence of a mode of "governmentality" with closer ties to Schmittian sovereignty than to Foucauldian bio-politics. Thus, the Australian government could blame the weak condition of the Lebanese state – its inability to disarm Hezbollah – for the war itself and for the humanitarian crisis that it triggered. From another angle, however, the bio-political regime of an increasingly weak post-Fordist state continues to spread its practical ideology of agency and value deeper into the tissues of everyday life. New organizations of production, circulation, and consumption produced in the wake of the Keynesian state continue to dismantle any "collective structures which may impede the pure market logic."[32] Even Australia, with its strong history of social equity (as opposed to the more vapid value of social equality), is slowly installing neoliberal markets and cultivating the neoliberal subjects who will occupy them.

It is at the intersection of these state and market forms and forces that the lethal condition of late liberal societies must be understood. They also must be understood not merely in terms of the facts on the ground but also in terms of our scholarly attachments to certain modes of time, eventfulness, and ethics. The security state's ability to capture countervailing energies and imaginaries is not restricted to those who march, protest, and organize against the security state; it also includes those who think critically inside and outside the universities.

---

[32] Pierre Bourdieu, "The Essence of Neoliberalism," trans. Jeremy J. Shapiro, *Le Monde diplomatique* (December 1998), http://mondediplo.com/1998/12/08bourdieu (accessed February 15, 2008).

How do we critically reflect on the conditions of lethality in late liberal societies when life and its imaginaries are located at the catachresis of these strong and weak states? It seems to me that two avenues must be pursued. Along the first, we would examine violence and lethality from a perspective that does not assume the qualities, vitalities, and borders on which neoliberalism defines life itself. Several scholars have been pursuing this project. In her recent book, *Life and Words*, Veena Das notes on anthropological attachment to the kind of violence that characterizes the catastrophe. Concentrating on social being in the wake of two catastrophic events – the gendered violence during the partition of India and Pakistan and the massacre of Sikhs in the wake of the assassination of Indira Gandhi – Das argues that it is not only the events themselves that are world annihilating but other modes and slow rhythms of death in their wake.[33] How do scholars find the right distance or right scale from which to sketch the "slow rhythms" of this lethal violence? This is indeed the question: how do we focus attention on the broom closets of late liberalism in the context of the spectacular machine of the killing state? Likewise, in a recent essay, Lauren Berlant juxtaposes forms of bio-power within the current regime of capitalism to the forms of sovereign power accumulated by the terror state.[34] Her case study is obesity. Her aim is to make visible endemic forms of death that are experienced as the attenuated background conditions of ordinary life and are resistant to typical accounts of causality, subjectivity, and life making.

One tactic that all of us use to make visible and compelling the nature of dying in these zones of slow death is statistics. By design, statistics transfigure one kind and mode of eventfulness into another. They transform borders, qualities, scale, and agency of one kind of eventfulness – if we can even use the term *event* in the domain of the chronic, slow, but as-yet unrealized form of lethality found in indigenous worlds – into another. As I am sure Das and Berlant are well aware, however, the deployment of a statistical imaginary to awaken a slumbering critical public and reason faces a central paradox. By transforming the invisible, dispersed, and uneventful into the visible, compact, and eventful, statistics obliterate the

[33] Veena Das, *Life and Words: Violence and the Descent into the Ordinary*. Berkeley: University of California Press, 2006.
[34] Lauren Berlant, "Slow Death (Sovereignty, Obesity, Lateral Agency)," 33.4: *Critical Inquiry*, 754–780 (2007).

very nature of this kind of death. Rather than understand this kind of lethality within its own terms (its dailiness, ordinariness, "livedness"), we demand that it conform to the spectacular event and the ethical dictates of empathic identification. As a result, nothing new happens. No alternative ethical formations are initiated. It is not even very clear how these statistics puncture the inured nature of suffering in local communities. Many indigenous friends of mine do not see the deaths in their communities as a form of state killing, unless an agent of the state – such as a police constable – literally kills them. The cruddy, cumulative, and corrosive aspects of life have spread so deep into the everyday that, as Ludwig Wittgenstein says, nothing more I can say other than that is what is.

This takes me to the second avenue that we might pursue. On this avenue, life is defined not by some redemptive future but by the understanding that *this is what is*. No future will have made it anything else. No present can be divided in such a way that what I have – my body and its health, my things, my affects – is not cosubstantial with what you have and do not have. We hardly have to have the same things, the same desires, tastes, languages, or aspirations, but the tighter the neoliberal market ties us all to one scale of value, the looser the post-Fordist state's grip on any ethical obligation to the health and welfare of its citizens and the more wakeful late liberal subjects are to what time it is and the more gripping Le Guin's simple ethical paradox becomes. Everyone must decide if his or her happiness is worth the suffering of those within the fetid broom closet. In this world where we live, there is no exit. We can change only the distribution of life and death so that some have more and some have less.

8

The Lethality of the Canadian State's (Re)cognition of Indigenous Peoples

Mark Antaki and Coel Kirkby*

In 1982, the Canadian state constitutionally "recognized and affirmed" the "existing Aboriginal rights and treaty rights" of its indigenous peoples. The constitutional turn to recognition promised reconciliation between nonindigenous Canadians and Canada's indigenous peoples. This chapter uses "recognition" as an entry point to reconsider some of the (legal) events marking the Canadian state's relations to indigenous peoples. More specifically, this chapter traces recognition's failure to overcome the Canadian state's lethal cognition of indigenous peoples. Because we dwell on how *re*-cognition discursively repeats cognition in one specific context, we seek neither to show that the discourse and practice of recognition are always and necessarily lethal nor to contribute directly to the theoretical literature that treats the classic texts on recognition. First, we identify the state as the political form of lethality, locating the lethality of the state in "cognition," in how the state knows, and hence how it sees and speaks. Second, we turn to the *Royal Proclamation*, the *Indian Act*, and the *White Paper* to show cognition at work in the attempt to make indigenous peoples legible, so as to rewrite them as members of a simplified Indian population. Finally, we illustrate the persistence of cognition in recognition by considering the constitutional promise of an honorable speech grounded in a proper sight of indigenous peoples. By examining the Supreme Court of Canada's interpretation of section 35 of the *Constitution Act, 1982*, we

---

* Assistant Professor, Faculty of Law, McGill University. Doctor of Philosophy (Ph.D.) candidate. University of Cambridge, Faculty of Law. We thank Kirsten Anker, Brenna Bhandar, Benjamin Berger, Jennifer Culbert, Robert Leckey, Alexandre Lefebvre, Stewart Motha, Alexandra Popovici, and Grégoire Webber for their helpful comments.

show how recognition continues to reduce indigenous peoples to populations and is tied to an understanding of reconciliation as submission to Crown sovereignty.

The Lethality of State Sight and Speech

Off the mainland coast of the northeast Pacific lies an archipelago shaped like an inverted thunderhead. Its islands seem to mirror the ever-present cumulonimbus clouds that cling to the mountains curling down their western shores. Constant showers feed the thick rainforests covering the land. Spruce, pine, and hemlock rise up from the sodden forest floor. The tallest of all is the red cedar, which grows to over 200 feet high, tall enough to block the sun. To the uninitiated, the endless procession of red-brown columns appears marred by occasional trunks bearing ancient wounds. These marks have healed imperfectly, enveloped by successive annual rings. Archaeologists have named these "culturally modified trees"[1] to acknowledge the people who marked them, the Haida. The Haida have relied on the trees for at least as long as the oldest of the marked trees. The red cedar was especially prized. Haida chiseled out planks for houses and blocks for canoes, and harvested bark in long strips peeled from the living tree. Cedar bark was so useful that it was called "every woman's older sister".[2] These practices rarely killed a tree, and thus left the old-growth forests largely intact. Trees were felled only, and then rarely, to carve *gyáa'aang*, or "totem poles," that once lined the seaward shores.[3] Wrought by master carvers from flawless red cedars, the *gyáa'aang* linked the Haida – translated as "the people," like many other names of indigenous peoples[4] – to their misty archipelago, Haida Gwaii, "the Islands of the People."

---

[1] Nancy J. Turner, Marianne Boelscher Ignace and Ronald Ignace, "Traditional Knowledge and Wisdom of Aboriginal Peoples in British Columbia," *Ecological Applications* 10 (2000), p. 1275.
[2] Marrianne Boelscher, *The Curtain Within: Haida Social and Mythical Discourse*. Vancouver: University of British Columbia Press, 1988, p. 22.
[3] Robin K. Wright, *Northern Haida Master Carvers*. Seattle: University of Washington Press, 2001, pp. 5–7.
[4] Indigenous polities who call themselves by names that translate as "the people" include the Anishinabek, Gitxsan ("people of the Skeena"), Innu, Inuit, and Tlingit. Not all refer to themselves by a word translated as the people, however. Roy Fabian, chief of K'atlodeeche, explains regarding the Dene, "'De' meaning river or the radiance of the sun, and 'Ne' meaning

The death of peoples *as* peoples – just as the death of forests *as* forests – is not accidentally related to the state. Indeed, to ask about the statehood of a state is to ask about lethality: "A state? What is that? Well! open now your ears to me, for now I will speak to you about the death of peoples," says Nietzsche's Zarathustra.[5] In Nietzsche's account, "state" appears as the name of a historically situated political form – not as the timeless name of political entities. Moreover, "state" might be better understood as the name of a way of being-in-the-world than as the name of an (albeit abstract and mysterious) entity or actor. The death of peoples is tied to how the state knows (cognition) and sees. In *Seeing Like a State*, Scott uses the "invention of scientific forestry in late eighteenth-century Prussia and Saxony" as a "metaphor for the forms of knowledge and manipulation" that characterize the state.[6] Scott describes how the state came to see its forests and also, crucially, "the degree to which it [state seeing] allowed the state to impose that logic [state speaking] on the very reality that was observed."[7] The sovereign speech of the state seeks to remake *what* it sees, according to the logic of *how* it sees.[8]

How does the state see? In our words, the state sees "statically." With the rise of "static" sight, "nature" is transformed into, and known as, "natural resources."[9] This way of seeing differs radically from the naturalist's or

earth; we believe we're from mother earth": 'The Meaning of Dene' Arctic Peoples Website. Visited 13 February 2008 <http://www.arcticpeoples.org/2005/12/28/the-meaning-of-dene>.

[5] Friedrich Wilhelm Nietzsche, *Thus Spoke Zarathustra*. Baltimore: Penguin Books, 1969, p. 75

[6] James C. Scott, *Seeing Like a State: How Certain Schemes to Improve the Human Condition Have Failed*. New Haven: Yale University Press, 1998, p. 11. We do not properly dwell on the nature of the relation between knowing and seeing in the present chapter. In Ancient Greek, to know (*eidenai*) is to have seen. See, for example, Liddell and Scott, *An Intermediate Greek-English Lexicon*. Oxford: Clarendon Press, 1889, at 226–227.

[7] Op. cit., p. 14.

[8] Compare with the sequence of "Understanding, Taking Possession, and Destroying," a chapter title in a work dealing with the Spanish conquest of the Americas: Tzvetan Todorov, *The Conquest of America: The Question of the Other*. New York: Harper &Row, 1984.

[9] Scott, *Seeing*, p. 13. The O.E.D. traces "state" to the Latin *stare*, to stand, and "static" (by way of the Latin *staticus*) to the Greek *statikos*, causing to stand. A proper thinking through of "static sight" would likely include some struggling with Heidegger's reflections on technique. With technique, what is is revealed as *Bestand*, or "standing reserve." *Bestand* is to be distinguished from *Gegenstand*, or "object." In this chapter, we do not dwell on the important, yet difficult, distinction between *Gegenstand* and *Bestand* – two ways in which beings come to stand for or before human beings; however, our pairing of object and static sight is more easily seen or heard in the German. See Martin Heidegger, "The Question Concerning Technology" in *The Question Concerning Technology and Other Essays*. New York: Harper & Row, 1977, p. 3.

The Lethality of the Canadian State's (Re)cognition

anthropologist's way of seeing the forest.[10] A state looks at a forest and sees a natural resource: a cedar becomes lumber; a copse of young firs, a wood lot; and the forest itself, a timber supply area. State sight does violence to the forest *as* a forest. It rationalizes and transforms what it sees into objects amenable to calculation and mastery. In the state's eyes, an ancient red cedar is not "every woman's older sister" but so many cubic feet of lumber. As Scott points out, "[a]t the limit, the forest itself would not even have to be seen; it could be "read" accurately from the tables and maps in the forester's office."[11] "Legibility," a keyword in Scott's characterization of state sight, emerges as a solution to the "blindness" of the "premodern state" that "knew precious little about its subjects."[12] The newfound legibility brings with it its own willful blindness: "simplification."[13]

As the state sees (or reads), so it in turn speaks (or [re]writes). To borrow Nietzsche's words, "[c]oldly lieth it also."[14] Through its speech, the state seeks to transform the legible objects of its cognition to conform better to its vision. Just as the forest is denatured into a "one-commodity machine,"[15] so too do standard measures and national languages tied to "uniform, homogenous citizenship" displace varieties of local knowledge, sight, and speech.[16] Contemporary international law illustrates this displacement by understanding statehood in part through the two principle criteria of "a permanent population" and "a defined territory."[17] States see and speak populations and not peoples, territories and not homelands.[18] By its very sight and speech, the state kills peoples *as* peoples.[19]

---

[10] Scott, *Seeing*, pp. 12–13.
[11] Op. cit., p. 15.
[12] Op. cit., p. 2.
[13] Part I of *Seeing Like a State* bears the title "State Projects of Legibility and Simplification."
[14] Nietzsche, *Zarathustra*, p. 75.
[15] Scott, *Seeing*, pp. 19–20.
[16] Op. cit., p. 32.
[17] Article 1 of the Convention on Rights and Duties of States, 26 December 1933, 165 L.N.T.S. (the Convention's criteria reflect customary international law).
[18] This displacement is tied to Foucault's account of bio-politics in which "population" is a keyword. The state's lethality towards peoples is tied to its power to make live, to manage biological populations. See, e.g., Part Five, "Right of Death and Power over Life" of Michel Foucault, *The History of Sexuality, Volume 1: An Introduction*. New York: Vintage Books, 1978. As Nietzsche puts it, "a death for many here has been devised that glorifies itself as life." Nietzsche, *Zarathustra*, p. 76.
[19] We turn to Nietzsche (and Scott) to emphasize the state's lethality toward peoples as peoples and not simply toward indigenous or so-called non-Western peoples.

The Haida felt the lethal gaze of Nietzsche's "cold monster"[20] when colonial authorities declared Haida Gwaii to be the "Crown Colony of the Queen Charlottes." A smallpox epidemic struck the islands a few years later and killed at least one in five Haida.[21] Some survivors, newly converted by an Anglican missionary whose first rule was for his converts to "give up deviltry (sic)," pulled down the *gyáa'aang* of their villages to erect crosses in their place.[22] Not all Haida rejected their *gyáa'aang* as pagan idols, however, nor did they all embrace Nietzsche's "new idol": the state.[23] *Gyáa'aang* were finally condemned when a federal law banned the potlatch, a complex ceremony that often culminated in the raising of a new *gyáa'aang*.[24] The few surviving *gyáa'aang* were uprooted and transported to the colonial capitals of Victoria (on Vancouver Island) and, across the Atlantic, in London. One especially fine pole reached the British Museum in 1903, where an academic lamented "[t]he decline, in the native estimation, of the importance of these totemic columns."[25] Looking back over a century later, Charlie Swanson, a chief of the neighboring Nisga'a people, recalled "when the potlatch was banned, along with totem poles, and dance blankets. Our culture was condemned at that time."[26] Grasping the death of peoples as the condemnation of culture might itself reflect state lethality. As we shall see, rather than belonging to a people, "culture" is often better grasped as an attribute of a member of a population.[27]

---

[20] Nietzsche, Zarathustra, p. 75.
[21] Boelscher, *The Curtain Within*, p. 13.
[22] John R. Henderson, "Missionary Influences on the Haida Settlement and Subsistence Patterns, 1876–1920," Ethnohistory 21 (1974): 303, p. 305; Robin Fisher, *Contact and Conflict: Indian-European Relations in British Columbia, 1774–1890*. Vancouver: U.B.C. Press, 1977, pp. 140 and 204; W. H. Collison, *In the Wake of the War Canoe: A Stirring Record of Forty Years' Successful Labour, Peril & Adventure amongst the Savage Indian Tribes of the Pacific Coast, and the Piratical Head-Hunting Haidas of the Queen Charlotte Islands, B. C.* London: Seeley & Service, 1915.
[23] Nietzsche, Zarathustra, p. 75.
[24] *An Act Further to Amend 'The Indian Act*, 1880, S.C. 1884, c. 27; for a look at the Haida potlatch, see Boelscher, *The Curtain Within*.
[25] T. A. Joyce, "A Totem Pole in the British Museum," *The Journal of the Anthropological Institute of Great Britain and Ireland* 33 (1903): 90, p. 95.
[26] David Neel, *Our Chiefs and Elders: Words and Photographs of Native Leaders* Vancouver: U.B.C. Press, 1992, p. 90.
[27] "They steal for themselves the works of inventors and the treasures of the wise: they call their theft culture – and they turn everything to sickness and calamity." Nietzsche, *Thus Spoke Zarathustra*, p. 77.

Cognition

Sovereign (Re)cognition: The *Royal Proclamation*

In 1763, Britain, France, and Spain signed the Treaty of Paris and ended the Seven Years' War. The European-designed peace saw the surrender of New France (Quebec) to the British. Not all indigenous peoples accepted this imposition, and some followed Obwandiyag ("Pontiac") in a "rebellion" against the British that raged along the frontier lands. To set up new governments for its recent gains but also to head off the "rebellion," the British Crown issued a *Royal Proclamation*.[28] Underlying its instructions to its colonial governors was the following policy:

> And whereas it is just and reasonable, and essential to Our Interest, and the Security of Our Colonies, that the several Nations or Tribes of Indians with whom We are connected, and who live under our Protection, should not be molested or disturbed in the Possession of such Parts of Our Dominions and Territories as, not having been ceded to or purchased by Us, are reserved to them, or any of them, as their Hunting Grounds....[29]

Following the *Royal Proclamation*, the Crown chose "to reserve under our [the Crown's] Sovereignty, Protection, and Dominion, for the use of the said Indians, all the Lands and Territories" beyond the colonies' expanding borders.[30] Through its Proclamation, the Crown interposed itself between "Indians" and settlers and required Indian consent for the cession of land.

The *Royal Proclamation* reads as a unilateral declaration of the Crown's "Royal Will and Pleasure" relating to its territory "for the present, and until"

---

[28] For the British authorities in 1763, the indigenous peoples stretching along the British imperial frontier from Quebec to Florida were seen as a major military threat. The Odaawaa, Haudenausaune, Lenape, Tsalagi, and Muskoke peoples were still powerful polities and treated as such by the British official and, grudgingly, the frontier settlers. Colin G. Calloway, *The Scratch of a Pen: 1763 and the Transformation of North America*. Oxford: Oxford University Press, 2006.

[29] R.S.C. 1985, App. II, No. 1. This chapter cites the most authoritative version of the *Royal Proclamation* reproduced in Appendix D of Canada, Royal Commission on Aboriginal Peoples, *Volume One of the Report of the Royal Commission on Aboriginal Peoples: Looking Forward, Looking Back*. Ottawa: Minister of Supply and Services Canada, 1996, p. 720 (Appendix D).

[30] Royal Commission, *Volume One*, p. 723 (Appendix D).

a "further Pleasure be known."[31] Although it provides for the protection of Indians, the Crown does so by inscribing its "mark of authority" on indigenous peoples, by rewriting their prior claims into the grants of a sovereign.[32] Thus, whatever "recognition" of indigenous peoples takes place in the *Royal Proclamation* (through such words as "connected to" and "Nations or Tribes") is mediated by, or even grounded in, a cognition that transforms them into objects of sovereign power.

Another history and another memory, however, belong to the *Royal Proclamation*. Shortly after the *Proclamation*, the British colonial authorities negotiated a peaceful end to "Pontiac's Rebellion." In 1764, leaders of the Haudenausaune and neighboring indigenous peoples met with Sir William Johnson, Superintendant of Indian Affairs, at Niagara to solemnize a relationship of peace and friendship through an exchange of wampum belts.[33] To the indigenous peoples present, John Borrows reminds us, the *Royal Proclamation* was not a "unilateral declaration of the Crown's will in its provisions relating to First Nations,"[34] but "part of a treaty between First Nations and the Crown ... which stands as a positive guarantee of self-government."[35] To the Haudenausaune, for example, the wampum belts were reminders of the renewed Covenant Chain between them and the British Crown. The two parallel beaded rows represented the First Nations and the Crown[36] and, when taken with the *Royal Proclamation* and oral exchanges, pointed to a promise of "colonial non-interference

---

[31] Op.cit.
[32] We borrow "mark of authority" from Marianne Constable, *The Law of the Other: The Mixed Jury and Changes in Conceptions of Citizenship, Law, and Knowledge*. Chicago: University of Chicago Press, 1994, ch. 4.
[33] John Borrows, "Constitutional Law From a First Nation Perspective: Self-Government and the Royal Proclamation," *University of British Columbia Law Review* 28 (1994): p. 1 at 22.
[34] Op. cit., p. 3.
[35] Op. cit., p. 4.
[36] Williams explains the *guswentah*, the two-row wampum belt, as follows: "There are three beads of wampum separating the two [outside] rows and they symbolize peace, friendship and respect. These two rows will symbolize two paths or two vessels, travelling down the same river together. One, a birch bark canoe, will be for the Indian people, their laws, their customs, their ways. The other, a ship, will be for the white people and their laws, their customs and their ways. We shall each travel the river together, side by side, but in our own boat. Neither of us will try to steer the other's vessel." R. A. Williams Jr., "The Algebra of Federal Indian Law: The Hard Trail of Decolonizing and Americanizing the White Man's Indian Jurisprudence," *Wisconsin Law Review* (1986), p. 219 at 291 cited in Borrows, "Constitutional Law," pp. 24–25.

in the land use and government of First Nations."[37] This solemnization became known to the Haudenausaune and others as the Treaty of Niagara.

Despite the intentions of Sir William and the Haudenausaune leaders at Niagara, the *Royal Proclamation* would be remembered for a long time by Canadian judges and statesmen as the source of Aboriginal rights. The turn to the language of recognition in the late twentieth century reenvisioned the *Proclamation* as a recognition of Aboriginal rights, yet the manner in which the *Royal Proclamation* grounded recognition in cognition would haunt judicial interpretation of its principal successor, section 35 of the *Constitution Act, 1982*. Indeed, in the words of the Royal Commission on Aboriginal Peoples, rather than reinvigorate an era of "contact and cooperation" with indigenous peoples, the *Proclamation* pointed forward to a stage of "displacement and assimilation"[38] through state cognition of indigenous peoples.

Simplification: The Indian Act

Cognition simplifies indigenous peoples into objects of state power, reduces their homelands to territories, and reduces them from peoples to members of a population. The *Indian Act* (in French, originally *The Law Relating to Savages*) was, and continues to be, the principal text through which the Canadian state cognized indigenous peoples. We trace some of the main legislative acts through which the Canadian state spoke (to), and so rewrote, indigenous peoples to make them more legible. This complex reading and rewriting took place through population censuses and registers, land surveys and reserve allocations, and other attempts to create an Indian population attached to isolated reserves with the final goal of assimilation. The era of cognition concludes with the reappropriation of the *Royal Proclamation* as a promise made between peoples that would usher in an era of recognition in the early 1980s.

The Mi'kmaq, Haudenausaune, Anishinabek, and other indigenous peoples along the rivers feeding the north Atlantic were the first to feel the

---

[37] Borrows, "Constitutional Law," p. 25.
[38] The Canadian government established the Commission, a group of notable jurists and indigenous people, in 1991 to report on the status of "Aboriginal peoples"; Royal Commission, *Volume One*.

rude shock of European settlement. In 1828, the military secretary to the Governor General of Lower Canada recommended settling Indians at specific locations, to better educate, convert, and ultimately transform them into Christian cultivators.[39] Interloping settlers and loggers soon squeezed these new settlements. The Bagot Commission, convened in 1844 to resolve this problem, recommended that the Indian reserves be "properly surveyed and illegal timber cutting eliminated by a timber licensing system."[40] The government would also replace the "treaty gifts and payments" tied to their recognition as peoples with the "training and tools" necessary for this envisioned population of sedentary planters.[41] The Commission also suggested a complementary system of boarding schools run by Christian orders to teach reading and writing in English to indigenous youngsters steeped in their parents' oral traditions.

To implement the Commissions' recommendations, the legislature of the newly formed Province of Canada[42] enacted two laws in 1850 to protect "Indian lands" by holding them in trust and exempting them from taxes and certain lawsuits.[43] The language of protection comes from the *Royal Proclamation*'s assertion of paternal power over indigenous peoples. In 1857, the same legislature went a step further and passed the *Gradual Civilization Act* to enfranchise male Indians. Rather than provide "protection," it aimed to simplify and assimilate indigenous peoples and their homelands. Its twin goals were the "gradual removal of all legal distinctions between them [Indians] and Her Majesty's other Canadian Subjects"[44] and the transformation of reserve land into fee simple plots under the general property law regime.[45] Candidates for the privilege of enfranchisement

---

[39] Royal Commission, *Volume One*, p. 265 (Part Two, Chapter 9, Section 3). The Royal Commission Report also briefly describes the different approach adopted in Upper Canada.

[40] Op. cit., p. 267 (Part Two, Chapter 9, Section 4).

[41] Op. cit., p. 268.

[42] In 1840 the colonies of Upper and Lower Canada were united into the Province of Canada. *Act of Union*, 1840, 3 & 4 Vict. c. 35 (U.K.).

[43] *An Act for the Better Protection of the Lands and Property of the Indians in Lower Canada*, Statutes of the Province of Canada 1850, Chapter. 42; *Act for the Protection of the Indians in Upper Canada from Imposition, and the Property Occupied or Enjoyed by Them from Trespass and Injury*, Statutes of the Province of Canada 1850, Chapter 74.

[44] *An Act to Encourage the Gradual Civilization of the Indian Tribes in this Province, and to Amend the Laws Respecting Indians*, S.C. 1857, Chapter 26.

[45] The 1860 *Indian Lands* Act continued this process by setting out a formal procedure for Indians to surrender their lands, a procedure that ostensibly flowed from the Royal Proclamation. This law ended the Crown's direct role in negotiating treaties with indigenous peoples and

The Lethality of the Canadian State's (Re)cognition

had to be over 21 years of age, educated, able to read and write English or French, "of good moral character," and "free from debt."[46] Because enfranchisement was voluntary, candidates were enticed by a grant of 50-acre plots in life estate from their band's reserve lands. On a candidate's death, the plot would pass to his children in fee simple or, if he were childless, revert to the Crown after passing to his wife in life estate. The "wife, widow, and lineal descendants"[47] of an enfranchised man were also automatically enfranchised. Over the next twenty-odd years, however, only one man voluntarily enfranchised himself.[48]

With confederation in 1867, the Parliament of Canada gained powers over "Indians, and Lands reserved for the Indians" through section 91(24) of the *British North America Act*.[49] Subsection 24 made indigenous peoples legible as objects of federal legislative power, similar in status to other objects of federal power such as the postal service or criminal law. The dangling comma in subsection 24 produced a wedge between indigenous peoples and their homelands. The federal government would not retain exclusive authority over indigenous peoples. In 1888, the Privy Council in *St. Catherine's Milling* held that surrendered treaty lands were provincial and not federal lands. Finding that the *Royal Proclamation* was the sole source of native title, the Privy Council stated that "the tenure of the Indians was a personal and usufructuary right, dependent upon the good will of the Sovereign,"[50] and emphasized the phrase "for the present" in the *Proclamation*.[51] Gordon Christie remarks that the judgment denied "any

---

replaced it with a bureaucrat directly responsible to the Canadian legislature. By shedding its role as protector of and negotiator with indigenous peoples, the British Crown seemed to sever the last frayed threads of its two-row wampum relationship of Niagara. *An Act Respecting the Management of the Indian Lands and Property*, Statutes of the Province of Canada 1860, Chapter 151, section 1; Royal Commission, *Volume One*, p. 273 (Part Two, Chapter 9, Section 6).

[46] Op. cit.

[47] Op. cit.

[48] Royal Commission, *Volume One*, p. 147 (Part One, Chapter 6, Section 1).

[49] *British North America Act*, 1867, 30–31 Vict., c. 3 (U.K.). The *British North America Act*, an Act of the Parliament of the United Kingdom, created the self-governing dominion of Canada.

[50] *St. Catherine's Milling and Lumber Company v. The Queen* (1888), 14 A.C. 46 (P.C.). See Sidney L. Harring, "'The Liberal Treatment of Indians': Native People in Nineteenth Century Ontario Law," 56: *Saskatchewan Law Review*, 297 (1992), for a discussion of the fascinating and complicated context of the case.

[51] Nearly a century later, the Supreme Court of Canada rejected the position that "Indian Reserves were enclaves which were withdrawn from the application of Provincial legislation,

legally enforceable obligation on the provincial Crown to release land to fulfill treaty promises for reserve land made by the Federal negotiators."[52]

After confederation, Parliament passed a series of laws consolidated in 1876 as the so-called *Indian Act*. This law regulated many aspects of the Canadian state's interactions with indigenous peoples. First, the *Indian Act* regime created a legal status of "Indian," limited to "[a]ll persons of Indian blood, reputed to belong to the particular tribe, band or body of Indians" and living on reserve land.[53] Among other things, the introduction of the racial notion of "blood" simplified the common yet varied practices of "adoption" in many indigenous polities. The regime established uniform patrilineal rules for all Indian "bands." If an Indian woman married a non-Indian man, for example, she lost her status, as did her children from that marriage.[54] If a woman married an Indian man, she automatically became a member of his band. An indigenous woman of a matrilineal polity had to choose between losing her Indian status if she married a nonstatus Indian or losing her people if she married a status Indian from another band. Parliament also tightened the definition of Indian to stress male lineage. Section 3(3) of the 1876 Act defined "Indian" as "First. Any male person of Indian blood reputed to belong to a certain band, Second. Any child of such person, Third. Any woman who is or was lawfully married to such person."[55] These simplified rules spoke to all Indians univocally as members of patrilineal Indian populations.

Second, the *Indian Act* regime introduced "municipal" institutions, whereby the Governor General could order the election of Chiefs.[56] By providing for elected chiefs in place of existing forms of "government," the Canadian authorities claimed, "intelligent and educated men, recognized as chiefs, should carry out the wishes of the male members of mature years

---

save by way of reference by virtue of Federal legislation." *Cardinal v. Alberta (Attorney General)*, [1974] S.C.R. 695, p. 702.

[52] Gordon Christie, "A Colonial Reading of Recent Jurisprudence: *Sparrow, Delgamuukw*, and *Haida Nation*" (2005) 23 Windsor Yearbook of Access to Justice 17, p. 24.

[53] *An Act Providing for the Organisation of the Department of the Secretary of State of Canada*, S.C. 1868, c. 42, s. 15 ["*Secretary of State Act*"].

[54] *An Act for the Gradual Enfranchisement of Indians, the Better Management of Indian Affairs, and to Extend the Provisions of the Act*, S.C. 1869, c. 42, s. 6 ["*Gradual Enfranchisement Act*"].

[55] *An Act to Amend and Consolidate the Laws Respecting Indians*, S.C. 1876, c. 18.

[56] *Gradual Enfranchisement Act*, s. 10. In 1884, the federal government introduced an alternative "municipal council" system for more "advanced" Indians bands. Instead of an elected or hereditary chief, this alternative created an elected council like those of Canadian settler townships. *Indian Advancement Act*, S.C. 1884, c. 28.

in each band."[57] Building on simplified patrilineal populations, the law reduced the complex and diverse political forms of indigenous peoples to a uniform patriarchal democracy modeled on neighboring nonindigenous municipalities.[58] The Royal Commission on Aboriginal Peoples explains that "the goal of the measures was specifically to undermine nation-level governance" as the "elective council system was not at all tribal in the larger sense of the nations or tribes referred to in the *Royal Proclamation of 1763*."[59] This goal also explains the reform seeking to create small, fractured reserve territories that precluded regional-sized "nations" with contiguous "homelands." By seeing indigenous peoples as distinct "bands," the law ascribed to each a distinct territory often, but not always, carved out of its erstwhile homeland.

Although its name was not as transparent as that of the *Gradual Civilization Act*, the *Indian Act* was also guided by the goal of assimilation. The simplification of indigenous peoples into members of an Indian population was an intermediate step, which preserved the separation of indigenous peoples from the broader Canadian population while rewriting indigenous peoples according to the logic of the broader population. Residential schools were particularly invasive, because they aimed to transform "savage" children – only children could undergo "the transformation from the natural condition to that of civilization"[60] – into "civilized" members of a single, homogeneous population, in part by eradicating indigenous languages.[61] The extent of this loss of language cannot be overstated. Barely one in ten self-identifying indigenous persons today has an indigenous language as his or her mother tongue.[62] On Haida Gwaii, barely a hundred people still speak *Xaat Kíl*.[63]

---

[57] Canada, "Annual Report of the Indian Branch of the Department of the Secretary of State for the Provinces," No. 23 in *Sessional Papers* (1871) at 4 cited in Richard H. Bartlett, *The Indian Act of Canada*, edition 2. Saskatoon: Native Law Centre, 1988, p. 18.
[58] Bonita Lawrence, "Gender, Race, and the Regulation and the Regulation of Native Identity in Canada and the United States: An Overview," *Hypatia* 18 (2003): 3 at p. 5.
[59] Royal Commission, *Volume One*, pp. 275–276 (Part Two, Chapter 9, Section 7).
[60] As found in op. cit., p. 338 (Part Two, Chapter 10, Section 1.1).
[61] Op. cit., p. 333 (Part Two, Chapter 10).
[62] Statistics Canada, 2006 *Census Profile of Federal Electoral Districts (2003 Representation Order): Language, Mobility and Migration and Immigration and Citizenship* Ottawa, 2007, pp. 2, 6, 10.
[63] Eung-Do Cook and Darin Howe, "Aboriginal Languages of Canada," in W. O'Grady and J. Archibald (eds.), *Contemporary Linguistic Analysis*, edition 5. Toronto: Addison Wesley Longman 2004, pp. 294–309 at p. 300.

The lethality of Canadian state sight and speech in this era of cognition denied a more nuanced view of indigenous people as distinct polities. In 1897, the pioneering anthropologist, Franz Boas, led an expedition to retrace the supposed migration routes of human beings from Siberia to the Canadian west coast. Boas skipped the distant Queen Charlotte Islands, but sent his young protégé, John Swanton, to collect stories and artifacts from the islands' people. Swanton spent the next ten months recording hundreds of stories and songs, and outlining the matrilineal structure of the Haida's heraldic clans.[64] Moreover, Swanton's description of Haida matrilineal structures helped bring Boas to doubt his earlier acceptance of the then-dominant cultural evolutionary theory. According to Lewis Henry Morgan, its leading proponent, primitive matrilineal societies evolved into more advanced patrilineal ones. Fieldwork by Boas and Swanton along the Pacific coast, however, revealed that the Kwakwaka'wakw, sandwiched between patrilineal groups to the south and matrilineal to the north, had slowly adopted matrilineal elements to their existing patrilineal structures – thus contradicting Morgan.[65] Boas's findings undermined the simplifying patrilineal pillar of the *Indian Act*. Not only was inexorable evolution toward patrilineality a fiction, but the theory also masked the complex plurality of indigenous polities before the *Indian Act* simplified and rewrote them.

The Canadian state's blindness to complex local knowledge did not go unresisted, especially along the west coast. One of Boas's former collaborators, the Scottish immigrant James Teit,[66] had married a Nlaka'pamux woman and learned her language. In the course of his ethnographic research for Boas and the Geological Survey of Canada, Teit witnessed the displacement of indigenous peoples along the Pacific shores in the late 1890s and then joined indigenous leaders advocating for their lands. The provincial government of British Columbia had already begun rationalizing indigenous lands with an 1874 law that sought to limit reserve

---

[64] John Swanton, *Haida Texts and Myths: Skidegate Dialect*. Washington, DC: Government Printing Office, 1905; Contributions to the Ethnology of the Haida. Publications of the Jesup North Pacific Expedition 5(1); American Museum of Natural History Memoirs 8(1). Leiden: E.J. Brill; New York: G.E. Stechert, 1905; Bringhurst, *A Story as Sharp*, 149.

[65] Franz Boas, "The Social Organization of the Tribes of the North Pacific Coast" *American Anthropologist* 26 (1924): 323, pp. 327–329.

[66] See Franz Boas, "James A. Teit," *The Journal of American Folklore* 36 (1923): 103; Wendy Wickwire, "'We Shall Drink from the Stream and So Shall You': James A. Teit and Native Resistance in British Columbia, 1908–22," *The Canadian Historical Review* 79 (1998): 199.

The Lethality of the Canadian State's (Re)cognition

allotments to 20 acres per Indian, less than one half the area recommended by the federal government and much less than the free 160-acre grants to settlers.[67] The federal government at first disallowed the law, but it eventually acquiesced to the province's reduced Indian land grants.[68]

Along the Pacific coast, the Haida and their Nisga'a, Gitxsan, and Tsimshian neighbors resisted the new reserves forced on them by chasing out government agents, land surveyors, and squatters.[69] As the Royal Commission writes

> Indian bands individually refused to fund schools whose goals were assimilative, refused to participate in the annual band census conducted by colonial officials, and even refused to permit their reserves to be surveyed for purposes of the 50-acre allotment that was to be the incentive for enfranchisement.[70]

In 1881, Chief Mountain led a Nisga'a delegation to Victoria, the provincial capital, to protest settlers coming into the Nass and Skeena river valleys. These peoples and others farther south had altered the potlatch to better organize themselves in resisting provincial land regulation. A few years later, the federal government amended the *Indian Act* to make it a misdemeanor for Indians to participate in potlatches. Uslick, a Sto:lo man, was the first man arrested under the potlatch provision for protesting growing pressure on Sto:lo lands and salmon-rich rivers in the Fraser Valley.[71]

With indigenous protest suppressed by the Royal Canadian Mounted Police, the leaders of the Sto:lo, Haida, and neighboring peoples resorted to the institutions and language of the Canadian state. After the federal government thwarted schemes to expand its land base, the province of British Columbia established the McKenna-McBride Royal Commission in 1913. A few years later the Commission finished its survey and recommended significant cuts to most reserves and complete elimination of others.[72] In

---

[67] *An Act to Amend and Consolidate the Laws Affecting Crown Lands in British Columbia*, S.B.C. 1874. no. 2.
[68] Order in Council (Canada) January 23, 1875 as found at <http://sisis.nativeweb.org/clark/oic1875.html> last checked February 26, 2008.
[69] Fisher, op. cit.
[70] Royal Commission, *Volume One*, p. 272 (Part Two, Chapter 9, Section 5).
[71] Cole Harris, *Making Native Space: Colonialism, Resistance, and Reserves in British Columbia*. Vancouver: University of British Columbia Press, 2002, p. 21.
[72] British Columbia, *Report of the Royal Commission on Indian Affairs for the Province of British Columbia* Victoria: Acme Press, 1916, p. 142.

response, several Indian bands came together to form the Allied Tribes of British Columbia (ATBC).[73] The ATBC, with James Teit as its "translator, scribe, and lobbyist," called on the provincial and federal governments to forestall reductions to reserve territory.[74] Nevertheless, Parliament implemented the Commission's recommendations shortly thereafter.[75]

The ATBC kept up its resistance, bringing its continued claims to land before the Special Joint Committee in Ottawa in 1927. The Reverend Peter Russell, the theologically – and legally – trained Chairman of the ATBC's Executive Committee, testified and described the Haida "government" as

> ... not a central government, a large central government such as you have, for instance, in a provincial government; it was more of a municipal government. Our government was something like the city state of the Greeks of long ago. There was no large central government, but there was a municipal government.[76]

This brief statement reflected both the success and failure of Canadian state cognition. Russell's Greek simile and municipal analogy probably reflected his own residential school experience with classical Western tropes, as well as the municipal-like band council imposed on the Haida. Despite speaking in the comfortable images of his interlocutors, he continued to press the claim of indigenous peoples to the lands. The government members dismissed Russell's images by turning the Haida practices against them. Referring to the Haida's raiding their neighbors and trading in slaves, a member of Parliament interjected, "The early Greeks again?"[77]

In 1927, the federal government amended the *Indian Act* to make that year the high-water mark of nonmilitary state suppression of "Indians" in Canada.[78] The most important amendment prohibited Indians from raising money or hiring lawyers to pursue land claims – a direct response to ATBC's legalistic defiance.[79] The federal government expanded the

---

[73] See generally Harris, *Making Native Space*.
[74] Wickwire, "'We Shall Drink from the Stream and So Shall You,'" p. 200.
[75] *British Columbia Indian Lands Settlement Act*, S.C., 1920, c. 51.
[76] Canada, Parliament, Special Joint Committee of the Senate and House of Commons Appointed to Inquire into the Claims of the Allied Indian Tribes of British Columbia, as Set Forth in their Petition Submitted to Parliament in June 1926, "Report and Evidence" in Appendix to the Journals of the Senate of Canada, 16th Parl., 1926–27 (June 1926) at 157.
[77] Op. cit.
[78] *Indian Act*, R.S.C. 1927, c. 98.
[79] Op. cit., art. 141.

definition of "potlatch" to cover almost any political gathering.[80] Indians were also required to request permission for a pass to leave their reserves from their Indian agents, who had discretion to grant or deny the request (although it was rarely enforced in practice).[81] These measures coincided with the end of the continuous treaty making flowing from the *Royal Proclamation* (and the treaty at Niagara). In 1921, the final treaty for a half-century, Treaty No. 11, ceded lands from British Columbia's northern border to the Arctic shores.[82] Not only had the Canadian state stopped negotiating with indigenous peoples as peoples, it had also legislated silence by denying them the means to demand the fulfillment of the *Royal Proclamation*'s promise of protection.

Not until 1951 did Parliament amend the *Indian Act* to remove the most conspicuous bans on potlatches, drinking alcohol (although it was still an offense to be drunk off reserve), suing the Crown for land claims, as well as now permitting on-reserve Indian women to vote in band council elections.[83] Nevertheless, the amended *Indian Act* continued the state's simplification of indigenous peoples into a population by rationalizing Indian status rules. The *Indian Act* consolidated Indian registers at each reserve into a central list that held the names of the entire population of (potential) status Indians.[84] Each eligible person was thus made legible to state officials sitting in federal offices in the capital, Ottawa, who never needed to set foot on a reserve road or forest floor. Because these people had only a limited time to register, however, "[t]he names of many people who ought to have been on the band lists or the general lists were never added."[85] Others were also stripped of their status by provisions like the new "double mother" rule. If a child had a mother and paternal grandmother who were not entitled to Indian status before they had married a status Indian man,

---

[80] Op. cit., art. 140.
[81] Royal Commission, *Volume One*, pp. 296–298 (Part Two, Chapter 9, Section 9.10).
[82] Whereas Treaty No. 11 marked the final westward expansion of the Canadian state into indigenous homelands, there was a series of three smaller treaties in 1923, the so-called Williams Treaties, for land already used by the government and settlers in southern Ontario: Robert J. Surtees, *Treaty Research Report: The Williams Treaties*. Ottawa: Treaties and Historical Research Centre, Department of Indian Affairs and Northern Development, 1986).
[83] *Indian Act*, S.C. 1951, c. 29, s. 8.
[84] Op. cit., ss. 5–9.
[85] Royal Commission, *Volume One*, p. 312 (Part Two, Chapter 9, Section 11).

then he or she would lose the right to Indian status on turning 21.[86] A single, centralized register drew a bright line that definitively captured every person as either within or without the Indian population.[87]

Indigenous peoples, however, still refused to make themselves legible to the Canadian state. In the Kahnawake reserve across the river from Montreal, for example, the Kanien'kehá:ka people removed all street signs and numbers to resist government efforts to conscript their young men into the armed forces in World War II.[88] Elsewhere, people resisted attempts to rewrite their polities through the *Indian Act*. After the imposition of a band council elected under the *Indian Act* on the Haudenosaunee Confederacy Council at the Six Nations reserve in 1959, a "Mrs. Logan" sought an injunction on behalf of hereditary chiefs to stop "Mr. Styres," the elected council chief, from surrendering reserve land to the government. Justice King wrote that, "[w]hile it might be unjust or unfair under the circumstances for the Parliament of Canada to interfere with their system of internal Government by hereditary Chiefs, I am of the opinion that Parliament has the authority to provide for the surrender of Reserve land."[89] The insistent overwriting of indigenous politics coincided with a resurgent interest in "Indian culture." During the early 1960s, for example, *gyáa'aang* began to be repatriated from the Royal British Columbia Museum to Haida Gwaii.[90] In 1969, a newly carved *gyáa'aang* was raised on Haida Gwaii – the first in the twentieth century.

Assimilation: The White Paper

State cognition of indigenous peoples led to a crisis in 1969 when the federal government introduced the "White Paper on Indian Policy," a

---

[86] *Indian Act*, 1951, s. 12(1)(a)(iv). See also Royal Commission, *Volume One*, p. 312. (Part Two, Chapter 9, Section 11).

[87] Section 87 of the 1951 *Indian Act* also explicitly provided for the application of provincial laws of general application to indigenous peoples. Although section 87 was meant to "address and acknowledge the widespread sense that provincial measures should not constrict the exercise of Indians' legitimate treaty rights," Wilkins explains, the unusual step taken regarding the application of provincial laws was tied to an earlier report's position that "the provinces had a role to play in achieving the recognized long-term goal of assimilation." Kerry Wilkins, "'Still Crazy after All These Years': Section 88 of the Indian Act at Fifty" *Alberta Law Review* 38 (2000): p. 458.

[88] There are still no street signs on the reserve. Thomas Deer (Teyowisonte) in conversation with Thomas McMorrow (Thursday 21 February, 2008).

[89] *Logan v. Styres et al.* (1959), 20 D.L.R. (2d) 416 (O.N.H.C.) at 424.

[90] Wright, *Carvers*, p. 321.

The Lethality of the Canadian State's (Re)cognition

policy document proposing the ultimate reduction of indigenous people to members of a population.[91] For the federal government, the archipelago of Indian reserves was embarrassing and reminiscent of South African apartheid.[92] Its solution proposed abrogating the *Indian Act*, phasing out the federal Indian bureaucracy, and integrating Indians into Canadian society. The *White Paper* thus opened with the claim that, "[w]e can no longer perpetuate the separation of Canadians." Intolerable separation was to be remedied by equality. The *White Paper* embraced "an equality which stresses Indian participation in its creation and which manifests itself in all aspects of Indian life," an equality that "preserves and enriches Indian identity and distinction."[93] The government envisioned that "there be positive recognition by everyone of the unique contribution of Indian culture to Canadian life."[94] The *White Paper* thus deployed the language of recognition that would come to dominate indigenous-Canadian relations in the last quarter century.

Although the *White Paper* recognized "Indian culture" as worthy of protection, it no longer saw it necessary (or even desirable) to recognize indigenous peoples as peoples. "Recognition" here meant assimilation into a nominally multicultural population. "Culture" had replaced the "Land and Territories" of the *Royal Proclamation* as the object of the state's protection. Nevertheless, the Canadian state continued to speak in the language of the "continuity of people"[95] through a written document that envisioned the final death of indigenous people as peoples.

Indigenous peoples in Canada decried this lie told by the state, which masked assimilation with equality. Harold Cardinal, a Cree writer, captured the feeling of outrage:

> We do not want the Indian Act retained because it is a good piece of legislation. It isn't. It is discriminatory from start to finish. But it is a lever in our hands and an embarrassment to the government, as it should be. No just society and no society with even pretensions to being just can long tolerate such a piece of legislation, but we would

---

[91] Canada, Minister of Indian Affairs and Northern Development, *Statement of the Government of Canada on Indian Policy*. Ottawa: Queen's Printer, 1969, "White Paper."
[92] *Apartheid* is translated from Afrikaans as "separateness."
[93] Canada, *White Paper*, p. 6.
[94] Op. cit.
[95] Op. cit.

rather continue to live in bondage under the inequitable Indian Act than surrender our sacred rights.[96]

By rejecting assimilation, indigenous peoples forced the Canadian state to retreat from equality toward "the anomaly of treaties between groups within society and the government of that society."[97] The *White Paper* was an instance of Taylor's "politics of universal dignity" as it emphasized the "equalization of rights and entitlements."[98] The step back from the *White Paper* introduced the "politics of difference."[99] If the politics of universal dignity were tied to the state's cognition of native peoples as members of a population, then the politics of difference raised the possibility and hope of recognition, of a proper sight of indigenous peoples.

In 1973, the Canadian Supreme Court's judgment in *Calder* invited a shift in government policy away from outright assimilation. The case was brought by Frank Calder and the Nisga'a people, who claimed that their Aboriginal title over the Nass river valley had never been extinguished. In a seminal ruling, seven Supreme Court judges split 3 to 3, with the last and deciding judge casting his vote against the Nisga'a appeal on a technical point. All the judges, however, shared the common view that Aboriginal rights to land and resources existed (the 3-3 split was over whether subsequent government actions had extinguished these rights).[100] In his dissent, Justice Hall admonished the Court of Appeal's characterization of the Nisga'a as "very primitive." The Nisga'a, he said, "are and were from time immemorial a distinctive cultural entity with concepts of ownership indigenous to their culture and capable of articulation under the common law."[101] Although he did not treat the *Royal Proclamation* as the source of aboriginal title, Hall J. referred to an earlier characterization of the *Royal Proclamation* as the "Indian Bill of Rights," adding that "[i]ts force as a statute is analogous to the status of Magna Carta."[102]

---

[96] Harold Cardinal, *The Unjust Society, The Tragedy of Canada's Indians*. Edmonton: M.G. Hurtig Ltd., 1969, p. 140, cited in the *Royal Commission on Aboriginal Peoples*.
[97] Canada, *White Paper*, p. 11.
[98] Charles Taylor, "The Politics of Recognition" in *Multiculturalism: Examining the Politics of Recognition*, ed., Amy Gutmann, Princeton: Princeton University Press, 1994, p. 37.
[99] Op. cit., p. 39. Taylor writes that "[t]he politics of difference grows organically out of the politics of universal dignity...."
[100] *Calder v. British Columbia (Attorney-General)*, [1973] S.C.R. 313.
[101] Op. cit., p. 375.
[102] Op. cit., p. 395.

The Lethality of the Canadian State's (Re)cognition

After the *Calder* decision, the federal government reversed its position on indigenous land claims.[103] The first treaty negotiated in this new era was the 1975 James Bay and Northern Quebec agreement involving the Cree and Inuit. The next year, the federal government agreed to negotiate a comprehensive land claim with the Nisga'a Tribal Council. The Council of the Haida Nation, formed in 1974 from members of the Skidgate and Masset band councils, resolved to "seek the formalization and retention of aboriginal title rather than the surrender of their aboriginal rights forever."[104] The Council and several other First Nations in British Columbia in 1980 and 1981 submitted comprehensive land claims to the Canadian government, which responded by publishing its policy on land claims.[105]

Recognition

The imperative of recognition was constitutionally enshrined when Canada patriated its Constitution in 1982. Section 35(1) of the *Constitution Act, 1982* states that "[t]he existing aboriginal and treaty rights of the aboriginal peoples of Canada are hereby recognized and affirmed."[106] Thus, like the *Royal Proclamation*, section 35 constitutes an "Indian Bill of Rights," but it uses language less straightforward than section 1 of the Constitution Act, 1982, which explicitly guarantees the individual rights enumerated in the *Canadian Charter of Rights and Freedoms*. In part because of its uncertain legal force and content, the two leading national indigenous organizations initially supported and then opposed the clause.[107] Nevertheless,

---

[103] Department of Indian Affairs and Northern Development, "Statement Made by the Honourable Jean Chrétien, Minister of Indian Affairs and Northern Development on Claims of Indian and Inuit People," Communiqué, 8 August 1973.

[104] From the minutes of the Council of the Haida Nation, Executive Meeting Saturday, December 7, 1974, Council of the Haida Nation, "History of the Council" (last visited 8 May 2008), <http://www.haidanation.ca/Pages/CHN/History.html>.

[105] Union of BC Indian Chiefs, "Historical Timeline" (last visited 26 February 2008), <http://www.ubcic.bc.ca/Resources/timeline.htm>; Department of Indian and Northern Affairs, *In All Fairness: A Native Claims Policy*. Ottawa: Supply and Services Canada, 1981. The Nisga'a, neighbors of the Haida, arrived at an agreement in 1998.

[106] *Constitution Act, 1982*, Schedule B to the *Canada Act 1982* (U.K.), 1982, c. 11.

[107] The National Indian Brotherhood represented status Indians and the Native Council of Canada (now called the Congress of Aboriginal Peoples) represented nonstatus Indians and Métis. The Brotherhood grew out of regional organizations across Canada in the 1960s that first united to oppose the 1969 White Paper. This loose confederacy of status Indian groups also contested the 1982 patriation of the Canadian constitution by, for example, organizing a protest by 300 status Indians in London, England. In 1982 the Brotherhood reformed as the Assembly of First

the wording "recognize and affirm" was striking and echoed constitutional politics in Canada in which "recognition" of Quebec as a "distinct society" featured prominently. This new era of constitutional recognition was complemented by an amendment to the *Indian Act* that attempted to eliminate the discriminatory status rules and restored status to those who had lost it.[108] These rules were both an affirmation of individual rights[109] and an attempt to redress a policy that had aimed at the simplification of indigenous peoples. By this single act of recognition, the population of status Indians swelled, compelling indigenous communities to confront the way they had come to know themselves through the *Indian Act*.[110]

The movement from the "Indian" of section 91(24) to the "Aboriginal" of section 35 suggests a movement from cognition (or misrecognition) to recognition, from population and territory, to peoples and homelands. The terms that have replaced "Indian" – "Aboriginal peoples," "indigenous peoples," "native peoples," "First Nations" – highlight both the peoplehood of indigenous peoples and their belonging to the land. Moreover, the language of "affirmation" in section 35 suggests more than grudging recognition. "Affirmation" emphasizes the importance of the "positive look" of others and taps into the psychological register of self-esteem.[111] This pairing of recognition and affirmation maps onto Taylor's discussion of the weaker and stronger claims of recognition. Although "recognition"

Nations, composed of the Chiefs of each First Nation in Canada. The Native Council of Canada was founded in 1971 as an umbrella organization of various provincial and territorial groups, but in 1983, the Métis of the west-central Canada separated to form the west Métis National Council. The Congress now represents off-reserve and non-status Indians, as well as those "Métis" excluded by the Council's definitions. The Inuit did not oppose section 35.

[108] An Act to amend the Indian Act, S.C. 1985, c. 27.

[109] The amendments aimed to bring the Act in line with the new *Canadian Charter of Rights and Freedoms*. They were also a response to a successful challenge before the United Nations Human Rights Committee that proved embarrassing to the Canadian government. In *Sandra Lovelace v. Canada*, Communication No. R.6/24, U.N. Doc. Supp. No. 40 (A/36/40) (1981), Lovelace had married a non-Indian and lost her status. She returned to her reserve after divorcing her husband. Because she was no longer a status Indian, her band council refused to provide her with a house. At 166: "[w]hatever may be the merits of the Indian Act in other respects, it does not seem to the Committee that to deny Sandra Lovelace the right to reside on the reserve is reasonable, or necessary to preserve the identity of the tribe." Moreover, the *Constitution Act, 1982* was amended almost immediately to clarify that rights flowing from modern land claim agreements would be constitutionally protected by section 35(3) and to guarantee section 35(1) rights equally to men and women by section 35(4).

[110] See, for example, Lawrence, "Regulation of Native Identity," p. 13 and ff.

[111] "It [due recognition] is a vital human need" in Taylor, "Politics," p. 26.

The Lethality of the Canadian State's (Re)cognition

appearing alone might not signify more than the will to let Aboriginal "cultures" "survive," the addition of "affirmation" leaves no doubt that their "worth"[112] is to be acknowledged. Furthermore, recognition, strengthened or completed by affirmation, raises the possibility of a reconciliation (or conciliation) grounded in a "fusion of horizons."[113] To recognize and affirm others is to accept the invitation to see as they see, to allow their sight to affect one's own. As we shall see, however, section 35 also carried within it the peril of the *Royal Proclamation*, which had grounded recognition in cognition.

Sovereign Reconciliation

By the 1990s, against the backdrop of treaty negotiations,[114] the first wave of section 35 cases, most of which concerned parts of British Columbia that were treaty-free, had reached the Supreme Court of Canada. In the first sentence of *Sparrow*, its first section 35 judgment, the Court announced that it bore the burden of indicating section 35's "strength as a promise to the aboriginal peoples of Canada."[115] The unanimous Court stated that section 35(1) "at the least, provides a solid constitutional base upon which subsequent negotiations can take place" and added that "[i]t also affords aboriginal peoples constitutional protection against provincial legislative power."[116] More than this, the Court explained, section 35 promised "a just settlement."[117] Evoking the "protection" of the *Royal Proclamation*,

---

[112] Taylor, "Politics," p. 64.
[113] Op. cit. p. 67. Taylor draws the "fusion of horizons" from Hans-Georg Gadamer, *Truth and Method*, trans. Garett Barden and John Cumming. New York: Crossroad, 1988.
[114] For example, in 1993, the six-stage British Columbia Treaty Process was established to negotiate treaties between the federal and provincial governments, and the First Nations of the Indian Act. The six stages of the process coordinated by the Commission are as follows: (i) statement of intent to negotiate, (ii) readiness to negotiate, (iii) negotiation of a framework agreement, (iv) negotiation of an agreement in principle, (v) negotiation to finalize a treaty, and finally (vi) implementation of the treaty. See British Columbia Treaty Commission, "Six-Stages: Policies and Procedures," Web site <http://www.bctreaty.net/files/sixstages.php>.
[115] *R. v. Sparrow*, [1990] 1. S.C.R. 1075, para. 1 The word *promise* evokes the practice of treaty making and its revival in the post-*Calder* era. What is more, the Court interpreted section 35(1) as a constitutional guarantee of Aboriginal rights precisely by invoking the principle, articulated in a 1983 Supreme Court decision, that "treaties and statutes relating to Indians should be liberally construed and doubtful expressions resolved in favour of the Indians." Para. 57.
[116] Op. cit., para. 53.
[117] Op. cit., para. 54. The words were borrowed from Prof. Lyon.

the Court confirmed a "trust-like, rather than adversarial"[118] relationship between government and indigenous peoples in which "the honour of the Crown"[119] was central. Inviting the hope of a fusion of horizons, the Court stated that it was "crucial" to be "sensitive" to the Aboriginal perspective on "the meaning of the rights at stake."[120] The Court's embrace of the Aboriginal perspective was tied to its labeling of Aboriginal rights as *sui generis*,[121] as it was to a willingness (manifest in the later cases of *Van der Peet* and especially *Delgamuukw*) to relax traditional rules of evidence.[122] In short, section 35 seemed to promise both proper sight and honorable speech.

Although much of the language of *Sparrow* was picked up by the majority in the 1996 *Van der Peet* decision, its words about a "just settlement"[123] gave way to a refrain of "reconciliation" and to the proposition that section 35 provides the "constitutional framework through which the fact that aboriginals lived on the land in distinctive societies, with their own practices, traditions and cultures, is acknowledged and reconciled with the sovereignty of the Crown."[124] Whereas reconciliation had barely appeared in *Sparrow*, variants of "reconcile" appear no less than thirteen times in the majority's judgment in *Van der Peet*, in sentences that are all versions of the sentence quoted here. The form of the sentences is always the same. Sovereignty is not to be reconciled with preexisting rights or peoples, nor are peoples to be reconciled with one another. Rather, Aboriginal peoples are to be reconciled with sovereignty. The majority judgment thus casts reconciliation as something that is done to Aboriginal peoples through section 35.[125] Furthermore, the "operation" of reconciliation appears "logical" rather than "existential" because one "fact," that of prior presence, is to be reconciled with an even weightier and more intractable "fact": Crown sovereignty or its "assertion."[126]

[118] Op. cit., para. 59.
[119] Op. cit., para. 64.
[120] Op. cit., para. 69.
[121] Op. cit., para. 59.
[122] *R v. Van der Peet*, [1996] 2 S.C.R. 507, para. 68 but especially *Delgamuukw* v. *British Columbia*, [1997] 3 S.C.R. 1010, para. 87 and ff.
[123] One would do well to remember "Juris praecepta sunt haec: honeste vivere, alterum non laedere, suum cuique tribuere." (The precepts of the law are these: to live honestly, to hurt no one, to give to each his own) Justinian's Institutes, Book 1, Title 1, Sec. 3.
[124] *Van der Peet*, para. 31. At most, "just" became an adjective that qualifies reconciliation (see para 50.). In her dissent, McLachlin J. finds "incomplete" this substitution of reconciliation for justice (para. 230). The Court uses "acknowledge" and "recognize" interchangeably.
[125] Op. cit., para. 50.
[126] Op. cit., para. 36.

The majority's words reveal the ambiguity of reconciliation. To reconcile is not simply "to bring (a person) again into friendly relations *to* or *with* (oneself or another) after an estrangement," but also "to bring into a state of acquiescence (*with*) or submission *to* a thing."[127] In some theological contexts, the two senses of reconciliation can be properly grasped as one, because submission to God is tied to the overcoming of human sin. Because humans are the sinful ones, it is always they who must be reconciled to or with God.[128] In the present context, however, to confound the two senses of reconciliation is to accept the state, wittingly or not, as the "new idol."[129] The Court's words reveal a section 35 analogous to the *Royal Proclamation* (that first "Indian Bill of Rights"). The "friendly relations" of reconciliation are grounded in submission to state sovereignty. Recognition carries cognition within it.

In the words of the Court, recognition and reconciliation appear as the twin goals of section 35[130] and as a sequence to follow when "applying" section 35 to specific cases. Thus, reconciliation appears to replace affirmation as the kind of speech act that is to issue from recognition, from proper sight. This sequence of sight to speech corresponds to the two principal laws of section 35: the law that identifies Aboriginal rights precedes the law that justifies limits to them. We name these laws the law of recognition and the law of reconciliation. We show how the law of recognition repeats the simplification of the *Indian Act* and how the law of reconciliation repeats the assimilation of the *White Paper*. Although we turn first to the law of recognition, we note that reconciliation emerges in *Van der Peet* as the overriding objective of section 35.[131]

Simplification: The Law of Recognition

The law of identification, or recognition, arose in *Sparrow*. Ronald Sparrow, a Musqueam man, invoked an Aboriginal right to fish as a defense against a charge for fishing with a net longer than permitted by his band's

---

[127] Oxford English Dictionary, senses 1 and 8 <www.oed.com>. Last visited February 26, 2008.
[128] See, e.g., "The Doctrine of Reconciliation" in Herbert Lockyer, *All the Doctrines of the Bible*. Grand Rapids, MI: Zondervan, 1988, pp. 191–192.
[129] Nietzsche, *Zarathustra*.
[130] *Van der Peet*, para. 43.
[131] E.g., op. cit., para. 36.

federal license. In construing section 35 "liberally," the Supreme Court ruled that "existing" rights included all rights not extinguished before 1982. It traced a long history of increasingly severe restrictions imposed on Indians in British Columbia, restrictions that limited them to fishing for food as commercial and sport fishing grew, until Indians were finally required to obtain licenses. Nevertheless, the Court found no requisite "clear and plain" intention to extinguish the right. It also rejected what it called a "frozen rights"[132] approach. First, the scope of a right was not to be determined by the state of its governmental regulation in 1982. Second, rights could "evolve" as, for example, modern means of fishing were adopted. Although these pronouncements were significant, the Court said little about the Musqueam right at issue. Echoing Justice Hall's words in *Calder*, the Court stated that the anthropological evidence suggested:

> ... for the Musqueam, the salmon fishery has always constituted an integral part of their distinctive culture. Its significant role involved not only consumption for subsistence purposes, but also consumption of salmon on ceremonial and social occasions. The Musqueam have always fished for reasons connected to their cultural and physical survival. As we stated earlier, the right to do so may be exercised in a contemporary manner.[133]

Although it affirmed an Aboriginal right, the Court refused to deal with the argument that "[w]hile no commercial fishery existed prior to the arrival of European settlers, ... the Musqueam practice of bartering in early society may be revived as a modern right to fish for commercial purposes."[134] Instead, it preferred to adopt the Court of Appeal's characterization of the right as a "right to fish for food and social and ceremonial purposes."[135]

These short passages in *Sparrow* grew into a full-blown test in 1996. Whereas the *Sparrow* court had barely used the word culture, the majority in *Van der Peet* borrowed a sentence from *Sparrow* to articulate a test featuring it: "in order to be an aboriginal right an activity must be an element of a practice, custom or tradition integral to the distinctive culture of the aboriginal group claiming the right."[136] The "Aboriginal rights" of

---

[132] Op. cit., para. 27.
[133] Op. cit., para. 40.
[134] Op. cit., para. 43.
[135] Op. cit., para. 45.
[136] Op. cit., para. 46.

The Lethality of the Canadian State's (Re)cognition

Aboriginal peoples were tied to the Aboriginality of Aboriginal peoples,[137] which was a matter of "culture." What, however, is Musqueam culture and how is it known? In what does the "being Musqueam" of the Musqueam reside?

Although the majority embraced the requirement that Aboriginal perspectives be considered in defining Aboriginal rights, it insisted that these rights must be taken into account "in terms which are cognizable to the non-aboriginal legal system."[138] This remark, quite tellingly, points to the cognition at the heart of recognition. For example, the majority also ruled that the significance of a practice to the Aboriginal peoples themselves could serve as evidence of the centrality of a practice but could not inform the description of the practice.[139]

Most telling, however, was the majority's mysterious decision to turn the moment of "contact" into the key moment: a present-day practice must have some continuity with a precontact practice if it is to ground a constitutionally protected right. The majority claimed that it chose this moment – rather than, say, the moment of the assertion of sovereignty[140] – "[b]ecause it is the fact that distinctive aboriginal societies lived on the land prior to the arrival of Europeans that underlies the aboriginal rights protected by section 35(1)."[141]

The majority's choice of the moment of contact shows cognition at work in recognition. The moment of contact appears as the moment after which Aboriginals are no longer easily identified *qua* indigenous peoples in their radical, uncontaminated otherness. Contact becomes a moment of cognition to which every subsequent recognition, or knowing again, must refer. The radical separation of self and other that precedes contact mirrors the subject–object relation that characterizes the static sight of cognition.[142] This static sight simplifies indigenous ways of life by seeing a set of discrete activities and separating significance from them. Echoing some aspects

---

[137] Op. cit., paras. 17–20. "Indianness" had emerged in division of powers adjudication to protect the core of federal legislative power over Indians from provincial legislation. See, for example, *Dick v. The Queen*, [1985] 2 S.C.R. 309.
[138] Op. cit., para. 49. See L'Heureux-Dubé J.'s dissent at para. 145.
[139] Op. cit., para. 58.
[140] As the judges of the British Columbia Court of Appeal had done.
[141] Op. cit., para 60.
[142] Moreover, the moment of contact evokes the "discovery" that purportedly grounded European claims to the "New World."

of the dissent, commentators criticized the majority's "essentialist" view of culture and the way it surreptitiously introduced the "frozen rights" approach that it had claimed to repudiate.[143] We name this persistence of cognition in recognition *hypostatization* rather than essentialism or reification. The static sight of the state hypostatizes all that it sees, even indigenous ways of life.

In *Van der Peet*, Dorothy Van der Peet, a Sto:lo like Uslick, had appealed her conviction for selling ten salmon for $50, contrary to the conditions of her band's food fishing license. The majority of the Court rejected her characterization of her right as a right "to sufficient fish to provide for a moderate livelihood" based on the claim of its significance to her community. Instead, it characterized her claimed right as "an aboriginal right to exchange fish for money or other goods"[144] and instead explained that the actual practices of her Sto:lo ancestors – whether and how they traded fish – were determinative.[145] The Court affirmed the trial court's findings that the exchange of fish (salmon) for money or other goods was not a defining feature of precontact Sto:lo. Although fishing might have been integral to the Sto:lo, exchange of fish was only "incidental" to fishing.[146] Because precontact Sto:lo had developed neither "a regularized trading system,"[147] nor specialization with respect to fishing, the exchange of fish for money could not be central to who they were.[148] In addition, the "qualitatively different" postcontact trade in fish that developed with employees of the Hudson's Bay Company obviated a finding of continuity.[149] Although the majority upheld Van der Peet's conviction, the dissenting judges found an Aboriginal right "to sell, trade and barter fish for livelihood, support and sustenance purposes" or "to provide the modern equivalent of the amenities which they traditionally have obtained from the resource, whether directly or indirectly, through trade."[150]

All of the judges in *Van der Peet* pointed to Aboriginal laws and customs as a source of Aboriginal rights.[151] In her dissent, Justice McLachlin

---

[143] See, e.g., op. cit., para. 165.
[144] This was in part because of the lack of evidence regarding the sale of fish on a broader scale. *Van der Peet*, para. 77.
[145] Op. cit., para. 79.
[146] Op. cit., para. 86.
[147] Op. cit., para. 88.
[148] Op. cit., para. 91.
[149] Op. cit., para. 89.
[150] E.g., op. cit., paras. 221 and 281.
[151] Op. cit. para. 40 for the majority.

The Lethality of the Canadian State's (Re)cognition

emphasized Aboriginal laws and customs when articulating a section 35 test that would also be workable for the Métis, who are themselves "products" of the encounter between Aboriginal peoples and Europeans. Disagreeing with the choice of the moment of contact, she stated "the better question is what laws and customs held sway before the superimposition of European laws and customs."[152] An inquiry into laws and customs holding sway invariably leads to the question of the self-government of peoples. However, even though the federal government had recognized an inherent right to self-government in 1995,[153] the Supreme Court was reluctant to follow suit. In its *Pamajewon* decision, the Court did not address self-government directly but stated that if self-government was a section 35 right, then its determination would fall under the *Van der Peet* test.[154]

The question of self-government resurfaced the following year in *Delgamuukw*, which involved a claim by Gitksan and Wet'suwet'en hereditary chiefs to some "58,000 square kilometres of northwestern British Columbia."[155] At the trial level, the chiefs brought their land claim forward on behalf of fifty-one Gitksan and Wet'suwet'en Houses. These Houses were organized along matrilineal lines of clans and houses, similar to what Swanton had described of their neighbors, the Haida, nearly 100 years earlier.[156] The trial judge had allowed a *de facto* amendment to translate the fifty-one Houses' claims to "ownership" and "jurisdiction" into claims to "aboriginal title" and "self-government."[157] The Supreme Court, however, found that the failure to amend the fifty-one individual claims into communal claims by two "nations" had prejudiced the respondent

---

[152] Op. cit., para. 248.

[153] Minister of Indian Affairs and Northern Development, *Aboriginal Self-Government: Federal Policy Guide – The Government of Canada's Approach to Implementation of the Inherent Right and the Negotiation of Aboriginal Self-Government*. Ottawa: Public Works and Government Services Canada, 1995.

[154] In R. v. Pamajewon, [1996] 2 S.C.R. 821, the Supreme Court heard an appeal from Anishinaabe ("Ojibwa") members of the Shawanaga and Eagle Lake First Nations who had been convicted for keeping a common gaming house. The members argued that both gambling and self-government (including the regulation of gambling) were section 35 rights. The Court, however, did not address the self-government claim. It stated that the proper characterization of the claim was the "right to participate in, and to regulate, high stakes gambling activities on the reservation" (para 26). It cited the lack of evidence regarding both large-scale gambling and its regulation by the Ojibwa to affirm the conviction.

[155] *Delgamuukw*, para. 73.

[156] See ch. 4, entitled "Witsuwit'en Institutions," by an anthropologist who also testified for the plaintiffs at trial. Antonia Mills, *Eagle Down in Our Law: Witsuwit'en Law, Feasts and Land Claims*. Vancouver: University of British Columbia Press, 1994.

[157] *Delgamuukw*, para. 74.

provincial and federal Crowns by denying them "the opportunity to know the appellants' case."[158] This fatal defect recalls the language of cognition that renamed indigenous peoples "Indian bands," a term replaced by "First Nation."[159] The Crown could know the Gitksan and Wet'suwet'en only as two First Nations. Much like Justice King's refusal to recognize Mrs. Logan's claims on behalf of the Haudenosaunee hereditary chiefs four decades earlier, the provincial and federal Crowns could not recognize a people as they saw and spoke of themselves.

Despite this persistent mis-sight, the Court took steps beyond *Van der Peet* with regard to Aboriginal title. Although the Court affirmed that Aboriginal title was a subset of Aboriginal rights, it found "that aboriginal title encompasses the right to exclusive use and occupation of the land held pursuant to that title for a variety of purposes, which need not be aspects of those aboriginal practices, customs and traditions which are integral to distinctive aboriginal cultures."[160] The Court chose the moment of the assertion of sovereignty, that is, the moment when underlying title shifts to the Crown, as the moment at which occupation had to be exclusive and to which present-day occupation must be traced. At least one aspect of culture remained, however: "those protected uses must not be irreconcilable with the nature of the group's attachment to that land."[161] The *Delgamuukw* Court thus moved away from the *Van der Peet* test yet built on that case's references to laws and customs by identifying "the relationship between the common law and pre-existing systems of aboriginal law"[162] as a source of Aboriginal title.

The *Delgamuukw* reference to pre-existing systems of aboriginal law raised the possibility of seeing Aboriginal peoples as peoples. As Kent McNeil points out, however, the Court tended to see preexisting Aboriginal laws and customs as means to determine exclusive occupancy at the moment of the assertion of sovereignty rather than as imbuing Aboriginal title with its content.[163] In other words, Aboriginal law was grasped more

[158] Moreover, the Court noted, the appellants had not had the benefit of the *Pamajewon* judgment and thus had "advanced the right to self-government in very broad terms, and therefore in a manner not cognizable under s. 35(1)." Op. cit., paras. 76 and 170.
[159] Indian and Northern Affairs, Canada, "Terminology," Indian and Northern Affairs, Canada, http://www.ainc-inac.gc.ca/pr/info/tln_e.html.
[160] Op. cit., para. 117.
[161] Op. cit.
[162] Op. cit., para. 114.
[163] Kent McNeil, "Aboriginal Title and the Supreme Court: What's Happening?" *Saskatchewan Law Review* 69 (2006): 282, paras. 15 and 18.

as fact than as law because it did not define title but was instrumental in proving it.[164] This use of Aboriginal law is similar to how the Aboriginal perspective was taken into account by the majority in *Van der Peet*. McNeil then argues that even if Gitksan and Wet'suwet'en law does not define title, it must have continued to apply after the assertion of sovereignty because "there was no official British presence in the Gitksan and Wet'suwet'en territories, apart from a few Hudson's Bay Company traders" in 1846.[165] A further complication is that until surrendered, title lands are supposed to be within federal – not provincial – jurisdiction. Because many of the claimed lands lie outside the *Indian Act* regime, these lands "should not have been subject to provincial land laws."[166]

McNeil argues that Aboriginal title necessarily has a "jurisdictional" quality to it because the lands are held communally.[167] When courts emphasize physical occupancy at the moment of the assertion of sovereignty, however, they overlook the necessarily lawful connection between a people and its homeland by unwittingly reproducing the dangling comma of section 91(24) that pries "Indians" from "Indian lands." This emphasis reduces living indigenous laws to historical matters of fact, repeating the cognition of the *Royal Proclamation* by "re-granting" to indigenous peoples their own homelands bereft of their jurisdictional ties to the land. McNeil points to the emphasis on physical occupancy in later cases but also to minority voices according to which Aboriginal perspectives must be allowed to reshape common law conceptions of property, the occupancy standard, and even Aboriginal title itself.[168]

Assimilation: The Law of Reconcilation

Because the Court subordinated recognition to reconciliation as the overarching goal of section 35, whichever recognition takes place in the first stage of its analysis is vulnerable to the reconciliation that takes place in

---

[164] The working out of this theme of the reduction of Aboriginal law to fact is prominent in the work of Kirsten Anker, to whom we are indebted.
[165] McNeil, "Aboriginal Title," para. 20.
[166] Op. cit., para. 21.
[167] Op. cit., paras. 23 and 22.
[168] Op. cit., McNeil cites Lebel J. in *R. v. Marshall; R. v. Bernard*, [2005] 2 S.C.R. 220, para. 130: "The role of the aboriginal perspective cannot be simply to help in the interpretation of aboriginal practices in order to assess whether they conform to common law concepts of title. The aboriginal perspective shapes the very concept of aboriginal title."

the second. Whereas the *Sparrow* Court read section 35 as a "guarantee" of rights, it ruled that section 35 rights could be limited. It thus treated section 35 as if it contained a provision similar to section 1 of the *Charter*, which states that Charter rights are subject "only to such reasonable limits prescribed by law as can be demonstrably justified in a free and democratic society."[169]

The Court elaborated a test for the justification of limits to Aboriginal rights akin to that elaborated in *Oakes* for *Charter* rights.[170] As in a Charter case, the first step is to see whether there is a governmental objective sufficiently important to warrant limiting the right in question. Whereas the second part of the *Oakes* test demands a proportionality analysis, the second part of the *Sparrow* test centers on "the honour of the Crown." In addition to considering proportionality, courts ask additional questions such as whether "the aboriginal group in question had been consulted" and whether "in a situation of expropriation, fair compensation is available."[171] The *Sparrow* Court rejected the "public interest" as a justification for limiting Aboriginal rights because it was "so vague as to provide no meaningful guidance" but accepted that "[t]he justification of conservation and resource management" was "uncontroversial."[172]

In *Gladstone*, a companion case to *Van der Peet*, the majority of the Supreme Court affirmed a right of the Heiltsuk to "to sell herring spawn on kelp to an extent best described as commercial."[173] The majority found it necessary to revisit the *Sparrow* test because, unlike the Musqueam right to fish for food and ceremonial purposes, the right of the Heiltsuk had no "internal" limitations. Without "internal" or "inherent" limitations, the majority reasoned, a strict approach to justification would turn a priority for Aboriginal fisheries into an exclusive right to fish.[174] The *Sparrow* test therefore had to be relaxed. In addition to conservation, the majority added other objectives "such as the pursuit of economic and regional fairness, and the recognition of the historical reliance upon, and participation in, the fishery by non-aboriginal groups."[175]

---

[169] *Constitution Act, 1982*.
[170] *R. v. Oakes*, [1986] 1 S.C.R. 103.
[171] *Sparrow*, para. 82.
[172] Op. cit., paras. 72–73.
[173] *R. v. Gladstone*, [1996] 2 S.C.R. 723, para. 28.
[174] Op. cit., paras. 57 and 59.
[175] Op. cit., para. 75.

The majority's approach in *Gladstone* was explicitly rooted in the "reconciliation" of "distinctive Aboriginal societies" with the "broader political community" of which they are a part and "over which the Crown is sovereign."[176] Limits to Aboriginal rights, the Court wrote, were just as important to this reconciliation as the rights themselves. Indeed, "the reconciliation of aboriginal societies with the rest of Canadian society may well depend" on the "successful attainment" of goals important to that community.[177] The words of the *Gladstone* majority mimic those of the *Royal Proclamation*, in which the relation of the Crown to Indian tribes or nations is overshadowed by their presence within territory claimed by the Crown. What is most striking, however, is not so much the judges' insistence on Crown sovereignty as their forgetting the distinctive character of Aboriginal rights tied to the Crown's honor and its promise of protection.

This judicial amnesia was resisted by Justice McLachlin in her *Van der Peet* dissent (where she answered the *Gladstone* majority). Her dissent was partially anchored in her belief that infusing the law of identification with internal limits would lead to a more reasonable approach to justifying limits to rights. She also brought attention, however, to the dangers of "treating the guarantee of aboriginal rights under section 35(1) as if it were a guarantee of individual rights under the Charter."[178] Requiring Aboriginal peoples be "taken into account" was not necessarily sufficient to uphold the Crown's fiduciary duty towards them. In fact, the "limited priority" given to the fishery in *Sparrow* could be made "meaningless" by failing to distinguish between limitations "required for the responsible exercise of the right" and those imposed "on the basis of the economic demands of non-aboriginals."[179] Justice McLachlin's dissent reminds us how forgetting the distinctive character of Aboriginal rights leads to the simplification of their rights into Charter rights and ultimately to the assimilation of indigenous peoples into the broader Canadian population.

Simplifying Aboriginal rights into Charter rights, reasoned Justice McLachlin, makes Aboriginal "interests" commensurable with the "interests" of Canadians at large and thus easily traded off in the ensuing

---

[176] Op. cit., para 73.
[177] Op. cit., para. 75.
[178] *Van der Peet*, para. 308
[179] Op. cit., para. 306.

governmental calculation to which judges will defer as long as the government decision "represents a 'reasonable' resolution of conflicting interests."[180] This line of reasoning recalls Harold Cardinal's fear that the *White Paper* would undo what little promise remained of the *Royal Proclamation*. Simplifying "Aboriginal rights" into Charter rights leads to a section 35 that can no longer provide a "solid constitutional base" for negotiations and relieves politicians of the burden of reconciliation.[181]

Just one year later, in the *Delgamuukw* case involving Aboriginal title, where internal limitations are much less present, Justice McLachlin joined Chief Justice Lamer (the author of the *Van der Peet*'s trilogy majority) in endorsing the revised approach to justification. Because Aboriginal peoples "exist within, and are a part of, a broader social, political and economic community"[182] to which they must be reconciled, the majority wrote, a "fairly broad" range of objectives can be of sufficient importance to limit Aboriginal title. The list that the Court gave included "... the development of agriculture, forestry, mining, and hydroelectric power, the general economic development of the interior of British Columbia, protection of the environment or endangered species, the building of infrastructure and the settlement of foreign populations to support those aims."[183]

The law of justification permits general objectives, like developing agriculture, logging, or mining, as McNeil notes, to justify the expropriation of a constitutionally protected and exclusive property right for private purposes.[184] This line of reasoning, he adds, is not surprising given the "reality" that most "private land rights" in British Columbia "were created without any surrender of that [Aboriginal] title."[185] Drawing on the Australian High Court decision in *Mabo*, he notes the judicial reluctance to overturn a past decision if to do so would "fracture a skeletal principle of our legal system," namely the protection of vested rights.[186] What is more,

---

[180] Op. cit., para. 309.
[181] Op. cit., paras. 309 and 313.
[182] *Delgamuukw*, para. 165. This passage is drawn from Gladstone.
[183] Op. cit., para. 175.
[184] Kent McNeil, "The Vulnerability of Indigenous Land Rights in Australia and Canada," *Osgoode Hall Law Journal* 42 (2004), p. 271, para. 35.
[185] Op. cit., para. 41.
[186] Op. cit., para. 40.

the danger posed by the Court's approach to justification is not simply that it ratifies the dishonorable actions of the past but that it justifies their repetition in the future.

The majority *Delgamuukw* decision ends with a return to *Sparrow*'s words about section 35 providing "a solid constitutional base upon which subsequent negotiations can take place." The Court sent the matter back to trial but invited the Crown, the Gitksan, Wet'suwet'en, and all the "other aboriginal nations which have a stake in the territory claimed" to negotiate. Anticipating or provoking future litigation, the majority asserted "the Crown is under a moral, if not a legal, duty to enter into and conduct those negotiations in good faith." The majority judgment ends with a further recitation of section 35's purpose as "the reconciliation of the pre-existence of aboriginal societies with the sovereignty of the Crown" followed by these final words: "Let us face it, we are all here to stay."[187]

Conclusion

This chapter has sketched the Canadian state's cognition of indigenous peoples and its persistence in the Supreme Court's adjudication of the constitutional recognition of Aboriginal rights. The persistence of cognition in recognition is bound up with what Nietzsche names *state idolatry*, that is, reconciliation as submission to Crown sovereignty. Indeed, aside from signifying knowing again, recognition is also properly grasped as a performance of a recognizer that inscribes a recognizee in an economy of sight. To recognize is to grant visibility. By granting visibility, the state makes something or someone legible with the mark of recognition, the mark of authority.[188]

As the static sight of cognition hypostatizes what it sees, it insulates the one who sees from the perils of experience, including the experience of others, and from the radical openness of the future. With the static sight

---

[187] *Delgamuukw*, para. 186.

[188] Markell writes, referring explicitly to Scott, that to ask for state recognition is to "further the state's project of rendering the social world "legible," "to present oneself as knowable," "to offer the state the reciprocal recognition of its sovereignty that it demands." Patchen Markell, *Bound by Recognition*. Princeton: Princeton University Press, 2003, p. 31, or, as Nietzsche puts the matter: "It will give *you* everything if *you* worship it, this new idol . . ." Nietzsche, *Zarathustra*, p. 76.

of cognition, the fantasy of sovereignty need not be surrendered.[189] To recognize others is to fix them, and to reconcile them to oneself is to secure one's future. The ambiguity of the *Royal Proclamation* is precisely that it presents itself as the latest link in a renewed Covenant Chain binding the Crown and indigenous peoples into an unknown future, while unilaterally inscribing Crown sovereignty and securing mastery over that future. Each event that we have considered is an attempt at finality, at fixity, by the Canadian state.

Today, a few thousand people of Haida and European ancestry live on Haida Gwaii, the Queen Charlotte Islands. Many cedars bearing Haida marks, although not all, have been cut down since the Council of the Haida Nation began their land claim nearly three decades ago.[190] In 2002, the Council lodged a statement of claim for Aboriginal title to Haida Gwaii, "the homeland of the Haida people," based on their continued "spiritual relationship with the beings and the spirits of the earth, the forests, the sea and the sky."[191] The Supreme Court narrowed their *prima facie* title claim to the single question of whether the Crown owed them a duty to consult regarding the forests – in this instance regarding a renewal and transfer of tree farm licenses for transnational logging companies - until their claim was proved. The Court found that no fiduciary duty attached to unproven title, but that there was a duty to consult rooted in the "honour of the Crown."[192]

The *Haida Nation* decision reaffirms the promise of recognition as a duty to indigenous peoples, a duty to see properly and speak honorably. This duty might ultimately require the surrender of the sovereign knowledge of cognition. The paradoxical promise of recognition without cognition might be the promise of a future, for all Canadians, "where the state *ceases*."[193]

---

[189] These concluding remarks are indebted to Markell, *Bound*, and gesture toward some of the themes raised therein.

[190] *Haida Nation v. British Columbia (Minister of Forests)*, [2004] 3 S.C.R. 511.

[191] Op. cit., para. 10(b).

[192] Op. cit., paras. 16, 39–41. This duty requires the Crown only to act in good faith by providing meaningful consultation appropriate to the circumstances, however.

[193] Nietzsche, *Zarathustra*.

PART II

INVESTIGATING THE DISCOURSES OF DEATH

9

Death in the First Person

Peter Brooks

The scaffold is the only edifice that revolutions don't demolish.
— Victor Hugo, 1832 preface to *Le Dernier jour d'un condamné*

The French debate on the abolition of the death penalty begins in late Enlightenment thinking, and abolition is called for in some of the *cahiers de doléances* (list of grievances) prepared for the meeting of the Estates-General that marked the inception of the first phase of the French Revolution. Abolitionists included Robespierre and others who would later use the guillotine heavily in their political purges. What if the Reign of Terror had forsworn capital punishment? The history of the world would have been startlingly altered. The abolition campaign did not succeed then, however, nor when it again became of acute interest following the bloodless French Revolution of 1830, nor quite after the February 1848 Revolution, despite a remarkably progressive set of legislative acts by the short-lived Second Republic, which was terminated by Napoléon III's coup d'état. In 1981, under the leadership of Minister of Justice Robert Badinter, the abolitionist goal was finally achieved, giving the French again the role that they have cherished since 1789, as proponents of universal ideals of human rights.

Victor Hugo's novel of a man about to be guillotined dates from 1829. It is the work of a 26-year-old who began his precocious writing career as a monarchist and Catholic, founder of a journal called *Le Conservateur littéraire*. *Le Dernier Jour d'un Condamné* (*The Last Day of a Man Sentenced to Death*) does not come from nowhere, but it is difficult to situate. The novel prepares for, rather than responds to, the legislative debate on the death penalty that would come a year later. Only in 1832, with a new edition of the novel, did Hugo add a long discursive preface in which he identified the novel as a pleading for the abolition of capital punishment.[1] The novel appears in many ways to be a visceral and personal work. It prepares Hugo's later "social" novels, especially *Les Misérables* (1862), and his self-appointed role as a political and social conscience for his century – a role that led, late in his career, to the novel written about the *année terrible* that saw French defeat in the war with Prussia, the siege of Paris, the insurrection of the Paris Commune, and its bloody suppression: *Quatrevingt-treize* (*Ninety-Three*; 1874). Named for the year of the Terror, *Quatrevingt-treize* was conceived as an act of reconciliation among his compatriots, bringing the partisans of revolution into a peaceful understanding with the royalists and authoritarians. The guillotine plays a large role in that novel, as well as in *Le Dernier Jour d'un Condamné*.

The guillotine is of particular importance, both in Hugo's work and in the French discourse on capital punishment. Dr. Joseph-Ignace Guillotin's proposal, early in the French Revolution, to use the machine that would bear his name gives a particular coloring to the French debate: capital punishment by means of the guillotine, after all, works by severing the head from the body. For intellectuals, this becomes a matter for thought, because the thinking part no longer is attached to the bodily part.[2] One could say that execution by the guillotine offers some sinister parodic realization of Cartesian dualism: the thinking self detached from the living self, in an impossible moment of reflection. Cogito ergo sum: does the detached head still think, if only for nanoseconds? Albert Camus' reflections on the guillotine rehearse the evidence for the horror of a momentary survival of sensation following the fall of the severing blade.[3] Asked by his guard what he is thinking, Hugo's condemned man replies, "I am thinking... that I will no longer be thinking this evening" ("Je pense... que je ne penserai plus ce soir"; 314). The separation of head from body by the guillotine seems to heighten, to intensify. This kind of anguished paradox posed by

---

[1] Victor Hugo, *Bug-Jargal et le Dernier Jour d'un Condamné*. Paris: Livre de Poche, 1970; hereafter cited parenthetically by page number. My translation. There is a recent English translation, *The Last Day of a Condemned Man and Other Prison Writings*, trans. Geoff Woollen. Oxford: Oxford World Classics, 1992.

[2] See, among other works on the imaginative role of the guillotine, Daniel Arasse, *La guillotine et l'imaginaire de la Terreur*. Paris: Flammarion, 1987; translated in English as *The Guillotine and the Terror*, trans. Christopher Miller. London: Allen Lane, 1989.

[3] See Albert Camus, "Réflexions sur la guillotine," in *Essais*. Paris: Bibliothèque de la Pléiade, 1965, 1021–1064. Camus' essay was earlier published with another by Arthur Koestler on hanging, in *Réflexions sur la peine capitale*. Paris: Calmann-Lévy, 1957.

death sentences of all sorts: the being that is now warm and capable shall have instantaneously ceased to be; the very thought process now carried forward will have ceased to be. As Georges Danton was supposed to have reflected on the eve of his own execution, you cannot conjugate the verb *to guillotine* in all its tenses: you can say, "I will be guillotined," but you cannot say, "I have been guillotined."[4]

The separation of *caput* from *corpus* seems in this manner to nourish an impossible dialogue of self and soul or of soul and body – traditional medieval literary practices. How can thought take place in the knowledge that it will cease with death, with the severing of head from body? It is an extreme version of a problem in traditional apologetics. See, for instance, the first of John Donne's *Holy Sonnets*: "Thou hast made me, and shall Thy work decay?" The traditional Christian answer is the resurrection, which is traditionally a bodily resurrection. That is why in the Roman Catholic Church bodies had to be buried integrally and in consecrated soil. The dismembered body – whether intentionally torn apart and scattered as in certain executions with added infamy or through accident – could be a source of anguish even in death. The use of the guillotine on a massive scale during the Terror brought various macabre rituals, such as holding the severed head up for the mob to see (note Danton's words to the executioner, "Be sure to show my head to the people, it's well worth it"[5]) or the wearing of scarlet or black ribbons around the neck, in imitation of the mark of the blade, at the "victims' balls" that followed the Terror. A curious consequence of the Terror is reported by Philippe Pinel, the remarkable "alienist" (as a specialist in mental disturbances tended to be called at the time) who took over the Salpêtrière Hospital for the insane during the Revolution and instituted his "dramaturgical" cures, in which patients were encouraged to act out their anxieties and obsessions. A patient in the Salpêtrière who had fallen under suspicion during the Terror (now past) remained unshakably convinced that he had lost his head on the guillotine and then had the wrong one restored to him. To those who told him this was an unreasonable belief, he replied with the story of Saint Denis, represented in traditional iconography carrying his head in

---

[4] Georges Danton, quoted in Stendhal, *Le Rouge et le Noir*. Paris: Garnier/Flammarion, 1964, 478.
[5] Georges Danton, quoted at www.brainyquote.com/quotes/g/georgesjac127530.html (accessed January 9, 2008).

his hands after suffering the martyrdom of beheading. Another inmate was coached to engage this man in dialogue about Saint Denis' relation to his severed head. Did he kiss it from regret and affection? Yes, but what did he kiss it with – his posterior, perhaps? The notion was to expose the obsession for what it was through ridicule and laughter.[6] In this case, we are told, the cure worked.

The decapitation obsession of Pinel's patient resonates with Hugo's condemned man, who at the outset of his narrative insists on the *idea* of his impending execution. "Sentenced to death! It's now five weeks that I have been living with this idea, always alone with it, always chilled by its presence, always bent under its weight" (265). So begins his account, started the morning of what will turn out to be his last day alive, as he awaits transport from his cell in Bicêtre prison to the Conciergerie, where he will be prepared for execution and taken to the Place de Grève, before the Hôtel de Ville, where the guillotine traditionally was erected: "My body is in irons in a cell, my mind is imprisoned in an idea. A horrible, a bloody, an implacable idea. I no longer have any but one single thought, one conviction, one certainty: sentenced to death!" (265–266). Nothing else can be thought in the face of the overwhelming imminence of the cessation of any thought, the idea of the self's extinction.

There is a sense in which the deep source of Hugo's anguish and resentment seems to be not only the death penalty but death itself. His condemned man recalls having read in a book that "all men are condemned to death, with an unspecified reprieve" (273). This sounds like Pascal's image of the human condition, in which we are all on death row, simply waiting for an end that is as arbitrary as it is inevitable.[7] The young Hugo, like his protagonist, appears to be haunted by the presence of death in life, the thought of his extinction. "What!" the condemned man reflects, "the sun, springtime, the fields full of flowers, the birds that wake up in the morning, clouds, trees, nature, freedom, life, all that is no longer mine!" (279). To the reflective consciousness, death is unthinkable, even

---

[6] On Pinel and on this case, see Jan E. Goldstein, *Console and Classify: The French Psychiatric Profession in the Nineteenth Century*. Chicago: University of Chicago Press, 1987, 83.

[7] "Let us imagine a number of men in chains and all condemned to death where some are slaughtered each day in the sight of the others, and those who remain see their own fates in that of their fellows and, looking at one another sorrowfully and without hope, wait their turn. It is the image of the human condition." Blaise Pascal, *Pensées*, ed. Louis Lafuma. Paris: Delmas, 1960, #314 (Lafuma), #199 (Brunschvicq).

Death in the First Person

scandalous. When in his holding cell the condemned man discovers the inscriptions left by previous occupants – including the authors of some notoriously bloody crimes – he is once again impressed by the reality of the unthinkable. The bodies of these predecessors lie in the potter's field at Clamart – his will too. As he waits in the Conciergerie, the condemned man asks himself

> Oh, is it really true that I am going to die before the end of this day? Is it true that it's me? This muffled sound of cries that I hear outside, this crowd of joyful people who are already hastening along the embankment, the policemen who are getting ready in their barracks, this priest in his black cassock, this other man with red hands, it's for me! I am the one who is going to die! Me, the same who is here, who is alive, who moves, who breathes, who is seated at this table, which looks like any other table, and could just as well be elsewhere; myself, in fact, this self that I touch and feel, whose clothing makes these very folds before my eyes. (325)

If we are all sentenced to death, as in Pascal's understanding of our condition, why should the death sentence imposed by a court of justice be so unbearable, so outrageous? Here I think we come close to the core of Hugo's revulsion at the death sentence: it doubles the natural, the inhuman outrage of death with the obscenity of a death intentionally imposed by human action. It is not only that the death penalty is an arrogation by humans of a power that is not properly theirs – that belongs to nature or fate or the deity or whichever other cosmic name one chooses – but also that willfully killing another human being is a violation of that wretched human community that Pascal describes as a bunch of convicts on death row. If we are all on death row, then there is all the more reason to refrain from doing nature's cruel work. To take an animate, breathing person with blood circulating in his or her veins and intentionally reduce that person to nonbeing is wrong and obscene. Death is something that humans should repudiate and stay away from; to build a machine for killing one's fellow men is barbarous.[8]

---

[8] For an interesting study of execution as abjection in this novel, see Allen Stoekl, "Hugo's *Le dernier jour d'un condamné*: The End as Contamination," *Diacritics* 30.3 (2000): 40–52. On Hugo's apparent dialogue with the poet André Chénier (guillotined during the Terror), during his table-tipping séances in Jersey in 1853–1854, see the notable essay by Suzanne Guerlac, "Phantom Rights: Conversations across the Abyss (Hugo, Blanchot)," *Diacritics* 30.3 (2000): 73–89.

One might think of the moment in Charles Dickens's *Great Expectations* when Abel Magwitch – the former convict who has been Pip's secret benefactor – is sentenced to death for having returned illegally from his transport to Australia. Severely wounded in his final attempt to flee from England before the law caught up with him, and indeed dying from his wounds, Magwitch at the climactic end of sessions is brought before the bar with a crowd of thirty-two prisoners, all to be sentenced to death:

> The sun was striking in at the great windows of the court, through the glittering drops of rain upon the glass, and it made a broad shaft of light between the two-and-thirty and the judge, linking both together, and perhaps reminding some among the audience how both were passing on, with absolute equality, to the greater Judgment that knoweth all things, and cannot err. Rising for a moment, a distinct speck of face in this way of light, the prisoner said, "My lord, I have received my sentence of death from the Almighty, but I bow to yours." There was some hushing, and the judge went on with what he had to say to the rest. They were all formally doomed.[9]

In Dickens's rendition (as implicitly in Pascal's) the death sentence is superfluous, because God has already done the work – superfluous in a bad way, in an encroachment of puny human justice (which in the case of Magwitch has missed the point) on that "greater Judgment that knoweth all things." Dickens's human judge is misguided, the dupe of a belief in the capacity of humans to hand out ultimate justice.

This surely is a deep source of objection to the death penalty. If one sets aside Dickens's confidence in that greater judgment – Hugo's novel evinces no belief in the consolations provided by the condemned man's priest and absolutely no promise of an afterlife – the problem is only the more troubling. In the name of what do we pronounce the death sentence on other living beings? The law of retaliation might apply to the immediate response to threat or provocation or outrage, but does this authorize the state's apparatus of death? Hugo's condemned man reminds us at several moments of the vast state machinery put into motion by execution: the police and even army corps mustered to keep order, the procession to

---

[9] Charles Dickens, *Great Expectations*. New York: NAL/Signet Classic, 1998, p. 462.

Death in the First Person

the guillotine, the walk-on parts of a whole cast of assistants in the death-dealing process. This scene becomes highly theatrical at the moment that the door of the Conciergerie is opened – "Hideous tableau, well framed in the prison door" (357) – to escort the prisoner to the tumbrel that will take him down the quay and across the river to the Hôtel de Ville: screaming populace, mounted police, soldiers in battle gear, and then the tumbrel, ladder angled against its back.

At the Hôtel de Ville, the condemned man claims that he has a declaration to make – which results in his momentary sequestration in a room of the Hôtel de Ville and the visit of a magistrate, to whom he pleads for clemency. The magistrate merely smiles and asks if that is all he has to say. The rope tying the condemned man's hands is removed, but it lies before him on the table where he writes, ready once again to bind his hands behind his back so that he can without resistance go on the movable plank that will lower his head into position on the guillotine. The executioner comes to say it is nearly the appointed hour; the magistrate leaves. The condemned man is alone with two gendarmes; the crowd outside howls in anticipation. "Oh, the wretches! It seems to me that someone is coming back up the stairs.... FOUR O'CLOCK" (363). With these capital letters – "QUATRE HEURES" – the text comes to an end. The appointed time names the fall of the blade. It is not that there is no more to be said; rather, the protagonist is not left to say it.

We realize that the last part of the condemned man's narrative has supposedly been composed in that room of the Hôtel de Ville, completing what he has jotted down in his other cells (at Bicêtre and the Conciergerie) on this final day. The coming of four o'clock brings us to the scaffold – to the threshold of extinction that is a final silence. It is implausible, you will say – even with a condemned man whom we know to be literate and thoughtful. It is a bit like the convention that has epistolary heroines such as Pamela and Clarissa, in Samuel Richardson's novels, scribbling letters in their private "closets" as a seducer is trying to force open the door. In the epistolary novel, Richardson boasted, narrations can be nearly instantaneous with the events they narrate. Epistolary novels provide more of a justification for this immediate writing, in the use of letters as communication, as a report to another on one's situation. The raison d'être of the condemned man's writing is harder to find: to whom does he address his words and why? If it is quite implausible that he would really be furnished with pen and paper in the three cells that he occupies during his last day, is it not equally implausible that he would seek to write at all at this point? The moment for writing would seem to have passed.

If you were setting out to write a novel about the last day of a man sentenced to execution, it is unlikely that you would choose to narrate the story in the first person. Of course, you might want to enter the consciousness of your condemned protagonist to track his inner reactions on the way to execution – this likely would be a large part of your interest in the story. You might also take your exploration of consciousness virtually all the way to its extinction, as, for instance, Arthur Koestler does with Rubashov in *Darkness at Noon*: "A second, smashing blow hit him on the ear. Then all became quiet. There was the sea again with its sounds. A wave slowly lifted him up. It came from afar and it traveled sedately on, a shrug of eternity."[10] Normally, however, you would want to leave yourself a margin from which to write your story: the margin provided by another consciousness, a narrative agency that lives on after the pistol shot or the fall of the blade. To choose to write a last-day story in the voice of the person whose last day it is strikes us as perverse or inept.

We are free to find Hugo's narrative stance in *Le Dernier Jour d'un Condamné* inept, and certainly it is perverse, with what I believe is a considerable awareness on Hugo's part of its perversity. Much of the power that this novel still delivers, nearly two centuries after it was written, comes from the first-person narration. This perspective is responsible for the crucial pathos of the novel, the excruciating experience it gives the reader. Our direct, unmediated access to this tortured consciousness facing its imminent extinction, its loss of the power to speak, makes the novel what it is. The implausibilities of the novel are less important than its terrifying immediacy. This is a novel that makes its reader uncomfortable. To be confined to this mind and self that we know will come to an abrupt and bloody appointed end brings a strange sort of claustrophobia. Like the condemned man, we want out, and out is what there isn't – the thing must inexorably continue to its end. Again, the word *obscenity* is the one that I find myself using: there is something obscene about being privy to the consciousness of someone about to be put to death.

---

[10] Arthur Koestler, *Darkness at Noon*, trans. Daphne Hardy. New York: Macmillan, 1941, p. 267.

Hugo's condemned man tells us little about himself and nothing about his crime. We know that he has a young daughter – he recounts a visit that she pays him in prison – but we learn nothing else about his family situation, his possible profession (he is not from the lower level of society like the other convicts around him, who often horrify him), and nothing about any story or condition that might have led him to crime. He does promise in Chapter 46 to write the history of his life for his daughter, so that she know later on "why the name I am leaving her is a bloody one" (353). When we turn the page to Chapter 47, however, we are given a "publisher's note": "We have not been able to find the pages that should have been attached here. Perhaps, as those that follow seem to indicate, the condemned man didn't have time to write them. It was already late when this thought came to him" (354). It was late, indeed, because when the next chapter begins he is in the Hôtel de Ville, and the guillotine outside is ready. The explanatory narrative – this one explicitly motivated as the explanation of his crime to be read by his daughter when she is an adult – is lost or never written. There is to be no *apologia pro vita sua*. The condemned man also is never named in the course of the novel. He is a kind of faceless, identity-less Everyman, defined only by crime and punishment.

Hugo has been much criticized for the seemingly generic quality of his condemned man and especially for eliding the crime that has brought him to this punishment. It is presumably a homicide of some sort – we know it is a bloody crime in any event – not the stealing of a loaf of bread, for which Jean Valjean is sent to the galleys in *Les Misérables*. There is no revisiting the crime; its existence is perfunctory. It is entirely different from Raskolnikov's murder in *Crime and Punishment*, for example. Hugo's project is evidently quite different from Fyodor Dostoevsky's epic examination of crime, conscience, confession, and expiation. It suits Hugo's purposes better to leave issues of guilt, remorse, and penance out of the equation. The author is interested in one thing only: the consciousness knowing that it will cease to be before the day is over. Near the beginning, as the condemned man asks himself whether his inward record of his last day will have any utility to others – should it survive – he calls his narrative "this history, necessarily incomplete, but as complete as possible, of my sensations" (277). The necessity of its incompletion – he intends to write until "it becomes *physically* impossible to continue" (277) – is of course the point. If narrative endings are always important, here it is precisely the impossible ending that matters – the inability to write "finis."

Contrast Hugo's insight here with the obscenely trivializing use of the idea of "closure" to a story evoked (to take only one egregious example from among many) by U.S. Attorney General John Ashcroft, at the execution of convicted Oklahoma City bomber Timothy McVeigh. Choosing to let the survivors of the bombing and the victims' relatives watch the execution on closed-circuit television, Ashcroft said, "I hope we can help them meet their need to close this chapter in their lives."[11] Here we have what you might call a humanistic insight perverted as it becomes a cliché of the culture. The idea that putting someone to death is necessary for others to be able to find tidy chapter endings in their lives strikes me as potentially monstrous. This concept takes us back implicitly to ritual stonings and similar scenes. It suggests that society needs human sacrifice for the rest of us to live better – rather, to understand our lives in more satisfactory and romantic crime-and-retribution ways.

Ashcroft strikes one as making an obscene, and Hugo a profound, comment on Walter Benjamin's insight in his notable essay "The Storyteller": "Death is the sanction of everything the storyteller can tell. He has borrowed his authority from death."[12] This is because a life takes on its meaning, becomes transmissible as wisdom, only at the moment of death. Only from that retrospective point one can speak of the meaning of a life that has been lived. Because knowledge of the meaning of our own lives is denied to us – we cannot stand beyond the ending that full stops the sentence – we seek such knowledge in the mirror of literature or, in Benjamin's terms, in the "flame" of literature. The fictional death is the "flame" at which the reader warms "his shivering life."[13] Our lives are shivering precisely because they do not equate to a transmissible wisdom. Especially in the modern era, lives do not tend to gain their meaning from traditional community assignments of role and value. Benjamin, writing in the wake of World War I and the experience of mass destruction and advanced technologies for wounding and killing, suggests that personal experience

---

[11] For a fuller comment on Ashcroft, McVeigh's execution, and the issue of closure to the story, see Peter Brooks, "A Tragedy in Search of an Ending," *The New York Times*, May 4, 2001.

[12] Walter Benjamin, "The Storyteller" ["Der Erzhäler"], in *Illuminations*, ed. Hannah Arendt, trans. Harry Zohn. New York: Schocken Books, 1969, 94.

[13] Ibid., 101.

Death in the First Person

itself is losing its transmissibility. Death as the "sanction" of the storyteller's narrative recovers meaning and transmissibility – but in the mode of fiction, the mode of the "as-if," which allows you to consider life from the perspective of its ending. Benjamin's insight is not a recipe for state executions.

I have argued elsewhere that narrative fictions organize meanings within time through the anticipation of a retrospective view that will illuminate what has led up to the end and make sense of the muddle of the middle.[14] Plot is what we bring to the unstructured temporality of life to give it shape and meaning. In some large sense, that meaning, as Benjamin claims, ultimately can come only from death. Narrative endings are thus often simulations of the ultimate ending: moments that bring resolution at least to a chapter of existence. The nineteenth-century novel very often stages formal death-bed scenes in which a member of an older generation transmits the wisdom accumulated during a life lived to a young protagonist seeking to forge his or her own significant destiny – promising implicitly that the protagonist's life will also eventually acquire meaning. The meaningful plot precisely stands opposed to the meaninglessness of a verb that cannot be conjugated in all tenses. This fact marks the very frustration of narrative.

Jean-Paul Sartre, another theoretician of narrative endings, recounts in his autobiography, *The Words*, that as a child who always felt contingent, unauthorized, and inauthentic, he found solace in the "poison" of a book entitled *The Childhood of Famous Men*, which recounted the daily lives of boys named Johann Sebastian or Jean-Jacques without ever mentioning who they became but nonetheless giving clues about their future greatness, as Bach or Rousseau, throughout the narrative. So Sartre's solution became one of authoring himself through the postulation of his future greatness, seeing each childhood act as somehow connected to a future identity. He ceases to live so that he can try to mean. As he succinctly states it, "I became my own obituary."[15] Hugo's condemned man is about to become his own obituary but cannot quite. The necessary incompletion of the narrative destroys the obituary form.

---

[14] See Peter Brooks, *Reading for the Plot* (originally published 1984). Cambridge, MA: Harvard University Press, 1995.
[15] Jean-Paul Sartre, *The Words* [*Les Mots*], trans. Bernard Frechtman. New York: Vintage Books, 1981, 206.

Hugo's decision to tell the story of his nameless condemned man's last day in the first person and up to the very moment when pen and paper are taken from him – so that his hands may be tied behind his back – might violate certain conventions of novelistic plausibility but nonetheless quite powerfully provokes a reader's reaction to the state's intentional death dealing. Although the original publication of Hugo's novel in 1829 had only a one-paragraph preface, the second edition, in 1832, came with a long preface in which the author "unmasks" the political and social "idea" that he intended to convey (369). His novel, Hugo says here, is to be read as "a general and permanent plea for all the accused, present and to come" (370). It is an absolute refusal ("cette suprême fin de non-recevoir") inscribed at the entrance to all criminal trials and a consideration of capital punishment not under the auspices of the courtroom but where it must be seen, on the scaffold and with the executioner. Hugo, in his most grandiose style, proclaims: "In the past the social edifice was supported on three pillars, priest, king, and executioner. Already long ago a voice said: the gods are leaving! More recently another voice was raised to cry out: the kings are leaving! Now it is time that a third voice be raised to say: the executioner is leaving!" (397). For Hugo, the very emergence of modern civilization requires this twilight of the executioner, which is in fact the most important disappearance. Hugo writes: "To those who regretted the disappearance of the gods, one could say: God remains. To those who regretted the kings, you can say: the nation remains. To those who might regret the executioner, there is nothing to say" (397). Hugo's grandiose vision goes on expanding. Of crime he says: "We will treat with charity this evil that we used to treat with anger. It will be simple and sublime. The cross takes the place of the gibbet. That is all" (397). Here the 1832 preface ends – with an implicit promise of the kind of romantic social democracy for which Hugo would become known.

"The scaffold is the only edifice that revolutions don't demolish" (373), Hugo notes earlier in the preface, in words that come as a sober reminder of a truth that our times have only engraved more indelibly. On their way to the reformation of society, most of our political and social revolutions have been murderous – not only in battle but also in the use of judicial murder. Could Hugo be right that the real sine qua non of a move forward into a world of social justice is not so much the abolition of priest and king as the abolition of the hangman? It was after all the perception of the leading reactionary philosopher of Hugo's time, Joseph de Maistre, that society reposed on the hangman. If you do not have someone to execute those whom you want to get rid of, the repressive society might be faced with problems, precisely in the execution of its will.

Hugo returned to the question of the guillotine in his final novel, *Quatrevingt-treize*, which he saw as his attempt to heal the deep wound in France caused by and revealed in the Paris Commune of 1871 and its draconian suppression. *Quatrevingt-treize* is an attempt to reconcile the revolutionary and reactionary traditions that had riven France since the Revolution – and would continue to do so despite Hugo's efforts. Hugo's theme is the royalist revolt in the Vendée, near Brittany, a major threat to the revolutionary government facing war on its eastern frontiers as well and one gradually suppressed with much harshness. In Hugo's novel, the royalist Marquis de Lantenac is pitted against his nephew Gauvain, who has become an apostle of revolution, and Cimourdain, an ex-priest and former tutor to Gauvain, who has become an inflexible Jacobin commissioner. The novel reaches its climax in the siege of the medieval fortress La Tourgue by the army sent from Paris, commanded by Gauvain. When Lantenac, in a gesture of self-sacrificing generosity, gives up his escape from the siege to rescue three children caught in the flames set by the battle, Gauvain responds with a corresponding piece of chivalry, letting his prisoner go free. Cimourdain presides at a drumhead tribunal that sentences Gauvain to death for treason, but this is not to be death before the firing squad or by hanging: the Jacobin masters of Paris have seen fit to send a guillotine by special escort to do justice to any and all royalist resisters who are captured. The idea is that revolutionary justice could be executed only on the guillotine.

So what we have toward the end of Hugo's novel is a grandiose symbolic confrontation of the medieval fortress La Tourgue and the guillotine: "A stone monster as pendant to a wooden monster."[16] Hugo continues, in one of his typically overheated prose passages, postulating large equivalences and antitheses:

> An edifice is a dogma, a machine is an idea. La Tourgue was the fatal result of a past called the Bastille in Paris, the Tower of London in England, the Spielberg in Germany, the Escurial in Spain, the Kremlin in Moscow, the Castel San'Angelo in Rome. In La Tourgue

[16] Victor Hugo, *Quatrevingt-treize*. Paris: Folio, 1979, 475; hereafter cited parenthetically by page number.

were compacted fifteen hundred years, the middle ages, vassalage, fief, feudalism; in the guillotine one year, 1793; and these twelve months made a counter-weight to those fifteen centuries. La Tourgue was monarchy, the guillotine was revolution. Tragic confrontation. On one side, the debt; on the other, the payment fallen due. (475)

Out of the tragic past of the medieval fortress – with its prisons and torture chambers and its seigneurial right of high and low justice over everyone and everything around it – comes something as "horrible as itself," this vengeful idea of the guillotine. Hugo writes that the guillotine has the right to say to the fortress, "I am your daughter" (477). The injustices of the medieval fortress have given birth to this ugly mechanism of vengeance.

When Gauvain's head is severed on the guillotine, Cimourdain, who has refused the army's appeal for clemency, pulls his pistol from his belt and shoots himself. The novel ends with their sister souls, the dark and the light, departing earth. It is supposed to offer an image of an end of medieval darkness and of the need for revolutionary justice: this should be the last action of the guillotine, the idea-machine the invention of which might be historically explainable and contextually justified, but that is nonetheless as inexcusable as the dungeons and oubliettes of La Tourgue. No more executions – the cross replaces the gibbet. Not long after the publication of *Quatrevingt-treize*, a young Henry James, residing in Paris, wrote of Hugo's political pronouncements during the electoral campaign of 1876, "Certainly France occasionally produces individuals who express the national conceit with a transcendent fatuity which is not elsewhere to be matched."[17] Hugo is fatuous, no doubt, yet his political-humanitarian program still has a certain sublime resonance to it. His claim that a just society must get rid of the executioner makes a resonant contribution to the debate that culminates in the abolition of capital punishment in France in 1981.

There are, of course, a host of other literary texts that would bear discussion in this context – *Darkness at Noon*, briefly mentioned previously, E. L. Doctorow's novel about the Rosenbergs, *The Book of Daniel*, and Norman Mailer's *The Executioner's Song*, to give a brief and arbitrary list. I want to conclude rather by asking why Hugo's vision of the end of the executioner has not been taken more seriously in the United States. Why

---

[17] Henry James, *Parisian Sketches*, ed. Isle Dusoir Lind. New York: New York University Press, 1957, 66.

has the abolitionist spirit so failed in its absolute claim against capital punishment that it now has become a piecemeal campaign that might indeed prove effective in reducing the number of executions but has a very long road to travel before it approaches abolition?[18] I know that there are a host of causative factors deeply rooted in American history, including racism and a certain addiction to violence, as well as religious traditions that apparently emphasize retribution over forgiveness, but there is also a failure in the moral imagination. Attorney General Ashcroft's decision to put McVeigh's execution on closed-circuit television (carefully encrypted so that it could not be copied) marked some kind of logical victory of the victims' rights movement over whatever one might want to call its opposite, the spirit that reached its apogee in *Furman v. Georgia* in 1972.[19] To insist that victims can achieve "closure" in their history of pain only through the witnessing of the execution of the perpetrator takes us back to a kind of primitive moral logic. This is the logic that presided over the U.S. Supreme Court's decision in *Payne v. Tennessee*, which in 1991 for the first time legitimated victim impact statements at the sentencing phase of capital trials. The opinion, written by Justice William Rehnquist, seems to delectate in the bloody details of the murderous rampage of Tyrone Pervis Payne, the better to ensure retribution.[20]

Recall *Louisiana ex. rel. Francis v. Resweber*,[21] where the failure of the electric chair to kill Willie Francis is characterized by Justice Felix Frankfurter as "an innocent misadventure."[22] Indeed everyone smoothes over the unfortunate mishap in Louisiana's death house until we reach the final footnote, which gives the affidavits of the eyewitnesses:

> Then the hood was placed before his eyes. Then the officials in charge of the electrocution were adjusting the mechanisms and when the needle of the meter registered to a certain point on the dial, the electrocutioner pulled down the switch and at the same time said: "Goodby Willie." At that very moment, Willie Francis' lips puffed out and his body squirmed and tensed and he jumped so that the chair

---

[18] New Jersey abolished the death penalty in 2007; it had not been used in this state for many years. There is not yet evidence that this admirable move by New Jersey will create any sort of abolitionist movement.
[19] *Furman v. Georgia*, 408 U.S. 238 (1972).
[20] *Payne v. Tennessee*, 501 U.S. 808 (1991).
[21] *Louisiana ex. rel. Francis v. Resweber*, 329 U.S. 459 (1947).
[22] Id. at 470.

rocked on the floor. Then the condemned man said: "Take it off. Let me breath [sic]." Then the switch was turned off. Then some of the men left and a few minutes after the Sheriff of St. Martin's Parish, Mr. E. L. Resweber, came in and announced that the governor had granted the condemned man a reprieve.[23]

The reprieve was, of course, ended by the Supreme Court's decision.[24]

Hugo might have recommended telling Francis's story in the first person. That would have been a chilling document and of course an impossible one for several reasons, starting with the unlikelihood that Francis was literate and continuing with the reluctance of the law, at the appellate level, to listen to personal narratives. Francis could have provided what Hugo's condemned man could not: a margin beyond attempted execution from which to speak. I intend this chapter not as a plea for narrative in the law – narratives are no good if no one listens to them – but as a plea to bring imagination back to a subject that has become the property of ideology, on the one hand, and statistical social science (and now to some extent medical science), on the other. Enlightenment thinkers, from Adam Smith to Rousseau, discovered the role of imaginative sympathy as foundational to ethics: it is only through being able to put ourselves imaginatively in another's place that we can act morally. Reason alone cannot do it. As we have seen in recent debates about the use of torture and cruel and inhumane treatment of prisoners in the so-called war on terror, a crabbed and narrow reasoning, including the parsing of statutes and conventions, can blind us to the human truth of pain and inhumanity. As Hugo perceived, the executioner and the torturer (in French, it is the same word for both: *le bourreau*) is fundamental to the repressive state. The killing state does not want us to think imaginatively and empathetically about its executions and its executioners. That is why pleadings such as Hugo's remain a necessary part of debate and why public discourse on state killing must be brought back, again and again, to the horror and obscenity of execution.

---

[23] Id. at 480–481 n. 2.
[24] See Austin Sarat, *When the State Kills: Capital Punishment and the American Condition*. Princeton, NJ: Princeton University Press, 2002, 70–72 (1984).

10

Open Secrets, or The Postscript of Capital Punishment

Ravit Pe'er-Lamo Reichman

The spectacle is not a collection of images; rather, it is a social relationship between people that is mediated by images. – Guy Debord, *The Society of the Spectacle*

Nobody bears witness for the witness. – Paul Celan, "Ashglory"

In his 1957 essay "Reflections on the Guillotine," Albert Camus recounts the story of how he came to know about executions. The incident involved his father, who was killed in World War I when Camus was only a year old and whom Camus knew mainly through his mother's recollections. Lucien Camus had gone to the center of Algiers to see the execution of a man convicted of killing his children in a particularly grisly, high-profile murder. Camus relates the incident half a century later:

> One of the few things I know about him, in any case, is that he wanted to witness the execution, for the first time in his life. He got up in the dark to go to the place of execution at the other end of town amid a great crowd of people. What he saw that morning he never told anyone. My mother relates merely that he came rushing home, his face distorted, refused to talk, lay down for a moment on the bed, and suddenly began to vomit. He had just discovered the reality hidden under the noble phrases with which it was masked. Instead of thinking of the slaughtered children, he could think of nothing but that quivering body that had just been dropped onto a board to have its head cut off.[1]

[1] I would like to thank Hannah Sikorski for her research assistance and Daniel Kim, Augusta Rohrbach, and Ted Weesner for their comments on this essay. Albert Camus, "Reflections on the Guillotine," in *Resistance, Rebellion, and Death*, trans. Justin O'Brien. New York: Alfred A. Knopf, 1961, 175.

It is a story in which one compulsion appears to be shockingly trumped by another, though the motivation for either remains unclear; the reader – like Camus himself – is left to fill in the gaping hole. Why exactly did Lucien Camus feel compelled to attend the execution? Did he support or oppose capital punishment? Did he believe that justice would be served? What drives the retelling, it seems, is less the spectacle of beheading than the father's desire to see it and his silence after doing so. If the son cannot say what his father saw, he can at least attest with certainty that he *wanted* to see it – "wanted to witness the execution, for the first time in his life." In satisfying his desire, however, the father creates it in his son, who will never see the scene that reduced his father to silence and must instead imagine it in prose. A gap forms between the father's experience and the son's fantasy, between the former's muteness ("What he saw that morning he never told anyone") and the latter's imagination ("he could think of nothing but that quivering body"). Indeed, the body could be that of the father himself. Camus' mother in the telling and Camus in the retelling are left with their own condemned man.

Between the father's experience and the son's narrative – between the act of witnessing and the hazards of imagining – lies a pocket of meaning, a place to work out the vicissitudes of what has become today a largely unseen, strictly imagined act. In this fissure, and rather than approaching the death penalty through arguments for or against it, I begin with the basic premise that executions today occur behind closed doors. With the abolition of public hangings in England in 1868 (and the last public execution in the United States in 1930), citizens have had to imagine, rather than witness directly, the death sentences carried out by their governments. Camus' depiction of his father suggests that the task of imagining an execution without the possibility of witnessing it produces not just the story of a "quivering body" but also the expression of an absence, a tabula rasa that no profusion of phrases, noble or otherwise, can quite fill. Pursuing this absence, I ask not how literature imagines the death penalty but how it does not – and what this narrative resistance can tell us about our culture's relationship to capital punishment.

What happens to the juridical and cultural imagination when acts carried out in the public's name take place in private? The short answer, at once historical, literary, and legal, is nothing at all. In an era saturated with images of explicit, gratuitous violence, the paucity of depictions of

Open Secrets, or The Postscript of Capital Punishment 247

executions appears as a curious blind spot. This is not to say that one never finds them. Truman Capote's *In Cold Blood*, Norman Mailer's *The Executioner's Song*, and E. L. Doctorow's *The Book of Daniel*, as well as films like *Dead Man Walking* (dir. Tim Robbins, 1995), *Dancer in the Dark* (Lars von Trier, 2000), and Errol Morris's *Mr. Death* (1999), present notably unflinching portrayals of capital punishment. Just as often, however – even more often – one encounters works that gesture toward the death penalty without representing it directly: from Richard Wright's *Native Son* to Vladimir Nabokov's *Invitation to a Beheading*, Joseph Conrad's *The Secret Agent* to Gerhard Richter's blurred Baader-Meinhof paintings and countless television shows of the *Law and Order* variety. Works such as these present execution in the form of a fantasy or allude to it by concluding with the moment of sentencing or the last conversation in prison, as though the execution itself were a mere formality, a fait accompli requiring no representation of its own. More telling are these less obvious texts in their turn away from direct representation – or, more precisely, in the mechanisms by which they suggest how our culture tolerates its most divisive juridical realities, narrating the modes through which we live with our deepest social ambivalences.

This is not to suggest that the matter of private executions has no bearing on the question of whether the death penalty is right or wrong in general. In "Reflections on the Guillotine," the two realities were intimately bound. A staunch opponent of the death penalty, Camus believed that people would reject it outright if they could only see it. The claims of his essay thus rest on the hypocrisy of a society that refuses to see the actions carried out in its name, accepting execution as a "regrettable necessity" as long as it is kept out of sight. When the curtain does part, as it did in the 2006 execution of Saddam Hussein, it does so in a way that exposes both the horror and the seduction of capital punishment. The grainy, unsteady cell phone camera footage of the execution, disseminated with astounding speed over the Internet, smacked of a base brutality, even a sense of illegality: one knew that one was not supposed to see it, which of course was part of its draw.[2]

---

[2] See, for instance, Marc Santora, "On the Gallows, Curses for U.S. and 'Traitors,'" *The New York Times*, December 31, 2006; and John F. Burns, "Hussein Video Grips Iraq; Attacks Go On," *The New York Times*, December 31, 2006. For a legal analysis of the hanging's implications, see Austin Sarat, "Pictures and Executions: The Real Scandal in the Hanging

The gradual transformation of punishment, as Steven Wilf has observed, occasioned not just a shift from what might be characterized as seeing to believing, and "not only from public to increasingly private forms of retribution, but from the visual senses to the imagination."[3] For Timothy Kaufman-Osborn, the change also constitutes a loss, a move away from the political. As he sees it, "Once removed from public view, absent the sort of public verification that might otherwise make it possible to contest official proclamations of unqualified success, hangings became a phenomenon of the depoliticized imagination."[4] What might thus appear as the law's invitation to the narrative imagination – a challenge for literature, journalism, art, or film to fill the gap left by the abolition of public executions – turns out to be a corollary that is far from guaranteed. Contrary to expectations that the imagination will picture what the state will not, literature repeatedly turns away from portraying the death penalty as anything other than the impossibility – or, at the very least, the remoteness and unlikelihood – of its representation.

Taking Executions Seriously

In England, the decision to move hangings behind prison walls was influenced chiefly by disdain for the "scaffold crowd" that flocked to London on execution days, an influx of the working class more invested in revelry and debauchery than in witnessing a solemn act of justice. Lawmakers consequently found themselves facing the need both to preserve public decency by eliminating the unruly crowd and to inculcate respect for the law by setting the right tone of sobriety at executions. The problem with public hangings and the festivities on their perimeter seemed to hinge on emotional register. "There must not be too much feeling; a polite nation's brutality must be camouflaged," the historian V. A. C. Gatrell writes of the decision for private executions.[5]

---

of Sad-dam Hussein," FindLaw, January 9, 2007, http://writ.news.findlaw.com/commentary/20070109_sarat.html (accessed January 30, 2007).

[3] Steven Wilf, "Imagining Justice: Aesthetics and Public Executions in Late Eighteenth-Century England," *Yale Journal of Law and the Humanities* 5 (1993): 78.

[4] Timothy Kaufman-Osborn, *From Noose to Needle: Capital Punishment and the Late Liberal State*. Ann Arbor: University of Michigan Press, 2002, 91.

[5] V. A. C. Gatrell, *The Hanging Tree: Execution and the English People, 1770–1868*. Oxford: Oxford University Press, 1994, 24.

Open Secrets, or The Postscript of Capital Punishment

The issue involved not "too much feeling" but rather the wrong kind of feeling – frivolity where gravitas ought to be, working-class rather than aristocratic sentiment. Consider the following exchange between Inspector of Police Thomas Kittle and members of the Royal Commission on Capital Punishment, which conducted an inquiry from 1864 until 1866:

Chairman: I have been told that as much as 25*l* has been paid for the windows of one room.
Kittle: I do not think that the witnessing an [sic] execution excites any fear.
Chairman: Not among the lower class of people?
Kittle: I think not. They look upon it as much as they would look upon any other exhibition for which there is nothing to pay to see. I think that they look upon it as they would look upon a prize fight, or any other exhibition of a like nature.
Chairman: An execution is a matter of interest to them to witness?
Kittle: I think so.
Mr. Neate: Do you mean to say that you do not see any seriousness and anxiety about them?
Kittle: There is a sort of anxiety and a straining to see the movement of the doomed man and the officials.
Mr. Neate: Do you see men turn pale at all?
Kittle: I have never noticed that, and I have watched their faces most intently.
Mr. Neate: Do such of the populace, as attend generally, show any feeling of terror or solemnity in consequence of witnessing the execution, or do they keep talking and chatting just as if nothing was the matter?
Kittle: I think that they seem to amuse and rather enjoy themselves previous to the sight which they come to see.[6]

Because we know the immediate and intended impact of the execution on the convicted, Kittle emerges here less as a witness to the hanging than as a lay anthropologist, scanning faces in the crowd for emotional responses. A strange confusion consequently arises as to which spectacle, the crowd or the prisoner, constituted the main event – a question that Foucault would

[6] Report of the Capital Punishment Commission, vol. 21, Cmnd. 3590 (1866) at 162.

answer resolutely in the crowd's favor. The condemned man might have been the spectacle's focal point, but he was not its hero. "In the ceremonies of the public execution, the main character was the people, whose real and immediate presence was required for the performance," Foucault writes. "An execution that was known to be taking place, but which did so in secret, would scarcely have had any meaning."[7] Following Foucault and Debord, whose epigraph began this essay, the spectacle no longer deterred but delighted; the law had failed in its objective.

As English lawmakers saw it, the key to retaining this meaning – or, rather, to transforming it into a more appropriate mood – was to let imagination dictate emotion. When Henry Fielding wrote in 1751, "A murder behind the scenes will affect the audience with greater terror than if it was acted before their eyes,"[8] his words gave the scaffold's abolitionists a fitting dramaturgical analogy for a more respectable, humane, and effective means of punishment. To some extent, of course, he was right: fear of the unknown would likely exert a tighter grip than the fear inspired by the ceremonial deaths that occurred with numbing repetition in the public sphere. Joseph Conrad indicated as much when he described the fear of hanging through the eyes of Mrs. Verloc in *The Secret Agent* after she has killed her husband and not long before she takes her own life:

> Mrs. Verloc was afraid of the gallows. She was terrified of them ideally. Having never set eyes on that last argument of men's justice except in illustrative woodcuts to a certain type of tales, she first saw them erect against a black and stormy background, festooned with chains and human bones, circled about by birds that peck at dead men's eyes. This was frightful enough, but Mrs. Verloc, though not a well-informed woman, had a sufficient knowledge of the institutions of her country to know that gallows are no longer erected romantically on the banks of dismal rivers or on wind-swept headlands, but in the yards of jails. There within four high walls, as if into a pit, at dawn of day, the murderer was brought out to be executed, with a horrible quietness and, as the reports in the newspapers always said, "in the presence of the authorities."... And how was it done? The

---

[7] Michel Foucault, *Discipline and Punish: The Birth of the Prison*, trans. Alan Sheridan. New York: Random House, 1995, 57–58.
[8] Henry Fielding, "An Enquiry into the Causes of the Late Increase of Robbers and Related Writings" (1751), quoted in Gatrell, *The Hanging Tree*, 23.

impossibility of imagining the details of such quiet execution added something maddening to her abstract terror.[9]

Not only does Mrs. Verloc's terror take hold from her inability to imagine a hanging in detail, but its force seems to stem from the language that communicates executions to the public – an officialese that confounds more than it clarifies, a rhetoric so understated in its "horrible quietness" that it could not but induce fear. Others, however, echoed Camus in "Reflections on the Guillotine," believing that state-sanctioned killing that went unseen would ultimately fade from consciousness and provoke little reaction, least of all fear. As Camus insists, "When the imagination sleeps, words are emptied of their meaning: a deaf population absent-mindedly registers the condemnation of a man."[10]

The prospect of a slumbering imagination was enough to undermine confidence in Fielding's assertion, leaving lawmakers bent on finding a public forum to replace the suspense of the gallows. The most obvious candidate was, of course, the courtroom scene, and the breathless anticipation in the moments before a sentence was pronounced. In 1866, the eminent judge Sir George Bramwell testified before the Capital Punishment Commission about the "striking effect" of this moment: "A sentence of death has a most serious effect upon all the people in Court. You have a perfect silence, as perfect as can be, all the people seem very much interested in it, and the sentence does create a very strong impression upon the persons present."[11]

Here, then, was an alternative to public hangings and the mob scenes that accompanied them – an opportunity to shift the weight of justice to the trial, to reframe the moment of suspense within the courtroom's reverential silence instead of the riotous commotion outside Newgate Prison. The novel, as Jonathan Grossman has argued, followed suit: literary works reinvented traditional plot lines to reflect the changing image of justice, and courtroom drama was born. "The old public spectacles became specters," Grossman notes, and punishment "became the postscript to the trial."[12]

---

[9] Joseph Conrad, *The Secret Agent*. 1907; Oxford: Oxford University Press, 2004, 196.
[10] Camus, "Reflections on the Guillotine," 177.
[11] Report of the Capital Punishment Commission, vol. 21, Cmnd. 3590 (1866) at 89.
[12] Jonathan H. Grossman, *The Art of Alibi: English Law Courts and the Novel*. Baltimore, MD: Johns Hopkins University Press, 2002, 14, 15.

The private life of punishment, it should be noted, was of a piece with the increasing privacy of death. As Walter Benjamin writes in "The Storyteller," "It has been observable for a number of centuries how in the general consciousness the thought of death has declined in omnipresence and vividness." Historically embedded in the life of community, death had been banished in the modern era to the farthest reaches of bureaucracy, "pushed further and further out of the perceptual world of the living."[13] For Benjamin, this decline was both symptomatic of the waning value of experience, which had been crowded out by newspapers and the rise of information culture, and a fundamental cause of the diminished ability to tell stories. Death gives the storyteller the authority, he writes, without which his stories lose their social force.

If the problem for Benjamin seemed to turn on the inability to perceive, for Foucault it became a problem of rights in the context of a legal order. In *Discipline and Punish*, Foucault depicted public executions as far subtler and more socially complex than a vengeful, Dionysian mob; as he saw it, they were distinctly political events:

> Not only must people know, but they must see with their own eyes. Because they must be made to be afraid; but also because they must be the witnesses, the guarantors, of the punishment, and because they must to a certain extent take part in it. The right to be witnesses was one they possessed and claimed; a hidden execution was a privileged execution, and in such cases it was often suspected that it had not taken place with all its customary severity.[14]

Take away this experience of witnessing, and the event's narrative shifts to another perspective, creating a vacuum that modernist literature recreates time and again. Virginia Woolf, E. M. Forster, and James Joyce, to name just a few, do away with traditional deathbed scenes, locating the

---

[13] Walter Benjamin, "The Storyteller," in *Illuminations*, trans. Harry Zohn, ed. Hannah Arendt. New York: Schocken Books, 1969, 93–94. Philippe Ariès writes similarly 40 years later: "Except for the death of statesmen, society has banished death. In towns, there is no way of knowing something has happened: the old black and silver hearse has become an ordinary gray limousine, indistinguishable from the flow of traffic. Society no longer observes a pause; the disappearance of an individual no longer affects its continuity. Everything in town goes on as if nobody died anymore." Philippe Ariès, *The Hour of Our Death*, trans. Helen Weaver. New York: Oxford University Press, 1991, 560.

[14] Foucault, *Discipline and Punish*, 58.

Open Secrets, or The Postscript of Capital Punishment

deaths in their novels outside the narrative frame.[15] Whereas the deaths in these novels and in Benjamin's critique are primarily social occurrences, however, the state-sanctioned killing of capital punishment is juridical in nature and should be treated as such. To say that it is removed from the public sphere is to make a social and political argument; to conceive of it as a postscript is to make a claim about narrative, suggesting how plots are reorganized to accommodate history's shifting sands.

Depicting this postscript became an ethical act rather than an elegiac or nostalgic one: in light of the changes in capital punishment, executions *needed* to be represented because they could no longer be witnessed. The burden had shifted from citizens to their surrogates – to journalists or select witnesses who attended executions by invitation only and to writers or artists determined to bring these executions to life. The terror that Fielding and others anticipated – that "a murder behind the scenes will affect the audience with greater terror than if it was acted before their eyes" – never fully took hold, however. In striking opposition to those who would champion the richness of the mind's eye, executions often appeared as distant, surreal images, as nostalgic fantasies or thought experiments – if they appeared at all. From this vantage, it is worth taking up Fielding's position conversely. If narratives resist depicting execution as content, what can we make of their form? What shape does the averse – but nonetheless ethical – imagination take?

First Words: Execution as Pretext

In addressing these questions, let us turn first to Sylvia Plath's *The Bell Jar*, which raises the specter of capital punishment by way of introduction, invoking the execution of Julius and Ethel Rosenberg in its opening paragraphs. Ten years before her novel was published, Plath observed in her diary on the eve of the electrocution:

> There is no yelling, no horror, no great rebellion. That is the appalling thing. The execution will take place tonight; it is too bad that it could not be televised... so much more realistic and beneficial than the

---

[15] Consider, for instance, Septimus Warren Smith's suicide in Virginia Woolf's *Mrs. Dalloway* (1925) and Mrs. Ramsay's death in *To the Lighthouse* (1927), Mrs. Moore's death in E. M. Forster's *A Passage to India* (1924) and Paddy Dingnam's death in the Hades episode of James Joyce's *Ulysses* (1922).

run-of-the-mill crime program. Two real people being executed. No matter. The largest emotional reaction over the United States will be a rather large, democratic, infinitely bored and casual and complacent yawn.[16]

Echoing the "horrible quietness" sensed by Conrad's Mrs. Verloc, Plath is disturbed by the resounding silence, the distinct feeling that the din surrounding the politics of treason – did they or didn't they? – had come to a mute, indifferent end with the execution itself. In drawing a parallel between a crime show and a televised execution, however, Plath records more than just the American public's waning interest in the Rosenbergs. She intimates something about the relationship between this interest and the execution's invisibility. The televised event seems to differ from a crime show in degree rather than in kind; it is "more realistic" than a fictional representation rather than simply real or immediate.

To navigate the indeterminate spectrum from less to more realistic, however, would be to miss the narrative point – namely the suggestion that "more realistic" is also "less interesting," that the execution seems utterly divorced from the Sturm und Drang of the trial. The execution must be represented, in other words, precisely because it is pure procedure and thus plotless rather than suspenseful; "real" thus amounts to "beneficial" in that it calls on viewers to fulfill a duty, to be edified rather than entertained. Cut off from a narrative arc, the execution becomes an event without a story, a nonevent. Is it any wonder that the executions garnering the most media attention today tend to be those that go awry, are delayed by the appeals process or halted by a presidential pardon – sometimes after the condemned has already been strapped onto the gurney?[17] As Hussein's 2006 hanging emphatically and grotesquely reminded us, bad behavior, medical mishaps, equipment malfunctions, or last-minute interruptions do more than twist the proverbial plot; they *are* the plot, lending a mechanically predictable event the conflict and resolution that it previously lacked.

---

[16] Sylvia Plath, entry on June 19, 1953, *The Journals of Sylvia Plath*, ed. Ted Hughes and Frances McCullough. New York: Ballantine, 1982, 81.

[17] Examples of such tragic failures abound. For a detailed list compiled by sociologist Michael L. Radelet, see "Some Examples of Post-Furman Botched Executions," Death Penalty Information Center, May 24, 2007, http://deathpenaltyinfo.org/article.php?scid=8&did=478 (accessed July 23, 2007).

Open Secrets, or The Postscript of Capital Punishment

If the modern execution has no plot, it can still serve as a vehicle for narratives of a vastly different order – not stories of crime, punishment, or power, but those concerned with the more private vicissitudes of an increasingly anonymous, atomized world. It is this world, rather than the political realm of the 1950s, that Plath unfolds in the opening pages of *The Bell Jar*, setting the tone of her novel beneath the pall of history that feels at once steadfastly real and eerily abstract:

> It was a queer, sultry summer, the summer they electrocuted the Rosenbergs, and I didn't know what I was doing in New York. I'm stupid about executions. The idea of being electrocuted makes me sick, and that's all there was to read about in the papers – goggle-eyed headlines staring up at me on every street corner and at the fusty, peanut-smelling mouth of every subway. It had nothing to do with me, but I couldn't help wondering what it would be like, being burned alive all along your nerves. I thought it must be the worst thing in the world.[18]

Execution here becomes a pretext in the most literal sense: a means of setting the stage for something dramatically different – or something dramatic, period.

Sounding a note symptomatic of the 1950s' shift from politics to the personal, the opening lines settle quickly into a narcissistic vein, despite the fact that the novel has a certain self-indicting quality about it, implicitly casting aspersions on the use of politics as a springboard for private torment and solipsism. The execution not only situates the novel in the era of McCarthyism – a time of paranoia, anxiety, and political uncertainty – but also serves as a barometer of Esther Greenwood's already precarious mental state. Despite its ominous tenor, however, the effect of these paragraphs has as much to do with a sense of hollowness surrounding the Rosenbergs as it does with the electrocution's omnipresence – its indelibility in newsprint, its pervasiveness in the air. An amorphous sensibility shapes the novel's beginning, gathering force as much from the impending executions as from Esther's peculiar New York aimlessness and her overwrought yet strangely barren idioms.

As though searching for something more specific or profound, her thoughts settle rather uncomfortably on bloated, adolescent statements:

---

[18] Sylvia Plath, *The Bell Jar*. New York: HarperCollins, 1996 [1963], 1.

that electrocution "made me sick"; that "it must be the worst thing in the world." One gets a distinct sense from these all-purpose phrases that however unavoidable the controversy might have been, the event itself remained frustratingly out of reach. Thus, even as Esther is quick to dissociate herself from the matter ("It had nothing to do with me"), she nonetheless feels the compulsion to imagine it viscerally. Just as her ruminations shift to a more graphic tone – the thought of "being burned alive all along your nerves" – she shuts them down with a statement as resolute as it is insipid: "I thought it must be the worst thing in the world." Her detached construction, set in the past tense, leaves a lingering sense that perhaps she no longer thinks this – that her conclusion, from the perspective of hindsight and twenty-something self-absorption, was not so terrible after all, compared with the electric shock treatment that she will undergo later in the novel. The Rosenbergs thus become a powerful way to foreground her own trauma, a deft sleight of hand through which the political does not become the personal but is obliterated by it.

Secrecy and Literary Form

It would be tempting, even logical, to suggest that the Rosenbergs' execution haunts Plath's text, pursuing Esther Greenwood with morbid thoughts and graphic images. As Marie Ashe argues, *The Bell Jar* is thick with references to Ethel Rosenberg, chief among them the repetition of Ethel Rosenberg's name before her marriage, Esther Ethel Greenglass, in Esther Greenwood.[19] Such a reading, however, obscures the larger social picture that the novel sketches, reducing the reference to the Rosenbergs to the status of a mere trope. As a political touchstone, the Rosenberg case polarized public opinion; as a social entity, it acquired a shape that is much harder to grasp:

> I kept hearing about the Rosenbergs over the radio and at the office till I couldn't get them out of my mind. It was like the first time I saw a cadaver. For weeks afterward, the cadaver's head – or what there was left of it – floated up behind my eggs and bacon at breakfast and behind the face of Buddy Willard, who was responsible for my seeing

[19] Marie Ashe, "*The Bell Jar* and the Ghost of Ethel Rosenberg," in *Secret Agents: The Rosenberg Case, McCarthyism, and Fifties America*, ed. Marjorie Garber and Rebecca L. Walkowitz. New York: Routledge, 1995, 215–231.

it in the first place, and pretty soon I felt as though I were carrying that cadaver's head around with me on a string, like some black, noseless balloon stinking of vinegar.

(I knew something was wrong with me that summer, because all I could think about was the Rosenbergs and how stupid I'd been to buy all those uncomfortable, expensive clothes, hanging limp as fish in my closet, and how all the little successes I'd totted up so happily at college fizzled to nothing outside the slick marble and plate-glass fronts along Madison Avenue.)[20]

What is striking about these reflections is how very general they are. This, I would venture, is the point. *What* she heard remains vague; the more important point is *how* she heard it, whether in the drone of ceaseless radio broadcasts or snatches of conversation at work, like white noise that one perceives dimly but does not comprehend. Although not suppressed, then, the execution is not exactly expressed either, certainly not with any specificity. It is here that we begin to understand how the execution functions, how it circulates among people without taking root or assuming a tangible shape. Everyone knows about it, but it fills the social space as form rather than substance. There is, in fact, little that feels substantial about it, surfacing as it does in halting, peristaltic fashion and successive approximations – the fragments of office talk, the cadaver, the eggs and bacon, the pungently stinking black balloon.

In making sense of the protean and strangely malleable quality of the Rosenbergs' execution, it bears considering Camus' comment in "Reflections on the Guillotine," "People write of capital punishment as if they were whispering."[21] The hush surrounding such public violence, in sharp contrast to the carnivalesque spectacles of the nineteenth century, suggests a connection between the modern death penalty and secrecy. Put simply, the discourse of capital punishment functions like a secret. Hannah Arendt defined culturewide secrets as facts that are "publicly known, and yet the same public that knows them can successfully, and often spontaneously, taboo their public discussion and treat them as though they were what they are not – namely, secrets."[22] A secret, unlike a suppressed fact, circulates

---

[20] Plath, *The Bell Jar*, 2.
[21] Camus, "Reflections on the Guillotine," 176.
[22] Hannah Arendt, "Truth and Politics," in *Between Past and Future*. New York: Penguin, 1968, 236.

among individual people but does so through unofficial channels and in illicit, unpredictable ways – between official lines of communication or, as Plath's narrative suggests, in parentheses. Its form, moreover, often says more than its content. A secret, in other words, serves as a structuring agent for a social or political discourse, as a means rather than an end: a purveyor of confidentiality, social standing, or moral lessons, a catalyst of intimacy and community.

It is only natural that the execution here becomes a vehicle for another form of pain: not the suffering of the electric chair but the story of a nervous breakdown. Transitioning abruptly from the political climate to her own story, the narrative veers from the Rosenbergs to "how stupid I'd been to buy all those uncomfortable, expensive clothes" and how all of Esther's accomplishments seemed to wither under Manhattan's bright lights. "It had nothing to do with me," she says, and yet her narcissistic empathy ("I couldn't help wondering what it would be like") suggests precisely the opposite. As a thought experiment that says more about Esther's vision of herself as sacrificial victim than it does about the Rosenbergs, the opening of *The Bell Jar* gestures toward the political but never quite gets there. From the beginning, the political reality of capital punishment was never its destination.

Last Words: *The Stranger*'s Failure of Imagination

If the death penalty in Plath serves as a pretext for a novel that never fully takes up the political stakes of capital punishment, Albert Camus' *The Stranger* rehearses Grossman's sense of punishment as a postscript. In keeping with Benjamin, the text's opening gesture invokes death but immediately makes it clear that no authority will derive from it. The famous opening lines announce the death of the narrator's mother, but, like the unspecified content of the newspaper stories in *The Bell Jar*, deliver precious little content: "Maman died today. Or yesterday maybe, I don't know. I got a telegram from the home: 'Mother deceased. Funeral tomorrow. Faithfully yours.' That doesn't mean anything. Maybe it was yesterday."[23] Laconically delivered, the news of Meursault's mother's death

---

[23] Albert Camus, *The Stranger*, trans. Matthew Ward. 1942; New York: Vintage, 1989, 3; hereafter cited parenthetically by page number.

anticipates his own impending execution at the end of the novel, after he is sentenced to die for killing an Arab on the beach in Algiers. The mother's death in the novel's unwritten past is as anonymous as her son's in its unwritten future. Whether in the retirement home or the prison cell, they live their last days behind thick and sterile institutional walls, "pushed further and further," as Benjamin observed, "out of the perceptual world of the living."

Meursault's deadpan first words inaugurate a text in which indifference features as the predominant register. His flat affect, juxtaposed with a plot that one could certainly imagine in very different, melodramatic terms – a man kills a stranger on a beach and is sentenced to death for his crime – unfolds through a steady, deadened listlessness, perhaps the closest thing to narrative inertia. A first-order reading of the novel reveals it as a map of moral failure: without repentance, a contemplative moment of reckoning, or an outpouring of guilt or sorrow. Meursault emerges at his trial as a man with no conscience – a characterization that, given his own internal monologue, is difficult to dispute. "I didn't feel much remorse for what I'd done," he thinks as the prosecutor makes the case against him. "But I was surprised by how relentless he was. I would have liked to have tried explaining to him cordially, almost affectionately, that I had never been able to truly feel remorse for anything. My mind was always on what was coming next, today or tomorrow" (100). Meursault's pathology runs deeper than an inability to feel or to think in moral terms. His greatest failure – indeed, the source of his ethical blindness – lies in his inability to imagine. "I've never really had much of an imagination. But still I would try to picture the exact moment when the beating of my heart would no longer be going on inside my head," he confesses (113). The unimaginative mind, Camus seems to suggest, is the indifferent one.

Meursault's creative limits consist of more than the inability to picture his final moments; they are thwarted too by the image of the machinery of execution, which for him seems entirely unreal: "The papers were always talking about the debt owed to society. According to them, it had to be paid. But that doesn't speak to the imagination. What really counted was the possibility of escape, a leap to freedom, out of the implacable ritual, a wild run for it that would give whatever chance for hope there was" (109). The law, however, proves far less exhilarating. Far from a wild run, this poetic leap takes the form of his appeal: the highly regulated, unromantic labyrinth of legal and bureaucratic procedure.

It comes as little surprise that the machinery of death remains for him enshrined in the historical glow of the guillotine as it once was: the scaffold with its attendant spectacle and the terror and grandeur of the French Revolution. The image can only disappoint, as it finally does when Meursault comes across a newspaper photograph of a modern guillotine, close to the ground and wholly unremarkable:

> You always get exaggerated notions of things you don't know anything about. I was made to see that contrary to what I thought, everything was very simple: the guillotine is on the same level as the man approaching it. He walks up to it the way you walk up to another person. That bothered me too. Mounting the scaffold, going right up into the sky, was something the imagination could hold on to. Whereas, once again, the machine destroyed everything: you were killed discreetly, with a little shame and with great precision. (112)

The problem for him seems to lie in the inability to imagine anything other than these two distinct guillotines, one romantically exaggerated and the other disappointingly plain. Nothing exists between them, no scenario that does not feel either larger than life or threadbare and inadequate. Meursault's attempts to visualize his execution thus come up empty time and again, to the point where his desire becomes a perverse yearning for the messiness of a bloody beheading, complete with the drama of public humiliation. Execution gets whittled down to its technical props; absent the drama of old, it appears as little more than a stage set. The successive failures of Meursault's imagination tell us much about the desire to see with one's own eyes and about the anemic quality of a mind with no direct experience of a political and legal reality.

Attempting once more to produce an image of the guillotine that affords a fuller vision, Meursault turns to a story at two removes: the story of his father attending an execution in Algiers, a narrative that Camus would rehearse over a decade later in the autobiographical passage from "Reflections on the Guillotine" with which this essay began:

> At times like this I remembered a story Maman had used to tell me about my father. I never knew him. Maybe the only thing I did know about the man was the story Maman would tell me back then: he'd

gone to watch a murderer be executed. Just the thought of going had made him sick to his stomach. But he went anyway, and when he came back he spent half the morning throwing up. I remember feeling a little disgusted by him at the time. But now I understood, it was perfectly normal. How had I not seen that there was nothing more important than an execution, and that when you come right down to it, it was the only thing a man could truly be interested in? If I ever got out of this prison I would go and watch every execution there was. (110)

What is striking about the two retellings is how little things change from one version to the next, how fiction and autobiography are presented in similarly stark, unembellished terms. Given their parallels, it seems important that the fictional narrative came first – as though the incident contained a fictional quality from the beginning, appearing as always unreal.

"Today there is no spectacle," Camus insists in "Reflections on the Guillotine," "but only a penalty known to all by hearsay and, from time to time, the news of an execution dressed up in soothing phrases."[24] The desire to become a witness explains the novel's last words and the fantasy of public execution that they describe. If Meursault cannot see an execution – his own or someone else's – then at least he will be seen:

As if that blind rage had washed me clean, rid me of hope; for the first time, in that night alive with signs and stars, I opened myself to the gentle indifference of the world. Finding it so much like myself – so like a brother, really – I felt that I had been happy and that I was happy again. For everything to be consummated, for me to feel less alone, I had only to wish that there be a large crowd of spectators the day of my execution and that they greet me with cries of hate. (122–123)

"There is no yelling, no horror, no great rebellion," wrote Plath of the Rosenbergs. This frenzy, albeit from a crowd hungry for the guillotine, is precisely what Meursault wants when he imagines the angry mob at his beheading. He craves something far simpler than melodrama: an encounter, one that pierces the thick blanket of alienation in the courtroom at the close of his trial – a detachment that pervades the novel from its beginning. "When the bell rang again, when the door to the dock

[24] Camus, "Reflections on the Guillotine," 181.

opened, what rose to meet me was the silence in the courtroom," Meursault observes, "silence and the strange feeling I had when I noticed that the young reporter had turned his eyes away" (107). In one of his more penetrating moments of self-consciousness, Meursault perceives himself – or, rather, sees himself being looked at – as the object of aversion. Rather than castigating him, however, the judge merely declares "in bizarre language that I was to have my head cut off in a public square in the name of the French people. Then it seemed to me that I suddenly knew what was on everybody's face. It was a look of consideration, I'm sure" (107). The hush in the courtroom is dramatic, as nineteenth-century jurists knew it would be, but its drama feels surreal to Meursault, as though a wide berth had been cut between the condemned and the audience that does not participate so much as gape. The man in the dock – in contrast to the one on the scaffold – becomes a spectacle in the purest sense of the word.

To imagine the angry crowd at his execution, then, is not only to rehearse this scene once more, with feeling. Unlike Esther Greenwood's attempt to feel "what it would be like, being burned alive all along your nerves," Meursault is consumed not by his own subjective experience but by the display of collective outrage. His fantasy ultimately consists of being lifted above his private identity, to be seen: public man revisited and revised in the shadow of state violence.[25] He resigns himself in these moments to the indifference of which he has been both source and receptacle, precisely to dream his way out of it. In this sense, he is not unlike Nabokov's Cincinnatus C. in *Invitation to a Beheading*, who experiences perfect lucidity as he lies on the execution block. As Nabokov's novel closes, Cincinnatus simply wills the entire scene out of existence, seeing it as if from the outside, "with a clarity he had never experienced before – at first almost painful, so suddenly did it come, but then suffusing him with joy, he reflected: why am I here? Why am I lying like this? And, having asked himself these simple questions, he answered them by getting up and looking around."[26]

Nabokov's and Camus' execution fantasies, however different their respective outcomes, suggest a connection between modern execution

---

[25] See Richard Sennett, *The Fall of Public Man*. New York: Norton, 1974.
[26] Vladimir Nabokov, *Invitation to a Beheading*, trans. Dmitri Nabokov. 1959; New York: Vintage, 1989, 222.

practices and the literary imagination: gone is the realism of Charles Dickens, Alexandre Dumas, William Makepeace Thackeray, or Gustave Flaubert, the meticulous description of blades, ropes, or bodies. Executions take place for Meursault and Cincinnatus in the mind's eye, revealing the surreal fantasies of condemned men but leaving their readers with precious little of the particular. As narratives that gesture toward resolutions without describing them – what happens on the day of Meursault's execution? does Cincinnatus really cheat death? – these texts seem destined to end in fantasy and to imbue this fantasy with an air of perversity and inscrutability.[27]

Seeing for Oneself

The right of a witness is simply to witness.   – *KQED v. Vasquez*

If the public has a right to attend executions, invitations would not be required.   – *Halquist v. Department of Corrections*

If Camus and Plath voice a pressing and perverse wish to see an execution, the desire proves more than just the stuff of literary invention. Nowhere does this appear more forcefully than in lawsuits brought by journalists seeking to televise executions and in the fact that courts routinely reject their demands. I want to conclude by examining the stakes of such cases, to trace a shift from the language of desire to that of rights – a return to Foucault's conclusion that public executions derived their social force from the people, who took their "right to be witnesses" seriously. What does it mean for a desire to be translated into a right, for the wish to see to become a wish for the *right* to see?

We find one answer in *Garrett v. Estelle* (1977), in which Tony Garrett, a reporter in Dallas, cited First and Fourteenth Amendment rights in petitioning the Northern Texas District Court to film the state's first execution since 1964. The court granted his request, rightly setting constitutional guarantees ahead of purported claims to decency. Where freedom of the press is concerned, nothing justifies the "impenetrable veil of secrecy"[28]

---

[27] Indeed, as Mary Ann Frese Witt and Eric Witt point out, it remains unclear whether Meursault is in fact executed, because we never learn whether his appeal has been rejected. See Mary Ann Frese Witt and Eric Witt, "Retrying *The Stranger* Again," in *Literature and Law*, ed. Michael J. Meyer. Amsterdam: Rodopi, 2004, 1–20.

[28] *Garrett v. Estelle*, 424 F. Supp. 468 (1977) at 472.

that descends when the public is barred from seeing the actions carried out in its name. Elsewhere, however, the opinion assumes a dramatically different posture, turning from constitutional rights to the nature of an execution. Along these lines, the court reasoned that television cameras had been barred from courtrooms because they could potentially disrupt a trial, but an execution falls under a different category: "An execution... is an entirely mechanical process carried out only after all deliberative proceedings have been completed. It is not seriously contended that a single television reporter, carrying a compact, portable film camera requiring no special lighting, can in any way disrupt or interfere with this state proceeding."[29] Unlike trials, which demand concentration and deliberation, executions are perfunctory and thus impervious to the distraction that a camera might pose. If punishment in literature gradually became the postscript to the trial, *Garrett*'s formulation treats it as more of a script: a predictable event of stock characters and a plot that never fluctuates.

The Court of Appeals for the Fifth Circuit viewed the matter differently, reversing the decision based not on the nature of an execution but on that of televised images and, more broadly, on the nature of representation itself. As Judge Ainsworth reasoned, "In order to sustain Garrett's argument we would have to find that the moving picture of the actual execution possessed some quality giving it 'content' beyond, for example, that possessed by a simulation of the execution. We discern no such quality from the record or from our inferences therein."[30] Austin Sarat and Aaron Schuster have pointed out the strangely postmodern tenor of this arguably conservative ruling, "almost as if [Ainsworth] were embracing a postmodern understanding in which signs and referents float free of one another."[31] Indeed, the opinion registers no difference between an event and its simulacrum; to record an electrocution and to reenact it in a television studio amount to the same thing: "Garrett is free to make his report by means of anchor desk or stand-up delivery on the TV screen, or even by simulation. There is no denial of equal protection."[32]

---

[29] Ibid. at 13.
[30] *Garrett v. Estelle*, 556 F.2d 1274 (1977) at 10–11.
[31] Austin Sarat and Aaron Schuster, "To See or Not to See: Television, Capital Punishment, and Law's Violence," review of *Pictures at an Execution: An Inquiry into the Subject of Murder*, by Wendy Lesser, *Yale Journal of Law and the Humanities* 7 (1995): 419.
[32] *Garrett v. Estelle*, 556 F.2d 1274 (1977) at 15.

Open Secrets, or The Postscript of Capital Punishment

The question of rights comes down to one of aesthetics, to the difference between one form of representation and another, and to the law's indifference to these discrepancies. All forms of representation, the *Garrett* court implies, are equal before the law, a position that subsequent courts have upheld. "The right of a witness is simply to witness," a Northern California District Court judge, Robert Schnacke, asserted in *KQED v. Vasquez*, ruling against a California PBS station's petition to film an execution.[33] As designated witnesses, members of the press might be in a unique position to communicate the details of an execution to the public, but no inherent right or custom exists permitting them to film the event. Although *KQED* does not comment on how the press might relay this information, one can reasonably assume that the answer would draw on the same rationale invoked by the *Garrett* court – that any means will do, because one form of simulation is as effective as another.

Moreover, the fact that the media are allowed to attend executions does not establish the public's right to do so. In *Halquist v. Department of Corrections*, the Washington State Supreme Court rejected the claim to such a right, deeming Halquist's evidence apocryphal at best:

> Mr. Halquist's only other support for his contention is an anecdote about two sheriffs of Spokane County, one a lame duck and the other newly elected, who both gave out a set of invitations to a hanging. While this story suggests that hangings were once well-attended spectacles, it does not show that attendance is or ever was considered a right retained under Const. Art. 1, § 30. Indeed, if the public has a right to attend executions, invitations would not be required.[34]

Notwithstanding the resonance with Nabokov's *Invitation to a Beheading*, the story of the Spokane sheriffs – whether or not it is true – has a fictional ring, which becomes the grounds on which the court rejects it as substantial evidence. Whether or not one agrees with the decision in *Halquist*, this

---

[33] The decision, however, was based not on this reason, which was offered here as one possible argument against the petitioner. The judge added to this logic that journalists could not film executions because it was simply not the custom in California.

[34] The Washington State Constitution reads, "The enumeration in this Constitution of certain rights shall not be construed to deny others retained by the people." Washington State Constitution, art. 1, sec. 30. *Halquist v. Department of Corrections*, 113 Wn.2d 818; 783 P.2d 1065 (1989) at 5 n. 4.

particular point is hard to refute. Attending executions might have been a social rite, but it never acquired the status of a legal right.

In rejecting petitions to film executions time and again, the courts maintain an unwavering faith in the ability of representation to convey and contain a political reality. Whether executions or their representations are portrayed as mechanical and invariable, the question of the public's right to witness them returns time and again to questions of aesthetics, perhaps a sign of the shaky foundation of rights discourse beneath arguments in favor of publicly accessible executions. The aesthetic questions raised in law seem to have little to do with the ethical concerns of literary works such as *The Bell Jar* or *The Stranger*, however. The literary concerns ultimately make claims that, although obviously aesthetic, are irreducible to the pragmatic concerns of the death penalty. Rather than posing the question of whether one ought to see, these works call our attention to the quality of seeing – and of not seeing. Their preoccupations ultimately focus on the struggle to imagine what one cannot see and the ethical and psychological experiences born in the attempt.

Curiously, neither the legal nor the literary treatment of witnessing takes up the question of responsibility in relation to seeing or imagining execution. For the courts, the issue of how one witnesses is overshadowed by the question of whether one is allowed to witness at all. For Camus and Plath, the central preoccupations hinge on the psychological consequences of what one can or cannot see. As an ethically charged position, however, the witness to an execution – whether in law or literature – cannot avoid the question of how to see, and to record what one sees, responsibly.

Coda: Orwell as Witness

An impenetrable mystery seems destined to hang forever over this act of madness or despair. — Joseph Conrad, *The Secret Agent*

Thus far, my argument has traced two related phenomena: the abolition of public executions and the resistance of literature to depicting capital punishment as little more than stock images or foregone conclusions. I want to close by considering what it means to picture a death sentence without recourse to either melodrama or euphemism. In doing so, I draw on a 1931 essay by George Orwell that bears the straightforward title, "A

Open Secrets, or The Postscript of Capital Punishment

Hanging." The short piece details Orwell's experience of witnessing the execution of a man in Burma, "a Hindu, a puny wisp of a man, with a shaven head and vague liquid eyes,"[35] who made no attempt to resist as his captors prepared him for the gallows:

> Two of them stood by with rifles and fixed bayonets, while the others handcuffed him, passed a chain through his handcuffs and fixed it to their belts, and lashed his arms tight to his sides. They crowded very close about him, with their hands always on him in a careful, caressing grip, as though all the while feeling him to make sure he was there. It was like men handling a fish which is still alive and may jump back into the water. But he stood quite unresisting, yielding his arms limply to the ropes, as though he hardly noticed what was happening. (44)

The procedure appears as unreal even to those most involved in it; the less the prisoner resists, the more unreal he seems – like a fish or, following Orwell's description of the prison cells in the piece's opening, an animal.

He becomes a person not in the official procedure of the execution, but in a moment that overwhelms Orwell shortly afterwards, shifting the focus away from the state acting on the prisoner's body and fixing instead on a simple act of the prisoner himself. It is a moment of resistance – not the man's resistance to his execution but his unintentional resistance to becoming a symbol of its brutality. Following a group into the prison yard, Orwell's gaze is drawn not to the gallows but to a gesture far simpler and, for him, more arresting:

> It was about forty yards to the gallows. I watched the bare brown back of the prisoner marching in front of me. He walked clumsily with his bound arms, but quite steadily, with that bobbing gait of the Indian who never straightens his knees. At each step his muscles slid neatly into place, the lock of hair on his scalp danced up and down, his feet printed themselves on the wet gravel. And once, in spite of the men who gripped him by each shoulder, he stepped slightly aside to avoid a puddle on the path. (45)

---

[35] George Orwell, "A Hanging," in *An Age Like This: 1920–1940*, vol. 3, *The Collected Essays, Journalism, and Letters of George Orwell*, ed. Sonia Orwell and Ian Angus. Boston: David R. Godine, 2000, 44; hereafter cited parenthetically by page number.

This barely discernible movement of the condemned man avoiding a puddle moves Orwell in a way that the execution – despite the detail with which he subsequently portrays it – cannot. A powerful sense of mystery overtakes him in this quotidian act, laying bare something that defies expression or logical explanation. "It is curious, but till that moment I had never realized what it means to destroy a healthy, conscious man. When I saw the prisoner step aside to avoid the puddle, I saw the mystery, the unspeakable wrongness, of cutting a life short when it is in full tide" (45). The realization settles over Orwell curiously and mysteriously because it contains nothing of the brutality that he subsequently witnesses, the body of the hanged man "dangling with his toes pointed straight downwards, very slowly revolving, as dead as a stone" (47).

The stray but searing detail of the puddle delivers a gravity that cannot be felt by focusing solely on the moment of execution. Barely perceptible, it reveals the man not as the proverbial dead man walking but as a fully recognizable person, a human being simply stepping aside so as not to get wet.[36] "I saw the mystery, the unspeakable wrongness" – a mystery distinct from secrecy, from the silence that Camus and Plath detect surrounding the death penalty and the exaggerated images through which political reality becomes literary fantasy in their novels.

Indeed, the larger-than-life scenarios of "being burned alive all along your nerves" or facing the angry scaffold crowd derive their narrative force from what might well be described as Edmund Burke's idea of the sublime. The difference between sensing, with little fanfare, an injustice beyond words and savoring a horrific description of electrocution is precisely for Burke the fault line between life and art. Such a distinction, he suggests, turns on an inability to recognize the difference between our ideals and our desires: "I believe that this notion of our having a simple pain in the reality, yet a delight in the representation, arises from hence, that we do not sufficiently distinguish what we would by no means chuse to do, from what we should be eager enough to see if it was once done. We delight in seeing things, which so far from doing, our heartiest wishes would be to see

---

[36] As such, Orwell's account takes up the concerns raised by Desmond Manderson: "It is through a complex of practices of denial that the condemned man disappears from the scene of his own death, a convenient absence which allows us to think of execution as something abstract and inhuman." Desmond Manderson, *Songs without Music: Aesthetic Dimensions of Law and Justice*. Berkeley: University of California Press, 2000, 115.

redressed."[37] Burke thus implies that our politics ("what we would by no means chuse to do") exist in a strangely discordant, even blind, relationship with our desires. The tension between them accounts for the difference between "A Hanging" and *The Bell Jar* or *The Stranger*. For Orwell there is no "delight in representation" but rather an emphasis on just how hard it is to come by any pleasure at all. He recalls how those who had attended the hanging shared an uncomfortable laugh afterwards, as though trying to lighten a moment that was destined to remain in darkness. "Several people laughed – at what, nobody seemed certain" (47), and Orwell soon "found that I was laughing quite loudly" (48) as well – a discovery suggesting the profoundly alienating rather than the edifying or sublime quality of the event. The narrative gains in force, I would suggest, precisely because of what is *not* there: no desire, delectation, or political posturing – no sense, in fact, that he is acting as a witness. Embedding himself in a context rather than rising above it, Orwell looks and listens with little comment, taking stock rather than taking sides. Given this, one might certainly accuse him of being cavalier or irresponsibly apolitical. Such a reading, however, obscures the way in which seeing an execution for Orwell amounted to far more than recording it as a mechanical procedure – as the drop of the rope, the flip of the switch, the insertion of the needle. It means at once to narrow the field of vision to a man and a puddle and to widen it to include far more than the instant of his death.

To witness an execution in Orwell's terms, I submit, is to change the terms of what it means to witness it at all. There is no fantasy, no struggle over rights, and no claims to civic duty. What counts for Orwell is an openness to the details outside the spectacle's field of vision, to the humbler observations that undo one's expectations or fantasies. It is the capacity to find oneself, having stumbled through chance and mystery, in the midst of an encounter at once tragic and ethical.

---

[37] Edmund Burke, A *Philosophical Enquiry into the Origin of our Ideas of the Sublime and Beautiful*, ed. Adam Philips. Oxford: Oxford University Press, 1990, 43–44.

11

Ethical Exception
Capital Punishment in the Figure of Sovereignty

Adam Thurschwell

Capital Punishment: Moral or Political

These are again interesting times to be thinking about the death penalty. Signs and portents seem to be everywhere. Closest to home, where only a few short years ago it was considered political suicide for a politician to be anything but gung ho in favor of executing wrongdoers, it has now become (almost) equally *de rigueur* to at least nod one's head in the direction of concerns about "making sure you get the right guy," DNA testing, and other methods of lowering the near-certain probability (based on recent experience) of executing the factually innocent. It has even become politically feasible to advocate abolition.[1] There are stronger indications as well, from former governor George Ryan's commutation of Illinois's entire death row, to moratorium efforts around the country, to legislative reforms that have been introduced at both state and federal levels.[2] Even the current U.S. Supreme Court, not exactly the capital defendant's best friend despite the "death is different" mantra that has ostensibly guided its capital jurisprudence for 30 years, has begun to narrow the scope of the death penalty's application[3] and to express impatience with incompetent capital

---

[1] For example, the governor of Maryland recently announced his support for ending the death penalty in his state. See Ovetta Wiggins and John Wagner, "O'Malley Voices Support of Bill to End Death Penalty," *The Washington Post*, January 26, 2007.
[2] New Jersey became the first state to abolish its death penalty in more than 40 years on December 17, 2007. Death Penalty Information Center, *The Death Penalty in 2007: Year End Report*, December 2007, www.deathpenaltyinfo.org/2007YearEnd.pdf (accessed January 25, 2008).
[3] See, for example, *Roper v. Simmons*, 543 U.S. 551 (2005), which prohibited execution of people who were under the age of eighteen at the time they committed a capital crime.

My thanks to my colleagues at Cleveland-Marshall College of Law for their helpful comments, to the Cleveland-Marshall Fund for support, and to Laurent Gloerfelt for research assistance.

Ethical Exception

counsel[4] and lower courts whose cavalier attitude toward procedural irregularities in capital cases exceeds even its own.[5]

Widening the focus and the historical framework a little, one finds even more significant signs of change. A growing number of nations are abolishing their death penalties, including some that were fervent practitioners of it in the recent past. Notably, the impetus for these changes has largely come from the pressures of globalization, as in the case of the former Soviet bloc nations that have abandoned the death penalty to become eligible for membership in the Council of Europe and similar supranational security and economic governance organizations.[6] International law is edging toward declaring capital punishment to be a human rights violation (many human rights treaties already do so),[7] and none of the various international criminal courts provides for the death penalty. The United States stood all but alone, even among fellow members of the "coalition of the willing," in affirming the appropriateness of executing as thoroughly demonized a mass murderer as Saddam Hussein.[8]

One might hope and expect that such dramatic changes in the political reality of capital punishment on the ground would be reflected in contemporary philosophical discussions of the death penalty. To a certain extent this has occurred, albeit primarily in the philosophical discourse that is at the furthest intellectual remove from the courtrooms where capital punishment is still practiced – that is, in the writings of continental theorists such as Michel Foucault, Jacques Derrida, and Giorgio Agamben. If one focuses on the Anglo-American debates, however, until very recently (and still for the most part today) one finds a surprising and disappointing disconnect from these real-world developments and from the realities of capital litigation as it is experienced today by capital defendants, capital attorneys, and nonabolitionist governments and their court systems.

---

[4] See, for example, *Rompilla v. Beard*, 545 U.S. 374 (2005); and *Wiggins v. Smith*, 539 U.S. 510 (2003).

[5] See, for example, *Miller-El v. Dretke*, 545 U.S. 231 (2005). The decision reversed the Fifth Circuit Court of Appeals for the second time in the same case for its failure to discern palpable racism in the selection of the defendant's jury.

[6] See Peter Hodgkinson, "Europe – A Death Penalty Free Zone: Commentary and Critique of Abolitionist Strategies," *Ohio Northern University Law Review* 26 (2000): 625–664.

[7] See generally William Schabas, "International Law, Politics, Diplomacy, and the Abolition of the Death Penalty," *William and Mary Bill of Rights Journal* 13 (2004): 417–444.

[8] See, for example, "Europeans Opposed to Death Sentence," *Der Spiegel Online*, November 7, 2006, www.spiegel.de/international/0,1518,446924,00.html (accessed February 5, 2007).

The reasons for this disconnect, moreover, are clear. Capital punishment has been analyzed as a moral and not a political-philosophical question. That is, the overwhelming tendency of the literature has been to analyze the legitimacy of capital punishment by asking if it can be shown to be an appropriate punishment for an offender as a matter of *individual moral desert* – when, if ever, the heinousness of a crime justifies the imposition of death as a matter of retributive justice; when, if ever, the deterrent consequences of a sentence of death will outweigh the punishment's deleterious consequences from a utilitarian perspective; and so on. Yet even the most cursory examination of the cultural, legal, and political roles of capital punishment as it is actually institutionalized (or not institutionalized) and practiced (or not practiced) around the world today demonstrates that this theoretical orientation gets it precisely backward. The most fundamental issues are neither individual nor moral but the profoundly political ones of the constitution and exercise of state sovereignty.[9]

This is not to say that political considerations never enter into these debates; they do. They appear, for example, in the form of arguments based on the pervasive racism of the capital justice system or the distorting effects of elected criminal justice officials (judges and prosecutors) who might bias the system in favor of death to gain reelection. When such appear, however, they are mostly adduced as nonphilosophical add-ons to the philosophical discussion, second-order issues suggesting the impossibility of institutionalizing capital punishment in a just manner even if it could be justified in principle on moral grounds. More subtly, even when political issues are presented in ostensibly political-philosophical terms, they end up being deployed and analyzed under the rubric of moral-philosophical categories instead. In other words, it is precisely what is specifically and essentially political in the question of capital punishment that is glossed over in the analysis.

It did not have to be that way. Several years ago, criminal law theorist George Fletcher called for a shift from understanding criminal law

---

[9] I would include in this generalization even the superficially moral objection to the execution of the actually innocent, which has played such a significant role in political debates in the United States. In fact, on closer examination, this is not a moral objection at all but an objection to the state's failure to select the right person to kill, which is one reason why many prominent abolitionists find themselves uneasy with this strand of the abolition debate. See, for example, Carol Steiker and Jordan Steiker, "The Seduction of Innocence: The Attraction and Limitations of the Focus on Innocence in Capital Punishment Law and Advocacy," *Journal of Criminal Law and Criminology* 95 (2005): 587–624.

exclusively through moral-philosophical categories to a focus on its political-philosophical underpinnings.[10] Fletcher's point was that criminal punishment (whether capital or noncapital) is not simply something that happens to someone deservedly or undeservedly but also is something that the *state*, as a state, does to someone and that the involvement of the state in the moral fate of individuals ought therefore to be an independent area for philosophical inquiry. With a few equivocal exceptions, there has not been much response to Fletcher's suggestion within the U.S. legal academy, and – at least until very recently – that has been almost equally true within the broader theoretical discussions of capital punishment.[11] Death penalty debates, to the extent that they resort to philosophical arguments, have for the most part remained resolutely committed to moral categories of justification and desert that are far removed from the realities of capital punishment on the ground.

Very recently, however, there have been signs of change. In what amounts to a discovery *après la lettre* of Foucault's theses about biopolitics and governmentality,[12] a few U.S. legal commentators of a retentionist or agnostic bent have begun to argue, in more and less serious forms, that capital punishment ought to be analyzed and evaluated as simply another form of government regulation like any other. Foucault famously argued that the essential characteristic of sovereignty was its "power to exercise the right to decide life and death."[13] In its earlier, premodern form, the state exercised that power in "the right to *take* life or *let* live" – that is, in its power to kill its subjects (e.g., for transgressing its laws) or allow

---

[10] George Fletcher, "The Fall and Rise of Criminal Theory," *Buffalo Criminal Law Review* 1 (1998): 275–294; and George Fletcher, "The Nature and Function of Criminal Theory," *California Law Review* 88 (2000): 687–703.

[11] There are a few notable exceptions. Austin Sarat and Timothy Kaufman-Osborn in particular have focused on the relationship of capital punishment to political sovereignty in their recent work. See Austin Sarat, *When the State Kills: Capital Punishment and the American Condition*. Princeton, NJ: Princeton University Press, 2002; Austin Sarat, ed., *The Killing State: Capital Punishment in Law, Politics, and Culture*. New York: Oxford University Press, 2001; Timothy Kaufman-Osborn, "A Critique of Contemporary Death Penalty Abolitionism," *Punishment and Society* 8.3 (2006): 365–383; Timothy Kaufman-Osborn, *From Noose to Needle: Capital Punishment and the Late Liberal State*. Ann Arbor: University of Michigan Press, 2002.

[12] See Michel Foucault, *The History of Sexuality*, vol. 1, *An Introduction*, trans. Robert Hurley. New York: Vintage Books, 1978, 135–146; Michel Foucault, *"Society Must Be Defended": Lectures at the Collège de France, 1975–1976*, ed. Mauro Bertani, trans. David Macey. New York: Picador, 2003, 239–256; and Michel Foucault, "Governmentality," in Graham Burchell, Colin Gordon, and Peter Miller, eds., *The Foucault Effect: Studies in Governmentality*. Chicago: University of Chicago Press, 1991, 87–104.

[13] Foucault, *History of Sexuality*, 1:135.

them to live. Natural death retained its own power over life that the state could emulate but not attack at its roots. The advent of techno-scientific modernity, however, gave the state the opportunity for the first time to contest natural mortality by prolonging and improving the lives of its citizens beyond simply threatening them. Accordingly, in this new bio-political state, sovereign power took on new functions that were not simply negative and prohibitory (transgress the law and you will die), but were affirmatively directed at promoting and enhancing life itself. In Foucault's formula, the modern state now concerned itself with the welfare and productivity of its population by exercising its "power to *foster* life or *disallow* it to the point of death" through its regulatory interventions into the social fields of medicine, education, public hygiene, food production, and so on.[14] By the same token, however, these interventions meant that state law necessarily subordinated its authority, at least to some extent, to the technical expertise of the various sciences and disciplines that it sought to employ in its new role of "fostering life." Hence we see the emergence of the techno-bureaucratic state, staffed and largely run by experts rather than political leaders in the traditional sense of the term (the state form that Foucault called "governmentality").[15]

As Foucault also noted, this mutation in the form of the state's "exercise of the right to decide life and death" necessarily resulted in a change in the political meaning of capital punishment as well. "How could power exercise its highest prerogatives by putting people to death, when its main role was to ensure, sustain, and multiply life, to put this life in order?" The answer was that capital punishment could no longer be justified by "the enormity of the crime" but only by the "monstrosity of the criminal, his incorrigibility, and the safeguard of society." That is, "one had the right to kill those who represented a kind of biological danger to others" – a shift in understanding of state killing from the punishment of evil to just another biopolitical regulation intended to foster the health of the body politic.[16] Thus Foucault in 1976.

Thirty years later and closer to home, two recent articles by U.S. legal academics have also attempted to subsume (and thereby justify) capital punishment under the rubric of "government regulation." Cass Sunstein

---

[14] Ibid., 1:138, 1:143.
[15] Foucault, "Governmentality."
[16] Foucault, *History of Sexuality*, 1:138.

and Adrian Vermeule's article is the better known of the two because of its provocative thesis that capital punishment might be morally obligatory under certain circumstances.[17] For my purposes, their argument is marred by their insistence on continuing to justify the practice on moral grounds even while theorizing it as government regulation – a move that obscures an otherwise useful insight into the political significance of capital punishment. Although it has received less attention, a 2005 article by Ronald Allen and Amy Shavell does not make this mistake and thus poses a greater challenge to the abolitionist position.[18] Their main target is the currently potent abolitionist argument that emphasizes the demonstrable risk of executing the innocent. Why, they ask, should capital punishment, in which the state could err in deciding who to kill, be treated as morally distinct from all the other government practices in which the state consciously decides to grant some innocents life and others death? As they point out, these practices are the routine fodder of government action: "Although it seems to have escaped the attention of the death penalty debate, a common feature of social planning is that it affects the incidence of death. Virtually all social policies and decisions quite literally determine who will live and who will die."[19] Their main example is highway and vehicle regulations, and they also point to decisions pitting health care and science research against educational funding allocation, but the list is virtually inexhaustible. Government regulations, from mundane fire and building codes to emergency disaster relief funding levels, effectively allocate life and death through policy planning that calculates the effects of the regulation on the population,

---

[17] Cass Sunstein and Adrian Vermeule, "Is Capital Punishment Morally Required? Acts, Omissions, and Life-Life Tradeoffs," *Stanford Law Review* 58 (2005): 703–750. This idea was spurred by recent studies suggesting that capital punishment might, after all, have a significant deterrent effect on homicide. That hypothesis is open to doubt, but it is not my aim to get into such an empirical debate here. For work questioning the studies that find a meaningful deterrent effect, see Jeffrey Fagan, "Death and Deterrence Redux: Science, Law, and Causal Reasoning on Capital Punishment," *Ohio State Journal of Criminal Law* 4 (2006): 255–320; Jeffrey Fagan, Franklin E. Zimring, and Amanda Geller, "Capital Punishment and Capital Murder: Market Share and the Deterrent Effects of the Death Penalty," *Texas Law Review* 84 (2006): 1803–1867; John J. Donohue and Justin Wolfers, "Uses and Abuses of Empirical Evidence in the Death Penalty Debate," *Stanford Law Review* 58 (2005): 791–846; and Richard Berk, "New Claims about Executions and General Deterrence: Déjà Vu All Over Again?" *Journal of Empirical Legal Studies* 2 (2005): 303–330.

[18] Ronald Allen and Amy Shavell, "Further Reflections on the Guillotine," *Journal of Criminal Law and Criminology* 95 (2005): 625–636.

[19] Id., 628.

including, more and more commonly, calculations about the likely resulting incidence of deaths. Why then, ask Allen and Shavell (and Sunstein and Vermeule), should innocent deaths that predictably result from the state's adoption of fallible capital punishment procedures be viewed differently from the innocent deaths that predictably – indeed, quite consciously – result from the government's calculated adoption of (other) regulatory policies?

Carol Steiker, in a response to Sunstein and Vermeule, believes that she can answer this question.[20] What is interesting here is the manner in which she inadvertently sidesteps the most profound political significance of capital punishment at the very moment that she is purporting to attack it from a political angle. In that sense, her article is exemplary of the traditional elision of the political in these debates. In sum, she argues that capital punishment differs from the state's regulatory decision to allow some to die because it is not "regulation" at all but a different state practice – "punishment" – that is subject to evaluative criteria that differ from those applied to nonstate killing. This point is fundamental because the necessary premise of Sunstein and Vermeule's (and any utilitarian's) argument in favor of capital punishment is the moral equivalency of state and nonstate killing – otherwise, the calculated deterrent trade-off of guilty (and some innocent) individuals executed by the state for the sake of (private) murders prevented would be a meaningless apples-and-oranges category mistake. That premise is incorrect, Steiker claims: capital punishment is "a practice of state punishment that can be unjust in ways quite distinct from the general wrongness of killing.... Being an act done by the state in the name of the collective, it requires not only moral but also political justification."[21]

Nevertheless, when Steiker goes on to offer ostensibly political arguments for the injustice of capital punishment – that capital punishment is so frequently disproportionate given the limited cognitive and moral capacities of most capital defendants, that it is so frequently administered

---

[20] Carol Steiker, "No, Capital Punishment Is Not Morally Required: Deterrence, Deontology, and the Death Penalty," *Stanford Law Review* 58 (2005): 751–789.

[21] Id., 755, 764. I am leaving aside her other arguments – with which, on their own (moral-philosophical) terms, I mostly agree – for the sake of my larger point. For an argument that none of these debates matters – a position with which I am obviously in sympathy – see Daniel Williams, "The Futile Debate over the Morality of the Death Penalty: A Critical Commentary on the Steiker and Sunstein-Vermeule Debate," *Lewis and Clark Law Review* 10 (2006): 625–640.

Ethical Exception

in a racially discriminatory manner, and that it necessarily erodes the humanity of the body politic – what is least clear is why she calls these arguments "political." The requirement of a proportional response to violence is equally applicable to killing by individuals – it is the fundamental premise of the law of self-defense, for example – as is the notion that racially motivated killings are more culpable than non–racially motivated killings (a principle that is enshrined in so-called hate crime legislation enacted in most United States jurisdictions). The dehumanizing trauma inherent in the act of killing is familiar to all who have read individual soldiers' accounts of battlefield experiences. Of course it is true, as Steiker says, that capital punishment, unlike an individual killing, is "an act done by the state in the name of the collective." If, however, the two acts (by the state, on one hand, and an individual, on the other) are to be evaluated under the same set of moral criteria, then what is essential about the state *qua* state – which is to say, what is essentially political – seems to have dropped out of the analysis. By focusing exclusively on the legitimacy of state actions rather than the nature of the state itself, the specificity of what is political about the political state is elided and moral categories necessarily remain privileged (whether or not they are dubbed "political" for these purposes).[22]

That said, the omission of the political question would be of no particular importance were it not for the fact that what is omitted seems to call into

---

[22] A recent article by Guyora Binder (which is cited by Steiker in "No") is paradigmatic in this regard, although it concerns the justification of criminal punishment generally, not just capital punishment. See Guyora Binder, "Criminal Theory: Moral or Political?" *Buffalo Criminal Law Review* 5 (2002): 321; and Steiker, "No," 764 n. 41. Binder argues that although they were traditionally labeled as species of moral philosophy, utilitarianism, and retributivism were in fact originally formulated to evaluate state rather than individual action and thus ought to be considered political as well as moral philosophies. I have no quarrel with Binder's historical genealogy, but (as I elaborate later) I believe that they obscure the more fundamental political-philosophical question of the nature of state sovereignty as such by aiming solely instead at the moral-normative evaluation of particular sovereign acts. Relatedly, intellectual historian Richard Tuck has argued that the classical contract theorists – from Hugo Grotius and Samuel von Pufendorf through Locke, Hobbes, and Kant – drew their model of liberalism's morally autonomous person not from an abstract metaphysical concept of the subject but from the norms of behavior that governed the really existing state sovereigns of the theorists' contemporary international order. Richard Tuck, *The Rights of War and Peace: Political Thought and the International Order from Grotius to Kant*. Oxford: Oxford University Press, 1999. The implications of Tuck's argument are potentially quite profound – among others, it seems to turn the contractarian legitimation of political sovereignty on its head – but are beyond the scope of this essay.

question the abolitionists' entire project. In fact, the political specificity of the state has not disappeared in Steiker's argument at all. Rather, her argument presupposes an implicit model of state sovereignty, but one that is so familiar and taken for granted as to be rendered all but invisible. In distinguishing "punishment" from "regulation," Steiker has recapitulated the Foucauldian distinction between the ancient state that exercises the right to kill or let live and the modern state that exercises the right to foster life or allow to die. Thus, by arguing for abolition in terms that understand it as "punishment," she (and the mainstream of abolitionist discourse, which I am using her work to represent) is unwittingly affirming a view of the state that makes its power to kill its own citizens its primary and essential attribute.

Indeed, Timothy Kaufman-Osborn makes precisely this point in a 2006 article in which he criticizes other abolitionists from a similarly Foucauldian perspective.[23] He points to a split between the current discourse and practice of capital punishment that breaks down precisely along the lines of Foucault's typology of state sovereignty. On the one hand, in their arguments about capital punishment, both its adherents and opponents posit a state whose power over the lives of its citizens is a special and defining element of its sovereignty – in which "punishment" must be distinguished from "regulation," in Steiker's terms. On the other hand, the actual practice of capital punishment by the state has increasingly come to resemble the modern bio-political sovereign. This split between the myth and reality of capital punishment, Kaufman-Osborn argues, is epitomized by the ideology of retribution and vengeance that provides the political capital for the maintenance of the death penalty, on one hand, and the reality of its cold, deliberately affectless pseudomedical implementation in the form of lethal injection, on the other. Kaufman-Osborn's concern is that in unconsciously embracing the older conception of sovereignty, abolitionists might unintentionally provide aid and solace to their enemy: "However unwittingly, abolitionist arguments premised on this conception may reinforce the representation of sovereignty that sustains this anachronistic myth and so its title to kill." Thus, he argues, "if the governmentalization of the state has advanced as far as Foucault would have us believe,"[24] abolitionism must take a different form today, one that undermines the killing state's mythical self-representation rather than affirming it.

[23] Kaufman-Osborn, "A Critique."
[24] Id., 382.

There is much to be said in favor of the call for abolitionists to turn their attention to the bio-political disciplinary matrix that supports the death penalty today rather than jousting with (and unintentionally reinforcing) an image of sovereignty that defines itself by its power to kill. One recent and astonishing – although temporary – vindication of Kaufman-Osborn's Foucauldian prescription was the initial success of legal challenges to capital punishment based entirely on the medical-technical issue of the state's faulty implementation of the lethal injection procedure.[25] Prior to these successes, most in the abolitionist community viewed legal attacks on the technical procedures of execution – except when these procedures resulted in truly spectacular failures, as in the case of the Florida defendant who caught fire during his electrocution[26] – as the hopeless last resort of those on the verge of execution. Even in the wake of the U.S. Supreme Court's decision overturning one of these favorable lower court decisions, litigators have continued to challenge the death penalty based on biomedical-ethical objections to lethal injection.[27]

Nevertheless, there are at least two reasons for hesitating to endorse Kaufman-Osborn's Foucauldian approach. If, as Kaufman-Osborn suggests, "the governmentalization of the state has advanced as far as Foucault would have us believe" – that is, in his view, to the point at which the biopolitical imperative to cultivate life has eclipsed the older sovereign form of threatening death – then Sunstein, Vermeule, Allen, and Shavell's utilitarian focus on net lives saved over lives lost would in fact crudely define the general terrain in which battles over capital punishment now must be fought. That would be an unfortunate concession for abolitionists to make, both from the perspective of their moral intuitions about the specific evil of capital punishment and from the pragmatics of contemporary political argument.

---

[25] Prior to the Supreme Court's decision in *Baze v. Rees*, 128 U.S. 1520 (2008), twelve states had put executions on hold because of constitutional challenges to their lethal injection procedures. Karen Kaplan, "Reliability of Execution Drugs Is in Question," *Los Angeles Times*, April 24, 2007. For a recent study finding the implementation of lethal injection in two states (California and North Carolina) to be faulty, see Teresa A. Zimmers et al., "Lethal Injection for Execution: Chemical Asphyxiation?" *PloS Medicine* 4.4 (April 2007): 1–8.

[26] The defendant was Pedro Medina. For accounts of Medina's and others' botched executions, see Michael L. Radelet, "Some Examples of Post-Furman Botched Executions," Death Penalty Information Center, May 24, 2007, www.deathpenaltyinfo.org/article.php?scid=8&did=478 (accessed January 25, 2008).

[27] *See Baze v. Rees*, 128 U.S. 1520 (2008). Information on continuing lethal injection litigation after *Baze* is compiled at Lethal Injection.org (http://www.law.berkeley.edu/clinics/dpclinic/LethalInjection/index.html) (last visited on December 17, 2008).

More fundamentally, however, Kaufman-Osborn (like, it should be said, many of Foucault's followers) overreads Foucault's distinction between the spectacular sovereignty of killing or letting live and the bio-political sovereignty of making live or letting die. Foucault himself never endorsed the notion that the latter had entirely eclipsed the former.[28] Instead, he interpreted the old sovereign power to kill as having migrated *within* the new sovereign power in the form of "racism," which he defined as "primarily a way of introducing a break into the domain of life that is under power's control: the break between what must live and what must die."[29] My purpose here is not to discuss Foucault's idiosyncratic definition of racism (although, it seems to me, it provides a potentially powerful tool for comprehending the role of race in the United States' history of capital punishment).[30] The point is simply that Foucault himself did

---

[28] See, for example, Foucault, "*Society Must Be Defended*," 241: "I wouldn't say exactly that sovereignty's old right – to take life or let live – was replaced, but that it came to be complemented by a new right which does not erase the old right but which does penetrate it, permeate it." In fairness, it should be said that Kaufman-Osborn elsewhere expresses his own awareness of this nuance. *See.* Timothy Kaufman-Osborn, *From Noose to Needle: Capital Punishment and the Late Liberal State.* Ann Arbor: University of Michigan Press, 2002, 190–192.

[29] Id., 254; see also 256.

[30] Foucault's distinction between spectacular and disciplinary punishment regimes, and his account of the different role of the death penalty in these regimes, has been attacked by some who point to the persistence of spectacular racist violence in the United States long after the period of spectacular punishment supposedly came to an end. See, for example, Joy James, "Erasing the Spectacle of Racialized State Violence," in *Resisting State Violence: Radicalism, Race, and Gender in U.S. Culture.* Minneapolis: University of Minnesota Press, 1996, 24–43. The role of race in Foucault's political theory deserves a lengthy discussion, one that unfortunately lies beyond the scope and purpose of the present essay. That said, while agreeing with James that it is dangerous to draw too sharp a line between the spectacular and governmental forms of sovereignty, as a preliminary matter I would still point out three flaws in her critique, whatever its other merits. The first two are closely related: she elides the difference between violence and spectacular violence, and she elides the difference between private spectacular violence and governmental spectacular violence. As to the first, specifically with regard to the death penalty James says, for example, "Behind prison walls, state executions take place as private spectacle" (Id., 35). "Private spectacle" is a contradiction in terms, however; the movement of executions behind prison walls is perhaps the clearest confirmation of Foucault's thesis of a sea change in the meaning and purpose of criminal punishment from a display of sovereign power to an exercise of bio-political expurgation. Nor are James's other examples of ostensibly spectacular racist violence convincing. Even the quasi-military destruction of the MOVE compound in Philadelphia was not intended to be a public spectacle – it became one only through the grotesque callousness and incompetence of the Wilson Goode administration and the Philadelphia police. This is of course in no way a defense of private executions or public bombings, nor is it to deny that private executions and (nonspectacular) public bombings can be just as racist and just as violent as the spectacular varieties. It is simply to point out that the goal of (genuinely) spectacular punishment was to advertise sovereign power to the public, whereas James's examples are either not public or not intended to be public

not believe that the "older" form of sovereignty had been superseded by bio-power. Thus, even if the state assumed the additional (bio)power of

> displays in this sense and become controversial and subject to public criticism precisely to the extent that they come to resemble such displays. As to the second point, James rightly argues that public lynchings exemplified the persistence of spectacular racist violence well into Foucault's modern age of "disciplinary" punishment (Id., 28–30). When thinking about Foucault's account of sovereignty, however, it is necessary to analyze the complex relationship between the official governmental penal ideology – which generally condemned extralegal violence even if that condemnation often amounted to lip service in practice – and the private, if pervasive, pseudo-penal rationalization of private lynchings, which were in reality motivated by a desire to maintain the system of racial subordination. James tends to elide the governmental and the nongovernmental with phrases such as "[t]he convergence of mobs and sheriffs [who] oversaw the branded, dismembered black body that symbolized the rage of the prosecuting crowd and state" (Id., 29) and torture "executed by self-appointed lawmen and government employees" (Id., 30). From the perspective of the black body, it did not and could not make any difference that his or her torturers were "self-appointed [i.e., private rather than official] lawmen" and "government employees" (and sheriffs) who were acting in their private rather than public capacities. If one is trying to sort out the role of state sovereignty in this matrix of public and private violence, however, it becomes important to make these distinctions to avoid a monolithic view that misses the political meanings of the racist violence. See, for example, David Garland, "Penal Excess and Surplus Meaning: Public Torture Lynchings in Twentieth-Century America," *Law and Society Review*, 39 (December 2005): 793–834.
>
> Finally, James's analysis of Foucault omits his discussion of race and racism in "*Society Must Be Defended*" (understandably, one should add, because James's essay was published in 1996 and Foucault's lectures were not published in French until 1997 and English in 2003). The notion of racism as "a break in the domain of life that is under power's control ... between what must live and what must die" (Foucault, *Society*, 254) corresponds very closely to James's own understanding of the role of race, as when she suggests that "bodies matter differently in racialized systems" (James, "Erasing the Spectacle," 34) when it comes to state executions. That is precisely Foucault's point, except that unlike James, he rids "race" of all traces of biologism and essentialism by defining it in terms of the decision over life and death rather than by trying to analyze the effect of an (implicitly) essentialized and prior notion of "race" on that decision. Without attempting to trace (or endorse) all its implications, it is clear that linking race to the sovereign power over death in this manner allows for a more nuanced understanding of the relationship of capital punishment and race. Capital trials and lynchings were not just reflections of a racist society but were themselves extremely important social mechanisms for imposing the meaning of racial difference in the first half of the twentieth century in the United States. Moreover, this perspective also offers an account of the racializing effect of capital and other criminal prosecutions in the contemporary war on terror. Does anyone think of Zacarias Moussaoui as French (his nationality) or even Moroccan (his ethnic heritage), or do they instead think of him as a (vaguely Arabic) "Islamic fundamentalist"? John Walker Lindh, a white man from California, is best known as "the American Taliban," and Jose Padilla – an American of Puerto Rican descent – is also more closely identified by most people today with al-Qaeda and Islamic fundamentalism than with his U.S. citizenship or Puerto Rican ethnicity. These diverse individuals, welded together in the public imagination under the rubric of "Islamic fundamentalism" through the medium and mechanism of criminal prosecutions (whether capital or not), exemplify the logic of Foucault's notion of "racism" as the line drawn between the friend and the enemy, those whom the state nurtures and those whom it kills. For all of these reasons, it seems to me that James's critique of Foucault, however trenchant her own emphasis on the role of race in capital punishment and other forms of state violence, fails to do full justice to the analytical virtues of his account.

"making live" during the course of the eighteenth century, it continues to be the case that its power to take life – however mutated in form – remains a, if not the, defining essence of its sovereignty. According to Foucault himself, sovereignty defined by its "title to kill" is neither anachronistic nor mythological – at least not yet – and abolitionist arguments that presuppose such a conception are not reinforcing a fiction but reflecting a continuing reality.

That conclusion provides no solace for abolitionists, however; instead, it only deepens the conundrum that Kaufman-Osborn identifies. If Sunstein, Vermeule, Allen, Shavell, and Kaufman-Osborn are wrong and the "title to kill" is no myth but actually defines a unique and essential element of the concept of sovereignty that is irreducible to its regulatory/governmental functions, it would appear that abolitionism – or at least its philosophical justification – has a much higher hurdle to jump than previously recognized. Not just the weight of history but the essential nature of state sovereignty itself would appear to have to be overcome to achieve its ends. It is to the implications of that conundrum that I turn in the following sections.

Sovereignty and the Right to Death

The notion that the state's "title to kill" is the very essence of its sovereignty is in no way unique to Foucault. Foucault himself traced the genealogy of this title to the ancient Roman law principle of *patria potestas*, which granted a father the absolute authority to kill his own children.[31] Regardless of its origins, however, there is a remarkable consensus in Western political philosophy, from the beginnings of post-Westphalian modernity to the present day, that identifies the essence of political sovereignty with the sovereign power to kill – or, to be more precise, the sovereign's right to claim the death of the citizen, whether in the form of direct killing or in the form of demanding that the citizen sacrifice his or her own life for the life of the state by submitting to military conscription. This consensus is not only consistent over time, but more remarkable yet, it is consistent across widely divergent traditions of thought, from liberal social contract theory, to Carl

---

[31] Foucault, *History of Sexuality*, 1:135. For a more extended discussion of the specific Roman law principle (*vitae necisque potestas*), see Giorgio Agamben, *Homo Sacer: Sovereign Power and Bare Life*, trans. Daniel Heller-Roazen. Stanford, CA: Stanford University Press, 1998, 87–90.

Schmitt's antiliberal decisionism, to contemporary continental political philosophy.

To cite only the liberal contractarian canon, in *Leviathan*, Thomas Hobbes defines the sovereign as he who alone retains the natural "right to everything, and to do whatsoever he thought necessary to his own preservation; subduing, hurting or killing any man in order thereunto," after the subjects had forsworn their own similar natural rights to enter into the commonwealth.[32] Jean-Jacques Rousseau, in the section of *The Social Contract* entitled, "Of the Right of Life and Death," states that under the social contract, the citizen's "life is not now, as it once was, merely nature's gift to him. It is something that he holds, on terms, from the State."[33] Perhaps most clearly, John Locke, in *Two Treatises of Government*, defines *"political power"* as *"a Right* of making Laws with Penalties of Death, and consequently all less Penalties, for the Regulating and Preserving of Property, and of employing the force of the Community, in the Execution of Such Laws, and in the defence of the Common-wealth from Foreign Injury."[34] I have already discussed Foucault's version of this thesis; more recently, Agamben has been the most prominent but hardly its only contemporary expositor.[35]

The point is not that these philosophers and traditions all say the same thing. There are enormous differences among them, with enormous practical consequences for the conclusions that one might draw from them about the legitimate exercise of political power. Nor is the point that the particulars of different states' self-imposed constraints on their power to kill are unimportant; on the contrary, these constraints are critical precisely because the state's power to kill is its essential and thus unavoidable attribute. My point is rather that however much these philosophical traditions might differ in the normative conclusions that they draw about the exercise of political power and the concomitant restraints on the exercise

---

[32] Thomas Hobbes, *Leviathan, or the Matter, Forme and Power of a Commonwealth, Ecclesiaticall and Civil*. Oxford: B. Blackwell, 1957, 203.

[33] Jean-Jacques Rousseau, *The Social Contract*, in *Social Contract: Essays by Locke, Hume, and Rousseau*, ed. Sir Ernest Barker, trans. Gerard Hopkins. London: Oxford University Press, 1947, 199.

[34] John Locke, "An Essay Concerning the True Original, Extent, and End of Civil Government," in *Two Treatises of Government*, ed. Peter Laslett. Cambridge: Cambridge University Press, 1988, 268.

[35] See generally Agamben, *Homo Sacer*; see also, for example, Achille Mbembe, "Necropolitics," *Public Culture* 15.1 (Winter 2003): 11–40.

of that power, they all posit "political power" itself – sovereignty as such, prior to any normative evaluation – in essentially the same way: as the sovereign's right, on one hand, to kill its citizens (and others on its territory as well) and, on the other, to conscript its citizens to fight and die in its own defense. To put the point another way, this "right" is a defining power and not a legal or moral right; its possession by the state implies nothing about the state's legal, ethical, or moral legitimacy or normative entitlement to exercise this power. It is simply the attribute that makes the state "the state" and not some other entity or institution within civil society.[36]

Apart from the convergence of these different philosophical traditions, this conception of sovereignty is consistent with most people's intuitions about the meaning of "the state," at least insofar as it is "sovereign." What is it that makes the state sovereign – supreme among all other social institutions – if not, ultimately, its right to kill (however limited to particular cases and constrained by particular procedures) and to demand the sacrifice of its citizens' lives in its defense? Moreover, although capital punishment is the focus here, it is important to separate out capital punishment as such from the state's power to kill (or rather, its right to the citizen's death), because this is only one aspect of the power. Even abolitionist states retain legal distinctions between justifiable killings by state actors in various situations (e.g., police killings of armed felons during arrests, the killing of political enemies by soldiers during wartime) and nonstate actors in similar circumstances.[37] Similarly, involuntary conscription in the service of

---

[36] For a recent work that takes up the issue of torture, rather than capital punishment, from this perspective, see Paul Kahn, *Sacred Violence: Torture, Terror, and Sovereignty* (Ann Arbor: University of Michigan Press, 2008). Kahn derives his very rich notion of sovereignty from a cultural-symbolic analysis of the citizen's relationship to the state rather than from a reading of canonical philosophical texts, but he arrives at essentially the same understanding as the one advanced here. Unfortunately his book came to my attention too late to engage with it further in this essay.

[37] This point took on a very concrete form in the course of the legal arguments in *State v. Makwanyane*, Case No. CCT/3/94 (So. Afr. Const. Ct. June 6, 1995), the case in which South Africa's Constitutional Court held the death penalty unconstitutional under South Africa's new constitution. The Constitutional Court rejected the death penalty in part because of the South African Constitution's unqualified declaration of the existence of a "right to life" on the part of its citizens. In attempting to counter this plain constitutional language, the government attorneys defending capital punishment raised some of the same government practices mentioned in the text above (justifiable killings of felons by government actors and killing the enemy during wartime, for example) as demonstrating that the assertedly absolute "right to life" could not in fact be absolute. Id., ¶¶ 136–140. Notably, the Constitutional Court did not disagree, holding only that whatever limitations might exist on the citizen's claim

Ethical Exception

an individual or institution – that is, slavery – is banned everywhere today except in one area: conscription for military service to the state. Finally, the state guarantees itself a monopoly on these quintessentially sovereign powers by forbidding them to all other actors in society and by criminalizing homicide and, traditionally, suicide and assisted suicide as well.

Again, my claim is emphatically not that all states are "the same" from the perspective of their moral, ethical, or political legitimacy. The point is that, to get at the most fundamental significance of capital punishment – and therefore to be able to make truly informed moral and ethical judgments about it, as well as to formulate effective political strategies aimed at its eventual abolition – one must separate the question of the state's sovereignty from its legitimacy. If, as I have been arguing (and as the consensus of Western political philosophical traditions also holds), the very concept of political sovereignty is intimately and essentially tied to the state's power to kill, this ought to have consequences for how we think about capital punishment.

Let us schematize the argument so far. The concept of political sovereignty is necessarily prior to any particular moral or ethical evaluation of its nature or actions: one cannot evaluate the state as "a state" and not some other social actor unless and until one knows that it is in fact a state that one is evaluating. To the extent that the state's power over the citizen's life (of which capital punishment constitutes one component part) is the defining essence of this sovereignty, then one can say that this power has a purely political status that stands outside any normative regime of moral, ethical, or legal judgment that one might (subsequently) apply to it. Sovereignty itself is thus, strictly speaking, not an ethical-moral concept. In that sense, the sovereign's defining power over death is excepted from such normative regimes. Considered solely in its relationship to political sovereignty, the state's power over death is an exception to the ethical, a political-philosophical concept that stands independent of the categories of ethical-moral philosophy. In short, we seem finally to have reached the purely political-philosophical perspective on capital punishment that I suggested was needed at the outset.[38]

---

of a "right to life" against the state, those limits did not extend to capital punishment. Id., ¶¶ 139–140.

[38] It is worth noting that the leading attempt to articulate the concepts of "sovereignty" and "the political" as pure philosophical categories in their own right, distinct from all other

Three Insights

What then do we learn by such a strictly political-philosophical perspective? Is there some practical or theoretical payoff to approaching capital punishment from this direction? Here, I suggest three areas that appear in a different and more instructive light when capital punishment is viewed through the lens of sovereignty, before concluding with one more political-philosophical and practical-political conundrum that this analysis seems to create.

Abolition or Reform?

The first such area is the prospect for, and indeed the meaning of, the abolition of capital punishment within a state. Here the results of the political-philosophical analysis are chastening. If the state's power to kill is (or is at least part of) its essential attribute, the attribute that makes it a "political state" in the first instance, then a complete and total abolition

> philosophical concepts with which they tend to become confused (i.e., moral, economic, religious, or aesthetic), concludes in the same notion of political sovereignty as the one derived here. See Carl Schmitt, *Political Theology: Four Chapters on the Concept of Sovereignty*, trans. George Schwab. Chicago: University of Chicago Press, 2005; and Carl Schmitt, *The Concept of the Political*, trans. George Schwab. Chicago: University of Chicago Press, 1996. Both Schmitt's concept of the political and his concept of sovereignty – which famously defined the sovereign as "he who decides on the exception" (*Political Theology*, 5) – ultimately turn on what he calls "the real possibility of physical killing" (*Concept of the Political*, 33). This insight also forms the starting point for the recent and highly influential political-philosophical work of Giorgio Agamben, Schmitt's most important contemporary interpreter. See generally Adam Thurschwell, *Specters of Nietzsche: Potential Futures for the Concept of the Political in Agamben and Derrida*, September 1, 2004, http://papers.ssrn.com/sol3/papers.cfm?abstract_id=969055 (accessed February 15, 2008), 58–61. There has been a resurgence of interest in the relationship between sovereignty and the rule of law (and in Schmitt's notion of the "sovereign exception" in particular) in the aftermath of the U.S. government's recent, repeated willingness to except itself from its own laws and treaty obligations on the ostensible grounds of the need for extreme measures in the "war on terrorism." See, for example, Christopher Kutz, "Torture, Necessity, and Existential Politics," *California Law Review* 95 (2007): 235–276; and Oren Gross, "Chaos and Rules: Should Responses to Violent Crises Always Be Constitutional?" *Yale Law Journal* 112.5 (2003): 1011–1034. My point is not to endorse this recent scholarship, nor is it to endorse Schmitt's or Agamben's analysis of the problem of sovereignty, no matter how much light they might shed on it. (I have criticized both. See Thurschwell, *Specters of Nietzsche*; Adam Thurschwell, "Cutting the Branches for Akiba: Agamben's Critique of Derrida," in *Politics, Metaphysics, and Death: Essays on Giorgio Agamben's* Homo Sacer, ed. Andrew Norris. Durham, NC: Duke University Press, 2005, 173–197.) The point is simply that, insofar as this currently influential branch of political philosophy necessarily passes through the question of the state's power to kill, the ostensibly narrow issue of capital punishment is highly relevant here as well.

Ethical Exception 287

of capital punishment would appear to have to wait on a complete and total transformation of the essential nature of political sovereignty. That is rather a taller order than mustering a political majority to enact legislation abolishing the death penalty or convincing five justices of the Supreme Court that it constitutes "cruel and unusual punishment."

That is in no way to say that the effort to abolish capital punishment through the legislature or the courts is not a worthwhile political goal – it is. Indeed, short of that complete and total transformation, such self-imposed legal limitations on the state's power to kill are the only means available to keep the state's killing to a minimum. What the focus on sovereignty suggests, however, is that such legal limitations are themselves necessarily limited to forestalling the state's power to kill rather than eliminating it. That power remains in reserve even in ostensibly abolitionist states, always ready to bubble up as a political option under the pressure of a particularly heinous crime or a political threat to the state itself – for example, in the form of terrorism. Here we see the fundamental connection between the practice of capital punishment and the state of emergency or state of exception in which a threat to the state's existence causes it to suspend the ordinary legal and constitutional constraints on its actions, as in the case of a declaration of martial law.[39] However much capital punishment is made part of the ordinary law of the state (what theorists of the state of emergency like Schmitt called the "normal situation"),[40] it also necessarily remains an exception to such ordinary law. In this regard, it is telling that when Carol and Jordan Steiker – two of the leading abolitionists in the U.S. legal academy – wrote an article titled "Abolition in Our Time" in the form of a fictional Supreme Court opinion from 2022 ruling the death penalty to be unconstitutional, the most favorable holding that they could imagine was one that abolished death as a penalty for all "ordinary crimes" but continued to uphold its constitutionality for "terrorism, political assassination, or other 'extraordinary' crimes" – that is, those crimes that pose a threat to the sovereignty of the state.[41]

There is, however, a silver lining to the cloud of difficult prospects for total abolition – a silver lining, at least, for the capital defense lawyers and anti–death penalty legislators who, working as they must within the

---

[39] See Kutz, "Torture, Necessity"; Gross, "Chaos and Rules"; and note 38 generally.
[40] Schmitt, *Political Theology*, 13.
[41] Carol Steiker and Jordan Steiker, "Abolition in Our Time," *Ohio State Journal of Criminal Law* 1 (2003): 323–344, 334.

constraints of the existing legal system and political climate, seek to increase the legal hurdles to execution without tilting futilely at the windmill of total abolition in every death penalty case or legislative debate. There is a tendency among at least some abolitionists to dismiss progressive reforms in the law of capital punishment as serving ideological ends and making the ultimate goal of total abolition more difficult by further entrenching the system.[42] If capital punishment is so intimately tied to the sovereignty of the state, however, then – again, short of a total transformation in the nature of sovereignty – all that one can do is continue to reform the practice. That need not be a pessimistic conclusion. It simply means that if and when the institution of the death penalty itself expires someday, it will more likely be a slow death by arteriosclerosis than (as some antireformist abolitionists seem to hope) sudden death by lightning bolt from on high (e.g., in the form of a definitive Supreme Court opinion). That is reassuring, at least, for the lawyers, legislators, and activists who are in the trenches today, trying to save individual lives and hoping that their efforts serve (rather than hinder) the larger project of abolition.

A Detour through Doctrine: The Problem of Death Penalty "Volunteers"

What of these reforms and individual efforts, however? Beyond suggesting that reform in general should not be dismissed, does the "sovereignty perspective" contribute anything to our thinking about the particular directions that the law of capital punishment ought to take? I think it does, as I now shall try to illustrate in one area of the law that has proved particularly intractable to analysis up to this point – the problem of so-called volunteers for the death penalty.

Volunteers are capital defendants who at some point in the criminal process choose to abandon their sentencing defense and ask to be executed. Volunteering for death is remarkably common; 132 of the 1,145

---

[42] See, for example, Carol Steiker, "Things Fall Apart, But the Center Holds: The Supreme Court and the Death Penalty," *New York University Law Review* 77 (2002): 1475–1490, 1477: "Since 1976, most of the major innovations in the Supreme Court's death penalty jurisprudence have both dissipated popular discomfort with the retention of capital punishment and insulated death penalty practices from more sweeping constitutional challenges by ameliorating or appearing to ameliorate some of the more obviously problematic features of capital punishment administration."

individuals – 11 percent – executed in the United States since the death penalty was reinstated in 1976 have been volunteers (including Gary Gilmore, the very first).[43] This number, moreover, dramatically understates the actual number of defendants who at one time or another decide to waive their right to defend against execution, because there are many who volunteer and then change their minds. (Indeed, among the numerous areas of conflicting precedent arising out of the volunteer phenomenon is the question of whether and when defendants may be allowed to change their minds and when they are stuck with their initial waiver.[44]) Volunteering raises a host of difficult issues, but for my immediate purposes it is enough to note that it wreaks havoc on well-established doctrinal approaches to otherwise run-of-the-mill legal situations.[45]

To cite only one example (from a case that the Supreme Court decided in 2007), it sometimes occurs that defendants specifically instruct their lawyers at the death-sentencing hearing not to present any "mitigating evidence" – the evidence introduced by the defense at the hearing to convince the jury to impose a sentence less than death. Not surprisingly, such defendants are almost always sentenced to death. In *Schriro v. Landrigan*,[46] one such defendant subsequently claimed that his lawyer's failure to investigate possible mitigation strategies adequately or to introduce any mitigating evidence at the hearing violated his Sixth Amendment right to

---

[43] Death Penalty Information Center, Execution Database, www.deathpenaltyinfo.org/executions.php (accessed February 6, 2009). The totals here are combined for states and the federal government.

[44] See Note, Recent Cases, *Harvard Law Review* 120 (2007): 1386–1393, regarding *Wilcher v. Epps*, no. 06-70043, 2006 WL 2986476 (5th Cir., October 17, 2006), *cert. denied*, 127 S. Ct. 466 (2006). See also Welsh White, "Defendants Who Elect Execution," *University of Pittsburgh Law Review* 48 (1987): 853–878, 855: "If electing execution is defined as expressing a clear preference for the death penalty over life imprisonment, then probably a majority of those on death row have at some point elected execution."

[45] There is an extensive law review literature on the problem of volunteering. See, for example, Daniel Williams, "Mitigation and the Capital Defendant Who Wants to Die: A Study in the Rhetoric of Autonomy and the Hidden Discourse of Collective Responsibility," *Hastings Law Journal* 57 (2006): 693–758; J. C. Oleson, "Swilling Hemlock: The Legal Ethics of Defending a Client Who Wishes to Volunteer for Execution," *Washington and Lee Law Review* 63 (2006): 147–203; John H. Blume, "Killing the Willing: 'Volunteers,' Suicide, and Competency," *Michigan Law Review* 103 (2005): 939–1009, 939–40; and Anthony J. Casey, "Maintaining the Integrity of Death: An Argument for Restricting a Defendant's Right to Volunteer for Execution at Certain Stages in Capital Proceedings," *American Journal of Criminal Law* 30 (2002): 75–106, 76.

[46] *Schriro v. Landrigan*, 127 S. Ct. 1933 (2007).

the effective assistance of counsel (a claim frequently made by volunteers who change their minds). The Supreme Court held that the defendant's express instruction not to introduce any such evidence precluded such a claim.[47] That conclusion seems at first blush unexceptionable – after all, why should any defendant be allowed to complain about the constitutional deficiency of an attorney who simply did exactly what the client told him to do?

What makes the result problematic is that presentation of mitigating evidence to the jury is a critical element that makes a death sentence constitutionally valid.[48] Without hearing about the defendant's life – who he or she was, is, and might yet become – the jury cannot make the ultimate decision about whether this particular individual deserves to live or die. Under current law, however, the presentation of mitigating evidence is a constitutional right that belongs to the defendant, and at least under proper circumstances, constitutional rights may be waived.[49] By waiving his or her right to present mitigation, the defendant can very effectively throw a monkey wrench into the constitutional death sentencing process. The spectacle of volunteering – what some commentators refer to as "state-assisted suicide" – thus arises when an otherwise run-of-the-mill principle of criminal procedure (waiver) is applied to a capital defendant. The fundamental legitimacy of the state, which stands or falls in most people's eyes first and foremost on the manner in which it chooses to go about killing its own citizens, has been placed in the hands of an individual, indeed, one who has already been convicted of abusing that ultimate power – a murderer.

When turned on the problem of volunteers, the political-philosophical perspective thus brings to light a conceptual gap in the law, a gap that is the source of the confusion around this issue. At a critical moment in the legal system – the moment when the system authorizes the taking of life – the individual rights–based understanding of justice that underlies

---

[47] Id. at 1941: "If Landrigan issued such an instruction, counsel's failure to investigate further could not have been prejudicial under [the Sixth Amendment]."
[48] *Abdul-Kabir v. Quarterman*, 127 S. Ct. 1654, 1674 (2007): "Before a jury can undertake the grave task of imposing a death sentence, it must be allowed to consider a defendant's moral culpability and decide whether death is an appropriate punishment for that individual in light of his personal history and characteristics and the circumstances of the offense."
[49] In general, those circumstances occur when the defendant is competent and the waiver is knowing, intelligent, and voluntary. See *Johnson v. Zerbst*, 304 U.S. 458 (1938).

and implements this system breaks down, because the only check on the absolute and defining power of the state, its power to kill, has been assigned to a person who might choose not to use that check. This paradox of rights-based systems is general; it comes into play and calls into question the legitimacy of every waiver of rights, even in the most routine of plea bargains, insofar as such waivers are, by definition, a free pass for the state to do what the U.S. Constitution otherwise says that it may not. Waivers are nevertheless routinely accepted in these other contexts, up to and including the waiver of rights in exchange for life imprisonment, and justified on grounds of respect for the defendant's autonomy.[50] The real question, then, is why the exaltation of individual autonomy suddenly becomes so controversial when extended to the capital waiver.[51] Part of the answer is the critical symbolic role that capital punishment plays in the legitimacy of the state *qua* sovereign. That, at least, is what the Supreme Court appears to have meant when it stated, "From the point of view of society, the action of the sovereign in taking the life of one of its citizens... differs dramatically from any other legitimate state action."[52]

Approaching the problem of volunteers from the perspective of sovereignty also suggests a doctrinal solution. If the problem arises because the law places the state's interest in its own legitimacy in another's hands, then the solution must involve *legal* recognition of this independent sovereign interest. Note that this interest is independent; it neither supersedes nor trumps the defendant's own independent interest in self-preservation, which is protected in the form of his or her Eighth Amendment right to introduce mitigating evidence. A procedure that conformed to the independent sovereign interest, however, would permit – indeed, it

---

[50] See generally Robert Toone, "The Incoherence of Defendant Autonomy," *North Carolina Law Review* 83 (2005): 621.

[51] The waiver doctrine has a fascinating history, one that is itself, not surprisingly, bound up with the courts' views of the prerogatives of sovereignty and with the practice of capital punishment. The trend has been a steady increase in the ability to waive criminal procedural rights, with the exception of one area in which the trend has lagged considerably – the waiver of rights in capital proceedings. One small but exemplary legacy of this history is contained in Federal Rule of Criminal Procedure 7, which requires that all crimes punishable by either death or imprisonment of more than one year be prosecuted by indictment but allows waiver of this requirement by the defendant only in noncapital prosecutions. Fed. R. Crim. P. 7(b). On the history of the waiver doctrine, see Nancy King, "Priceless Process: Nonnegotiable Features of Criminal Litigation," *UCLA Law Review* 47 (1999): 113, 118–125.

[52] *Gardner v. Florida*, 430 U.S. 349, 357–358 (1977).

would require – the sovereign to investigate the defendant's background and introduce mitigating evidence *on its own behalf*, in the service of its own independent interest, even over the defendant's objection. It is precisely that logic that has led a few state courts to formulate this very solution to the dilemma posed by death penalty volunteers.[53]

There is obviously much more to say about the potential doctrinal implications, and complications, of this solution. The point here is simply that an approach to capital punishment that views it as an element of sovereignty enables us to understand the confusion around the issue of death penalty volunteers and to formulate and justify doctrinal responses that might otherwise be difficult to imagine.

The International Perspective

To this point I have been arguing that inasmuch as the state's power to kill is an essential element of its sovereignty, short of a transformation in the nature of sovereignty itself, abolition will remain at best only partially or temporarily achievable. Of course, the nature of sovereignty *is* being transformed, or at least so we are told on a regular basis by theorists of globalization. If that is in fact the case, then one would expect that this transformation would have an impact on the administration of capital punishment. That is what one sees when one looks around the globe – in particular, when one looks at the global changes in capital punishment described at the outset.

The states that have gone farthest in abdicating their sovereignty to supra-sovereign organizations – the states of the European Union and the Council of Europe – are the very ones that have abolished capital punishment most thoroughly, to the point of making abolition a condition of membership. At the same time, the state that most resembles the European states in its history and culture, except for its traditional insistence on its own sovereignty and related distrust of international law – the United States – remains a retentionist state. From the sovereignty perspective, moreover, it

---

[53] See *State v. Koedatich*, 112 N. J. 225, 331–32, 548 A.2d 939, 994–95 (1988); and *Muhammad v. State*, 782 So.2d 343, 363–64 (Fla.), *cert. denied*, 534 U.S. 944 (2001). Other courts have recognized the logic of such a solution as well. See *Morrison v. State*, 258 Ga. 683, 686, 687, 373 S.E.2d 506, 509 (Ga. 1988); and *People v. Deere*, 41 Cal.3d 353, 364, 710 P.2d 925, 931, 222 Cal. Rptr. 13, 20 (Cal. 1985).

is predictable that international law, both treaty based and customary, currently leans significantly toward classifying capital punishment as a human rights violation, without yet definitively so holding. Like all law, international law reflects as well as provides normative guidance for its underlying political reality. Whatever the inroads made by suprasovereign principles of justice, the reality of the current international order remains founded on the sovereign nation-state. It is thus hardly surprising that international law would not yet generally treat capital punishment as a human rights violation, any more than it would treat military conscription as one.[54]

Closer to home, it is also consistent with this perspective that the case that sparked the current debate over the use of international law as legitimate authority in domestic constitutional litigation was a death penalty case, *Roper v. Simmons*.[55] I have been arguing that the political legitimacy of a state turns, for essential reasons, on its manner of employing its inherent power to kill. With respect to sovereignty, the notion of "political legitimacy" has two faces, domestic and international. Because international law comprises the norms that sovereigns expect other sovereigns to abide by, it is no coincidence that the legal regulation of capital punishment proves to be the point at which it is most difficult to keep international law separate and distinct from the law of the United States.

Finally, it is worth mentioning that there are other indications of a mutation in the sovereign power over death, outside the sphere of capital punishment proper, that seem to confirm the value of this notion as an index for the globalization process. The trend in the legislative abolition of military conscription, for example, closely corresponds to the international trend in abolition of the death penalty. The significant majority of European states and Western democracies more generally, including the United States, currently rely on a volunteer rather than a conscripted

---

[54] See, for example, *International Covenant on Civil and Political Rights*, article 6, recognizing both an "inherent right to life" and continuing, legitimate existence of the death penalty, while also stating, "nothing in this article shall be invoked to delay or to prevent the abolition of capital punishment by any State Party to the present Covenant"; article 8, exempting from a general ban on forced labor, "any service of a military character." U.N. Office of the High Commissioner for Human Rights, *International Covenant on Civil and Political Rights*, General Assembly resolution 2200A (XXI), December 16, 1966, www.unhchr.ch/html/menu3/b/a_ccpr.htm (accessed December 19, 2007).

[55] See, for example, comment, "Introduction: The Debate over Foreign Law in *Roper v. Simmons*," *Harvard Law Review* 119 (2005): 103–108.

army. It is worth reflecting on what such a shift means in terms of the globalization of this fundamental sovereign power over the life of its citizens, especially given the political difficulty in reversing course and reinstituting the draft.[56] At the same time, in what might appear to be a far corner of the legal system, the notion that assisting a person's suicide ought not to be subject to criminalization is gaining ground in essentially the same parts of the world.[57] What these trends share is an encroachment on the traditional sovereign's monopoly over the citizen's life. The outcome of each is equivocal (as is the trend toward the abolition of capital punishment), and there are individual considerations within each area of legal regulation and each sovereign state that make any consistency among them rough at best. Nevertheless, the sovereignty perspective on capital punishment suggests a subterranean connection among these otherwise disparate phenomena that adds a significant dimension to theoretical discussions about globalization and its effects on the law.

Ethical Exception?

I began this essay with the hypothesis that the traditional moral-philosophical perspective fails to speak to any of the issues that really matter today in the field of capital punishment, and I have tried to defend the notion that a pure political-philosophical perspective, one that focuses on capital punishment's relationship to political sovereignty, provides far greater insights. I would like to conclude with a conundrum that, it seems to me, complicates this alternative hypothesis. That conundrum arises directly out of the law of capital punishment as it has developed in the Anglo-American tradition.

Capital punishment is best understood as an essential attribute of state sovereignty, one that precedes – conceptually at least – any moral-ethical

---

[56] The relationships among conscription, nation building, and political sovereignty have not been lost on the military and its historians. See, for example, General Rupert Smith, *The Utility of Force: The Art of War in the Modern World*. New York: Alfred A. Knopf, 2007, 92–93.

[57] See, for example, *Washington v. Glucksberg*, 521 U.S. 702, 718 n. 16 (1997), which discussed then-current legislative and judicial debates about the issue in various countries; Kurt Darr, "Physician-Assisted Suicide: Legal and Ethical Considerations," *Journal of Health Law* 40 (2007): 29, 44–52; and Richard Parks, "A Right to Die with Dignity: Using International Perspectives to Formulate a Workable U.S. Policy," *Tulane Journal of International and Comparative Law* 8 (2000): 447–482.

normative evaluation of the state or its actions. And yet, as soon as one turns to the law of capital punishment both in its current and historical forms, one is struck by the vocabulary of moral judgment and moral responsibility that the legal doctrine incorporates quite consciously and explicitly and indeed makes central to its rules of decision. Since the U.S. Supreme Court reinstated the death penalty in 1976, it has said repeatedly that the state's decision to take life is and must remain a "reasoned moral response"[58] to the evidence. The Court has similarly emphasized on numerous occasions the "truly awesome responsibility of decreeing death for a fellow human" and has even, in one case, overturned a death verdict on the grounds that the trial procedure had unconstitutionally lifted that responsibility from the jury's shoulders.[59] Nor is this a modern development in the law. Long before the Eighth Amendment was written, the common law expressly incorporated similar moral sentiments into its doctrines and holdings.[60]

Such express reliance on moral judgment is itself exceptional in this age of "neutral principles" and positive law. If the state's right to the death of its citizens is pure political power, an "exception to the ethical," then why does capital punishment in practice (at least in aspiration, if too rarely in reality) also seem to be an "exception that is ethical," indeed, an exception to the general separation of morality from law?

Reconsidering the proposals in the previous section, one can expand the scope of this puzzle. How is it possible that reform of an absolute sovereign power is even thinkable? That is, how can the law, which is itself declared by the sovereign, turn back on that sovereign and legally bind it to (normative) criteria of legitimacy? Why and how, for example, if the sovereign right to death is a pure matter of power and not of "right" at all, would the law incorporate a self-imposed moral limit on this power? Why and how could a sovereign incorporate international law considerations into its domestic lawmaking (as the U.S. Supreme Court did in *Roper*) or even bind itself to protect international human rights?

This is obviously not a question of the possibility of these phenomena – they are all happening today, in however imperfect and criticizable a

---

[58] *Abdul-Kabir*, 127 S. Ct. at 1669.
[59] *Caldwell v. Mississippi*, 472 U.S. 320, 329–330 (1985).
[60] See Adam Thurschwell, "Federal Courts, the Death Penalty, and the Due Process Clause: The Original Understanding of the 'Heightened Reliability' of Capital Trials," *Federal Sentencing Reporter* 14.1 (2001): 14–24.

fashion. It is rather a question about whether the political-philosophical approach can actually remain distinct from questions of morality or ethics. Can the concept of sovereignty remain "purely" political, based solely in its power over death, or is there something intrinsic to the concept that opens it up to critique from within – to an auto-critique that allows or insists that sovereignty call itself and its own actions into moral, ethical, or legal question?[61]

These are questions that the current political and legal reality of capital punishment put to political philosophy, however, and not the other way around. The main point that I hope to have made in this essay is that a philosophical approach to capital punishment that begins from the fundamental questions and categories of the political will bear more fruit, both philosophical and practical, than one that approaches it from a moral-normative perspective. The fact that the light thus shed on practice runs in the other direction as well is a topic for another essay.

---

[61] For one account of such an ethical opening "within" sovereignty itself, see Jacques Derrida, *Rogues: Two Essays on Reason*, trans. Pascale-Anne Brault and Michael Naas. Stanford, CA: Stanford University Press, 2005, 142.

12

No Mercy

Adam Sitze

In the book that Gilles Deleuze called a "new philosophy of law," François Ewald suggests that the primary task for the philosophy of law is to inquire critically into the conditions under which various societies reflect on, throw into question, and strip self-evidence from – in short, problematize – their own juridical experience.[1] Capital punishment is a particularly interesting matter for the philosophy of law that is so construed. The question, as Norberto Bobbio formulates it, of "whether it is morally and/or juridically permissible for the state to kill in order to punish" was not raised by any of the religions of the book, by classical political philosophy, or by the modern political philosophies that otherwise broke so decisively with both religious tradition and classical political philosophy.[2] Only when thought within the horizon of eighteenth-century political economy, where its wasteful ineffectiveness could suddenly be raised as a problem for the government of the emergent modern state, does it seem that the abolition of the death penalty became intelligible as a distinct juridical possibility.[3]

---

[1] Gilles Deleuze, *Negotiations, 1972–1990*, trans. Martin Joughin. New York: Columbia University Press, 1995, 84. François Ewald, *L'Etat Providence*. Paris: Bernard Grasset, 1986, 41–43.

[2] Norberto Bobbio, *The Age of Rights*, trans. Allan Cameron. New York: Polity Press, 1995, 143 and also 128, 140–141, 144, 149–150, 160; Albert Camus, *Reflections on the Guillotine*, trans. Richard Howard. Michigan City, IN: Fridtjof-Karla Publications, 1959, 44–47; and Jacques Derrida, "Capital Punishment: Another 'Temptation of Theodicy,'" in *Pragmatism, Critique, Judgment: Essays for Richard J. Bernstein*, ed. Seyla Benhabib and Nancy Fraser. Cambridge, MA: MIT Press, 2004, 202–203.

[3] Bobbio, *Age of Rights*, 128–130, 137, 152, 160.

For their comments on the longer essay of which this chapter is a part, I thank Joshua Barkan, Timothy Campbell, Jordana Haviv, Warren Montag, Sayres Rudy, and the participants of the "Killing States" conference, which was convened by Jennifer Culbert and Austin Sarat at Amherst College, November 3–5, 2006.

The conditions for this problematization, however, are at best poorly understood. Thanks in large part to Michel Foucault's *Discipline and Punish*, there is today a theoretical consensus that Cesare Beccaria's 1764 criticism of the death penalty, *On Crimes and Punishments*, focused less on its cruelty or inhumanity than on its simple uselessness for the well-being and security of the public (*salute pubblica*).[4] Because Beccaria held state executions to be, in Foucault's words, a "bad economy of power,"[5] he argued that the death of a citizen should be limited to those exceptional situations in which internal enemies threaten the very existence of the *salute pubblica* (66–67). Under normal juridical conditions, Beccaria recommended, a more efficient economy of power should pertain: the death penalty should be replaced with perpetual forced labor, the continuous example of which will deter crime much more effectively than will the occasional execution (67).

Yet Beccaria's argument to this effect is not original, and in a sense it is surprising that it should be so widely accepted as abolitionism's primary intellectual origin.[6] Raphael Hythloday offers a similar argument in Book 1 of Sir Thomas More's 1516 *Utopia* as part of his fearless speech to the cardinal archbishop against the execution of thieves. Hythloday, like Beccaria, does not argue for the elimination of the death penalty as such. He merely suggests (like Beccaria) that the death penalty does not effectively deter crime and that the *salus publica* would be better served were the state to exploit, rather than eliminate, criminals' corporeal potencies.[7] Despite this resemblance, however, Hythloday's opposition to the death

---

[4] Cesare Beccaria, *On Crimes and Punishments and Other Writings*, ed. Richard Bellamy. Cambridge: Cambridge University Press, 1995, 10, 30, 31, 68, 112; hereafter cited parenthetically by page number.

[5] Michel Foucault, *Discipline and Punish: The Birth of the Prison*, trans. Alan Sheridan. New York: Vintage, 1979, 79.

[6] On the tradition of abolitionism inaugurated by Beccaria's *On Crimes and Punishments*, see Coleman Phillipson, *Three Criminal Law Reformers: Beccaria, Bentham, Romilly*. Montclair, NJ: Patterson Smith, 1970, 69, 83–106. On *contemporary* abolitionism and neoabolitionism, see Austin Sarat, *When the State Kills: Capital Punishment and the American Condition*. Princeton, NJ: Princeton University Press, 2001, 246–260; and Timothy Kaufman-Osborn, "A Critique of Contemporary Death Penalty Abolitionism," *Punishment and Society* 8.3 (2006): 366–373.

[7] Thomas More, *Utopia*, trans. Clarence H. Miller. New Haven, CT: Yale University Press, 2001, 19–30, cf. 99, 100, 107. On the conditions under which Hythloday turns to the Roman law concept of *opus publicum*, see Thorsten Sellin, "Penal Servitude: Origin and Survival," *Proceedings of the American Philosophical Society* 109.5 (October 1965): 277–279.

penalty rests on a radically different premise than Beccaria's. Whereas Hythloday does not openly question the Thomistic principle that human laws should be continuous with God's laws (from the Mosaic commandment not to kill to Christ's "new law of clemency" [*noua lege clementiae*]),[8] the opposite is true for Beccaria. He not only explicitly criticizes the idea of a bond between the political and the theological (11, 22–23) but also calls into question the most theological of all political powers: the sovereign right of clemency (111). Clemency might be "the most desirable endowment of sovereignty," Beccaria writes, and it might seem especially necessary in states with atrocious and absurd laws, but because it is needed only to the degree that punishments are unnecessarily severe, and because the very idea of clemency encourages illusions of impunity and hence too the commission of crimes, clemency would have to be completely excluded (*esclusa*) from any state that finally instituted a predictable and geometrically rigorous system of crimes and punishments (111; translation modified). Under a finally civil and rational legal system, the sovereign right to let live would no longer stand apart from law as a rare, gentle exception to its otherwise cruel penalties; it now would be resplendent in the legal code itself. This "most beautiful prerogative of the throne" would then no longer be isolated to occasional absolutions; it would serve as the general norm for a penal law that henceforth would be uniformly mild (111–112).

Beccaria's criticism of the death penalty is thus distinct from Hythloday's in a small but important way: unlike Hythloday, Beccaria problematized not only the sovereign right to *kill* but also the sovereign right to *let live*. Given the very different diagrams of knowledge and power under which each author wrote, this distinction is perhaps not surprising. More wrote at a moment when sovereign power received its intelligibility from its continuities with and parallels to divine power.[9] In a text that marks the twilight of this moment in more ways than one, Shakespeare's Portia could

---

[8] More, *Utopia*, 27; translation modified. For the implicitly economic and nontheological basis of Hythloday's explicitly theological discourse, see Louis Marin, *Utopics: Spatial Play*, trans. Robert A. Vollrath. Atlantic Highlands, NJ: Humanities Press, 1984, 146 and also 153, 163.

[9] Compare Michel Foucault, *Security, Territory, Population: Lectures at the Collège de France, 1977–1978*, ed. Michel Senellart, trans. Graham Burchell. New York: Palgrave, 2007, 232–33; and J. G. A. Pocock, *The Machiavellian Moment: Florentine Political Thought and the Atlantic Republican Tradition* Princeton, NJ: Princeton University Press, 1975, 28–30.

thus claim that mercy "is an attribute to God himself. / And earthly power dost then show likest God's, / Where mercy seasons justice."[10] Beccaria, by contrast, wrote under conditions in which capital's need for labor power spurred the politicization of life and hence, too, the emergence of a new concept of sovereignty.[11] Under these conditions, as Foucault has claimed, sovereign power consisted less in the right to *take life* or *let live* than in the power "to *make live* or *reject* [*rejeter*] into death."[12] For Beccaria, clemency thus registered within a drastically different epistemic horizon than it did for More. Clemency was desirable not as the attribute through which sovereign power could become most like divine power but merely as an especially fitting means to the end of preserving the sacred lives of individuals and populations.[13] This *deconsecration* of clemency implies a conjunction of sovereign power and bio-politics that would have been almost unthinkable for More. Beccaria considers clemency to be beautiful not because its exercise is emblematic of a sovereign who is and ought to be God's vicar but simply because it is the sovereign exception that most

---

[10] William Shakespeare, *Merchant of Venice*, 4.1.183–197. Compare Isabella's appeal to Angelo in *Measure for Measure*:

> No ceremony that to great ones 'longs,
> Not the king's crown, nor the deputed sword,
> The marshal's truncheon, nor the judge's robe,
> Becomes them with one half so good a grace
> As mercy does. (2.2.59–63)

Rousseau, by contrast, writing after the epistemic break Foucault indicates (*Security, Territory, Population*, 236), can say little more about the sovereign right to pardon except that its juridical foundation is "not very clear." Jean-Jacques Rousseau, *The Social Contract and the First and Second Discourses*, trans. Susan Dunn. New Haven, CT: Yale University Press, 2002, 177. See also note 13 below.

[11] Michel Foucault, *The History of Sexuality*, vol. 1, *An Introduction*, trans. Robert Hurley. New York: Vintage Books, 1977, 140–45. See also Paolo Virno, *A Grammar of the Multitude*, trans. Isabella Bertoletti, James Cascaito, and Andrea Casson. New York: Semiotext[e] Foreign Agent Series, 2004, 81–84.

[12] Foucault, *History of Sexuality*, 1:136, 1:138; Michel Foucault, *Histoire de la Sexualité: La volonté de savoir*. Paris: Éditions Gallimard, 1976, 181. Compare, on the sovereign power to reject or cast off, Thomas Hobbes, *De Cive*. Oxford: Clarendon Press, 1983, 116.

[13] One could also pose the problem this way: although More and Beccaria both silently reiterate Cicero's maxim "salus publica suprema lex esto" ("the safety, security, or well-being of the public is the highest law"), More does so under a diagram of pastoral power that has as its objective the *salvation* of the souls of the flock, whereas Beccaria does so with reference to the doctrine of *Ragion di Stato*, which had as its goal the *safety* and *security* of the public. See Foucault, *Security, Territory, Population*, 126, 162, 234–237, 262–266, 348; and Andrew R. Dyck, *A Commentary on Cicero, "De Legibus."* Ann Arbor: University of Michigan Press, 2004, 458–459.

fully expresses the basic principle of the bio-political, namely that life is the highest good.[14]

Unfortunately, the possibility of grasping this distinction has been complicated by the censorious reception that Beccaria's text suffered from the first moments of its publication.[15] In the initial, anonymously published 1764 edition of *Dei delitti e delle pene*, Beccaria's criticism of clemency occupied a privileged place as the text's penultimate chapter. Beccaria's French translator André Morellet, however, found this arrangement to be unnatural and unclear. In his 1766 translation of *Dei delitti*, which would for two centuries serve as the basis for many later editions of the text (up to and including Faustin Hélie's 1856 French translation, which Foucault used in his research for *Discipline and Punish*), Morellet moved Beccaria's criticism of clemency from the end of *Dei delitti* to the middle, where he buried it in a chapter called "On Prompt Punishments."[16]

Because Morellet's translation appeared in the same year in which the Vatican placed Beccaria's text on its *Index Librorum Prohibitorum*,[17] it is plausible to suppose that Morellet's intervention was in some way designed

---

[14] Beccaria, *On Crimes and Punishments*, 66 (referring to "life itself" as "the greatest of all goods"). On the concept of "life as the highest good," see Hannah Arendt, *The Human Condition*. Chicago: University of Chicago Press, 1958, 312–319. My claim here is not, to be clear, that the modern right of mercy is somehow a "secularized" theological concept. To the contrary, Seneca's pre-Christian letter to Nero, *De clementiae*, already construes clemency as an exclusively political power to grant life. For Seneca, clemency is a desirable virtue for the emperor not because it refers to a theological foundation but because it is the best way to preserve the *salus publica* and because it is the proof positive that an emperor is a true king and not a tyrant (or that he possesses not only *potentia* but also *auctoritas*). Clemency is also, in this discourse, an exclusively masculine virtue. Whereas any woman or beast is capable of taking life, only a true imperial prince can give life, and in this he resembles a father. "On Clemency," in Seneca, *Moral Essays*, vol. 1, trans. John Basore. Cambridge, MA: Harvard University Press, 1935, 373, 377, 389, 399, 411, 416, 423, 427. That the imperial power of clemency so construed internally excludes life within law, in the Agambenian sense, is perfectly clear. Nowhere is this better exemplified than in the simple command through which the emperor grants clemency: "Live" [*Vitam*] (Id., 372, 386). For a more detailed account of these problems, see Melissa Barden Dowling, *Clemency and Cruelty in the Roman World*. Ann Arbor: University of Michigan Press, 2006, 18, 195–209.

[15] On the way Beccaria's work has been misread from the very moment of its publication, see David B. Young, "'Let us content ourselves with praising the work while drawing a veil over its principles': Eighteenth-Century Reactions to Beccaria's *On Crimes and Punishments*," *Justice Quarterly* 1.2 (June 1984): 158–59, 162–63, 169; and Piers Beirne, "Inventing Criminology: The 'Science of Man' in Cesare Beccaria's *Dei delitti e delle pene*," *Criminology* 29.4 (1991): 778, 785–786.

[16] See, on this point, Beirne, "Inventing Criminology," 780 n. 5.

[17] Ibid., 782.

to rescue Beccaria's text from being banned. But especially if this is so, we must conclude that Morellet saved Beccaria's text only by stifling its most decisive argument. All translations of *Dei delitti*, including Morellet's, conclude with a basic teleological claim about the *potentiality* of penal law: the more a nation develops out of a state of savagery into civilization, the more its power to punish should be actualized in, through, and as a power *not to* punish (113). In the 1764 edition of *Dei delitti*, however, this teleological claim is reinforced by the very form of Beccaria's text. In this, its initial arrangement, Beccaria's text *opens* with a Hobbesian discourse on the origin of the sovereign right to punish and *closes* with a proposal for negating and elevating the sovereign right of clemency into the basic principle governing penal law as such.

There is in this textual form a silent claim about what it means for a society to achieve or accomplish its modernity. In Volume 1 of *The History of Sexuality*, Foucault argued that a society's "threshold of modernity" is reached when its "subtractive" or "deductive" sovereign right to kill is displaced by bio-power's "positive" or "productive" apparatuses.[18] According to Foucault, the emergence of bio-power gave rise to the notion that the purpose and essence of law is not to take life but instead to preserve, multiply, and sustain it; this, in turn, rendered the very idea of a legally administered death penalty a contradiction in terms.[19] Bio-power modified more than just the sovereign right to kill, however, and herein lies the importance of reading Beccaria's initial edition of *Dei delitti* to the letter. For Beccaria, it seems, a society accomplishes its modernity when, as Deleuze might say, it "varies the coefficient"[20] on the old right to let live, breaking with the limited use of this right as an exception to a law that is ordinarily deadly and giving it a new and augmented use as the internal norm of a law the intrinsic purpose of which is now, precisely as a result of that augmentation, to preserve or prolong life. The singular modernity of

---

[18] Foucault, *History of Sexuality*, 1:143.

[19] Id., 1:137–138. Slavoj Žižek has argued that contemporary opposition to the death penalty is predicated on a hidden biopolitics, but this puts the cart before the horse: before abolitionists could presuppose a hidden biopolitics, the politicization of life already modified law in such a way as to predispose it to abolitionism. Slavoj Žižek, *Welcome to the Desert of the Real!* New York: Verso, 2002, 90; and Slavoj Žižek, *The Puppet and the Dwarf*. New York: Verso, 2003, 95.

[20] Gilles Deleuze, *Foucault*, trans. Seán Hand. Minneapolis: University of Minnesota Press, 1988, 41.

Beccaria's text, from this standpoint, consists neither in its criticism of the death penalty (which, in some ways, is less rigorous and consistent than Hythloday's) nor in its substitution of an economics of corporeal potencies for the spectacle of the scaffold. (Hythloday, after all, also embraces penal servitude as an alternative to the death penalty.) It lies rather in the claim that the goal of all civilized penal law is and ought to be the *extinction* of the sovereign right of clemency in and through its *indistinction* with a fully actualized sovereign power *not to* punish.[21] Beccaria's criticism of the "savagery" of the sovereign right to kill is, in short, grounded in his *profanation* of the sovereign right to let live.

For readers who were able to consider *Dei delitti* in its initial arrangement, this emphasis seems not to have been in doubt.[22] More recent readers of Beccaria, by contrast, seem to maintain a curious silence on the point on his criticism of the right of clemency.[23] This silence has several serious consequences for contemporary abolitionist theory and practice. I will here limit myself to one: the Morelletian misreading, as we might call it, establishes the conditions under which some abolitionists today not only

---

[21] This, for example, explains why Beccaria can argue that penal laws should be *both* gentle *and* inexorable. Just as the harshness of penal law must henceforth be tempered by the gentleness of clemency, so, too, must the right of clemency be exercised with unswerving lawlike regularity and uniformity. See Beccaria, *On Crimes and Punishments*, 63, 112; compare James Whitman, *Harsh Justice: Criminal Justice and the Widening Divide between America and Europe*. New York: Oxford University Press, 2003, 50.

[22] In his 1778 "Bill for Proportioning Crimes and Punishments," for example, Thomas Jefferson cites Beccaria repeatedly and by name in support of his proposal that, with several exceptions, "no crime shall be henceforth punished by the deprivation of life or limb." Jefferson's manifestly Beccarian criticism of capital punishment is that it "weaken[s] the State by cutting off so many, who, if reformed, might be restored sound members to society, who, even under a course of correction, might be rendered useful in various labours for the public, and would be living and long-continued spectacles to deter others from committing the like offences." Significantly, Jefferson also proposes that the pardon power "totally be abolished," on the strictly Beccarian grounds that an abolition of this type would increase proportionality between crime and punishment and, by removing any hope of reprieve, decrease the incentive to commit crimes in the first place. See Thomas Jefferson, *The Writings of Thomas Jefferson*, vol. 2, ed. Paul Leicester Ford. New York: G. P. Putnam's Sons, 1893, 204–205, 219. Other eighteenth-century English readers of Beccaria also criticized the pardon power in these terms. See Anthony Draper, "Cesare Beccaria's Influence on English Discussions of Punishment, 1764–1789," *History of European Ideas* 26 (2000): 185, 188–189, 191; and Whitman, *Harsh Justice*, 163–164, 184. It is worth noting that the first English translation of *Dei delitti*, which was published in 1767, openly criticized Morellet and remained faithful to the original 1764 arrangement of Beccaria's text. Beirne, "Inventing Criminology," 780 n. 5.

[23] See, for example, Marcello Maestro, "A Pioneer for the Abolition of Capital Punishment: Cesare Beccaria," *Journal of the History of Ideas* 34.3 (1973): 463–468.

appeal to but also praise the sovereign right of clemency, as if this right were somehow a self-evident or even sufficient antidote to the right to kill.

The blind spot in this praise of clemency can be outlined with brief reference to the social contract thinkers from whom Beccaria derived his basic theoretical premises. For Jean-Jacques Rousseau, capital punishment takes as its object not a moral person but "simply a man," which is to say, a living being who has been stripped of the conditional gift of life and can therefore be treated less as a citizen of the republic than as an enemy who endangers its safety or security from within.[24] On these terms, the juridical basis of capital punishment is less the right to punish than the sovereign right, in war, to kill a vanquished enemy. The counterpart of this right is, of course, the equally martial sovereign right to spare the life of the vanquished enemy. But for Jean-Jacques Rousseau's predecessors, if not for Rousseau himself, the sovereign right to spare the life of the vanquished enemy remained the central premise of the conquest theory of justified slavery.[25] Mercy, as the sovereign power that corresponds and gives juridical expression to the slave's preference for life over death,[26] is thus in this line of thought not an *antidote* to sovereign cruelty. On the contrary, the sovereign's reprieve is the primary juridical basis precisely for *reseizing* the defeated enemy as a slave and for maintaining the slave as a living tool for increasing the wealth of the republic.

This correlation between mercy and slavery receives a subtle but decisive twist in Beccaria's thought. Beccaria follows Rousseau by considering the death penalty to be an act of war against an internal enemy of the republic.[27] He breaks with Rousseau, however, by construing commerce not merely

---

[24] Rousseau, *Social Contract*, 177.

[25] See also Dowling, *Clemency*, 16–18; Hugo Grotius, *The Law of War and Peace: De jure belli ac pacis libri tres*, vol. 3, trans. Francis W. Kelsey. Washington, DC: Carnegie Institution of Washington, 1916, ch. 7; Thomas Hobbes, *The Elements of Law Natural and Politic*, ed. J. C. A. Gaskin. Oxford: Oxford University Press, 1994, part 1, ch. 14; and John Locke, *Two Treatises of Government and a Letter Concerning Toleration*, ed. Ian Shapiro. New Haven, CT: Yale University Press, 2003, 110, cf. 104; cf., William Blackstone, *Commentaries on the Laws of England, Volume 1: Of the Rights of Persons*. Chicago: University of Chicago Press, 1979, 411–412. On pardon and mercy as the juridical basis for the regulation and oversight of penal labor, see also More, *Utopia*, 30, 95.

[26] Michel Foucault, *"Society Must Be Defended": Lectures at the Collège de France, 1975–1976*, ed. Mauro Bertani, trans. David Macey. New York: Picador, 2003, 94–95.

[27] Beccaria, *On Crimes and Punishments*, 66. Compare Michel Foucault, "Truth and Juridical Forms," in *The Essential Works of Foucault, 1954–1984*, vol. 3, *Power*, ed. Paul Rabinow et al. New York: Free Press, 2000, 53–54.

as one among many organs of the body politic (its "digestive system") but as the most humane and reasonable form of warfare of which a civilized republic is capable.[28] Where warfare is framed in these terms, the republic's relation to its internal enemy necessarily also appears in a new and different light. The warlike hostility that defines that relation now need not express itself only through killing (although it bears repeating that Beccaria retains this possibility for exceptional cases in which a criminal endangers the very existence of the republic). Under normal juridical conditions, this same hostility can and should be expressed in and through a specifically economic claim on the life – the labor power – of the internal enemy. It is on this basis that Beccaria can claim that perpetual penal servitude is not only *more economic* for the *salus publica* than is the death penalty (both because of its use of the internal enemy's corporeal potencies and because of its value as a continuously deterrent example) but also *more hostile* – crueler and more warlike – toward the republic's internal enemy (because suffering is no longer concentrated into a single intense instant but is now extended over, and coextensive with, the internal enemy's entire lifetime; 68–69). Abolitionist activists are right to criticize Beccaria's account of the death penalty for being premised on an affirmation of penal slavery.[29] But for the purposes of fully comprehending Beccaria outside of the terms established by the Morelletian misreading, we must today intensify that criticism by extending it to the twisted path by which Beccaria arrives at this premise. Beccaria's opposition to the death penalty joins a *governmentalization of mercy* (in which the sovereign right to let live is no longer a Christ-like exemption from an intrinsically life-threatening law but instead the innermost norm of a law the objective of which is now to preserve and prolong life) to a *militarization of governmentality* (in which the political economic management of things, bodies, and goods now figures as the most reasonable and humane way to express hostility against any enemy). The result is an *internalization* of the martial sovereign right of merciful reprieve (so that mercy, rather than the right to wage war, is

---

[28] Beccaria, *On Crimes and Punishments*, 8, 56; and Jean-Jacques Rousseau, "On Political Economy," in *The Social Contract; or, Principles of Right*, ed. Charles M. Sherover. New York: Meridian, 1974, 256. More generally, see Foucault, *"Society Must Be Defended,"* 225–226.

[29] For a reading of Beccaria that makes a claim of this type, see Barbara Esposito, Lee Wood, and Kathryn Bardsley, *Prison Slavery*. Silver Spring, MD: Committee to Abolish Prison Slavery, 1982, 36–39.

now the juridical basis of the republic's relation to its internal enemy) that is simultaneously a *normalization* of that same right (such that penal slavery, for Beccaria, is and ought to be a permanent and ordinary part of any civilized republic's management of its things, goods, and populations).

One might object to this reading by pointing to Beccaria's argument that, in cases of theft, "the *temporary* enslavement of the labor and person of the criminal to society... is the only sort of slavery that can be called just" (53; emphasis mine) and by observing that the conquest theory of slavery is distinct from both the Aristotelian notion that some beings are slaves by nature and the chattel slavery practiced in the United States. But Beccaria's abolitionism lends itself to these theories of slavery too. One of the distinctive marks of Beccarian abolitionism is the notion that the death penalty should be opposed because its savage or barbarian quality is not appropriate for civilized nations.[30] A civilized nation, in Beccaria's terms, is one that is capable of *excluding* the sovereign exception of clemency from its legal system by *internalizing* that exception as the legal system's most fundamental norm.[31] This internal exclusion is not only the underlying juridical schema that quietly shapes Beccaria's understanding of the humane way in punishment. It is also the basic dynamic that gives motion and direction to Beccaria's teleological concept of legal history. When clemency is dethroned from its emblematic place and function in premodern eschatology, it does not after all disappear from jurisprudence altogether; it silently reemerges as the worldly or immanent standard by which historical progress in the humanitarian reform of penal laws can be measured. Within the horizon of eighteenth-century European revolutionary

[30] Beccaria, On Crimes and Punishments, 70. "The death penalty is not useful because of the example of savagery it gives to men." See also A. G. L. Shaw, *Convicts and the Colonies: A Study of Penal Transportation from Great Britain and Ireland to Australia and Other Parts of the British Empire* London: Faber & Faber, 1966, 128–129; and Bobbio, *Age of Rights*, 132; cf. Alpheus Todd, *Parliamentary Government in the British Colonies*. Second Edition. London: Longmans, Green, & Co, 1894, 365–6; and Arthur Berriedale Keith, *Imperial Unity and the Dominions*. Oxford: Clarendon Press, 1916, 69–70. For Beccaria's definitions of civilization, savagery, and barbarianism, see his "Reflections on Barbarousness and Civilization," in *On Crimes and Punishments and Other Writings*, esp. 143–144.

[31] Here, as elsewhere, Beccaria's arguments derive in part from Rousseau. See Jean-Jacques Rousseau, "Second Discourse," in *Rousseau: The Discourses and Other Early Political Writings*, ed. Victor Gourevitch. Cambridge: Cambridge University Press, 1997, 166. For an account of Rousseau's related argument about law's supplementation by pity, see James Swenson, *On Jean-Jacques Rousseau: Considered as One of the First Authors of the Revolution*. Stanford, CA: Stanford University Press, 2000, 100–103.

thought, this internal exclusion of clemency no doubt heralded a radically egalitarian and specifically modern concept of the political.[32] At the limit of that horizon, however, this same internal exclusion had viciously inegalitarian implications. For, on the terms of Beccaria's humanitarianism, it follows perfectly that the less a given nation develops out of a savage or barbarian state, the less it deserves penal laws in which clement exceptions are the norm. Indeed, the more savage or barbarian a given nation is the more unswervingly harsh its penal laws must be and the more rarely should clement exceptions to those laws be granted. In the United States (where, from the beginning, Beccaria's thought was enthusiastically received[33]), this teleology lent itself to a fatal limit on abolitionism's pursuit of its own desired juridical objective. Angela Davis has described the way that

> slavery as an institution, during the end of the eighteenth century and throughout the nineteenth century... managed to become a receptacle for all of those forms of punishment that were considered to be barbaric by the developing democracy. So rather than abolish the death penalty outright, it was offered refuge within slave law. This meant that white people eventually were released from the threat of death for most offenses, with murder remaining as the usual offense leading to a white man's execution. Black slaves, on the other hand, were subject to the death penalty in some states for as many as seventy different offenses. One might say that the institution of slavery served as a receptacle for those forms of punishment considered to be too uncivilized to be inflicted on white citizens within a democratic society.[34]

It is not difficult to comprehend how Beccaria's discourse on clemency contributes to the racist dynamic that Davis describes here. For Beccaria,

---

[32] The French revolutionaries' Penal Code of 1791, for instance, abolished the sovereign right of clemency outright, on the argument that clemency was an intrinsically monarchical power at odds with the principles of republican governance. The ban lasted until 1802. See, variously, Arlette Lebigre, "Pardon, Grâce, Amnistie: Deux Mille ans D'Arbitraire," *L'Histoire* 143 (April 1991): 88; Kathleen Dean Moore, *Pardons: Justice, Mercy, and the Public Interest*. Oxford: Oxford University Press, 1997, 24; and Whitman, *Harsh Justice*, 143–145.

[33] Compare, on this point, David Brion Davis, "The Movement to Abolish Capital Punishment in America, 1787–1861," *American Historical Review* 63.1 (October 1957): 25–39; Maestro, "A Pioneer for the Abolition of Capital Punishment," 465–467; and Beirne, "Inventing Criminology," 781 n. 8.

[34] Angela Davis, *Abolition Democracy: Beyond Empire, Prisons, and Torture*. New York: Seven Stories Press, 2005, 36–37.

clemency is the sovereign exception that, once integrated within penal law as its general norm and measure, not only entails the permanent existence of penal slavery (as the enduring humanitarian alternative to the death penalty) but also permits the survival of the very penal cruelties to which it is ostensibly opposed (because, on Beccaria's terms, it is unthinkable that clemency could become the internal norm for the penal laws governing savage or barbaric populations). Especially where it is internally excluded as the fundamental norm of a finally civilized penal code, clemency cannot then be considered an escape from thanatopolitics. For Beccaria, as for some of his unwitting heirs, clemency functions both as an alternative to the cruelty of the sovereign right to kill and as its *double* or *rival*, which is to say, as the juridical basis for a theorization and justification of a cruelty worse than death.[35] It is no doubt an inescapable part of our juridical experience today that, to stay the hand of the executioner, we are forced at certain moments to appeal for clemency in urgent and unequivocal terms. But to critically inquire into that experience is to realize that the sovereign right to spare life is by no means a self-evident antidote to the sovereign right to kill. It is instead the site of an intricate theoretical and practical predicament. To the extent that abolitionist discourse today remains governed by Beccaria's problematization of the sovereign right to kill, its juridical possibilities – up to and including its capacity to contribute to the broader political program that Davis, quoting W. E. B. Du Bois, calls "abolition democracy"[36] – will remain silently constrained by the terms in which Beccaria problematizes the sovereign right to let live. Absent a rigorous theoretical reflection of this predicament, it will be impossible to conceive of a future for abolitionist practice that is more than a dismal repetition of its equivocal Beccarian past.

[35] On the mercilessness of George Ryan's 2003 clemency, see Austin Sarat and Nasser Hussain, "On Lawful Lawlessness: George Ryan, Executive Clemency, and the Rhetoric of Sparing Life," *Stanford Law Review* 56.5 (2003–4): 1339–1340; and Austin Sarat, *Mercy on Trial: What It Means to Stop an Execution*. Princeton, NJ: Princeton University Press, 2005, 135. On the more general place and function of penal slavery in post-Emancipation "neo-slavery," see Douglas Blackmon, *Slavery by Another Name: The Re-Enslavement of Black Americans from the Civil War to World War II*. New York: Doubleday, 2008.

[36] See George Lipsitz, "Abolition Democracy and Global Justice," *Comparative American Studies: An International Journal* 2.3 (2004): 273, 276–278; and Davis, *Abolition Democracy*, 73, 95–97.

Index

abolition/abolitionism. *See also* death penalty
    American campaign, 18, 242–244
    death penalty/execution focus, 19–20
    French debate on, 229
    international perspective, 292–294
    and justifiable killings, 284
    of public executions, 248
    public feasibility of, 270
    vs. reform, 286–288
    and state killing/clemency, 20–22
    and state sovereignty, 278–282
"Abolition in our Time" (Steiker and Steiker), 287
aboriginal peoples. *See* Australia, indigenous life; Canada, lethal cognition of indigenous peoples
Aboriginal Public Health Improvement Program, 173
Aboriginal rights, 199. *See also* Canada, lethal cognition of indigenous peoples
Abu Ghraib (prison), 124
Aeschylus, 60
Afghanistan, 41–42
African Americans, 89–90
Agamben, Giorgio
    homo sacer, 112, 121
    sovereign power, 11, 87–88
    zone of indistinction, 156, 162, 167
Ainsworth, Judge, 264
Al-Kateb v. Godwin, 187–188
Allen, Ronald, 275–276
Allied Tribes of British Columbia (ATBC), 205–206
Al Odah v. United States, 131–132
al-Qaeda, 42–43
Althusser, Louis, 169

Altman, Jon, 181
American Civil Liberties Union, 141
Amnesty International, 141, 187
Antaki, Mark, 15–16
Anti-Christ, The (Nietzsche), 150
Antigone (Sophocles), 54–55, 66
antiwar demonstrators, 108–110
Apollonian individuation, 60–63
Arendt, Hannah
    citizens, rights of, 71–72
    human finitude, 53–54
    legality, claims of, 132
    life, priority of, 162–164
    persons, legal definition of, 11–12
    private/family life, 107
    "right to have rights", 128
    secrets, culturewide, 257
Arnold, Jeremy, 8–10
Aryan Brotherhood. *See Koch v. Lewis*
Ashcroft, John, 238, 243
Ashe, Marie, 256
"Ashglory" (Celan), 245
assassination, as self-defense, 44
assimilation, of indigenous peoples, 209–210. *See also* Canada, lethal cognition of indigenous peoples
asylum seekers, 185–186
Australia
    death penalty opposition, 184
    forms of governmentality, 172
    humanitarian efforts, 184–185
    lethality in, 14
Australia, indigenous life
    Community Development Employment Project (CDEP), 181
    and ethics of empathy, 181–182

309

Australia, indigenous life (*cont.*)
  health crisis, 173
  illness, types of, 175
  infections, treatment of, 180–181
  riots, 184
  risk, privatizing, 177–179
  since colonization, 173–174
  social life example, 177
  socioeconomic status/health relationship, 174–177
  withdrawal of federal support, 179–180
Australia, state security measures
  and Lebanon humanitarian crisis, 188–189
  mandatory detention, 186–188
  power to detain, 183–184
  public protest against, 184–185
  terrorist spectacle, 183
Australian Bureau of Statistics, 174–175
Australian Capital Television v. Commonwealth, 183–184
Australian Institute of Health and Welfare, 174–176
Azmi, al- (Guantanamo Bay detainee), 114, 116

Bagot Commission, 200
Bartleson, Jens, 29, 49–50
Bataille, Georges, 118, 121
Beccaria, Cesare
  clemency criticism, 299–304, 306–308
  death penalty criticism, 20–22, 297–298
  penal slavery, 304–306
  Vatican's censorship of, 301–302
Behrooz and Ors v. Secretary of the Department of Immigration and Multicultural and Indigenous Affairs, 187
Bell Jar, The (Plath), 253–257
Benjamin, Walter, 238–239, 252, 258–259
Berlant, Lauren, 190
bin Laden, Osama, 41–42, 44
"biopower", 6
Blackstone, William, 12, 148
Blackwater, Nordan v., 88
Blackwater contractors, 10–11. *See also* private military contractors
  Fallujah attack on, 94–100
  immunity for, 101
  litigation response, 98–99
  Nordan v. Blackwater, 88
  "sacrifices" for the company, 93–94
Boas, Franz, 203–204

Bobbio, Norberto, 297
body count. *See* dead bodies
Borrows, John, 198
Boumediene v. Bush, 131–132
Bramwell, Sir George, 251
Bremer, Paul, 101
Brigades of Martyr Ahmed Yassin, 96
British Columbia, Calder v., 210–211
British Columbia, Delgamuukw v., 219–220, 224–225
British North America Act, 201
Brooks, Peter, 16–18
Brooks, Rosa Ehrenreich, 43
Bunck, Julie, 29–30
Burke, Edmund, 19, 268–269
Burke, Kenneth, 38
Bush, Boumediene v., 131–132
Bush, George W.
  9/11 commission convocation, 41–42
  and Cindy Sheehan, 108–110
  and declared wars, 44
  and Terry Shiavo's death, 162
  use of private military contractors, 92–94
Bush, Rasul v., 118, 130
Bush administration
  9/11 Commission report, 35–36
  competency, criticism of, 77–78
  due process, redefinition of, 127–128
  on fighting terrorists, 69
  intentions of, 78–79
  persons, legal definition of, 128–129
  political documents of, 26–27
  privacy, protection of family, 106–110
  rogue state concept, 39–40
  suspected terrorists, treatment of, 134. *See also* due process
Bussolini, Jeffrey, 49

Calabresi, Guido, 125
Calder, Frank, 210–211
Calder v. British Columbia, 210–211
Calhoun, Craig, 178
Cameron, James, 153
Camus, Albert, 18, 230, 245–246, 257–260
Camus, Lucien, 245–246
Canada, 15–16
Canada, lethal cognition of indigenous peoples
  enfranchisement, 200–201
  and European settlement, 199–200
  fixity, attempt at, 225–226

Index

Indian Act of 1876
  amendments to, 206–208
  assimilation goal, 203
  legal status of "Indian", 202
  "municipal" institutions, 202–203
  resistance to, 208
  land grants, 204–205
  legislative acts, 199
  polity distinction, 203–204
  recognition, law of
    constitutional enshrinement, 211–212
    Delgamuukw v. British Columbia, 219–220
    language of, 212–213
    Pamajewon, R. v., 219
    R. v. Sparrow, 215–218
    R. v. Van der Peet, 218–221
  reconciliation, law of
    and justification, 224–225
    limitations to Aboriginal rights/title, 221–224
    sovereign reconciliation, 213–215
  Royal Proclamation, 197–199
  visibility, granting of, 225
  "White Paper on Indian Policy", 208–211
capital punishment. *See also* abolition/abolitionism; death penalty; execution; guillotine
  abolition vs. reform of, 286–288
  bio-politics/governmentality relationship, 273–274
  as closure, 17
  as culturewide secret, 257–258
  as ethical exception, 294–296
  as government regulation, 274–276
  guillotine in, 17
  international perspective, 292–294
  narrative resistance to, 18–19
  political arguments, 276–278
  political-philosophical domain, 19–20, 271–273
  political reality of, 270–271
  "right to kill", 282–285
  and state sovereignty, 278–282
  volunteers, problem of, 288–292
Capital Punishment Commission, 251
Cardinal, Harold, 209–210, 224
Cartesian dualism, 17, 230
Catholicism, 154–155, 231
Celan, Paul, 245
Center for Constitutional Rights, 113–114, 141

Cetina, Karin Knorr, 43
chairs, emergency restraint, 114–115
Chang, Gordon, 37–38
Chomsky, Noam, 39–40
Christian fundamentalist faith
  bodily resurrection, 231
  death, understanding of, 13–14
  immortality, idea of, 167
  and Jesus' death, 152–153, 166
  judgment, issue of, 152–153
  and Terry Shiavo's death, 162–166
Christie, Gordon, 201–202
CIA, 44
citizenry, government dependence on, 83–84
Clarke, Richard, 42
clemency. *See also* Beccaria, Cesare
  internal exclusion of, 306–307
  and penal slavery, 304–306
  sovereign right of, 21–22, 299–304
Clement, Paul D., 133–134
Clinton, Bill
  and declared wars, 44
  rogue state concept, 39–40
  use of private military contractors, 92–93
Clinton administration
  bin Laden training camps, 42
  "Mogadishu effect", 95
closure, concept of, 238
cognition. *See* Canada, lethal cognition of indigenous peoples
Cohen, William, 42
Collins, Randall, 31
combatants, enemy, 11–12. *See also* detainees, enemy
Commentaries on the Laws of England (Blackstone), 148
Commonwealth, Australian Capital Television v., 183–184
Community Development Employment Project (CDEP), 181
Concept of the Political, The (Schmitt), 66, 160–161
confinement, solitary. *See* solitary confinement
Conner, DeMont, 136–140
Conner, Sandin v., 136–140
Connolly, William E., 164
Conrad, Joseph, 250–251, 266
conscription, 104, 282, 284–285, 293–294
Constitution Act, Section 35 (Canadian), 16
Cover, Robert, 128

Crimes Act (Australian), 183–184
criminal sentencing. *See* sentences/sentencing
Cushman, Thomas, 70–75

Daihani, Mr. (Guantanamo Bay detainee), 116
Darkness at Noon (Koestler), 236
Das, Veena, 190
Davis, Angela, 307–308
Dayan, Colin, 11–12, 152, 167–168
dead bodies
    counting of, 9–10, 51
    hiding of, 80–81
    from war in Iraq, 67–68
death
    and Christian fundamentalist faith, 13–14
    civil, 11
    dignity/indignity in, 158
    grief and consolation, 159
    "letting die", 171–172
    in modernist literature, 252–253
    nothingness, experience of, 160
    physiological process of, 156–158
    political meaning of, 160–161
    as sacrifice, 10–11
    as "sanction" of storyteller's narrative, 238–239
    and security relationship, 54–56
    and sovereignty relationship, 56–59
    of Terry Shaivo, 162–166
    untouchable character of, 159–160
    as withdrawal from the world, 158–159
death penalty. *See also* abolition/abolitionism; capital punishment; execution; guillotine
    closure, concept of, 238
    French debate on, 229
    and imaginative sympathy, 244
    in narrative/literary works. *See also Dernier jour d'un condamné, Le* (Hugo)
        Darkness at Noon (Koestler), 236
        epistolary novels, 235–236
        first-person narration, 236
        Great Expectations (Dickens), 233–234
        guillotine, importance of, 230–231
        Hugo's "social novels", 229–230
        meaningful plot, 239
        Quatrevingt-treize (Ninety-Three) (Hugo), 229–230, 241–242
        soul/body dialogue, 231–232
        "Storyteller, The" (Benjamin), 238–239
    volunteers, problem of, 288–292
    as war against internal enemy, 304–306
Debord, Guy, 245, 249–250
De Cive (Hobbes), 64
defense, concept of, 49
Dei delitti e delle pene (Beccaria), 301–302
Deleuze, Gilles, 297
Delgamuukw v. British Columbia, 219–220, 224–225
Democracy in America (Tocqueville), 129
"Democratic Realism", 70
Department of Aboriginal Affairs, 173. *See also* Australia, indigenous life
Department of Corrections, Halquist v., 263, 265–266
Department of Defense, on detainee suicide, 119–120
Dernier jour d'un condamné, Le (Hugo)
    death as idea, 232
    epigraph quotation, 229
    explanation of crime, absence of, 236–238
    presence of death in life, 232–233
    reader discomfort, 16–18
    as social novel, 229–230
    state's apparatus of death, 234–235
Derrida, Jacques
    dead, counting of the, 51, 72
    rogue state concept, 39–40
    on sovereignty, 25, 35
desecration, 97–98
detainees, enemy. *See also* due process
    countersacrificial posture, U.S., 123
    destruction/alienation claims, 121–122
    habeas corpus cases, 131–132
    hunger strikes/forced feeding, 113–118, 166
    and popular sovereignty, 122–123
    and "preservation of life", 118
    "prestige of sacrificial body", 121
    sacrifice, exclusion from, 11
    suicide/suicide attempts, 111–112, 118–121, 123–124
Dickens, Charles, 233–234
Dillon, Michael, 58
Dionysian impulse, 60–63
Discipline and Punish (Foucault), 5–6, 81, 252, 298
Dobson, James, 162
documents of state
    as means discourses, 36
    publicizing of sovereignty, 34–35
    template/structure of, 32–33

Index

domination, within given territory, 28–32
Donne, John, 231
Dossari, Jumah al-, 111, 123–124
draft, military. *See* conscription
Dred Scott v. Sandford, 12, 89–90, 134–135
Du Bois, W. E. B., 308
due process
  and civil existence, 128
  in constitutional law, 134
  Dred Scott v. Sandford, 134–135
  Hamdan v. Rumsfeld (2006), 133–134
  Hamdi v. Rumsfeld (2004), 132–133
  Koch v. Lewis, 141–148
  legal imagination, 134
  Meachum v. Fano, 135–136
  meaning of, 135
  Military Commissions Act (MCA), 129–131
  persons, legal definition of, 11–12, 128–129
  persons, legal status of, 132
  Sandin v. Conner, 136–140
  Slaughter-House Cases, 135
Dulles, Trop v., 127
Dumm, Tom, 12–14
Duncanson, Ian, 185

Eckstein, Timothy, 143–144
Elias, Norbert, 30–31, 39
Ellison, Harlan, 166–167
Emancipation Proclamation, 90
"Emergency Restraint Chairs", 114–115
Emerson, Ralph Waldo, 160
enemy, fragmented idea of, 46. *See also* detainees, enemy
ESS Support Services Worldwide, 94
Estelle, Garrett v., 263–265
ethics
  of empathy, 14
  fiction-based wager, 169–171
  of responsibility, 28
Euben, J. Peter, 76–77
Ewald, François, 297
execution. *See also* abolition/abolitionism; capital punishment; death penalty; guillotine
  Albert Camus on, 245–246
  and courtroom drama, 251
  as cultural practice, 16–18
  as culture-wide secret, 257–258
  emotional responses to, 248–249
  as event/nonevent, 254
  focal point of, 249–250

imagination, role of, 250–251
imagined vs. witnessed, 246
in narrative/literary works
  Bell Jar, The (Plath), 253–257
  courtroom dramas, 251
  "Hanging, A" (Orwell), 266–269
  Invitation to a Beheading (Nabokov), 262–263
  "Reflections on the Guillotine" (Camus), 245–247, 251, 257, 260–261
  representation, impossibility of, 248
  secrets, culturewide, 256–257
  Stranger, The (Camus), 18, 258–262
and privacy of death, 252
public vs. private, 246–249
right to see/witness, 263–266
sovereign distance from, 5–6
surrogate witnesses, 253

Fallujah, attack on Blackwater contractors, 94–100
Fano, Meachum v., 135–136, 138
fate, and sovereignty, 79
Fielding, Henry, 250, 253
Fletcher, George, 272–273
forced feeding/hunger strikes, 113–118, 166
foreign policy, and state violence, 49–50
Foucault, Michel
  bio-politics/governmentality relationship, 150, 162, 273–274
  death penalty, 298
  public execution, 5–6, 249–250, 252
  sovereign power, 61–62, 81, 278–282
  "threshold of modernity", 302
  tragedy, purpose of, 59–60
Fowler, Michael, 29–30
Francis, Willie, 243–244
Frankfurther, Felix, 243–244
freedom, 38, 47
free trade, 38
Friedman, Milton, 185
Furman v. Georgia, 243

Garrett, Tony, 263–265
Garrett v. Estelle, 263–265
Gatrell, V. A. C., 248
Geneva Conventions, 88, 129–130
Georgia, Furman v., 243
Gettysburg Address, 88–90, 103
Giddens, Anthony, 29
Ginsburg, Ruth Bader, 139

Girard, Rene, 73–74
Gitxsan (Gitksan), people and land, 205, 219–221. *See also* Canada, lethal cognition of indigenous peoples
Gladstone, R v., 222–223
globalization, and capital punishment, 293
Gnostic Gospels, 155
Godwin, Al-Kateb v., 187–188
Goldwater-Nichols Department of Defense Reorganization Act, 32–33, 37–38
government. *See also* sovereignty
  dependence on citizenry, 83–84
  monopoly on sacrifice, 84–85
Gradual Civilization Act of 1857 (Canada), 200–201, 203
Grassian, Stuart, 142–143
Gray, M. C., 181
Great Expectations (Dickens), 233–234
Greenwood, Esther. *See* Rosenberg, Ethel and Julius
Grossman, Jonathan, 251
Guantánamo Bay. *See also* detainees, enemy; due process
  description of, 112–113
  epigraph quotations, 111
  executive control of, 113
  persons, categorization of, 12
  supermax detention in, 148–149
guillotine
  and Cartesian dualism, 17
  in narrative/literary works, 230–231
  "Reflections on the Guillotine" (Camus), 245–247, 251, 257, 260–261
  in Reign of Terror, 231–232
  and soul/body dialogue, 231–232
  in *Stranger, The* (Camus), 260

habeas corpus, 11–12, 130–132. *See also* due process
Haida, people and land. *See also* Canada, lethal cognition of indigenous peoples
  conversion of, 196–209
  and forests, 193
  government of, 206
  homeland claim, 226
  matrilineal structure, 203–204
  resistance of, 205
Hall, Justice, 210, 216
Halquist v. Department of Corrections, 263, 265–266

Hamdan v. Rumsfeld (2006), 127, 129–130, 133–134
Hamdi v. Rumsfeld (2004), 132–133
Hamilton, Lee, 35–36
"Hanging, A" (Orwell), 266–269
Harlan, Marshall, II, 144–145
Harris, Harry, 111, 119–120, 168
Hassan, Emad, 114–115
Haudenausaune, people and land, 198–199, 208. *See also* Canada, lethal cognition of indigenous peoples
Heidegger, Martin, 53–55, 160
Heiltsuk, people and land, 222–223. *See also* Canada, lethal cognition of indigenous peoples
Hippocrates, 156
History of Sexuality, The (Foucault), 302
Hobbes, Thomas
  death, fear of, 58
  security threats, 4
  on sovereignty, 63–65, 283
  state of nature, 2–3
Holy Sonnets (Donne), 231
Howard, John, 172, 184–186. *See also* Australia, indigenous life; Australia, state security measures
Hugo, Victor
  on capital punishment, 16–18
  Dernier jour d'un condamné, Le
    death as idea, 232
    epigraph quotation, 229
    explanation of crime, absence of, 236–238
    presence of death in life, 232–233
    reader discomfort, 16–18
    as social novel, 229–230
    state's apparatus of death, 234–235
  executioner, exit of, 239–241
  Les Misérables, 229–230
  Quatrevingt-treize (Ninety-Three), 229–230, 241–242
  on revolutions, 229
  "social" novels of, 229–230
Human Condition, The (Arendt), 162–164
Human Rights Watch, 141
hunger strikes/forced feeding, 113–118, 166
Huntington, Samuel, 105
Hussein, Saddam, 73, 247, 254

"I Have No Mouth, and I Must Scream" (Ellison), 166–167
incarceration. *See* solitary confinement

Index

Index Libororum Prohibitorum (Vatican), 301–302
Indian Act of 1876 (Canada), 16. *See also* Canada, lethal cognition of indigenous peoples
"Indian culture". *See* "White Paper on Indian Policy" (1969)
indigenous communities/life. *See* Australia, indigenous life; Canada, lethal cognition of indigenous peoples
International Covenant on Civil and Political Rights, 187
Invitation to a Beheading (Nabokov), 262–263
Iraq. *See also* National Strategy for Victory in Iraq
  civilian deaths/displacements, 67–68
  supermax detention in, 148
  terrorism, spread of, 68–69
  U.S. invasion of, 8–10, 51–52
Iraq, war in. *See also* private military contractors
  contradictions of sovereignty, 67–69
  instrumental rationality, 75–82
  liberal-humanitarian justification for, 69–75
Iraq Body Count project, 67

James, William, 170
Jay, Nancy, 103
Jesus, 13, 100, 153–156
Johns Hopkins University, 67
Johnson, Sir William, 198–199
Joudi, Majid al-, 116
judges/judgment. *See also* sentences/sentencing
  and Christian fundamentalist faith, 152–153
  responsibility to sentence, 150–151
Jurisprudence of Power: Victorian Empire and the Rule of Law, A (Kostal), 134

Kagan, Robert, 69–70
Kahn, Paul, 84, 97, 104
Kahnawake, people and land, 208. *See also* Canada, lethal cognition of indigenous peoples
Kanien'kehá:ka, people and land, 208. *See also* Canada, lethal cognition of indigenous peoples
Kaufman-Osborn, Timothy, 248, 278–282
Kean, Thomas, 35–36
Kennedy, Anthony, 129–130

killing, state. *See* state lethality
King, Justice, 208, 220
Kirkby, Coel, 15–16
Kittle, Thomas, 248–249
Knox, Bernard, 57–58
Koch, Mark, 141–148
Koch v. Lewis, 141–148
Koestler, Arthur, 236
Kostal, R. W., 134
KQED v. Vasquez, 263, 265
Krauthammer, Charles, 70
Kristol, William, 70
Kwakwaka'wakw, people and land, 204. *See also* Canada, lethal cognition of indigenous peoples

Lamer, Justice, 224
Landrigan, Schriro v., 289–290
Langley Air Force Base fighter pilots, 42
Lebanon humanitarian crisis, 188–189. *See also* Australia, state security measures
Le Guin, Ursula, 169–171, 182–183
Les Misérables (Hugo), 229–230
lethal force, sovereign use of, 5–6
lethality, conditions of, 14–15
lethality, state. *See* state lethality
"letting die", 171–172. *See also* state lethality
Leviathan (Hobbes), 3, 63–65, 283
Lévi-Strauss, Claude, 40–41, 83, 87
Lewis, Koch v., 141–148
Life and Words (Das), 190
Lincoln, Abraham, 88–90, 103
Lingis, Alphonso, 158–160
Litwak, Robert, 39–40
Locke, John, 3–4, 283
Logan v. Styres, 208, 220
Los Alamos, 49
Louisiana ex. rel. Francis v. Resweber, 243–244
Lutz, Catherine, 30
Lynch, Jessica, 105–106

Man, Paul de, 170
Mann, Michael, 39–40
Mary Magdalene, 153–154, 156
Mary (mother of Jesus), 153–154
McDonnell, Wolff v., 138
McKenna-McBride Royal Commission, 205–206
McLachlin, Justice, 218–219, 223–224
McNeil, Kent, 220–221

McVeigh, Timothy, 238, 243
Meachum v. Fano, 135–136, 138
means discourses, 36
Mehan, Hugh, 37–38
mercenary. *See* private military contractors
mercy. *See* clemency
Military Commissions Act (MCA), 129–131
military draft. *See* conscription
"Mogadishu effect", 95
Mohammad, Sheikh Feiz, 188–189
Mohammed, Khalid Sheikh, 123, 148–149
"Moral Philosopher and the Moral Life, The" (James), 170
Moran, James B., 141–142, 145–147
More, Sir Thomas, 298–299
Morellet, André, 301–302
Morgan, Lewis Henry, 204
Musqueam, people and land, 215–218. *See also* Canada, lethal cognition of indigenous peoples

Nabokov, Vladimir, 262–263
Nancy, Jean-Luc, 79–81
National Commission on Terrorist Attacks upon the United States. *See 9/11 Commission Report, The*
National Intelligence Estimate (2006), 68–69
National Intelligence Estimate (2007), 68
National Security Council, 36
National Security Strategy of the United States of America (NSSUSA) 2002
  freedom, repetitive reference to, 38
  innocuousness of state violence, 26–27
  means/ends contradictions, 40–41
  president's message, 37
  preventive war policy/model, 33–34
  rouge state concept, 39–40
  territory monopolization, 7–8, 40
  theological underpinnings, 37–38
  verbs, use of, 38–39
National Security Strategy of the United States of America (NSSUSA) 2006
  freedom, associations of, 47–48
  innocuousness of state violence, 26–27
  Iran focus, 34
  offense vs. defense theme, 48
  preventive war policy/model, 7–8
  sovereignty, movement of, 48–49
National Strategy for Victory in Iraq, 28, 36, 45–47
nature, state of, 2–4

Nauru (Pacific island of), 185–186
Niagra, Treaty of, 198
Nietzsche, Friedrich
  Anti-Christ, The, 150
  on Greek tragedy, 62–63
  human finitude, 53–54
  sovereign knowledge, 60–61, 65
  state idolatry, 225
  state sight and speech, 194–209
9/11 Commission Report, The
  American interests as global, 43–44
  enemy identification, 42–43
  fatwa against America, 44
  innocuousness of state violence, 26–27
  publication/authorship of, 35–36
  spatial disorientation, 43
  technological misrepresentation/miscalculation, 42
  textual genres/point of view, 41–42
Nisga'a, people and land, 196–197, 205, 210–211. *See also* Canada, lethal cognition of indigenous peoples
Nixon, Richard, 90
Nlaka'pamux, people and land, 204–205. *See also* Canada, lethal cognition of indigenous peoples
Nordan v. Blackwater, 88
NSSUSA (*National Security Strategy of the United States of America*) 2002
  freedom, repetitive reference to, 38
  innocuousness of state violence, 26–27
  means/ends contradictions, 40–41
  president's message, 37
  preventive war policy/model, 33–34
  rouge state concept, 39–40
  territory monopolization, 7–8, 40
  theological underpinnings, 37–38
  verbs, use of, 38–39
NSSUSA (*National Security Strategy of the United States of America*) 2006
  freedom, associations of, 47–48
  innocuousness of state violence, 26–27
  Iran focus, 34
  offense vs. defense theme, 48
  preventive war policy/model, 7–8
  sovereignty, movement of, 48–49
nuclear weapons, 104
Nuland, Sherwin, 157

Oakes, R. v., 222
O'Connor, Sandra Day, 132–133

Index

Oedipal sovereignty
  and death
    knowledge of, 67
    Oedipus, story of, 53–54, 56–58, 62, 76, 80
    and security relationship, 54–56
    and sovereignty relationship, 56–59
    vs. Hobbesian sovereignty, 63–65
    vs. Schmittian sovereignty, 65–67
    structure of, 59–63
  and the War in Iraq
    contradiction/paradox of sovereignty, 8–10, 67–69
    instrumental rationality, 75–82
    liberal-humanitarian justification for, 69–75
Oedipus, story of, 53–54, 56–58, 62, 76, 80
Oedipus at Colonus (Sophocles), 53–54, 56–58
Oedipus the King (Sophocles), 53–54, 60, 66
On Crimes and Punishments (Beccaria), 297–298
"Ones Who Walk Away from Omelas, The" (Le Guin), 169–171, 182–183
Oresteian Trilogy (Aeschylus), 60
Origins of Totalitarianism, The (Arendt), 132
Orwell, George, 266–269

"Pacific solution", 185–186
pacified social spaces, 30–31
Pamajewon, R. v., 219
parenthetical words/phrases, use of, 27–28
Pascal, Blaise, 232–233
Payne v. Tennessee, 243
Pearson, Noel, 179–180
Pelican Bay (prison), 140, 142–143
Pentagon
  on force feeding of prisoners, 115
  and Jessica Lynch, 106
  and photo ban on caskets, 106–107
persons, redefinitions of, 11–12
Philpott, Daniel, 29
physical force, state use of, 25–26
physical pain. *See* torture
Pierce, Charles Sanders, 170
Pinel, Philippe, 231–232
Plath, Sylvia, 253–254, 258. *See also* Bell Jar, The (Plath)
Pochoda, Daniel, 143–144
Poe v. Ullman, 144–145
Political Theology (Schmitt), 65–66
"Politics as a Vocation" (Weber), 25

"Pontiac rebellion", 197–199
Potts, Jack, 142
Povinelli, Elizabeth, 14–15
Prince, Erik, 99–100. *See also* Blackwater contractors
prisons, supermax, 11
private military contractors. *See also* Blackwater contractors
  deaths, recognition of, 91–92
  Fallujah attack on, 94–100
  and immunity, 100–101
  legal/cultural position of, 89
  Nordan v. Blackwater, 88
  as unsacrificeable subjects, 88–89
  in U.S. foreign policy, 92–93
  as veterans, 99–100
Pruett, Tammy, 109
punishment. *See also* sentences/sentencing
  denial of freedom, 151
  sentencing trends, 12–14
  torture as, 151–152
Putting Liberalism in Its Place (Kahn), 84

Quatrevingt-treize (Ninety-Three) (Hugo), 229–230, 241–242

Rasul v. Bush, 118, 130
Rawlsian contractualism, 151
reconciliation, ambiguity of, 214–215
Red Zone Web site, 83
"Reflections on the Guillotine" (Camus), 245–247, 251, 257, 260–261
Rehnquist, William, 136–138, 243
Reichman, Ravit, 18–19
responsibility, ethic of, 28
restraint chairs, 114–115
Resweber, Louisiana ex. rel., Francis v., 243–244
Rice, Condoleezza, 35–36
Rice, Susan, 39
risk, privatizing, 177–179
rogue nations/states, 33–34, 39–40
Rogues (Derrida), 25
Roper v. Simmons, 293
Rosen, Nir, 96
Rosenberg, Ethel and Julius, 253–256, 258
Rousseau, Jean-Jacques, 283, 304
Royal Commission on Aboriginal Peoples, 203
Royal Commission on Capital Punishment, 248–249

Royal Proclamation (Canada), 197–199
Rumsfeld, Hamdan v., (2006), 127, 129–130, 133–134
Rumsfeld, Hamdi v., (2004), 132–133
Russell, Peter, 206
Russia, 42
R. v. Gladstone, 222–223
R. v. Oakes, 222
R. v. Pamajewon, 219
R. v. Sparrow, 213–214, 222
R. v. Van der Peet, 214–216, 218–221, 223–224
Ryan, George, 270

sacrifice/sacralization. *See also* detainees, enemy; private military contractors
  ambiguous meaning, 102–103
  and citizenship, 83–84, 89–90
  as controlled actions, 124–125
  counter-sacrificial policy, 86
  deaths as, 10–11, 110–111
  and desecration, 97–98
  family, privacy protection of, 106–110
  gendered conception of, 103, 105–106
  legal/policy forms, 86, 125–126
  meaningful loss, 126
  official avoidance of, 85
  outsourcing of, 85–86, 93–94, 100
  and popular sovereignty, 97, 111
  privatization of, 86
  as ritual, 86–87
  sacrificial energy, manipulation of, 102
  shared vulnerability, 104–105
  of soldiers, 90–91
  and sovereign power, 87–88
  substitution of victim, 100
  unauthorized actors, 87
  victims' status, 96–97
  "Vietnam gap", 90
Sandford, Dred Scott v., 12, 89–90, 134–135
Sandin v. Conner, 136–140
Sarat, Austin, 264
Sartre, Jean-Paul, 239
Savage Mind, The (Lévi-Strauss), 83
Schmitt, Carl
  citizen/state relationship shift, 162
  depolitization of life, 13
  and John Howard's foreign policy, 185
  political concept of death, 160–161
  on sovereignty, 65–67
Schnacke, Robert, 265

Schriro v. Landrigan, 289–290
Schuster, Aaron, 264
Scott, James C., 194–195
Secret Agent, The (Conrad), 250–251, 266
Secretary of the Department of Immigration and Multicultural and Indigenous Affairs, Behrooz and Ors v., 187
security threat groups (STGs), 140–141. *See also Koch v. Lewis*
Seeing Like a State (Scott), 194–195
Segal, Charles, 63
sentences/sentencing
  and Christian fundamentalist faith, 152–153
  as denial of freedom, 151
  etymology, 150
  guidelines/mandatory minimums, 150–151
  vs. prisoner suicides, 168
Shaivo, Terry, 162–166
Shavell, Amy, 275–276
Sheehan, Casey, 108–110
Sheehan, Cindy, 108–110
Shehri, Yousef al-, 114, 116
Shelton, Henry Hugh, 42
Simmons, Roper v., 293
Simon, Jonathan, 150–151
singularity, of beings, 79–80
Sitze, Adam, 20–22
Slaughter-House Cases, 135
SMU II (Special Management Unit II), 140–141. *See also Koch v. Lewis*
Social Contract, The (Rousseau), 283
social contract theory, 4, 304
social spaces, pacified, 30–31
Society of the Spectacle, The (Debord), 245
Socrates, 100
solitary confinement
  condemnation of, 141
  and debriefing, 146–147
  and due process, 136–140
  Koch v. Lewis, 141–148
  segregation decisions, 141
Sophocles, 52–54. *See also* Oedipal sovereignty
Souter, David, 133–134
sovereignty. *See also* Oedipal sovereignty
  compromise, types of, 29–30
  and death penalty volunteers, 291–292
  and death relationship, 56–59

Index

instrumental effectiveness of, 10
migration of, 155
paradox of, 52
popular, 97
practice of, 59–63
publicizing, 34–35
right to citizen's death, 282–285
and right to kill, 81–82
and state violence, 4–6
Soviet Union, 42
Sparrow, Ronald, 215–216
Sparrow, R. v., 213–214, 222
Special Management Unit II (SMU II), 140–141. *See also Koch v. Lewis*
Starr, Kenneth, 99
state. *See also* sovereignty
and blood spilling, 1
documents of, 32–33, 35–36
right to kill, 282–285
"state killing". *See* state lethality
state lethality. *See also* Australia, indigenous life; Australia, state security measures
in late liberal societies, 189–191
legitimacy of, 27–28
physical force, use of, 25–26
state sight and speech, 193–209
"within a given territory", 28–32
state of nature, 2–4
state violence
academic interest in, 1–2
and defense models, 49
and foreign policy, 49–50
and sovereignty, 4–6
from state of nature, 2–4
and suffering, 10–11
St. Catherine's Milling and Lumber Company v. The Queen, 201–202
Steiker, Carol, 276–278, 287
Steiker, Jordan, 287
Stevens, Anthony, 127
Stevens, John Paul, 129–130, 136, 139
Stewart, Terry, 140
STGs (security threat groups), 140–141. *See also Koch v. Lewis*
Sto:lo, people and land, 205. *See also* Canada, lethal cognition of indigenous peoples
"Storyteller, The" (Benjamin), 238–239, 252
Stranger, The (Camus), 18, 258–262
Strauss, Leo, 185
Strong, Tracy, 160–161
Styres, *Logan v.*, 208, 220

Sunstein, Cass, 274–275
supermax detention, 148. *See also Koch v. Lewis*
"supermax syndrome", 142–143
Swanson, Charlie, 196–197
Swanton, John, 203–204

Tampa (Norwegian ship), 185–186
Taney, Roger, 12, 89–90, 134–135
Task Force Platinum, 148–149
Taussig-Rubbo, Mateo, 10–11
Taylor, Charles, 210
Teit, James, 204–206
Tennessee, Payne v., 243
territory, 7, 28–32
terrorism, 33–34, 68–69
Thomas, Clarence, 127
Thurschwell, Adam, 19–20
Thus Spoke Zarathustra (Nietzsche), 194
Tocqueville, Alexis de, 129
torture
acceptance of, 12, 130
as punishment, 151–152
in science fiction, 166–167
and sentencing trends, 13
sustaining life as form of, 166
withdrawal of law as, 166
trade, free, 38
tragedy, purpose of, 59–60
Trop v. Dulles, 127
Trotsky, Leon, 25
Tsimshian, people and land, 205. *See also* Canada, lethal cognition of indigenous peoples
Two Treatises of Government (Locke), 283

Ullman, Poe v., 144–145
United National Working Group on Arbitrary Detention, 187
United Nations Commission on Human Rights, 115
United Nations Committee against Torture, 141
United Nations Human Rights Committee, 187
United Nations World Conference against Racism (2001), 185–186
United States, Al Odah v., 131–132
U.S. Army Rangers, 95
Utopia (More), 298–299

Van der Peet, Dorothy, 218
Van der Peet, R. v., 214–216, 218–221, 223–224
Vasquez, KQED v., 263, 265
Vatican, 301–302
Vermeule, Adrian, 274–275
victims, sacrificial status of, 96–97
victory, deconstruction of term, 45–46
Vietnam conflict, 36, 42, 90
violence, extraterritorial deployment of, 30–31. *See also* state violence
Violence and the Sacred (Girard), 73–74
volunteers, for death penalty, 288–292

Wagner-Pacifici, Robin, 7–8
waiver, of rights, 291
war
  antiwar demonstrators, 108–110
  centrality of, 31
  preventive policy/model, 7–8, 33–34
  territorial extensiveness of, 31–32
  on terror/terrorism, 37–38, 104
Warren, Earl, 127
Waxman, Henry, 99–100
Weber, Max
  authority, sources of, 31–32
  freedom, invocation of, 47–48
  state, definition of, 25–28

state violence
  innocuousness of, 26–27
  physical force, 4–5
  and sacrifice, 93
  and territory, 7
  words/phrases, parenthetical use of, 27–28
Wet'suwet'en, people and land, 219–221. *See also* Canada, lethal cognition of indigenous peoples
White, Byron, 135–136
"White Paper on Indian Policy" (1969), 208–211. *See also* Canada, lethal cognition of indigenous peoples
Wilf, Steven, 247–248
Witherington, Ben, 153–154
witness, right to, 263, 265
Wittgenstein, Ludwig, 191
Wolff v. McDonnell, 138
Words, The (Sartre), 239
World Islamic Front, 44
World Medical Association, 115

Yassin, Sheikh Ahmed, 96

Zarathustra, 194
Zelikow, Philip, 35–36